D1614091

MARGARET CHASE SMITH

BEYOND CONVENTION

Patricia L. Schmidt

MARGARET CHASE SMITH

BEYOND CONVENTION

Orono, Maine / The University of Maine Press / 1996

Photographs in this book are reproduced with permission from Northwood University Margaret Chase Smith Library, Skowhegan, Maine.

ISBN: (cloth) 0-89101-088-2

This book has been smyth-sewn for permanence. The paper used in this publication meets the minimum requirements of the American National Standard for Information Sciences—Permanence of Paper for Printed Library Materials, ANSI Z39.48-1984.

Book design by Michael Alpert. Manufactured in the United States of America.

Library of Congress Cataloging-in-Publication Data

Schmidt, Patricia L., 1942-
      Margaret Chase Smith : beyond convention / Patricia L. Schmidt.
         p.   cm.
      Includes bibliographical references and index.
      ISBN 0-89101-088-2 (alk. paper). — ISBN 0-89101-089-0 (pbk. :
alk. paper)
      1. Smith, Margaret Chase,—1897-1995   2. Women legislators—United States—Biography.   3. Legislators—United States—Biography.
4. United States. Congress. Senate—Biography.   5. Maine—Politics and government—1865-1950. 6. Maine—Politics and government—1951-
7. Anti-communist movements—United States—History.   I. Title.
E748.S667S36   1996
328.73'092—dc20
   [B]   96-31038
                                            CIP

CONTENTS

ILLUSTRATIONS

Frontispiece: Portrait of Margaret Chase Smith, 1940. *Photograph by Hesler Henderson*

The photograph facing page 334 shows Margaret Chase Smith at the site of her newly acquired property on Norridgewock Avenue, Skowhegan, Maine, prior to building her new home, June 1948. (Photograph by Huff Studios, Skowhegan)

Additional photographs follow page 146

For my parents, Wesley Schmidt and Hilda L. Schmidt

PREFACE

THIS BOOK FIRST TOOK SHAPE in December 1982 when I travelled to Skowhegan, Maine to examine the papers of Margaret Chase Smith. I remember still my first deep gulp of near-freezing air and the glimpse of a wild duck on a not yet iced-in lake on the country road from Bangor to Skowhegan, his dark green, glossy head and light underparts as distinctive as his sudden dive beneath the lake's surface. As I wound through Maine's hilly northern midsection I caught up with the mighty Kennebec River, Margaret Chase Smith's Kennebec, the river her ancestors had walked and ridden hundreds of miles to reach, a once wild, untamed river, momentarily peaceful. How like the senator herself, I thought, once I met her, for both she and the river seemed eternal, permanent, enduring. The following summer I returned to begin a labor that would span thirteen years—an account of her fascinating life.

Part of the summer of 1983 was spent driving Margaret Chase Smith across Maine's Second District. "Would you like to come with me?" she asked one day at the end of the morning interview. "Where?" I asked. "To see Maine." At eighty-five she wanted to see the face of Maine once more, the small towns of the interior which had sent her to Congress and then to the Senate. I was to do the driving. Together we travelled through the farming country of Canaan, past the grove of birch trees and the bridge where Clyde Smith had taken the Chase family to camp when he was courting Margaret, on to the paper mill towns of Madison and Anson. By the time we arrived in Farmington she had revealed that if she were younger she would build another house. "I still don't have what I want," she said. And she told me about her husband Clyde. "He was a captivating man, almost to the point of being hypnotic." Dead for more than forty years, and she still felt the pull of his charm. There were other trips: to Augusta and Cundy's Harbor (on the coast above Portland), to the small towns of the lake region, to Lewiston and Auburn, to Smithfield and Athens. As we drove, we talked of Maine's church spires and of her dream to see that each small town had money to buy a spotlight so that at night the white spires could be seen for miles. She told me about the Abnaki who had lived in Maine before the English and French arrived and of their brutal massacre by the English at Norridgewock.

Unfolding before us in the clear and crystalline Maine summer was the
raw beauty and drama of Maine—a landscape as strong and vital as the
spirit of its people, a force that had pulled on the earliest settlers and drawn
countless artists and painters and writers to explore the nexus of interplay
between nature and intellect. In the serenity of these long, uninterrupted
journeys, paradox, distortion and much truth emerged. Margaret Chase
Smith's need to invent a character of mythic proportions co-existed with a
self that was essentially honest and straightforward. A streak of parsimony,
the need for control, a relentless struggle for perfection and an expectation
of absolute loyalty were juxtaposed against humor, kindness, and even, at
times, selflessness. Especially were these latter qualities revealed when she
spoke of her beloved Chihuahuas, Minnix and Betty, as precious as children, now long dead. For a time that summer, she showered my two
Westies with the same kind of attention and affection that I imagine
Minnix and Betty received, and in doing so she revealed a self far more
human than the political icon she strove to become.

One weekend in August, I drove Senator Smith to a farm belonging
to her secretary and her husband. With us were Buffy, then barely more
than a puppy, and Chivas, a dignified adult Westie. The dogs were chasing each other in the pasture and Senator Smith had settled into conversation on the wide porch of the farmhouse when I went for a horseback ride. In my absence, the dogs found cowpods and by the time I
returned were splattered from snout to tail. At the sound of my scream,
they sheepishly crawled toward the wire fence that surrounded the cow
yard and slowly began to ease under it. Buffy, who was the less cautious,
failed to drop low enough, and the electrically-charged lowest strand
stung him. At first he stood frozen. And then, yelping, he ran straight for
the closest refuge he could find.

Fifty yards away, Senator Smith in a crisply ironed summer dress was
sitting on the porch, rocking and laughing and reminiscing. The end of
my project was a nineteen-pound Westie covered with fresh cow dung.
Jolted by the fence, he sprinted across the mint-colored lawn, and when
he reached the porch, up he flew, past the iced tea glasses and into the
starched lap of a very surprised Margaret Chase Smith. My foot hung in
mid-step and the green of the lawn turned black. Then suddenly laughter like crystals tinkling spilled off the porch and into the yard and around

the dogs. "Oh my, Oh, my," as if nothing unusual had just happened, as if dogs and cowpods landed in her lap every time she drank tea. With poise born of a lifetime, she turned to her host: "You know, we used to have dogs. Took them everywhere, even out to eat. Did I ever tell you the story of our first Chihuahua?"

After daubing at Senator Smith's dress, I grabbed Buffy and Chivas and followed the resident children to Lemon Creek to clean up before supper and assess the situation. But there was nothing to make of it—at least nothing negative. I had undertaken the study of the life of a woman whose grace could be as disarming as her frown was unnerving, whose solitary journey had the stamp of great adventure, and who wasn't inclined to judge small dogs, or other helpless things, too harshly—at least not in a setting so bucolic and pastoral.

When summer ended, I returned to Florida, though over the next ten years I saw her fairly frequently. We visited in Silver Spring, Maryland, and I entertained her on 4 July in my small cottage in Lakewood, Maine. She invited me to her 90th birthday celebration, and we kept in touch over holidays and during summer vacations. She showed me her summer home at Cundy's Harbor from the water as well as the land, and she made certain that I experienced the fine lobsters caught in those very waters. With the passage of time, however, came a distance sufficient for me to balance her view of the past with the views of others.

I have withstood the temptation to discuss Margaret Chase Smith as a pioneer. Because she was the seventh woman to enter the Senate and the only one to be elected after first serving eight years in the House, the label of pioneer seems apt. But that is not how she perceived herself, despite her conscious exploitation of the identity of a pioneer between 1948 and 1952 when she was attempting to win the number two slot on the Republican ticket. Most of the time, Margaret's sense of self had less to do with pioneering—in Webster's terms, "preparing the way for others"—than with a grand adventure all her own. She wanted to see what she was capable of achieving.

Had she come to Washington committed to issues—rather than to a region, a way of life, a personal quest—her career would have been easier for biographers to assess. Instead, she eludes definition and frustrates analysis. In the end, Margaret Chase Smith exceeded her wildest dreams, though not without a high price in isolation and alienation—from her class, her Party, maybe even her gender.

At an early age, Margaret had reason to question the patriarchy. Her father, George Chase, who seems to have favored her younger brother, despite some early evidence of father-daughter bonding, became over the course of his life increasingly dependent on alcohol and unable to provide adequately for his family. Margaret's mother, Carrie, thus became the financial backbone of the Chase family. From the household of an emotionally unstable father, who also suffered from excruciating headaches, Margaret entered the house of a charming but unfaithful husband, Clyde Smith, who eventually died of complications from a sexually transmitted disease. By the time of Clyde's death, Margaret had little reason to put much faith in a system which perpetuated the myth of male superiority and ample reason to turn to sources of security which existed within herself. Even so, she avoided the labyrinth of the feminism of her times and embraced convention, even a she embarked on an adventure that carried her well beyond conventional boundaries. Despite the potential challenge she posed to the status quo in deciding to run for public office in 1940, she carefully distanced herself from those who stridently demanded immediate social change, for even though she was herself an agent of change, she preferred not to call attention to that fact. Women who referred to men as "oppressors" and to the home as a "prison" especially had the potential to fracture her carefully constructed coalition of men and women from the great middle, women like my own mother, who had her own private reservations about woman's place and thus could identify with the precariousness of Margaret's positioning. In this way, she paradoxically represents what some have referred to as the first stage of twentieth century feminism: challenging daddy—a phenomenon intertwined with the major themes of a life that remained throughout its duration a work in progress.

ACKNOWLEDGMENTS

IN WRITING THIS BOOK, I have often felt that I had no words left, that I had used up every one I ever knew in sketching my subject's life. But upon reflection, I find that the most important words have yet to be uttered. They are, both simply and profoundly meant, thank you.

My research for this book depended on generous financial assistance from the University of Florida, through the Division of Sponsored Research and the Graduate School, and from the Southern Regional Educational Board. I especially want to thank former UF provost Robert Bryan and former Dean of the Graduate School, Madelyn Lockhart, whose support never wavered.

Further, I am indebted to generous and thoughtful people from Florida to Maine who enriched my research. For their assistance during the winter months when I was teaching, I want to thank the staff of the UF Library, with special thanks to Leilani Freund, John Van Hook, Dolores Jenkins, and Dale Canelas. In the Special Collections of the Miller Library at Colby College, I was the recipient of the tireless help and insights of P. A. Lenk. Associates from Special Collections of the Fogler Library at the University of Maine responded promptly and cheerfully to numerous requests, as did librarians at the Skowhegan Public Library. I am indebted as well to librarians who made available to me archival collections at Yale, Syracuse, Radcliffe, the University of Michigan, the Library of Congress, the Presidential libraries, Bowdoin, the Portland (Maine) Public Library, Bates and the Maine State Library.

At the Margaret Chase Smith Library, I was fortunate to work with two fine directors, James MacCampbell and Gregory Gallant. Gallant, especially, went out of his way to make materials available and provide support services. Without the friendship of the library staff, my job would have been far more difficult and much less fun. For their friendship and quiet good will, I thank Reggie Collins and Pat Spivey. For taking me into her family and letting me experience the decency, warmth, humor and pride of Maine people, I thank Angela Stockwell and the Hall family of Athens, Maine.

I have been especially fortunate to have received the help and criticism of scholars who have shared with me their craft and their wisdom. Patricia

Craddock, an Edward Gibbon biographer, provided generous encouragement and uncompromising standards throughout numerous rewrites. Historian Hillel Schwartz similarly held me to his high standards and constantly enriched my analysis; Bob Mautz (now deceased) cheered me on as no one else quite could and enhanced my prose by his careful reading; historian Gus Burns commented on parts of the work with enthusiasm and insight, as did Robert Bryan and John Seelye, whose knowledge and understanding of the Puritans was invaluable in my assessment of Margaret Chase Smith's ancestral legacy. To historical sociologist Ann Neel, I am indebted for an especially close reading of the final draft. Smith Kirkpatrick shared a lifetime of knowledge about the craft of writing. To him, I owe more than I can repay.

I am grateful for the advice and enthusiasm of Neeti Madan at the Charlotte Sheedy Agency, and for the help of numerous colleagues and friends, including Jane Bailey Sanders, whose intrepid reading of an early draft inspired me to keep on, Melissa Herman, who has generously given this project hours of her time, Cathryn and John Lombardi, Paul and Polly Doughty, John Cech, Kevin McCarthy, Patricia Haynie, Debi Gallay, George Bedell, Pat Dunn, James Twitchell, Ron Carpenter, Sue Fisher, Judy Waldman, G. E. Rice, Yancey Walters, Jack Wheat, Mary Leigh Jones, Barbara Wingo, Cappy Longstreth, Billye Boselli, Ruth Trobe, Raymie McKerrow, Sue Whiddon, Ruth Alexander, Jeannine Webb, Carolyn Hufty, and Charlie Reed. To Fred and Mary Stuart and to Barbara Specht, whose faith in this project has remained constant for over a decade, my special thanks.

Michael Alpert's enthusiasm for the book created a climate that has made it a joy to work with the University of Maine Press. His tact, wit and precision have earned my deepest respect. I also thank editorial assistant Margaret Miller and indexer Mary E. Lawrence for their conscientious work, and my typists Susan Lewis and Elizabeth Williams, without whose support and competence this book would never have been completed.

To Buffy, Chivas, B. J. and Alex, who lived the book with me and without whom it could not have been written, and to my father, who taught me to whistle and throw a ball, and my mother, who will doubtless find a way to display this book on the refrigerator, this book is fondly dedicated.

P. L. S., June 1996

INTRODUCTION

1. *Nineteen seventy-two*

HER FACE WAS SOFTER than it had been in 1940 when she first ran for office. She was all angles then and sharp lines, her jutting jaw a sculptor's dream. A small woman whose straight back always made her seem taller than 5'3", whose crisp, nasal Maine twang brought special weight to her words.

Even at 74, time had not obscured the high cheek bones and prominent jaw which made her recognizable well beyond the boundaries of her beloved Maine—a ship's figurehead in proud profile. Nor after 32 years in public office and a crushing defeat had her force of will diminished, or her strength of character. They still punctuated the way she carried herself and the way she carefully framed her sentences. Integrity is what some called it. Others thought it was pure stubbornness. Both views were correct.

But integrity was the quality most evident in the house which she had built for herself high above the Kennebec River and to which she had now retired. Clean of line, without ostentation, but solid and well constructed, the house had many windows to brighten gloomy winter afternoons and to capture the sun on shimmering days in May when all of Maine becomes young again. Gray clapboard with white trim, it sits securely below the crest of Neil Hill and overlooks the town in which she had grown up. The town in which her father had been a handyman and barber, the town in which she had married Clyde Smith, a local politician who ended up a congressman, the town which had helped her launch her career in 1940 and which in 1972 had failed her.

From Neil Hill she could not see the house on North Avenue where she had been born. The house which always seemed to need paint, inside and out, the austere two-story, shutterless house with its stoop and plain door, the house which Grandfather Murray had built with his own hands, and which upon his death became the Chase house.

Nor could she see most of the houses of those who had dominated Somerset County's political and economic life from the time of earliest remembrance. The sprawling 19th century houses with wide porches, mansard roofs, and bay windows, or the stately Philander and Abner Coburn mansion on Baptist Hill with its Greek-columned front and sweep of lawn. Hidden from view as well was the house which sat at the foot of her hill and presided over Coburn Avenue and Pleasant Street. The Stephen Coburn house was perhaps not the grandest in Skowhegan, but it was one in a constellation whose understated elegance conveyed not just wealth, but old money. Its charm lay in its balance and scale, its worldly resemblance to a French country house. It suggested sophistication and sense of place, and it represented membership in a charmed circle to which by birth Margaret Chase Smith was not entitled to belong.

Sense of place had not been the legacy of the cavernous Pooler house on Fairview Avenue where Margaret and Clyde Smith had taken up residence after their marriage. Nor scale either. The Pooler house was dark, even on long summer days, and its rooms were quick to take on the chill of evening. It was larger than the Stephen Coburn house and, some would note, much more grand. A sure sign of "new money," tongues would wag, even though it was built by one of the town's earliest families. In ten years of marriage, the Pooler-Smith house never felt as though it belonged to her. Clyde's stepmother, Albra, who lived with them, was much more its mistress. Margaret remained a poor girl from North Avenue whose presence was tolerated only because she was Clyde's wife, and his second wife at that. But over time she prevailed.

Eventually, acceptance came even from people like the redoubtable Louise Coburn, Stephen's daughter. Though some knew her best from her role in administering the Coburn Land Trusts and others recognized her as the author of a two-volume history of Skowhegan, she was most widely known for her activities in the Maine Society of Mayflower Descendants, D.A.R., and Colonial Dames of America. To Margaret, she was a model of much that Margaret was not, and everything she wished she could be.

As a young woman, Louise Coburn had been softly pretty, but by the time Margaret came to know her, she was every inch a dowager—from her ample bosom, to her starched posture, to her pince-nez. She had not been the first woman graduate of Colby College in nearby Waterville but was the only woman of the four in Colby's class of 1877 to receive a degree. And in 1890, when Albion Woodbury Small, Colby's tenth president, announced his plan for "coordinate education" which would exclude women from "male" studies such as natural and social sciences, she joined forces with Mary Low Carver, class of 1875, to wage a campaign to keep Colby truly co-educational.[1]

As the battle lines formed, Small avoided the argument that women were intellectually inferior and therefore should be denied a full education. Instead, he claimed that Colby believed in "the old-fashioned idea that the typical woman is not one who finds her sphere in public life, but . . . one whose ambitions center in the family. . . ." Hence, she had no need of the sciences or mathematics. Both Low, who had been the valedictorian of her co-ed class, and Coburn believed that men and women should "attain to the same end—mental culture," but they couched their argument in terms that suggested an acceptance of traditional nineteenth-century views of women. Arguing that because woman's proper role was that of a wife and mother, women needed to "have the best and truest culture"—a condition which could not be achieved without entering "the charmed circle of the sciences"—Coburn and Low effectively used Small's position against him without sounding like radicals.[2] Their embrace of tradition, even as they undermined and rejected it, foreshadowed the path Margaret Chase Smith would follow throughout her public career.

Though Coburn and Low were committed to the "recognition of selfhood" which was at the heart of the struggle for woman's rights, they were not feminists. Their motivation stemmed more from a belief in parity than from a commitment to the "separatist . . . impulses which affected vast numbers" of feminists.[3] In this matter, too, Margaret followed in their footsteps. Moreover, Coburn, who never married, provided a model of someone who put her mind "at work at other purposes than refining [her] subordination to men," an impulse which may have played a significant role in Margaret's marriage to a much older man and her unwillingness to remarry after his death.[4]

When in 1944 Margaret Chase Smith was awarded an honorary degree from Colby (her first), she knew that it could only have happened with Louise Coburn's support. The Coburns and the few who were like them made such things happen—or prevented them. They always had, and they always would. That she could never become a Louise Coburn, however, was clear to Margaret from the time she was quite young.

The Coburns were a founding family in Somerset County, and they lived suspended between gentility and small town nobility. The Chases and the Coburns came to the interior of Maine at about the same time, and both families rather quickly acquired land. After the Civil War, the Chases lost theirs, while the Coburns increased their few hundred acres to many thousands. By the end of the century, because of their shrewd investments in land, the Coburns had become fabulously wealthy. As the business prospered, Abner became President of the First Bank of Skowhegan, and director and President of the Maine Central Railroad. In 1862, he was elected Governor. When Abner died in 1885, he left the then-staggering sum of nearly $1,000,000 to educational and missionary organizations.

Abner's brother and Louise's father, Stephen, became a lawyer. Although he dabbled in politics and served a short term in Congress, Stephen was not a politician. He enjoyed reading and thinking, and as a young man served as principal of Bloomfield Academy. His first love was the law, and it was as a small town attorney that Stephen Coburn chose to make his living. The worldliness and sophistication of his house on Pleasant Street suited this bookish Coburn. And it whispered ever so quietly that Stephen Coburn held membership in the "club" which dominated Somerset County and even Maine itself for a time.

The club. She had known she could never be one of them and had not even thought of them for years. And now when she had finally come home to stay, most of them were gone. Those bewitching people who had inhabited the well-lit rooms on Pleasant Street and Baptist Hill, who posed for Christmas pictures at front porticos framed by snow, shielded from the cold by their fur hats and muffs, who married each other and who took privilege for granted, and who had opposed her and helped her, snubbed and embraced her, and who—just when she needed them most—had abandoned her, but who had never succeeded in keeping her just the girl from North Avenue.

2. View from the Kennebec

MARGARET CHASE SMITH was no ordinary woman, and her dream was no ordinary dream. But the pattern of it was buried deep within the soil of central Maine, a soil from which it was difficult to make a living, much less move with ease from one social stratum to another. The region was born in a confluence of migration to the frontier by people so poor it was said that had they not migrated, they "must have remained a public charge in the respective town" from which they came.5 The lure was land, free land to those who would settle and carve civilization out of the wilderness. To understand Margaret Chase Smith, the Senator and Congresswoman, it is necessary to understand the land's effect on the values of the region in which she was born. It was from the egalitarian, independent farmer and village dweller that Margaret sprang, and it was this group that shaped her present-past.

These yeomen were more of a tribe than a state, even with their individual differences. They preferred "a society where many small producers engaged in exchange as equals, where no white man had dominion over another," and where tenancy and wage labor were the exception, rather than the rule.6 They shared a love of the land and clung to the independence it nurtured, a value which endured not only on rural farms but in Maine's villages as well, where many a small house lot boasted a vegetable garden, a cow and chickens. As the rest of the country experienced an influx of immigrants from all over the world, Maine's percentage of foreign-born in 1900 remained a low 13.4% (as compared with Boston and New York's 35% average), many of whom, like Margaret's maternal grandfather, were from Canada and could quickly become assimilated.7 Even as late as 1946, Maine still saw herself as a state "of open country" in which villages and farms formed "the backbone of her income, with fully 60% of the people living in rural towns" and villages.8 Margaret Chase Smith, descendant of Puritans and granddaughter of immigrants, absorbed at an early age the tribe's shared moral principles. Though her ambition would carry her far beyond the confines of Maine, the hold of rural Maine and its values remained bone deep.

At her moral center was an impulse spawned by Yankee Protestantism, the legacy of her Puritan forebears. To her, measures of right and wrong were to be found within herself, not in a political climate whipsawed between economic considerations and political passions. Co-existing with her genuine highmindedness, however, was an essentially negative, judging presence which often caused her to assess the positions taken by others in the least generous light. At its worst, her preference for the moral high road became an exercise in imperiousness. At its best, it became her attack on McCarthyism and her continuing campaign to goad Eisenhower into showing some courage in his dealings with McCarthy, even though that meant she was all but banished from the White House during much of the Eisenhower presidency.

A second, even broader pattern was Margaret Chase Smith's quest for standing, with politics the means by which she could achieve it. Her style reflected the model of statecraft she saw from her husband's office in Skowhegan, where local problems always had a name and a face and where direct intervention was expected. The character of the quest derived from the Yankee Protestant belief that a true state of grace is possible only if one holds oneself to the "highest imaginable excellency."⁹ She was not merely seeking to redress an accident of birth by becoming rich or famous or powerful, as others like Richard Nixon or Lyndon Johnson, shaping themselves in the mold of Horatio Alger heroes, seem to have done. She was striving to prove herself one of the elect, a model of perfection. Hence her pride in a perfect record of roll call votes and an unmatched number of honorary degrees. These were outward signs of accomplishment of an inward quest, though for others they became symbols of her lack of sophistication and proof of her tendency to mistake form for substance. But to Margaret Chase Smith, they were sign posts that the road on which she was travelling was the correct one. The city on the Potomac was a secular substitute for the "City upon a Hill" envisioned by John Winthrop in 1630.¹⁰ Her "hidden personal myth"—a term coined by biographer Leon Edel—thus was more than mere ambition. That was the obvious myth. The hidden part of the myth was the inadequacy that drove the quest, that fueled the need to best herself, to prove that she was of singular quality. Once that is understood, her rise to the Senate and her bid for the Republican nomination for president make a great deal of sense, as does her acute sensitivity to slights and defections. Even the special character of her defeat after thirty-two years in public office can be better understood.

The way from Skowhegan to Washington was long, even by airplane. But if the physical distance could be easily traversed by plane, the psychic distance between these two points, especially for a woman, was vast. Margaret was not well educated, had little in common with other congressmen and senators, was not a feminist, nor even a very good Republican, according to her critics. She was a woman operating in a male domain, and despite the constant presence after 1948 of a politically astute male administrative assistant, who was also her companion in private life, she remained, through most of her life, virtually alone. By what means did this woman "invent her own destiny?" How can her career and her success in defying the restraints of female role be explained? One answer is suggested in Carolyn Heilbrun's *Writing a Woman's Life,* though her construct applies to women artists rather than to women in the public domain. For women artists "to live a quest plot, as men's stories allow, indeed encourage them to do, some event must be invented to transform their lives, all unconsciously, apparently 'accidentally,' from a conventional to an eccentric story," writes Heilbrun. In this way, a woman can escape "the social demands, the compulsion to motherhood, and despair at her lack of accepted sex appeal." This transforming event (usually a sexual, or at least a social sin) will carry her far outside conventional boundaries and thereby liberate her from the bonds of her role to become a creative force.[11]

For the public woman as well, a transforming event is important, though she is not free to ignore convention. Indeed in the public domain, convention is an ally, respectability an imperative. Thus Heilbrun's paradigm must be shifted. As with Heilbrun's artists, a leap from the private to the public domain requires a felt need to excel. In addition, prior success is necessary so that opportunity can be effectively exploited. In Margaret Chase Smith's case, she had learned early how to excel and had achieved eminence in two women's groups, the National Federation of Business and Professional Women [BPW] and Sorosis. She had also moved steadily upward in the Maine State Republican organization before the death of her husband—the "transforming event of her life"—occurred in 1940. At that moment, her life was freed just as were the literary lives about which Heilbrun has written. Ten years earlier, at the age of thirty-two, when she wed a man twenty-one years her senior, Margaret had met the social demands expected of her without automatically creating an expectation of motherhood. Widowed at forty-two, she was elevated to an unassailable position of moral purity and protected from having to worry about the issue of sex appeal. Having early adopted the community's values, she was free to pursue her own unconventional adventure without the wind-drag of deviancy dogging her path. Ironically, in contrast to the creative women of Heilbrun's essay, her very *acceptance* of society's norms provided the means by which to *escape its boundaries*, a choice perhaps as generically central to the ascent of public woman as rejection of conventional boundaries is to the quest of female artists for creative independence.

Much of Margaret's life was spent fashioning a self that existed apart from class and gender, apart from her role as wife, and apart from society's veering opinions about woman's role. The pattern can best be described as a series of disguises, each one useful in pushing beyond the confines of what was acceptable for women. Margaret Chase Smith found it easier to explore who she was through costume and disguise—basketball uniforms, white gloves and hats, a WAVES military uniform, an Air Force jump suit, a red rose and pearls—than to directly challenge society's conception of womanhood. Her intuitive understanding of the need for camouflage thus makes her advocacy—particularly of the Equal Rights Amendment and Regular Status for Women in the Military—decisions of special daring, containing within them as they did the potential for exposing her carefully constructed persona.

In fact, gender shaped most aspects of Margaret's political career. By the forties, when it had become clear that the "woman vote" was not to be a decisive factor in national elections, and both parties began to turn away from including women at the highest levels, the GOP's reversal cost Margaret a potential platform from which to launch a national career. Nor did the pattern change during the Eisenhower presidency. Margaret's attack on Joe McCarthy and her continuing unwillingness to be a "team player" exercised Eisenhower almost as much as his failure to criticize Joe McCarthy irritated her. Thus Eisenhower—especially galled by a *scolding woman* who didn't know her place—allowed her to remain in exile throughout the fifties.

In the sixties, as America struggled for its political soul, Margaret's role became that of political presence, a remnant of America's fonder past. At her best, she was the voice of order, candor, and fair play, someone who spoke from conviction and weighed in on the side of principle, rather than self-preservation. At her worst, she grew fearful of civil disorder and disruptive change, intolerant of protest and protesters, receptive to the arguments of those who feared anarchy more than repression. She belongs in the category of business and professional women who found ways to excel in the years immediately preceding and following World War II and is a link between suffrage activism and the re-emergence of feminism in the 1960s and 1970s. In her refusal to accept the limitations of gender, she represents one of the most significant trends of the twentieth century. And in her capacity to understand that politics is both translation and transcendence, a vehicle for the most sublime aspirations of the home folks, she has few peers.

Where Margaret Chase Smith's story began was in the village, where everyone knew everyone else's business, just as their grandparents before them had known, all set in the midst of the desolate, sweeping beauty of central Maine.

PART I CANAAN

1. *The Maine Woods*

TWENTY MILES SOUTH OF SKOWHEGAN on a broad terraced plain
which slopes gently down to the Kennebec River is an ancient Abnaki
burial ground, now obscured by the town of Waterville. Long before 1629
when the Kennebec Proprietors (known also as the Plymouth Company)
laid claim to the three million acres which ran fifteen miles deep on
either side of the Kennebec, the Abnakis, whose language and culture
tied them to the Algonquian tribe, were the land's stewards and fishers of
the Kennebec and Sebasticook Rivers.[1]

Along the banks of these rivers they trapped beaver and built cabins
which they set up very quickly by planting poles joined at the top and
covering them with large sheets of bark. In the account of a priest who
lived among them for many years, they were described as a "tall, strong"
people "of a swarthy complexion," with black, braided hair and "teeth
whiter than ivory." He also noted that they were accomplished hunters.[2]
When game grew scarce they travelled the Kennebec-Chaudiere River
highway the whole way to Quebec, where they came to know the French
Jesuits. As early as 1633, the Abnakis invited the Jesuits to establish a mission between Waterville and Skowhegan at Nanrantsouack, which the
English later called Norridgewock. Their first priest was Gabriel
Druillettes, who travelled to Norridgewock from Quebec in 1646. He was
succeeded by several other Jesuits, the last of whom was Father Sebastian
Rasles, who took over the mission from 1694 to 1724. From the moment
Father Rasles arrived in New France from Lyons in 1690, Abnaki life fascinated him, particularly Abnaki language. "It cannot be denied that the
language of the Savages has real beauties," he wrote to his brother in
France, after spending two years in an Abnaki village near Quebec, "and
there is an indescribable force in their style and manner of expression."[3]
After five months of continuous study, he could understand all of their
terms but was having difficulty with "the form of expression and the spirit of the language." He repeated to them some passages from the catechism, and they gave them back "with all the nicety of their language."

Rasles immediately wrote these down and thus began a French-Abnaki dictionary "and also a Catechism which contained the precepts and Mysteries of Religion."4

Once he arrived in Norridgewock, he continued to record the Abnaki language, and in order to hear as much of it as possible, to spend countless hours in individual cabins. In this way he became an integral part in the life of the village. Wrote Rasles to his brother with unabashed admiration, "There is nothing equal to the affection of the Savages for their children."5

Nine years after his arrival in Norridgewock, the always-uneasy relationship between the French and the English finally erupted into what was called Queen Anne's War, an armed struggle between the French, who claimed all of the land east of the Penobscot river, and the English who claimed all of the province of Maine. Caught between these two contenders for empire were the Jesuit priest and his flock. When orders came from the English colonial government in Boston that all French missionaries should leave Maine, Father Rasles refused. In 1704-05 the village was attacked by the English and the church burned to the ground. Undaunted, Father Rasles held services in a temporary bark chapel and saw to the construction of a new church, which was finally completed in 1718. In 1723, Rasles informed his brother that the English were promising "a thousand pounds sterling to the man who should bring them my head."6

In the winter of 1721-22, a party of English troops under the command of Colonel Thomas Westbrook was sent to Norridgewock to capture Father Rasles. They were spotted by the Abnaki and an alarm was sounded which gave Rasles and the old men of the village time to hide and watch as the soldiers pillaged the church and the priest's dwelling and carried off Father Rasles's manuscript, the product of Rasles's thirty years among the Abnakis.7

Since English "warnings" had not weakened Father Rasles's resolve, on 23 August 1724, a third force was sent to Norridgewock. Once again they pillaged and set fire to the village. But this time, as Father Rasles tried to see to the welfare of his flock, the man who loved the Abnakis was killed.8

After 1724, the banks of the Kennebec no longer sheltered the Abnakis. Those who did not flee north to the Mission of St. Francis de Sales in Canada migrated east and joined the Penobscot Tribe at Old Town on the Penobscot River.9 The Abnakis' belief in Christianity, which had been cruelly tested by the English, was soon all but washed from memory and fused into a mottled landscape of blood and tears and love.

By the time Margaret Chase Smith's forebears built their cabin along the Kennebec in 1771, only the river carried the Abnaki memory, as carved pipes and bits of pottery sometimes washed up on shore. Only the bear and the owl bore witness to the passage of "the people of the dawn," until men like Thoreau, more than a century later, began to celebrate the intangible qualities of the wilderness and the superiority of the Indian, to whom "Nature must have made a thousand revelations . . . which are still secrets to us." Of the Abnakis, Thoreau confessed that he had much to learn, of the missionary, nothing. "I'm not sure, but all that would tempt me to teach the Indian my religion would be his promise to teach me *his*." From the Indian alone, Thoreau could learn the language of Nature, "the ancient level of communication [which] still existed in the forests of Maine" at the time of Thoreau's visits, between 1846 and 1857, long after the Abnakis left Norridgewock.10

Of such transcendental sensibilities the English settlers probably knew little and understood less, though the Maine wilderness had a hold on them as complex as introspection. Perhaps more so. Their habit of survival included an Indian's knowledge of the woods, and an Indian's knowledge of plants for medicinal purposes. But their impulse to tame the wilderness, to fell trees, to enlarge their cabin, and to expand their farm had nothing in common with the culture of the red man.11 "The Anglo-American can indeed cut down, and grub up all this waving forest, and make a stump speech, and vote for Buchanan on its ruins," Thoreau wrote in 1857, "but he cannot converse with the spirit of the tree he fells, he cannot read the poetry and mythology which retire as he advances. He ignorantly erases mythological tablets in order to put his handbills and town meeting warrants on them. Before he has learned his abc in the beautiful but mystic lore of the wilderness which Spenser and Dante had just begun to read, he cuts it down, coins a *'pine-tree'* shilling (as if to signify the pine's value to him), puts up a deestrict [sic] schoolhouse, and introduces Webster's spelling book."12

In the unbroken line of progress decried by Thoreau and others who loved the wilderness, Margaret's paternal forebears, the Chases and the

Emerys, proudly marched. Like many Puritan immigrants who left England in the early part of the seventeenth century to establish themselves in the new world, they were originally "excised from the broad ranks of the middle classes, coming from the towns and villages of several regions" of England.[13] With them they brought what historians Perry Miller and Thomas H. Johnson have called "the culture of England at that moment." They were thus likely to have been "just as patriotic as Englishmen who remained at home. They hated Spain like poison, and France only a little less." The Puritans also contended that the Bible was the supreme law "a hard and fast body of arbitrary law."[14] But it is not Puritan theology which is central to this story. It is the Puritan's habit of mind, which by 1771 had become, along with Calvinism, that pattern of thought we identify with the Yankee type.

The "strength of Puritanism," write Miller and Johnson, "was its realism. . . . It is impossible to conceive of a disillusioned Puritan; no matter what misfortune befell him, no matter how often or how tragically his fellowmen failed him, he would have been prepared for the worst, and would have expected no better." Yet there was nothing "lukewarm, halfhearted or flabby about the Puritan; whatever he did, he did with zest and gusto," a characteristic which the Abnakis of Norridgewock discovered for themselves far too late.[15]

The archetypal Puritan thus was "a visionary who never forgot that two plus two equals four; he was a soldier of Jehovah who never came out on the losing side of a bargain. He was a radical and a revolutionary, but not an anarchist; when he got into power he ruled with an iron hand, and also according to fundamental law. He was a practical idealist with a strong dash of cynicism; he came to New England to found the perfect society and the kingdom of the elect—and never expected it to be perfect, but only the best that fallible men could make."[16] To this construct should be added a love of order and an active suspicion of those who were "contrary minded." Even in the twentieth century, many of these values remain intact and have become "one of the continuous factors in American life and American thought."[17] Nowhere is their hold more evident than in rural Maine, and on no public figure of the twentieth century more than on Margaret Chase Smith.

The Chase branch left England sometime around 1630. Aquila Chase, who was a pilot or a fisherman, arrived in Hampton (in what is now New Hampshire) sometime around 1638-9. The Puritan settlement was located between the Piscataqua River and the northern boundary of the Bay Colony, and its spiritual leader was the Reverend Seaborn Cotton, son of "the famous John Cotton of the first Puritan generation."[18] Records show that Aquila was granted six acres for a house lot in 1640, and then in 1644, coinciding with his marriage to Ann Wheeler of Hampton, an additional six acres of "upland meadow and swamp."[19]

Most likely lured by the promise of more land, Aquila soon sold his six acres of meadow and swamp to his brother and moved from Hampton to Newbury, Massachusetts where he was granted four acres of land for a house lot and six acres of upland, along with six acres of marsh—all on the condition that he "go to sea and do service in the town with a boat for four years." He had increased his holdings by two acres and pocketed the sum received from his brother for his six acres in Hampton. It seems he had made a good Puritan bargain. For four generations the Chases remained in Newbury.

Newbury was also the home of the Emerys, who formed the second branch of Margaret Chase Smith's paternal line. After arriving in Boston in 1635 from England, John Emery and his wife Mary left almost immediately for Newbury, where they had been offered a town grant of half of acre for a house lot. On 2 December 1642 John Emery was recorded as one of the ninety-one freeholders of the town, and in the same year he was appointed with three others to "make valuation of all property in the town, for the purpose of proportioning each man's share in the new division." His contribution must have been valued, because within two years he received a grant from the town in excess of twenty-two acres which was to be shared with another resident. In 1661 at the age of 63 he was elected selectman, a powerful and prestigious office which controlled every aspect of local administration, including the levying of taxes and the resolution of questions of property rights—such as location and access to one's fields.[20]

On 16 September 1648, seven months after the birth of John and Mary's third child, Mary died. One and one-half years later, John remarried and on 13 May 1652 he and his second wife, Mary Webster, added a fourth and final child to the Emery household. For two generations the

Emerys remained in Newbury. Then sometime after 1753 John Emery's great-grandson Jonathan chose a path similar to the one which Aquila Chase's great-great-great grandson Isaac Chase would follow thirty years hence. He and his wife Jerusha set out for the frontier to build a new life together in the Province of Maine.

The first leg of their journey was probably completed aboard one of the wood coasters which regularly sailed from coastal Massachusetts to Maine, and which provided "cheap transport" to migrants.[21] The second probably began at the mouth of the Kennebec at Hallowell, where the couple set off for Maine's interior. Ahead of them to the north was an almost wholly uninhabited wilderness which stretched to the Canadian border. It was, in Thoreau's words (one hundred years later), a "bran-new country; the only rooms were of Nature's working, and the few houses were camps."[22] Where roads did exist, they were hardly more than foot-paths through the forest. So the couple travelled on foot most of the time, using horses whenever they were available. The journey was grueling and the elements cruel. The forests were cavernous. White pines, which were slowly being cut down for masts for the Royal Navy, soared to two hundred and forty feet, while eighty-foot tall red spruce commanded the forest's mid-light. At dusk a stealthy panther might be seen, and timber wolves could be heard at night. Always there was a specter of being caught without shelter as winter came on, making any delay on the jour-ney a potential tragedy. By April, when iced-over rivers and ponds began to thaw, the hazards of travel became even greater. Wrote Father Rasles of one such journey:

> In the meantime, we [Father Rasles and his small group of Abnakis] came to a lake which was beginning to thaw, and where there was already four inches of water on the ice. We were obliged to cross it with our snowshoes on; but as these snowshoes are made of strips of skin, as soon as they were wet, they became very heavy and rendered our walking more difficult. Although one of our men went in advance to sound the way, I suddenly sank knee-deep; another man, who was walking by my side, suddenly sank waist-deep, crying out: 'My father, I am a dead man.' As I was approaching to give him my hand, I myself sank still deeper. Finally it was not without much dif-ficulty that we extricated ourselves from this danger, on account of

the impediment caused us by our snowshoes, of which we could not rid ourselves. Nevertheless, I ran much less risk of drowning than of dying from cold in the middle of this half-frozen lake.

New dangers awaited us the next day at the crossing of the river, which we were compelled to pass on floating cakes of ice.[23]

Fifty years after Rasles's account, the Emerys survived the perils of their trip, and when they reached a place called Pond Town Plantation (now Winthrop) in the center of Maine, they stopped for a time. The area was beautiful. The forests were a composite of birch, maple, beech and evergreen. To the north was Lake Maranacook, to the south Lake Annabessacook. Scattered about were smaller lakes which filled with water lilies each summer. Soon the Emerys became restless, and they set out for less populated regions to the north. Thirty-five rugged miles away they stopped, and on a plot of ground which would eventually become Fairfield, they decided to homestead. There, in 1771, they built a rude cabin on the west bank of the Kennebec River, just eight miles downstream from Norridgewock, where the ruins of a chapel, an old grave surmounted by a cross, and a covered passageway to the river were all that remained of Father Rasles's mission.

After the Emerys had lived in Fairfield for four years, Benedict Arnold led an ill-fated expedition up the Kennebec and stayed at Jonathan Emery's home for two weeks in 1775, while his boats and baggage were portaged around the rapids of the Kennebec. Jonathan, who was a carpenter as well as a farmer, worked with Arnold's men to repair his boats, while David, his eldest son, listened to talk of war with England and decided to enlist. Before the year was out, David had become a soldier in the Continental Army. There he saw duty for five years, travelling with Arnold's Canadian expedition, serving at the siege of Boston in 1777 and finally transferring to Valley Forge (near Philadelphia, Pennsylvania). In 1780, he was discharged in New Jersey, whereupon he travelled straight home to Maine to live for the next fifty years with his wife Abigail and their ten children, including a set of twins, Miles and Rachel.

In 1825, Rachel married Isaac Chase, the son and namesake of Captain Isaac Chase, who had left lower New England for Maine around 1786 and earned the rank of Captain when he commanded a company of artillery in 1812. With the marriage of Isaac and Rachel, the

Chases and the Emerys were joined. Though the marriage merged two hardy Puritan families, the match did not prove brilliant. By now the Emerys especially, but the Chases as well, belonged to a small group of settlers who had made a start in the Maine wilderness. And in theory, for those who had made such a start, early nineteenth-century Maine offered expanding economic opportunities. But Isaac and Rachel were not able to exploit them.

In 1784, as a measure for settling Revolutionary War debts, Massachusetts had embarked on a course to encourage settlement in the District of Maine. Veterans received warrants, and lotteries were established to attract settlers. Restrictions on timber cutting "especially of large mast trees" were lifted, and the loggers arrived. At the same time, an increasing number of draft animals in urban centers created a booming market for oats and hay.[24] Between 1784 and Maine's subsequent separation from Massachusetts and admission to the Union on 15 March 1820, the state's population quintupled, exploding from 56,321 in 1784 to 298,335 by 1820.[25] Now was the time for established settlers to parlay land already owned into more acreage and to capitalize on a boom economy. Great fortunes and foundations for family wealth were to be built in this period, with results that would be felt well into the twentieth century.

With the dramatic influx of people into Maine, northern Maine timberlands became more valuable, as most of the old forests along the lower coast had been depleted by the turn of the century. Soon lumber operations had moved north into the interior, and small towns like Skowhegan boasted four sawmills. By 1841, families like the Skowhegan-based Coburns, who had large holdings in timber, were positioned to become the closest thing Maine had to royalty. The Isaac Chase family, on the other hand, chose a different path, and that, as the poet says, "made all the difference."[26]

Why the Emery-Chases did not seize opportunity is not clear. Perhaps fear constrained Rachel and Isaac. The slender hold which had been so painstakingly established over five generations might be snapped in less than one. Or perhaps financial gain was just not important to them, though this seems highly unlikely. What is more plausible is that they had built up a staggering debt in carving their homestead out of the wilderness which kept them too close to poverty to capitalize on the boom.

Merchant creditors, often willing to advance a settler and his family the provisions, livestock and tools needed in their first years, were also likely to charge high prices and high interest which kept the settlers in penury.[27]

In 1807 when the English traveller Edward Kendall toured the Kennebec Valley, he observed that "the farmer is commonly in debt to the merchant to an amount exceeding the value of his whole property. The merchant considers the farm, the crops, the oxen and the utensils of his debtor as his own," he wrote, "but reckons upon the industry of the farmer, and on the security of the property; and so long as he is satisfied with these, he reckons on his outstanding debts as on money put out to use, and from which he is to derive yearly interest."[28]

From those who did not have the resources to pay on their debts, merchants acquired improved homesteads very cheaply. Large landowners were easily able to obtain capital for more land by selling their timber, but small farmers like Rachel and Isaac Chase were consumed by the effort required to coax a crop out of the thin and rocky soil, tend to the livestock, clear the land and fell enough trees so that pine boards could be sold for cash and their debts reduced. Many homesteaders similar to the Chases lived in abject poverty, so poor that they lived "on bread alone for days, and sometimes [had] to make a dinner of herbs."[29]

Though the state of the Chase finances cannot be ascertained, it is likely that Isaac and Rachel did not invest in ways that would have brought them wealth because they lacked the capital, rather than the will, to do so. In any case, whatever the basis for their choices, during the first half of the nineteenth century the Chases occupied themselves with farming their land in Fairfield and rearing their six children, the oldest of whom was born in 1826, the youngest in 1837.

When the War of Rebellion, as the Civil War was called in Maine, began, the First Maine Regiment, consisting entirely of volunteers, was mustered into service.[30] Skowhegan (including Fairfield) felt it a point of honor to fill its quota without a draft, so the town paid recruits a bounty to volunteer. The bounties ranged from $100 at the beginning of the war to $300 by 1864.[31] So at the age of 24 John Wesley Chase—Rachel and Isaac's youngest child—enlisted and became a soldier in the Union Army. His wife, Margaret Nolan Chase, to whom he had been married less than a year, was three months pregnant. Sons of prominent citizens and leading citizens paid "commutation" for others to serve in their places. But John Wesley Chase and some 72,000 other Maine men, marched off to defend the Union.

As soldiering goes, John Wesley Chase was lucky. He came home even before the war's end and stayed there. When the conflict finally ended, 7,320 Maine men, or more than ten percent of the number Maine had sent off to fight, lay dead.[32] But marching off to war and living afterward required different sets of skills, and adjustments which some men were not able to make.

John Wesley Chase was one of those who faced down the nightmares of war. The army had purportedly instructed him in the rudiments of civil engineering, but the lessons that stuck with him were the far more searing ones about good and evil, sin and redemption, order and chaos. Man's dualities, more than the business of making money or building roads, would thenceforth hold his attention. It was as though, like his Puritan ancestors, he was searching "for an inherent rationality in things, in the mind, in the order of the universe." And like them, he turned to the church. At the age of 26 he became a clergyman in the Methodist church. At the core of his choices was most likely a belief akin to that which had first brought his forebears to Boston and then to Newbury. "The material world is transitory and deceptive, the passions of men ebb and flow, men make mistakes, accidents happen, and God can override or turn aside all natural processes; but something eternal and immutable does exist, and by that we must live."[33]

For fourteen years he served the Methodist Episcopal Church, until he died of pneumonia at the age of 39.[34] Left to mourn and survive were his wife, Margaret Nolan Chase, and four children. The youngest of these, George Emery Chase, would become Margaret Chase Smith's father.

For many families, the years following the war were hard times indeed. Robbed of a provider when John Wesley Chase died in 1876, the Chase family barely had the means of survival. Margaret Nolan Chase inherited nothing aside from the heavily-mortgaged 150-acre Chase homestead and sole responsibility for her four children, who were, at the time of their father's death, ages fifteen, nine, five, and two. After struggling for a time, she lost the homestead to the bank and with the children moved into nearby Fairfield to live. The two older children, Alice and Franklin, worked their way through school, and their younger brother, Charles Wilbur, went on to study civil engineering. When he was twenty-five Charles drowned in the Kennebec River during the big freshet of that year. The youngest son, George Emery Chase, left school after only a few years and set off for the West to make his way in the world.[35]

The Chase children had no head start in life. Time had bought them no advantage. Six generations of struggle had improved not one whit the family's fortunes, while new obstacles such as deepened class distinctions and the disappearance of cheap land made the Chase family's ascent out of poverty even more difficult than it had been for their forebears.

2. *The Father and Mother*

BY THE TIME George left for the West, many frontiersmen-farmers in Maine had not survived. Their lands had been sold for debts and back taxes at a fraction of their worth. Between 1870 and 1900 Maine's brief dominance in the cattle industry was eclipsed by the West, where land was less costly per acre and huge herds could be more cheaply fed. And so it was with wheat. Millions of acres of flatland where wheat could be harvested with combines, along with improvements in transportation which allowed for cheap transport, had brought Maine's wheat producers to their knees within a decade. The lives of frontiersmen-farmers and their families had been lost to Maine winters, to childbirth, and disease. After the Civil War, their financial well-being was destroyed by economic forces beyond anyone's control. Some, of course, who became storekeepers or lumbermen or mill owners grew wealthy. Others, who continued to depend for a living on Maine's stony soil, teetered on the edge of abject poverty. A few of these, in William Faulkner's idiom, "endured." The Chases endured.

George's dreams were too big for him. His trip West was a disaster. He returned to his mother's home penniless, despondent and with few prospects for employment.[36] Life had beaten him early. The role of the hero was not one he would ever tackle again.

George Chase's early set-back in the West and the loss of self-esteem which accompanied it were made worse by blinding headaches which afflicted him throughout his adult life. These occurrences could have been the result of something as simple as needing eyeglasses, or as complex as a nervous system disorder like neurasthenia, which is characterized by fatigue, depression, worry and often localized pains without apparent objective cause. Probably his father's untimely death, coupled with the loss of the family home, the ensuing dislocations of his childhood, and the drowning accident which took his brother Charles' life had all exacted a greater toll than anyone realized, though a genetic basis for the headaches seems likely, as his daughters inherited his tendency to suffer severe headaches.[37]

After a few months stay in Fairfield, George recovered enough from his misadventure to look for work, and he set off for Skowhegan, sixteen miles away. There he found employment as a waiter at a fine old hostelry, the Hotel Coburn, and he met the woman he would marry, Carrie Matilda Murray.

Carrie was beautiful, and she was winsome. She was a small woman who weighed less than one hundred pounds. She had beautiful dark hair and large eyes, and she loved to play the banjo. She would sit on a stool, holding her instrument and humming, her shapely legs and ankles more exposed than was customary, her Gallic charm completely mesmerizing the round-faced and unprepossessing George Chase.[38]

She was not, however, *of* the culture. Her father was an assimilated French Canadian who had left St. George Parish, in the Province of Quebec, as a boy and never looked back. By the time he himself had grandchildren, there was no trace of his native French, his Catholic faith, or the customs and traditions of a people who, less than one hundred and fifty years earlier, had been the English's most hated enemies. What he had given up to become an American was all that he was, as if his past were a great black hole at the center of which was something foul and unworthy—too embarrassing even to acknowledge. And so, his grandchildren, vaguely aware that their origins were French, as well as English, grew up knowing only his Anglicized, adopted name of Murray, not sure, but sensing that in their past was something darkly mysterious and unknowable. For Margaret, that void became part of who she was—part of the dark side which impeded her and the spur which was the key to her success. In some elemental ways, it kept her from feeling as though she truly belonged; and at the same time it kept her striving to be central. It reinforced her dislike for humanities courses like history — which were the preserve of people who knew they belonged, the socially elect — as it fed her drive to excel outside the classroom. It fueled her anxiety, her ambition, and her need for perfection, for surely if she did everything perfectly no one would ever guess the possible flaw.

And if she never probed too deeply into John Murray's past, she could not be shamed by his secret. Thus, Margaret was seventy-five before she began to explore the Murray line, though she knew all about the Chases and Emerys before she was thirty. Only after her career had ended did she make a pilgrimage to Quebec, there to discover that her grandfather's dark secret was that he had been christened Lambert Morin, that his father did not attend his baptism, and that his godparents had not signed the baptismal certificate because they could not write.[39] She had waited more than half a century to peer in at the void — perhaps unconsciously waiting until she was seasoned — only to discover that he was a child of poverty, born into a culture despised by the English, a refugee forced to leave much of himself behind and all the richness described by Lionel Trilling as "the hum and buzz of implication . . . that part of a culture which is made up of half-uttered or unuttered or unutterable expressions of value."[40]

Ironically the single most important legacy of Lambert Morin to his granddaughter Margaret was a keen respect for his adopted culture. By the time she came under his influence, he had become an archetypal Yankee Protestant. From his wages of $1.25 per day at the sash and blind factory, John Murray always deposited a specific amount in a savings account. The local banker reported years later that he always knew when Saturday noon came because this "little quiet man, John Murray, came through the door at exactly 12:15 [and] handed his bankbook and fifty cents to the teller for deposit in his account."[41] Personal responsibility, hard work, and thrift would characterize Margaret's personal, adult choices, as unswerving loyalty would characterize her relationship to the Maine culture. Because the Murray line was not essentially of the culture, she did not experience the kind of suffocating security within it which sometimes vitiates drive or fosters rebellion. Instead, she would spend her life striving to keep the culture on which her claim to membership was rather tenuous, safe from outside forces that would change it.

When George Chase met Carrie Murray, she was working at the local shoe factory and living at home. Over her father's protests, she had dropped out of high school a few weeks before graduation to go to work. Her father, who never went to high school, valued education far more than did his fun-loving daughter, and he was violently opposed to her decision. "I want you to graduate," he told her, but if you are determined to go to work you will be expected to pay your board, five dollars a week, as I will [only] support you as long as you are in school."⁴² Carrie was not to be dissuaded, however. And she went to work at the shoe factory, where she learned to be a fancy stitcher.

Her income by the standards of the day was good, and she paid her board regularly. But John Murray's "concession" was anathema to her, for she had imagined that her wages would be hers to do with as she pleased. Though she could hardly refuse to pay him, she did not forgive John Murray for charging her board until the day she married. On the occasion of her wedding, he handed her a bankbook with all of those payments for board deposited in her account.⁴³

Clearly Carrie could be stubborn, and perhaps that streak of willfulness contributed as much as anything to her choice of George Chase as a life partner. From John Murray's perspective, however, George was not a particularly desirable son-in-law. His job at the Coburn Hotel did not provide financial security, much less prosperity, nor was it an obvious steppingstone to a responsible position. By Murray's standards, George was too scattered, too preoccupied with schemes and far too fond of drink, which made him ugly and hot-tempered, and which, as Murray feared, grew worse with age. Even though Carrie enjoyed him, and he made her laugh, the side of George that was moody, petulant and jealous of anyone who paid any attention to Carrie was not lost on John Murray, and he did not approve.⁴⁴ Nonetheless on 25 October 1896 — only six months after the death of George's younger brother — Carrie Matilda Murray and George Emery Chase were married.

After the marriage, despite any lingering misgivings John Murray may have had, he did what he could to help the newlyweds get off to a good start. Fourteen months after her wedding date, Carrie gave birth to an infant girl in the same house that John Murray had built and in which Carrie herself had been born.

Though the day on which Carrie's daughter entered the world, 14 December 1897, was gray and sodden, soon it was to be white. White on the rooftops of white frame houses, white covering seldom-used paths, white muffling the hooves of horses pulling wagons and carriages on the street, white in mens' beards, framing flushed white faces. White-draped trees and white-roofed barns framed against an ashen sky—white the visible symbol of a chilling, numbing Maine December. The Kennebec which had taken the life of an uncle she would never know would soon be frozen over, the homestead along its banks that had been the Chase farm—now the Hinkley School, a home for needy boys and girls—blanketed in soft white snow, its outbuildings blurred to roundness by the snow against its walls. Soon all of the children, and parents, and grandparents who had gone before would slumber under a clean white covering, their graves part of a muted landscape in which all who had cleared the land and all who had fought that rending were one. As if in tribute to that present-past, George and Carrie named their infant daughter Margaret Madeline, for George's mother, who had died in Fairfield eight years before Margaret's birth.[45]

3. Childhood

WHEN MARGARET was only six months old, George moved Carrie and Margaret to Augusta, where he took a job as headwaiter at the Hotel North Augusta. Margaret was a beautiful baby, with dark wavy hair, rosy cheeks and a wide smile. Since the family lived at the Hotel and took their meals in the dining room, Carrie, who didn't care for housework, had unlimited time to spend with her beautiful child. She pushed Margaret in a stroller up and down the hills of the capitol city, and she and Margaret drew attention wherever they went. Carrie, who loved to talk, but knew no one in Augusta, talked with Margaret constantly and gave Margaret her full attention.

Margaret's exposure to the world these early years thus told her that she was important and charming. In the hotel dining room where a high chair had been provided for her, she was the center of attention, and people often stopped to speak to the handsome young family.[46]

The job in Augusta, however, did not work out quite as George had planned. Exactly what happened is not known, but "after a short time" the family returned to grandfather Murray's house on North Avenue where Margaret's cultural tutorial continued. In these years Margaret called him "Banker," a name somewhat easier for a small child to say than "grandpa," and a fitting metaphor for the precepts he was teaching her.

Until Margaret was five, the family stayed in the Murray home on North Avenue and paid "Banker" rent. The white clapboard house of six small rooms and a barn, connected by a long wood shed, was situated close to town and surrounded by a lawn, maple trees and a white picket fence, all of which made the lot seem bigger than its quarter-acre.47 In a replication of rural life in miniature, a cow and chickens resided in the barn, and later a horse. At "Banker's," order and continuity prevailed. Each fall George butchered a hog and each spring he put in a vegetable garden. Eggs and milk and fresh vegetables were plentiful throughout the summer months, and in winter the family depended on the vegetables, fruits, jams and jellies Carrie had "put up" in Mason jars.48 Before Margaret celebrated her sixth birthday, George moved his family out again, this time to Shawmut, near the family seat in Fairfield, where he opened a barber shop. By now the Chase family had expanded to include Wilbur, who was born in 1899, a third child, Roland Murray, born in 1901, and a baby, Lawrence, who was born in 1903.

The Shawmut years were developmentally important ones for Margaret. The Chase house stood close to the center of village life, near the village store and close to the railroad depot, the hub of what must have seemed to a child of five a great terminus of activity. In later years, Margaret fondly recalled carrying mail to the post office and visiting an elderly lady who lived across the road. She often stopped to see the grocery store owner, who offering her penny candy sticks which she refused, as she generally did not care for any candy except chocolates. Such daily interactions were likely to have reinforced a sense of well being and taught Margaret that risk-taking and venturing into the unknown were opportunities from which to derive pleasure, rather than situations to be feared. The relative independence of these years, in fact, encouraged an explorations of her strengths and nurtured her spirit of adventure.

In Shawmut, Margaret became well-schooled in the mores of village life, and at an early age she mirrored the judgmental and inquisitive impulses of many of her neighbors. The Chases lived in a double tenement house, the other half of which was occupied by an alcoholic woman. The archives reflect that when Margaret spied her staggering around outside, she would loudly announce: "There she goes again," as if Margaret were the voice of the town.49

While the Chases were in Shawmut, Carrie hired a girl of eleven named Agnes Staples née Lamore to work for her as a domestic. Agnes became Margaret's first real friend.50

Agnes arrived at the house every day but Sunday at 7 A.M. and prepared breakfast for the family. During the day she did housework and tended to the children until around eight p.m., leaving only after Wilbur had not only gone to bed, but to sleep as well. Wilbur's bedtime tantrums were already legendary, and he could be very difficult to manage. He was certainly harder to manage than Margaret, who was herself no amateur, having mastered the fine art of throwing herself down on the floor and holding her breath to get her way with Carrie. Margaret later recalled that Wilbur's nighttime tantrums pleased her, for they delayed the departure of her beloved Agnes whose company she sorely missed, especially on Sundays. In fact, she came to dislike Sundays intensely because she did not get to see Agnes until Monday.

In Shawmut, early signs of Margaret's drive, quest for perfectionism and meticulous attention to detail can be observed. Quite often when Agnes arrived in the morning Margaret would be up and dressed and Agnes would say: "Why are you up? Why don't you stay in bed?" Margaret's answer, as Agnes remembered, was emphatic: "Because I want to do things!" Often Margaret would be waiting outside in the swing humming a tune when Agnes arrived. She was "always writing something make believe with pencil and paper" or "reading her children's books." Then she would beg Agnes to go someplace with her. On such outings, Margaret would carefully make sure that her doll, which she carried with her "when she went to call," was as spotlessly clean as her own dress and her leather shoes, which she rubbed with handkerchiefs tucked into her apron pocket.51

Archival materials reveal that by the age of five, Margaret did not choose to play with children but preferred talking and being with older people. She loved to listen to adults talk and often sat on the couch in the parlor, listening intently as Carrie and a neighbor chatted, rather than going out-side to play with other children. With the birth of Wilbur, Margaret's emo-tional life changed. She now had a rival for her parents' affection, and she appears to have become less central to George than she had once been. In Shawmut George did not permit his daughter to enter his adjacent barber shop, despite Margaret's pleadings, nor did he spend a great deal of time with her. It is telling that Wilbur, who was two years Margaret's junior, was one of Margaret's least favorite persons. According to Agnes' later recollec-tions, he was jealous of Margaret. Quite likely the jealousy worked in the other direction, for Margaret spent much of her time bossing him around, a pattern defended by the loyal Agnes, who observed that George and Wilbur were very much alike—a fairly damning statement since she thought Wilbur was "a spoiled brat."[52]

Margaret's youngest brother Roland, on the other hand, who suffered from convulsions of indeterminate origin, was much less of a threat than Wilbur and elicited from her an unconditional love. With Roland, Margaret became quite protective, warning Carrie when another attack was on its way and crying as she watched the one-year old struggle for his life. Throughout her life she was drawn to situations involving people whom she believed to be vulnerable or needy.

Even as Margaret's childhood omnipotence was crumbling, Margaret and Carrie remained close. Carrie, though not a traditional mother with strong domestic impulses, was nonetheless Margaret's protector and greatest admirer. She allowed her maternal duties to be somewhat usurped by the capable Agnes, who fed the children a hot breakfast (usu-ally oatmeal, toast and eggs) and made sure that Margaret was not going off unsupervised on jaunts to the post office or elsewhere. But Carrie made sure that Margaret had dolls and pretty dresses, even though she could ill afford them. "Carrie would spend her last cent on Margaret," Agnes remembered, "because she was so proud." Perhaps because Carrie saw in Margaret her own willfulness, determination, and brightness, she had trouble saying no to this beautiful child she had produced. "I always knew that with tears I could win her over," Margaret was to say later. "So I'd cry. I'd go into tantrums. I always thought my mother would have been so much better had she said no at the beginning when she meant no. She couldn't bear to see me unhappy."[53]

Early in 1903 at eighteen months of age, Roland Murray died in Shawmut from pneumonia. Shortly thereafter, Carrie knew that she was pregnant for the fourth time. After two years in Shawmut and the death of a child, the Chases were ready to move back to Skowhegan. Probably as much for herself as for the children, Carrie asked Agnes to come with them. Though Agnes was willing, her own mother did not agree. The Chases left for Skowhegan without her, and Margaret left behind her only friend and her own dear brother.

The return to Skowhegan was not a triumphant one for George Chase. Once again, things had not worked out as he had planned. George went to work for another barber on Madison Avenue, in Skowhegan, and the family took a house on Leavitt Street. Occupying the North Avenue home was Carrie's half-sister, Laura, who had recently married and who was, when the Chases came back to town, pregnant with her second child. Within a year, Laura would be dead, at the age of twenty-one.

After Laura's death, the Chases moved back to "Banker's" where they would remain for the rest of their lives. John Murray still owned the house and rented it to Carrie and George, living with them most of those years, which were tumultuous ones for the Chases, as George and "Banker's" differences became accentuated by their living arrangement.54 The two men had never gotten along, but now George showed open contempt for the mild-mannered, pipe-smoking "Banker."

George was more hot-tempered than he had ever been, a tendency which grew worse when he drank. He lost his temper easily with Wilbur and Margaret, once spanking Margaret with a shingle because she didn't get home from school as early as he believed she should. She was in the back of the school, playing. "My father came over with a shingle. He took that shingle and touched my buttocks with that once. I said I wasn't doing anything. He said 'you didn't come home when you're supposed to. I don't want you over there playing with those boys and girls. Your place to play is at home.'" He also objected to letting the children taste coffee. "Mother would give us milk in the morning, and when he wasn't looking, she would put a teaspoon of coffee in the milk," recalled Margaret. "He was so strict. He didn't have any education—but he was meticulous about everything. He insisted on table manners. And I'll tell you if you used a fork wrong or did anything wrong, you'd get your fingers touched a bit."

Wryly she noted, "I didn't have coffee until I was quite old."[55] The family's explanation for George's harshness was that he was racked with pain from severe headaches, a malady no doubt exacerbated by his increasing difficulty in feeding his family, coupled with the indignity of living in his father-in-law's house and compounded by the grief at the loss of his young son. Whatever was fueling his fury, its impact on Margaret was unlikely to have been positive. Increasingly, George's punitive and unpredictable behavior made him seem a remote male figure, more likely to inspire ambivalence about men, than to generate a sense of pleasure in their company.

For Carrie, too, life had become increasingly more difficult after the return from Shawmut. Gone forever, it seemed, were the earlier carefree days, with the steady Agnes to help with her home and children. Now Carrie not only took care of Margaret and Wilbur all by herself, but she had an infant son, Lawrence Franklin, born on 10 November 1903 — nine months after the death of Roland — to look after. She was also in charge of the Chase household — cooking, cleaning, washing and ironing — and in order to make ends meet, she sometimes took outside jobs, waiting tables at the Coburn Hotel, or working at Green Brothers' 5 and 10 cent store, or at the shoe factory as a fancy stitcher. But through all of this, Carrie did not complain, and that was one of the valuable lessons she taught her daughter, the positive side of stubbornness. By example, she taught Margaret the virtue of a stiff upper lip. In the words of Maine poet Edward Arlington Robinson, Margaret learned that nothing was so "futile as regret."[56] One can only do one's best day-by-day, whatever the circumstances, even when the circumstances seem almost unbearable.

On 18 September 1906, at the age of two years and ten months, Lawrence Franklin Chase died of dysentery. Carrie, who was determined to have small headstones on Roland's and Franklin's graves, ordered them from Edwin Marble, a well-known local stonemaker, even though she did not have money to pay for them. Instead, she paid by taking in the Marbles' washing and ironing and furnishing them with a quart of milk each day from the family's cow, delivery of which fell to Margaret. Each morning before school, sometimes in freezing weather, Margaret would deliver the milk to the Marbles who lived about a mile away. On especially cold mornings, the family's black maid and cook — the only one in town of the fewer than twenty-four African-Americans in Skowhegan—often took Margaret into the kitchen and rubbed her chilled hands in cold water before Margaret turned around to walk back to Skowhegan and go to school.

By Margaret's own assessment, however, her childhood though "difficult" was happy. The back yard was often full of children, and when one of the children had a birthday, the Chases would make ice cream on the back stoop in an old-fashioned, hand-turned freezer. Margaret, who had been given piano lessons, would play at these parties and everyone would sing. Her childhood friends still recall that "it was always fun to go to the Chase house. There were usually parlor games in progress, or masquerades, or dancing and singing, with Margaret at the piano." Harry Day, who as an adult became the Skowhegan grocer, remembers "how he used to take rolls of butcher paper from his father's store: the paper was tacked on the walls of the Chase barn and painted as scenery for exciting amateur theatricals."57

The schools Margaret attended were Lincoln and Garfield Elementary Schools on Leavitt Street, where she was an average, though somewhat indifferent, student. Until the end of third grade, she wore her beautiful dark hair in curls, at which time she had her father cut them off so that she could be in style, much to her mother's sorrow.58 Through fourth grade, she wore her hair in two braids, tied about an inch from the bottom with narrow, colored ribbon. During this time, there was a run of lice at the school, and the girl sitting in the seat behind her took some from her own hair and put them in Margaret's braids. For Carrie, this was the final indignity. The Chases might be poor, but they were neat and clean, and she complained with unusual vehemence to the teacher about classroom hygiene and decorum. 59At that moment, life had conspired to reduce Carrie and those she loved to a bleakness she had not imagined when she married George Chase a decade earlier. Just as her employment of Agnes and Margaret's piano lessons revealed Carrie's upper-middle-class impulses, her daughter's lice were an unmistakable sign that such aspirations were delirium and the Chases' slender hold on even middle class respectability was crumbling.

Despite their increasingly desperate circumstances, Carrie taught Margaret by her own example that poverty does not have to bring shame, nor is hard work, however menial, demeaning. Carrie Chase worked. It was that simple. Much later, when Carrie was sixty-five and free from the need to work, she earned a salary from her son-in-law, the congressman, collecting rents from his tenants.[60] For Carrie, just as for "Banker," and ultimately for her daughter Margaret, work, even when it ceased to be a necessity, was valued for its own sake. In this, mother and daughter were typical. An expectation of hard work was still rooted in the soil of central Maine when Margaret was growing up. Just as Skowhegan's heritage was agrarian, so were its impulses. Many men still worked their own land, and usually with their own hands, for not without effort did the thin and rocky soil of Maine yield its fruits.

By the beginning of the 20th century, manufacturing had become an increasingly important source of income to the community. The spinning, worsted, and woolen mills, shoe factories and lumber mills were important to the town's tax base and employed many of the town's citizens. In 1913, the combined payrolls of the three textile mills in Skowhegan were approximately $3000 per week. With 630 people employed, the average annual income was less than $250, and the average weekly salary less than $5 per employee. By comparison, the town newspaper, The Independent Reporter, listed average annual salaries in Chicago in 1913 as $1200 per year.[61]

Unlike Chicago, however, or the large manufacturing centers in southern New England, there was in Skowhegan something akin to what the historian Richard Hofstadter described as a "natural harmony of interests among the productive classes."[62] Of course, people who worked in the mills in Skowhegan were not immune to the inhumane treatment so often found in the textile mills of the day. In fact, when Margaret was thirty and took a job as office manager at the local Cummings woolen mill, she observed people laboring twelve to eighteen hours a day in the dye house or the carbonizer area for twenty-six cents to twenty-eight cents an hour, 108 hours a week. Later, when she tried to describe what she had seen, the only words that seemed to fit were "slave labor."[63]

But Skowhegan workers had an advantage over their urban counterparts. They were not totally dependent on the mills for their existence and few among them could be described as impoverished laborers. The meagerness of their income from the mills was offset by the relative steadiness of such work and the availability of foodstuffs from their own farms: apples, corn, potatoes, eggs, chickens, milk, butter, and meat from a slaughtered cow or hog, supplemented by game shot on their own land. These were not the wage slaves of Lowell factories or of New York sweatshops, but yeomen farmers with steady wages and personal autonomy. Even townspeople did not stray too far from their agrarian roots, for many, like the Chases, used their house lots to produce foodstuffs.

Their sense of place was connected by the umbilical cord of generational memory to the early struggles of their ancestors to carve small farms out of the wilderness. Continuity and commonality fused past to present in a timeless flow. So it was that in the early 20th century, villagers and farmers alike remained more of a tribe than a state, their genetic and cultural similarities merging with shared moral principles, leavened by the value they put on independence of action and the principles of hard work. From the darker side of their collective persona came a suspicion of strangers, those from "away." Linked as well to their agrarian tradition was an impulse toward populism, "an undercurrent of provincial resentments, popular and 'democratic' rebelliousness and suspiciousness, and nativism."[64]

And so, in this setting it was natural that Margaret Chase, descendent of Puritans and granddaughter of hard working emigrants, should fall heir to these impulses, their potency increasing as she grew older.

4. *Setting Off*

ON 25 JUNE 1909, when Margaret was six months short of her twelfth birthday, her mother gave birth to a baby girl, Evelyn Mary Chase. Margaret now had a sister, and the family another mouth to feed. Whether the financial strain produced by another child influenced Margaret's decision is not known, though it is likely, but within a year of Evelyn's birth, Margaret walked into Green Brothers' 5 and 10 cent store and asked for a job.

It was an uncommon display of assertive independence in a twelve-year old. "Would there be any opportunity for a part-time job?" she asked the manager. He looked her up and down and said, "Can you reach that top shelf?" Of course, she could not reach it because she was too short.

"When you can reach that top shelf," he told her, "you come back and I will talk to you seriously and we will see what we can find." A year later, just before Christmas, she went back to see the manager. He remembered that she had been there before, and he said, "Well, you've grown a little." Margaret said she hoped that she had and did he have anything that she could do. He told her to come in if she wanted to and work Saturday evening. She would get fifty cents from five o'clock to ten. Soon the job was extended to afternoon and evening, for which she was paid seventy-five cents, and then it was expanded to all day and evening for which she earned one dollar. Christmas vacation, she was offered employment the week before Christmas. She went in six days, and worked from eight o'clock in the morning until six at night.[65]

On certain nights including Saturday, she worked until ten o'clock and was paid $3.50 per week, a generous sum of money in those days. The next year she was delighted when they asked her to stay on the second week after Christmas to help with inventory, counting the number of screws, hooks and tacks in stock. The job was tedious, though she later claimed it taught her patience and accuracy. After all, the $3.50 she earned was too important to jeopardize with negative thoughts.[66] Already Margaret had embarked on a course of action which was hardly the norm for a thirteen-year-old female. She had begun to make her way in the world, well aware that her salary was important in providing some of the family's necessities, as well as contributing to the family's single luxury: Saturday night outings to Smithfield Pond.

Situated just a few miles outside of Skowhegan, the pond is one of the smaller lakes in the Belgrade Lakes chain. In summer, its sandy shores play host to swimmers and its shady banks provide a cool and soothing refuge for picnickers. When Margaret was a child, cabins could be rented for a dollar a day, and the Chases rented one as often as they could during Maine's short summers.

On Saturdays, George worked in the barber shop while Carrie prepared their food for the weekend—sandwiches and cookies for the trip, and a jug of lemonade when they got to Smithfield. They would "arrive about 11 or 12" in a "two-seater carriage, and some of us would sit on the floor and put our feet under the seat so we could pile the food onto the seat."[67]

George Chase loved to fish, and early morning perch fishing was best. So as soon as the family arrived at the cabin, everyone went right to bed. By 4 A.M. Margaret, who never minded getting up early, joined her father on the lake in a row boat where they trolled for perch, a scene which resonates with elements of male bonding. With luck, they would bring in a dozen or more by 6 a.m.. George "was very particular about the cleaning of the fish," remembered Margaret. "He would bring them in on the rocks and clean them." Then he'd "take them into the house and mother would be ready with her hot frying pan and salt pork, etc. She'd roll those fish in meal and we would have breakfast."[68] In the afternoon, George took the children swimming, or watched them from the white sandy shore. Carrie remained in the cottage, preparing meals and packing belongings for the return home by dark.

Margaret's second sister, Laura, was born on 20 December 1912, six days after Margaret's fifteenth birthday. That same year, Margaret decided to try her hand at other jobs, perhaps as much a continuing search for identity and accomplishment as it was a source of income. For a brief time, she waited tables at the Coburn Hotel, where her father had gotten his first job and her mother occasionally worked. But the pay was poor and the better customers who tipped more generously were assigned to the older waitresses. Then she tried her hand at being a domestic. There were homes in town where girls were hired to help in the evening with dinner and dishes, and Margaret thought that working there might be a good way to earn some money. When she asked a local dentist and his wife if they would let her work for them occasionally, they agreed and soon contacted her to work one evening from 5:00 to 10:00, serving dinner and washing dishes. By evening's end, Margaret's pay came to a mere thirty-five cents, a sum which so outraged Carrie that she forbade Margaret to continue. In a similar venture, Margaret worked all of Christmas Day in the Frank Briggs home, waiting on a houseful of people and washing mountains of dishes for the sum of one dollar for the day.[69]

Finally, Margaret fell into a job which seemed perfect. She was asked by the town's night telephone operator, who knew that Margaret was looking for part-time work, if she would like to come in and learn how to be an operator. The operator wanted someone as a substitute so she could get out once in a while. The hours were from eight o'clock in the evening to seven or seven-thirty in the morning, and the pay was ten cents an hour, or one dollar for the night. Margaret was ecstatic. She learned quickly, and by October 1915, she was substituting regularly for Mrs. Frances Kelly, the night operator.[70] In no time Margaret had mastered the manual switchboard, along with the names and numbers of those who called regularly and asked her to connect them with a person, rather than a number. Even in old age, she remembered that John Rippin's office number was 59, ring 2; his house was 312, ring 12.[71]

The job suited Margaret, not only because of the pay and the hours. She had few calls to handle during the night and plenty of time to talk with her friends or listen in on a wide range of phone conversations, so "you knew everything that went on in the town." On slow nights, she used to talk with operators all over the state "because you really couldn't go to bed," though she had "a dirty old couch there that she slept on."[72] She was dealing with the public in a more sophisticated way than she had at Green Brothers; and she was learning to identify people by their voices. By means of the telephone switchboard, the whole state opened up to her, as smaller stations called into Skowhegan and other operators around the state came to know her by name. She was at the center of things, connected at the very hub of the community by a network of wires and plugs, all of which led out to the world and then back to her.

By the age of seventeen, Margaret could be described as striking, though not a beauty. Her dark hair framed a finely chiseled face, dominated by chambray blue eyes which could be by turns luminous or coquettish. Willfulness and singlemindedness could be glimpsed in a too-prominent jaw, about which she was self-conscious throughout her life, while personality and dynamism could be seen in her walk and heard in her laughter. Even though great beauty eluded her, to Margaret, attention would be paid, that much was certain.

And though she was bright and a quick learner, it was not to be in the academic realm that she would make her mark. Margaret was drawn by the particular, rather than the abstract, by problem-solving rather than theory. Her attitude was reminiscent of Carrie's early disputes with Banker over quitting school to go to work, a story that is easily imagined to have become imbedded in family folklore. She regarded fundamentals as trivial and irritating details standing in the way of quick accomplishment.

"Learning for learning's sake" was a pastime for those who were privileged. Margaret, who clearly understood her station in life, did not waste time confusing who she was and what she could expect from life with that full range of choices available to the town's elect. Like Carrie, Margaret thought of school as "just like serving so much time in prison. I resented going to school," she said, "because I was so anxious to get a full-time job and start making my own living and my own way in the world."73 Margaret's educational deficiencies were to haunt her throughout her professional life.

5. *The Quest*

IN HER CLASS of fewer than twenty-five, others like Ray Boynton, who was valedictorian and school president and Florence Burrell, who was salutatorian and school secretary, were the class "brains." Margaret filled a different niche. She was well liked and dependable, a personable girl who had switched from the general course to the commercial course in her junior year after flunking history. Margaret was dubbed "Chase" by most of her friends, "Marcus" by a few and was described in the yearbook, "The Lever," by the phrase: "She walks as if she were stirring lemonade within herself," a description which seems to suggest a young Margaret who was erect, lively and acerbic.74 She displayed no tendency toward introspection, nor did she keep a diary during this period. She was happiest in the company of others, and adored extra-curricular activities, high school socials, and boys, even one named "Smith," who lived on a farm just off the Farmington road. Later on, after she had married Clyde, he used to tease her about "the time [she] was falling in love with someone else," meaning the other Smith boy.75

But the activity around which Margaret's life most deeply revolved was the Skowhegan High School girl's basketball team, a team which won the state championship her senior year. The basketball court was the arena in which she experienced adolescence, learned endurance and a respect for accuracy, and discovered the importance of teamwork, the benefits of physical discipline and the unparalleled exhilaration which comes with victory. And though it did not point the way to a real job, it did reveal to her the way she wanted a job to feel—indeed the way she wanted life to feel—exhilarating, and filled with variety and challenge and reward.

She was the team's manager and played running center on a team of six. In those early days of the sport, the court was divided into three zones. Two forwards played at one end of the floor and two guards played at the other. Neither the guards nor the forwards could cross the center line into the other's zone. The third zone was the center, and the players who occupied that zone were there primarily to relay the ball from the guards at one end to the forwards at the other end of the court. It was because women were not thought to be strong enough to throw the ball the length of the floor that the position of running center was created.

The game was started with a jump ball. At the jump, the ball was tipped to the running center who was to pass the ball to the team's forwards. Margaret's position was pivotal. The running center was truly the archetype of a team player because her primary function was to relay the ball to the forwards, who would ultimately score the points and receive most of the attention and applause. Centers did not score points; rather they made scoring possible. Even so, because of the success of the Skowhegan team, there was glory enough to go around for all six girls. The team was followed with enthusiasm by the town. "Both teams got into the game all over at the start," reported the *Independent Reporter* on page one of its 2 March 1916 edition, "Skowhegan starting out with an excellent lead." Then Coburn Classical "put up a fast game and out-classed Skowhegan in passing, nevertheless the local players beat [Coburn] 13 to 3 on sureshots and foul throwing [and] were well up in speed."[76] Their games were usually held on Friday or Saturday nights in front of scores of supporters, with a play-by-play reported enthusiastically in the pages of the town newspaper. Even away games were well attended by fans from Skowhegan, with the outcomes faithfully reported in the *Independent Reporter*'s next issue.

Margaret had never done anything she liked so well. She enjoyed everything about the sport—the discipline it imposed, the strategies of offense and defense, the awareness of the compression of time into three, ten minute periods, and her own role in making plays possible, the link between offense and defense. She learned from the game that she enjoyed competing, and even more, that she enjoyed winning. Like her job with the telephone office, it put her at the center of things and in control, and it brought her to people's notice.

The team had been formed in Verna McQuillen's backyard when Margaret was in ninth grade, and from that moment, her schooldays became synonymous with basketball.77 At first they had no coach and their schedule included fewer schools than the nine which comprised their Central Maine Championship season in Margaret's junior year. Practice, however, occurred at regular intervals during the season, and between practicing and playing, the girls ended up spending much of their time together in the winter months. By the time they won the state championship in her senior year, the team had been together for three years. Through the critical years of adolescence, they had become a natural source of support and strength for each other and had provided a pivotal experience in young Margaret's life.

The bonding which took place during these years was akin to the female friendships portrayed in Laura Lee Hope's Outdoor Girl Series and Helen Vandercook's Campfire Girls, Red Cross Girls and Girl Scouts, and for Margaret was a form of self-rehearsal. *The Campfire Girls at Sunrise Hill* (the first in the Vandercook series, published in 1913 when Margaret and her teammates were no more than sophomores) tells a tale of twelve girls from privileged backgrounds who attend summer camp in New Hampshire. After spending time together, they decide to form a club. The impulse for their decision comes from a vague dissatisfaction with their lot in life as girls and a desire to do something "different." "Oh dear," one of the main characters exclaims, "I do wish one would invent something new for girls." The person speaking is Betty, who is described as fifteen or sixteen, with gray eyes and a short, straight nose. Her face "conveyed an effect of refinement that was almost disdain. Her mouth was a little discontented and somehow she gave the impression that, though she had most of the things other girls wish for, she was still seeking something." Betty's restlessness gives birth to the idea of the Campfire Girls, a "club," with secret ceremonies, a secret call, and canons of behavior which include telling the truth, being loyal, being kind to one another, and displaying independence. The club becomes an antidote to passivity and boredom, and a means to achieving the status of fully evolved human beings.

In an interesting choice by the author, the potential of this sisterhood is first realized, or at least articulated, by Betty's brother, who supports the girls' undertaking. He observes that "living out of doors all summer . . . and learning to look after herself and rub up against other girls may be the best thing in the world for Betty. I am afraid she has been growing up more ornamental than useful." Most remarkable is his observation that "the modern world has no place in it but for useful people nowadays. And somehow it seems to me that even more is going to be asked of women than has been asked of men. They have got their own housekeeping and some of the world's too, pretty soon."[78]

The Campfire Girls and other series like it were creating the image of a "new woman." She was to be self-sufficient, able to 'build her own fires,' take her turn at chores and work with other women for the common good. Adventures were not only for men, these books seemed to say, new scripts were being written by women so that they could pursue their own adventures. Margaret and her teammates were experiencing female friendships in much the same way as were the girls at Sunrise Hill. The team relied on chants and cheers, drew on team loyalty, and expressed an easy affection for one another. By then Margaret was dubbed "Marcus," a choice which suggests the dominance of a confident, masculine persona. What was awakened among the girls on the basketball team as it was among the girls at Sunrise Hill, and especially in Margaret Chase, was a sense of empowerment, a heretofore unarticulated belief in her own abilities. One truly could take charge of one's life and make it what one wanted to. Hard work and total commitment were the secrets. The importance of this experience is hard to overestimate, for some years ago, at the age of seventy-nine, Verna McQuillen still expressed profound disappointment at missing the chance to play in her high school championship game because of an attack of appendicitis.[79]

But no one missed the team more than Margaret when they all graduated in 1916. Basketball enabled her to harness the impatience and drive which academic subjects merely frustrated and enlist these impulses in the cause of excelling. Eventually, her need to excel and win would become her own white leviathan, and their pursuit—as with the fictional Ahab—would dictate a life course that left little room for anything else.

Thus graduation from high school seemed to Margaret less a beginning than a cruel ending. College was not in her future, nor was Sargent's

School of Physical Education in Boston which for years she had hoped to attend.[80] The reality was that she was a girl from a respectable, but poor family whose resources barely covered the family's daily needs. And so graduation could mean only one thing—the loss of the very activity which had first liberated her. What she had discovered about herself and what had made her feel whole were soon to be tragically blunted by her real-life options. When she completed the high school's commercial course, she would be fortunate to find a job as a bookkeeper, a telephone operator, stenographer, typist or a secretary. And although within a few years, she might make twice the income of workers in the shoe factory or waitresses, she did not sense that any of these jobs would enable her to do more than earn a small paycheck.[81] But in her senior year, Margaret's life intersected with someone who seemed fully in command of the world in which he lived, and whose ability to create opportunities for Margaret were practically without limit, or so it seemed.

6. *The Man from Hartland*

CLYDE HAROLD SMITH was born in Harmony, Maine, in the spring of 1876. His arrival preceded the appearance of purple trillium, yellow violets and the scent of apple blossoms. His birthplace was a solid Cape Cod, built by his father and his uncle and perched on the highest hill in Harmony. In appearance the house was much like others in the region. It was a rectangular frame box with a pitch roof and no stoop, or porch, or overhang to soften its facade. On either side of a wide front door were two windows with small six-over-six panes.

And yet, the house had a charm about it which derived from its proportion: its balance of height and width, the relation of door and window openings to each other and to the house as a whole. All of these features suggested permanence—the result of a fierce struggle to impose order on the unruly wilderness of northern Maine. The interior of the house was finished simply, with white plaster walls and narrow moldings around each fireplace. It was an eight-room dwelling with a wide center stairway. Two chimneys flanked either side of the stair-well, their fireplaces providing the house's only heat.

From the upstairs windows, a sweeping vista of Maine unfolded. To the northwest, foothills stretched into mountains which led to Canada. South lay dense forest, inhabited by porcupine, bear, and deer. To the east stretched the pasture and fields which the Smiths had cleared stone by stone. Along the southern boundary of the pasture was stone fence, shaded by a windbreak of trees and following the course of a dirt road which sharply descended to Harmony.

In winter, the climb from Harmony to the Smith's farm, a journey of about three miles, was a test of character and endurance. When it snowed, the road was frequently impassable, and only a pressing need would precipitate a trip to Harmony, for the return home was filled with uncertainty and the real danger of getting lost in a blizzard and freezing to death.

On those cold winter nights the wind found every opening in the uninsulated house, and the pine floors offered only slightly more comfort than the frozen ground below. Sleep was fitful and best undertaken fully dressed, with passages between dreaming and waking dominated by attempts to keep warm. The hardy alone survived under such conditions. Clyde's mother did not.

Angie Bartlett Smith died shortly after the birth of her fourth child, Kleber, in 1882. With her death, two of the children went to relatives and neighbors. Clyde's sister, Lena Mae, went to her maternal grandmother's and the youngest child was boarded with friends. Clyde and his younger brother, Myron, stayed at home with their father.

Clyde was six years old when baby Kleber was born, and when his mother died, he unofficially took over the raising of Myron. The boys were left at home much of the time, with only a neighbor to look in on them. Together, they came to provide, one for the other, much of the affection and love that had been lost with the death of their mother.

When Clyde was thirteen, his father Willard Smith remarried and the children were reunited. Clyde's new mother, Albra Cook, was from nearby Athens, where the family moved briefly when Willard "became engaged in trade." Then, within six months of the move to Athens, Willard moved his family again—this time to Hartland, where he had purchased the Skinner Grocery Store.[82]

As Harmony had formed and shaped Clyde, Hartland would embrace him. It was there that he grew to manhood and it was there that his political gifts would flower. At fourteen, Clyde was practically a man. Though he was enrolled at Hartland Academy, much of his time was spent driving a grocery wagon for his father and delivering orders. Since telephones were few, he spent quite a bit of time talking with people and finding out what they needed. Delivering groceries was the classroom in which he first learned about politics.

Even though Clyde's attendance at Hartland Academy was limited by his job of driving a grocery team, Clyde managed to keep in touch with several young ladies with whom he had found favor. When he wasn't able to go to school, he exchanged notes with them and met them after work in the evening. After one such evening, a young lady wrote to Clyde the next day: "Are you so tired and sleepy today that you could not come into school this afternoon? I was quite sleepy this forenoon and feel better this afternoon, only I am a little lonesome." In a (presumably) later note, she wrote: "I told you it was the first time and would be the last. I'm willing to swear that on the *Bible*."[83]

The usual jealousies and slights, perceived and real, often had to be worked out by mail. Another letter from the same young lady begins: "I hardly know what to say, only that I feel very bad that you doubt me so. As for Henry, last night, I only thought of him as a school friend. Say, I told you about that. He was around under my nose all the time and the more I tried to get rid of him, the more he hung around. I know I ought not to have danced with him. If it depends on me, as you say, we will keep on as before, only better friends, so that the stories that some folks take pains to invent need not trouble us . . . but I['d] rather see you and talk than to write as I can't write all that I want to say."[84]

After high school Clyde took a course at an Augusta business college but he seems never to have considered a college education.[85] Presumably, for a while, he kept in touch with his high school sweetheart, who was still in school, but before long, Clyde discovered something that exhilarated him as much as amatory adventure—a talent for debate and public speaking. Soon he was expounding his views around the pot-bellied stove of his father's grocery store and on the public platform. "Not a few people living in the vicinity of Hartland," remembered a contemporary of Clyde's, "will recall those old lyceum days when Clyde Smith was the presiding genius, when readings and music were enjoyed and wholesome debates on conditions of the time was discussed pro and con."[86]

As a teenager, Clyde had developed an interest in public policy issues, and his sketchy notes from this period reflect at least a nodding acquaintance with the relevance of moral considerations, though in the following instance he does little more than work it into a sentence. "This not only a question of immigration, but it is one of morality," he wrote. "Weather (sic) we proceed with our ownward (sic) march which is landing us so far above our competitors, or shall we drop down inch by inch into degradation. Neither can my opponent dispute the law of nature which sanctifies my statement."[87]

Bill Brown, Clyde's first mentor and an attorney from nearby Madison, claimed that: "at age seventeen [Clyde] knew more about tariffs and the function of government than most anyone that wished to argue the point at his father's store in Hartland." Thus it was that Brown "ran" Clyde for his first post "at an age when most young men and women do not know how to mark a ballot." When ". . . we first put him up for office," Brown recalled, "it was against a man who at that time was a powerhouse in politics, and nobody conceded Clyde a chance. At that time he had a bicycle and while his opponent was basking in the sun, Clyde was travelling about the countryside, from morning until late night, talking to people. The result was that he won and that's why, as he gained experience and knowledge of what his constituency needed, no one was ever able to beat him."[88]

The prize Clyde won (in 1899) was a seat in the Maine House of Representatives from the district comprised of Hartland, Harmony, St. Albans, Canaan, Cambridge, and Ripley, a seat he held for two terms until 1903. Though he was not yet twenty-one when he began to campaign, his nomination coincided with his twenty-first birthday and by the time he won the election he was of legal age to take his seat, the youngest man ever elected to the Maine legislature.[89] Like his father, Clyde was a Republican, a choice which made his political future much brighter than it would otherwise have been in the rock-ribbed Republican state of Maine.[90]

In Augusta, he came to know the glories of politics, as he had come to know the glories of amatory conquests some years earlier. The city was his port of entry to roaring power and the companionship of men who were defenders of all things good in this life and of many which were not. It was a tuning fork for his emerging sense of self, and it consistently held up before him accomplishments of the past, as well as the present. As Clyde walked the halls that had seen the likes of Hannibal Hamlin, who became Lincoln's vice president; James G. Blaine, secretary of state under two presidents and Maine's first candidate for the presidency in 1876; and the indomitable Thomas Brackett Reed, who served in Congress for twenty-two years and dominated the U.S. House of Representatives for eight years as Speaker, Clyde was daily reminded of the far-reaching power and potential of politics.

Reed in particular caught Clyde's attention. Though Reed was stepping away from public life as Clyde entered it, his example of courage and independence was to linger in memory long after his departure. He had been sent to Congress by Maine's First Congressional District in the year Clyde was born, having served previously in the Maine House of Representatives and the Senate, and as Maine's attorney general. By the time Clyde was a young man, Reed had ascended to Speaker of the House of Representatives and was so much in control of that body that he was called by friends and enemies alike, "Czar Reed." For almost a decade he dominated the House only to be undone in the end by such lesser lights as William McKinley, who had served under Reed as a congressman from Ohio, and McKinley's chief supporter, Mark Hanna, whose economic theories one contemporary described as "rollicking economic lechery."[91] In 1896, Reed got presidential fever. Though his bid for the Republican nomination was unsuccessful, the journalist William Allen White observed that he "deserved the Presidency."[92] Some pundits had it that he was too good a man to be president, while supporters like Henry Cabot Lodge explained that he was too principled to exchange offices, from the cabinet on down, for votes, a decision which may have cost him the nomination but kept his "high conception of public duty unstained and unimpaired."[93]

By all accounts, Reed was a major figure in the closing decade of the nineteenth century. To young Clyde, he must have seemed heroic indeed. Reed was tall and of such girth as to make the streets on which he walked seem narrow. A great "porpoise of a man," was how the journalist William Allen White described him in his memoirs: "He must have weighed three hundred pounds," wrote White. "He stood six feet of blubber, and yet power exuded from his excess adipose, his triple chin, his big, jowled countenance, like visible electricity. He was a man of wide erudition and exceptional culture—New England Brahminism blowing a hundred miles an hour."[94] He had a debater's pugnacity, razor wit and a total command of parliamentary practice and law.

The same year Clyde went to Augusta to serve in the Maine House of Representatives, Reed had decided to abandon politics and accept a standing offer of a senior partnership in a New York law firm. Though the event was called a "calamity" for Congress and the *New York Tribune's* headlines screamed: "Congress without Tom Reed! Who can imagine it!" Reed left with hardly a backward glance. His decision was the culmination of diffused ill-will between himself and McKinley, and growing disillusionment with the party of Lincoln.[95]

The final straw had come with the peace treaty which ended the Spanish-American War. Specifically, Reed opposed transfer of sovereignty of the Philippines to the United States because it ensured domination of the Filipinos without their participation, an act in conflict with the Declaration of Independence and the foundation principles of the United States. After the treaty was ratified, he resigned. In the words of one of his biographers: "He was a Republican and had lived and worked forty years under its traditional tenets. He could not lead a revolt nor could he go over to the opposition. There was only one course he could follow and that was to abandon political life."[96] Had his independent streak not have taken over, he might have outlasted McKinley, for within three years Leon Czolgosz's bullet brought the McKinley era to an end.

There are hints that Reed strove for, and indeed achieved, something more than power alone, a kind of "tranquil greatness," perhaps.[97] Once, when a friend visited him to discuss politics, Reed read to him aloud from Sir Richard Burton's *Kasidah*:

> Do what thy manhood bids thee do
> from none but self expect applause
> He noblest lives and noblest dies
> who makes and keeps his self-made laws.[98]

By this code, it seems, he tried to live his life. He was himself to remark in a public address after retirement: "It is a very lonely life that a man leads who becomes aware of truths before their time."[99] Thus Reed became a law unto himself, a knight of the Republican Party, who provided young legislators like Clyde, and later, Margaret, with a measure by which to judge political courage.

Thomas Brackett Reed died suddenly in December, 1902. At a joint session of the Maine legislature on 28 January 1903, called to mourn the loss of their native son, Clyde shared his grief with his fellow legislators with characteristic expansiveness and sentimentality. "A hero is dead," he told them. "Not while on the battlefield, amid the rush of contending parties; nor while in gallant leadership, leading his party onward and onward in every charge, with victory ever in hand, for he had laid down the gavel and ceased to participate in the great political arena of his life. But we can never forget how we have known of him in this very hall, a leader of leaders, champion of champions."[100]

Clyde's awareness that he had stood in the presence of an uncommon man suggests much about the inner Clyde Smith. Like the clipper ships, whose heyday had passed before Clyde was born, politicians of the stature of Thomas B. Reed would not be seen again, or so at least it must have seemed to Clyde, whose impulse, even when he was young, was to revere and romanticize the past. Nostalgically, Clyde observed "that the dreams of childhood and visions of old age vanish, . . . flowers bloom, blush, and fade away. Stars fall from heaven and leave no trace behind them. But a life like Thomas Brackett Reed's can never run its course and be forgotten . . . and when the fettered fangs of eternity were bearing his soul away, his life was just beginning."[101] Beyond his wistful and romanticized vision of Reed, however, there resided in Clyde a sense of loss that went deeper than the shallows of nostalgia. Because of Reed's uncommon courage in public life, he was a genuine hero to Clyde and to many of his contemporaries as well. To Joe Cannon, his successor as Speaker of the House, Tom Reed was "the strongest intellect crossed on the best courage of any man in public life that I have ever known."[102]

Fifty years later, Margaret Chase Smith would display impulses similar to Reed's. Like him, she would be drawn to the slippery slope of moral outrage and high moral purpose. Like him, she was frequently iconoclastic and stubborn, much to the delight of her Maine constituents. Because she lacked Reed's education and nimbleness of mind, she would be drawn by issues of personality as much as by principle, and because she was a woman in a man's domain, she would be ignored rather than engaged in debate by her colleagues. Both of them progeny of Puritans and both of them born into families that had not prospered, Thomas Reed and Margaret Chase Smith conducted their public affairs in the belief that principle is all, that morality must guide policy, and that courage is the singular mark of character. Clyde shared such beliefs but was himself unable to sustain such pure moral fire, though he valued it all the more when he discovered it in others. Thus, for all three—though in quite different ways—the stony soil of Maine nurtured a singular kind of heroism.

After Reed's death, Clyde stayed to finish his second term but decided against seeking a third. At session's end, at the age of twenty-seven, Clyde looked homeward to Hartland and entered with "renewed interest into the public life of the town."[103] On the surface, it appeared that he had come home to Hartland to stay. He became superintendent of Hartland Schools and with his brother Myron opened two stores—a clothing store and a hardware store. Like a married man with a mistress, politics remained part of his life, too, and in 1904, he succeeded his father as selectman of Hartland, a position he held until 1907.

But Hartland did not offer enough challenges to hold him, and he decided to seek the office of sheriff of Somerset County. It was a decision which was to shape the rest of his life. The incumbent in the office, Alfred H. Lang, was a Democrat whose competence made him a difficult opponent. Nonetheless, Clyde was successful and at twenty-eight became the sheriff of Somerset County. Soon after his victory in 1905, Clyde left Hartland for the larger town of Skowhegan, less than twenty miles away, where he made his home in the jail residence, which his aunt Clara Bartlett came to Skowhegan to run for him.[104]

Clyde was a strikingly handsome young man in 1905. He had dark wavy hair, full lips, a prominent nose and a face made distinctive by high cheek bones and piercing eyes. He was not tall but he gave the appearance of tallness, as he stood erect and without stiffness, his feet slightly apart, his shoulders square. He favored three-piece suits and a tie, and he wore a watch chain and fob. In a family portrait from the period, Clyde stands astride, behind his seated father and step-mother and slightly apart from his two grown brothers and sister. His right hand is in his trouser pocket, his jacket is unbuttoned, and his left hand is lightly touching his watch fob. Though the eyes of the other family members are gazing to the left of the photographer, Clyde is looking straight at the camera. In his stare there is a force which draws one to him before the rest of the photo can be taken in. There is certainty in his eyes, and intelligence, and supreme self-confidence, though there is gentleness, too. His is the face of a young man with few repressed desires, who takes his pleasures and his opportunities as he finds them, and wakes up each day certain that many more will come his way again.

*　*　*　*　*　*

In 1908, with eight months left in his term as sheriff, Clyde and the daughter of one of the most prominent men in Skowhegan were married. In the sedate language of the *Boston Globe*, he and Edna Page had been "Quietly Wedded" in Portsmouth, New Hampshire. In Skowhegan, in a very small article on the front page of the town's newspaper, Clyde's neighbors read: "Skowhegan readers of the *Boston Globe* were surprised to see the following item in Saturday's edition of that paper, under the heading of Portsmouth, N.H. news: 'The marriage of Clyde H. Smith and Miss Edna C. Page, both Skowhegan, took place yesterday at the parsonage of the North Congregational Church.'" The author of the article then observed that "the prominence the contracting parties occupy in our town renders the nuptials of more than passing interest, the bride being the only daughter of the late Hon. Edw. P. Page and the groom the sheriff of Somerset County." In perhaps the most revealing statement in the article, the writer concluded: "We learned that Mr. and Mrs. Smith are passing the present week in Hartland as the guests of his parents, the newly-weds' choice of honeymoon location affected perhaps as much by the suddenness of their decision, as by their limited funds."[105]

Though the wedding itself was a quiet, understated affair, clearly the circumstances surrounding it were not. At twenty-four, Edna was almost ten years younger than Clyde and from one of the most prominent families in Skowhegan. The Pages were both wealthy and influential with ample holdings in the pulp industry—in 1903, for example, Edna's father, Edward Page, and two partners had bought the Richards Paper Company. Edward was also involved in one of several private water companies which supplied water to Skowhegan. And he was president of the First National Bank. For over seventy years, two generations of the Page family would give continuous service as executive officers of that bank, with Edward Page succeeded in 1924 by Blin Page, his son and Edna's brother.

The social circles in which the Pages moved were the very finest. Edna's mother, Lizzie, had served as president of the Skowhegan Woman's Club, was a member of the school committee, and was on the board of the Women's Aid Society, a group chosen by the town of Skowhegan in 1887 to "expend the income of the legacy provided in the will of Abner Coburn 'to aid and assist the worthy and unfortunate poor, and to save them from pauperism.'"[106] In addition to Lizzie's social and civic activities, she also wrote stories of Maine rural life which were published in *Redbook* and *Household*.[107]

Edna's Aunt Mary was involved with the establishment of Coburn Park, an activity which benefitted from the participation of Louise Coburn herself and Clementine Weston, wife of Levi Weston, descendant of one of Skowhegan's original settlers.

Edna's elopement with an upstart from Hartland was a blow from which the family did not recover. For many years, even after Clyde and Edna were divorced, the Page family didn't even speak of Edna.[108]

A more positive outcome of Clyde and Edna's union was the formation of a newspaper, which they established during the first year of their marriage. The *Somerset Independent* began publication on 19 May 1909, with the usual quantity of county and local news.[109] But unlike the existing *Somerset Reporter*, the *Independent*'s first page was devoted to lengthy articles on state and national events, and it appeared on Wednesdays. A town the size of Skowhegan was hard-pressed to support two local newspapers. So, five months after the *Somerset Independent* first appeared, the two newspapers merged to form the *Independent Reporter*. Controlling interest in the new company was held by Clyde and Edna. Clyde was to be the president of the corporation and Elmer Ellsworth McNeelie, who owned one-third interest and had owned and managed the *Somerset Reporter*, was to be in charge of the office. Quite likely it was rumored that Edna's money had bought the newspaper.

Edna and Clyde's involvement with the newspaper probably came as a surprise to their friends, for neither had served an apprenticeship as journalists, and neither was an aspiring writer or editor, though Clyde did oversee the paper's editorial policy.

What the newspaper offered Clyde and Edna besides risk and potential income, however, was political leverage, an outcome which might not have been their primary goal, but which could hardly have been entirely unforeseen. The tradition of mixing politics with the newspaper business had been established in Skowhegan by one of Clyde's predecessors at the *Somerset Reporter*. Thirty years earlier, J. O. Smith (no relation to Clyde), who was the editor of the *Somerset Reporter*, had been a power in the Republican Party. Eventually he became secretary of state for Maine, whereupon he left Skowhegan to live permanently in Augusta, turning the job of editor over to his partner and brother-in-law. Throughout J. O. Smith's stewardship of the paper, its pages reflected Republican orthodoxy. His self-proclaimed objective was that the paper should be "an exponent of Republican principles and an aid to the cause, particularly in Somerset County."[110] By all accounts, his attempt to mix politics and journalism was a success, for both he and the paper flourished.

Just as the paper was a potential springboard into politics, it was a magnifying glass as well which gave Edna and Clyde a privileged view of the life of Skowhegan. Access to information about the town's comings and goings suited them, for they were outgoing, social creatures who enjoyed the society of their fellows more than most. Despite the Pages' disapproval, through the paper they established a place even within the charmed circle of Skowhegan's leading citizens, for the paper was not a "crusading newspaper," but a town chronicle which reflected back to its readers a mirror image of a people whose equanimity was relatively undisturbed by crime, by class struggles, by the influx of immigrants or the rise of tenements. The persona of the newspaper thus suited the town, for it was the voice of an extended family which had not yet begun to experience the dislocations of the twentieth century.

Though the paper flourished, for reasons that are not clear, the marriage did not. In mid-1913, Edna began divorce proceedings, and on 27 January 1914 a divorce was granted.[111] The couple had no children.

Everyone in town knew the handsome, popular, recently-divorced Clyde Smith, who had been elected first selectman in March of 1915, and when he began to call the night operator to get the correct time, Margaret decided after talking with him that he was as impressive as she had been led to believe. "He had the most fascinating voice over the phone," she later recalled, and she tried "to answer him just as impressively."[112] Over the next months, Clyde's requests for the correct time moved to the level of more general conversation—a practice forbidden to operators by company policy—as increasingly he and Margaret found each other intriguing.[113]

Exactly when they met face to face is difficult to determine, but when Margaret ran for the U.S. Senate in 1948, her opponents accused her of breaking up Clyde's marriage. Smith supporters countered with a chronology showing that Margaret Chase did not meet Clyde until the spring of 1916, or more than two years after the divorce's final decree. What is likely, however, is that Clyde and Margaret talked on the phone at least as early as October 1915 when Margaret, who was nearly 18, was working on the night switchboard and Clyde had been a selectman for eight months.[114] That they met as early as 1914, before the divorce was final and Margaret was sixteen, is also possible. In any case, a relationship between the two was certainly in bloom by spring of 1916, even though Clyde was twenty-one years older than Margaret.

One night when they spoke on the phone, he asked whether she would be interested in helping in the town office during tax assessment time in April, explaining that the work would consist of writing names, property holdings, and taxes in a large book and would require twelve weeks at $12 per week.[115] The salary was well beyond any amount Margaret had ever earned or hoped to earn in the near future, so she was disinclined to refuse, even though there was school to consider, and she wanted to graduate with her class.

On the other hand, basketball had ended on 17 March with Skowhegan's stunning defeat of Cony High of Augusta, so the basketball schedule was not a consideration. But Carrie—perhaps remembering a similar decision that she had made at the same age—insisted that Margaret must be able to graduate. After a successful interview with Skowhegan's three selectmen, Margaret talked with her high school principal and was allowed to complete her high school work during evenings and on weekends. Though it cannot be confirmed, Clyde's intervention with the principal is likely. There is certainly no doubt that by this time he was actively helping to shape Margaret's life.

What drew the attention of the ambitious and increasingly powerful Clyde Smith to Margaret Chase is not entirely clear. Her sauciness and her efficiency both probably played a part. But youth, too, was in her favor. Clyde was known to be attracted to younger women, and he even took a classmate of Margaret's to a town dance during Margaret's senior year. One might speculate that his preference for women twenty to twenty-five years his junior was a symptom of a youth whose employment left him barely enough time for school, and even less time for the high school sweetheart who had been the love of his young life. His high school sweetheart's father was a teacher in the same school, so the notes back and forth and trysts between the two teenagers took on a special quality of intensity and furtiveness. Clyde's attraction to Margaret, and to other young women as well, suggests a preference for romance tinged with danger and threat of discovery. It was an indulgence which would continue after Margaret and Clyde were married and for which they would both pay a very high price.

But Clyde probably saw in Margaret special qualities that he did not find in others. She was very impressed by him, and she may have provided him with the admiration, applause and affection he had lost at the age of six with the death of his mother. And, since she had naturally enjoyed the company of older people ever since she was a young child, she probably treated Clyde as though he were the most important and fascinating man she had ever known—as indeed he was. Any such admiration would have been a welcome change from the disapproval of his first marriage.

She was, moreover, a young woman with enormous potential, in whose life Clyde knew he could make an important difference. In many ways, Margaret needed him as much as his baby brother Myron had. Without Clyde's intervention, the town's gradations in rank would most likely determine how Margaret would spend much of her life, and he could not, would not, let that happen.

For her part, Margaret found in Clyde the affection and unconditional love that came only sporadically from her volatile father. Clyde had much to teach her about the world, and she was a willing student. She observed that he moved with ease within the world and bent it to his will much of the time, as he was able to do when she was hired to help with the town tax rolls. The mystery of success and the acquisition of power—

which meant being at the center of things—were his to disclose, and in his hands were the tools with which Margaret could channel her restless ambition. Her early forays in search of a unique identity had all led her to this powerful and loveable man who flattered her with his attentions and gave back to her a treasured vision of her own importance and worth.

In April 1916 came the highlight of the senior year—the class trip to Washington, D.C. At first, because of the chronically pinched finances of the Chase family, Margaret had resigned herself to not going. The expense of the trip was to be sixty dollars, quite a sum in those times and for that family. Then grandfather Murray, "Banker," spoke up. He took Margaret with him to his bank, the Skowhegan Savings Bank, where he talked for a while with the cashier and then announced that he wanted to make a withdrawal. Margaret was elated at first and then surprised as the cashier passed her a pen and a note for sixty dollars, saying that she was to sign the note and pay with interest during the next year.[116] "Banker" never intended for Margaret to believe that success would come easy, but he did want her to realize that the game was worth the candle.

The excursion was made by train to Fall River, Massachusetts and then by boat to New York, an overnight trip. From New York the group travelled by train, with a stop in Philadelphia for lunch and sightseeing before arriving in Washington and the Pennsylvania Hotel. To Margaret, the hotel seemed very grand indeed, and the room she shared with three other students, a marvel.

A chill lingered in the Washington air. And there were few signs of the tulips and forsythia of a spring in full stride. But that did not matter to the Skowhegan High School Class of 1916. There was so much to see and do. The itinerary was a crowded one. The class not only met Maine Congressman John Peters and Mrs. Peters, as well as Senator Burleigh, but she and her classmates also went to the White House and met President Wilson.

The event which impressed Margaret most, however, and which she remembered in detail fifty years later was a visit in the home of Dr. and Mrs. George Otis Smith, nee Grace Coburn, on Bancroft Place, where the class was served "Harlequin ice cream," ice cream in three colors, the first the students had ever seen. The Smiths made an indelible impression on the eighteen-year old. In the first place, "Dr. Smith was head of the Geological Survey for years," she recalled, "and the Coburn-Smith families were well-known and prominent citizens from the early settlers in Skowhegan. Their son, Charles, was in my class." In the second place, even at the age of eighteen, she did not miss the fact that their influence extended well beyond the boundaries of Northern Maine and even New England. Clearly, they were comfortably ensconced in the genteel and clubby world of Washington insiders. Said Margaret of the experience with classic understatement: "This was an experience for most of us who did little socially."[117]

Washington was not her first trip outside of Skowhegan. She had travelled with the basketball team to several towns and cities in Maine, among them Augusta, where she had stayed with the family of Carl E. Miliken, who would subsequently become governor of Maine. The Milikens were a large family, and they lived in a rambling house on Western Avenue. The oldest daughter was Margaret's hostess, and the visit, in Margaret's words, had been "pleasant." Such trips, however, made Margaret painfully aware of the social distance between herself and some of the girls with whom she stayed. "Of course, I was just a little poor girl up there in Skowhegan," she remembered, "and all these girls wore raccoon coats and all that type of thing."[118]

Washington, on the other hand, simply intoxicated her. People looked different there. They dressed beautifully and ate dinner out. They shopped in department stores like Woodward and Lothrop, where Margaret, too, went shopping and bought some material for a skirt.[119] Too soon the trip ended. When the time came to leave, the group had their picture taken. There they all stood, twenty teenagers, the faces of the girls framed by hats, the boys wearing ties, all looking much older than their years. Near the end of the girls' row stood Margaret, posed against the skyline of Washington, looking serious, serene and hopeful.[120] At that moment, at eighteen, her whole life stretched ahead of her, as the adults were fond of saying.

After the school trip, the class turned its attention to finishing their senior year while Margaret went to the municipal building every day. There she sat all day long with Clyde and two other selectmen, updating the tax rolls and recording payments.[121] Her senior year was completed in the evenings and on weekends.

Progress on taxes was slow because of the many people coming in for help and advice from first selectman Clyde Smith. Occasionally at noon, Clyde would suggest that Margaret bring her notebook and accompany him in his big Maxwell on town business out of the office, after which he would drop her off at home. Margaret was not alone in being "impressed" with his "low, shiny El car." In the 1916 "Lever," Margaret's classmates 'gave' "to Ruby Dyer Margaret Chase's permission to ride in a Maxwell car."[122] While Clyde took care of his business, Margaret "would sit in the car or walk around, write a note or two and go home to lunch, getting back to the office at one o'clock."[123] One day he said: "I have to go to Athens [on Sunday]. Do you think your folks might like to ride out with me?" Margaret asked them and they agreed. Sunday came, and Carrie, who had reluctantly accepted the invitation, and George, who was fascinated with Clyde's car, both went along. The eleven-mile trip was a pleasant one, and it led to other short trips, for which Clyde was always careful first to issue an invitation to Carrie and George. Carrie, who was in Margaret's words, "a very wise woman," was always equally careful to accept, for from the beginning, she kept a watchful eye on Clyde. She even agreed to go camping with them, though "she was scared to death of mice." By the side of a stream, they cooked their supper, and then George and Clyde "went and cut the boughs and made a bed, and we slept on it. And didn't my mother hate it," Margaret recalled. "Of course, she didn't think much of my marrying Clyde. [But] she didn't want to do anything to show her dislike of it because she knew that it would make me all the more determined, which it wouldn't have."[124]

But Clyde's intentions were hard to misconstrue. When graduation morning came, Margaret found at her place in the office a small gold watch, with blue lettering, on a chain. "I could feel my face flush," she reported later, "and knew the two older gentlemen were looking at me, perhaps suspicious that Clyde's attentions might be other than good — they perhaps knowing him better than I did." Even then, she said, "Clyde had a reputation for liking girls, especially young girls."[125]

After graduation, Margaret worked through the summer in the Selectmen's office. Outings in the car with Clyde and her parents continued, even as Clyde remained attentive to one of Margaret's classmates, Mamie Haydenn, a young woman who bore a striking resemblance to

Margaret and whose parents also accompanied their young daughter on rides with Clyde.

Nevertheless, one afternoon, Ralph (Bob) Murrow, one of Margaret's high school beaux who had been invited for dinner, arrived at her house just before Clyde dropped Margaret off from work. As Margaret greeted Bob, he said: "I guess I have lost my girl." Margaret's quick denial, "Don't be ridiculous, he only took me home" suggests that Margaret's peers realized the relationship between Clyde and Margaret was "serious," even before Margaret admitted it to herself.[126]

On 22 June 1916, Margaret graduated with her class and in the following weeks grew increasingly anxious about finding a permanent job. Soon the job with the selectmen's office was to end, and she had no prospects for fall. She had hoped to work long enough to save the money it would take to go to Sargent, but with no permanent job in sight, that dream was quickly vanishing.

Clyde, who "didn't think much of . . . [her] interest in Sargent" intervened as he had with her summer job. One day, he asked her if she would like to teach school, saying that he thought it might be a good start, at least until she found a permanent position. He then talked with the superintendent of schools, who met with Margaret and offered her a job teaching at a one-room school, four miles south of town, on the back road to Waterville, known as the Pitts School. The pay would be $8.50 per week and she could be home on weekends. Margaret accepted.[127]

The Pitts School and its pupils gave scant encouragement to the hopes of self-fulfillment which her high school years had kindled. The austere life of a country school teacher was for her a hardship, and it transformed her at nineteen into someone who looked twice her age. She wore her hair back with a knot at the neck, favored flat heel shoes and a sailor suit type of dress. Photographs of her at the time reveal an expression that was both set and controlled, with all traces of coquettishness and joy and hope banished. As she later recalled: "I was as plain as the living."[128]

She took a room in the home of the Albert E. Jewitts, an older couple whose daughter, Lucy, had gone away to school. The house was immaculate and Mrs. Jewitt was a good cook who fixed plain country fare. Every morning, Mrs. Jewitt gave Margaret breakfast and fixed her a lunch of a thinly spread peanut butter sandwich and cookies. Then Margaret set off for school, one-half mile "down over the hill." Evenings were spent in front of a fire in the fireplace, listening to Mr. Jewitt recite Service's "The Shooting of Dan McGrew" and other popular doggerel while Margaret and Mrs. Jewitt crocheted. They didn't have a phone, and if Margaret wanted to use the telephone, she "had to go quite a ways." The tedium and loneliness were so unbearable that she willingly believed the story that was told about a neighbor who "used to keep a milk pan on the table by the telephone as she knitted. She'd take that receiver and put it down and she could hear all the neighbors talk," Margaret recalled years later, "she knew everything that was going on."[129]

The Jewitt house had no toilet facilities, though there was a "water-closet" at the end of the long shed to the barn. There was no central heat, either, though Margaret's room had a small wood stove in the middle of the room. Just before Margaret arose at sunup, Mrs. Jewitt lighted a fire, "hardly long enough to take the chill out of the air, and it was more than a chill—it was very, very cold," Margaret remembered. She paid the Jewitts five dollars a week for her board and room and Carrie $1.50 per week on the weekends, which left her two dollars with which to start her own school fund.[130]

When Friday came, Margaret left the Jewitts for Skowhegan. After a weekend at home, her room always seemed even colder and more cheerless than when she had left. How she dreaded Sunday nights!

The physical rigors of her life in the country were less difficult to handle than were the psychic ones. Ideas tended to bore her, and her own impatience with booklearning made it hard to instill a love of learning in her charges. Even had she been of a scholarly nature and more inclined to a life of ideas, however, her students would have been a formidable challenge.

She was in charge of nine pupils—the oldest, fourteen years old and the youngest (twins) four years old, neither of whom spoke anything but French. Fortunately, their brothers and sisters were also enrolled, and they helped Margaret with the twins. With nine pupils at nine different grade levels, Margaret figured that she was able to give each student two minutes apiece in each subject. Clearly she couldn't spend enough time with them to do much good. They were children of the rural poor, and with the exception of some "very, very bright . . . fourteen-year-old boys who could carry me away in history," Margaret saw them as slow and sluggish.[131] To them, school was drudgery to be endured, an interruption in the flow of the seasons. Education was more an indignity than a means to a better life.

Margaret remembered one boy in the class who could neither learn nor retain anything. She worked hard with him but he made no progress. Then she discovered that he was getting up in the mornings, doing chores from 4:30 A.M. until he came to school, and when he returned home, doing chores until dark. She also remembered one girl from a large family, "the only one in the school who was not clean," and she taught her how to wash her face and comb her hair.

Most of the students would not complete the tenth-grade. Many would marry very young and live out their lives wringing an existence from the land, supplemented by factory work in town. They would fish the rivers and lakes, hunt deer, grow their own vegetables and pick berries in the woods for pies and jam.

Later generations, up from the cities, would idealize their freedom. Children of a professional class who felt burdened by both parental success and parental expectation would find respite in the form rather than the substance of "pastoral life." Nostalgia for the "freedom of the countryside" blurred the hard edges of rural life for these privileged classes and caused them to buy weekend places, or become summer people, or move to Maine permanently. But no illusions of such "freedom" blinded Margaret Chase. She had grown up on the edge of poverty, and her lonely, stifling year in the country convinced her, even before spring came, that "she didn't care to teach school."[132]

Long after she left the Pitts School, she would remember how, by October, the walls became cold to the touch and the building felt as though it had begun to absorb the dampness of the earth. And she also remembered how, once the big woodstove which stood in the center of the room got going, the room grew heavy with smoke and the children with too many layers of clothing began to sweat. For Margaret and the children alike, the Pitts School was an irritating and largely irrelevant exercise, an unpleasant experience which at first seemed only to reveal to Margaret what she did not want, though in reality, it probably revealed to her just as clearly what she was seeking.

7. *Homecoming*

RESCUE FROM HER SOLITUDE came in "twenty-eight weeks" in the form of a job offer from the Skowhegan office of the New England Telephone Company, where she had previously worked as a part-time operator. She could start in the business office at twelve dollars per week, a sizeable increase in pay from the Pitts school.[133] The decision was not a difficult one. Back to her beloved Skowhegan, a town wonderfully the same as when she had left it and as yet largely unaffected by the nation's entry into World War I, which had occurred on Good Friday, 6 April 1917.

She would return to family and high school friends like Mildred Beale, Pauline Bragg Greene and Florence Burrell, who had remained in their Skowhegan hometown—to shopping and dates, gossip and a new career. With no more than a backward glance at the seven months of loneliness and daily frustration, and with little brooding over a decision which had not worked out, she returned home to take up where she had left off. Very quickly, her gregarious nature, which had found a steady diet of solitude unpalatable, blossomed, and she was savoring with special delight the parties and ice cream socials which characterized the years prior to the Roaring Twenties.

On 18 November 1917, it was announced in the *Independent Reporter*, that "Miss Margaret Chase has been engaged as coach for the girls' basketball team of Skowhegan High School. Miss Chase was formerly a member of the Skowhegan quintet and supporters of the team feel that she is capable of fulfilling her responsible position."[134]

During her year of exile from Skowhegan, Margaret's attraction to Clyde may have deepened. On those weekends when she travelled to Skowhegan through all kinds of weather, Clyde may have been her primary means of transportation. In such a circumstance, it would have been easy for her to feel important, valued, and even prized. And this was a state of grace to which she had been drawn from the time she was very young. To the extent that Clyde succeeded in making Margaret feel central, he probably became "family," though the precise meaning of that term would undergo many changes over time. As for Clyde, although Margaret entranced and attracted him, others whose company delighted him remained fixed stars in his galaxy, and he had no intention of abandoning them. Especially when it came to young women, the fountainhead of Clyde's "love" was virtually inexhaustible. In fact, by the time of Margaret's return, Clyde's passions were aroused by a different and equally young lady, with whom he would spend much time during the summer and fall of 1917, and to whom he would purportedly propose marriage.

Soon after Margaret returned to Skowhegan, Gertrude Noble arrived at her family's summer cottage in Cornville, five miles outside of Skowhegan. Though the Nobles had for some years been residing in New York City, they had maintained and continued to use the family summer place. How or when Clyde met Gertrude is not known, but when the summer ended and summer people left after Labor Day weekend, Gertrude stayed into November. On 6 December 1917 the front page of the *Independent Reporter* ran a story which began: "We have it on excellent authority that Clyde H. Smith, Skowhegan's first selectman, is to be married in New York City in the early future and will return to Skowhegan with his bride." The article ended with the observation that "his proposed marriage will come as a great surprise to his many friends."[135]

No record of Margaret's reaction is extant, though it is not unreasonable to assume that she was not pleased. Although the marriage never took place, the newspaper printed no retractions or apologies, thus giving weight to a belief that the report had some basis in fact. Much later, in a 1930 congratulatory letter to Clyde from editor Roland Patten on the occasion of Clyde's marriage to Margaret, Patten mentioned "the time I put in that front page piece about your marriage to the girl in New Jersey, or somewhere down that way." Although he was "much chagrined and humiliated to have made such a mistake," Patten said, "I can look back on it now and see the humorous side—although there must have been, for the time being, more or less tragedy in it."[136]

If the episode had the potential for tragedy for Margaret, she would not give into it. Over the next year, she turned her attention to her job at the Maine Telephone and Telegraph Company, to socializing with her friends, and to coaching basketball at Skowhegan High School. Once again she was where she liked most to be—in the center of things. Working in the commercial office enabled her to meet people when they paid their bills or placed telephone calls. Her hours were regular, her tasks well defined, and her pay of twelve dollars allowed her some extra money beyond what she paid Carrie so that she could indulge in her favorite activity—shopping.

Mildred Beale, a former teammate on the basketball team and her best friend, worked in an office not far from Margaret's, and the two frequently found excuses to run errands and meet at the bank. On Saturdays, they took the train to Waterville, eighteen miles away. The outings had a ritual sameness about them: a hot fudge sundae at Hagers, a sweep of all the store windows, a purchase at Emery and Brown's—usually a finely made handkerchief of the sort prized by Mildred—and then a return to Skowhegan on the afternoon train.[137] The trips were confirmation that Mildred and Margaret were grown up, sophisticated, and independent.

Margaret's coaching not only kept her occupied but confirmed her long-standing belief that she would be good at it. The 1918 basketball team boasted an 8-2 record, matched in 1919 by a 7-1 record. Reported the *Independent Reporter,* these victories were due to the efforts of coach Margaret Chase.[138]

In the same year, Clyde announced his candidacy for the Maine legislature. His resolve to run for state office, it seems, was little affected by the gaffe about Gertrude Noble, nor shaken even by the announcement of his former brother-in-law, Blin Page, that he would oppose Clyde for the seat. Between Blin and his now-remarried sister Edna, relations were formally distant. Between Blin and Clyde there remained only the most profound antipathy.

Although the tether of hatred which connected Clyde and Blin may have been sparked by Clyde and Edna's marriage and subsequent divorce, it was sustained by profound differences between the two men. Blin was the product of privilege, Clyde a product of opportunism. Blin grew up the son of a bank president and took over from his father when he came of age. Clyde, though from an old Maine family, was the very essence of a self-made man, who had depended for survival on his wits, his charm and his resourcefulness—qualities which created anxiety in men like Blin Page, who had no reason to cultivate them in themselves, or trust them in others. Even the appearance of the two men suggested antithesis. Clyde had an open, dashing style even at middle age, while Blin had a stern countenance and a sour demeanor which overshadowed his essentially handsome features.

At the core of their conflict was the reality that men like Clyde are upstarts who threaten to take from men like Blin privileges which are theirs by right of birth. It was a struggle between the old and the new, the maintenance of an imposed order and the inevitability of change. What hung in the balance was a whole range of social, economic and political privilege.[139]

Even the newspaper detected the generic tension between these two types of men. Embedded in an otherwise flattering sketch of Clyde in a 1917 newspaper article, for example, was the somewhat cryptic observation that "during his term in office, as First Selectman, Mr. Smith has introduced many new things into the civic life of the town, *perhaps the most acceptable* being the municipal fuel yard."[140] Clyde's other reforms—which included systematic building inspections (to reduce the likelihood of fires), improvement in the town streets and lighting system, and increased services for the poor and needy—were apparently far less "acceptable" to the entrenched powers of Skowhegan, who were often both landlords and taxpayers.

During his 1918 campaign Clyde took up the cause of de-privatizing ownership of Skowhegan's water supply. Two years earlier, a survey of the region had been made by some Waterville engineers to assess the feasibility of forming a water district for Skowhegan, either alone or with other towns. Their final recommendation was that unless the present town water could be improved in quality and quantity, the currently privately-owned system "should be acquired by the Water District either by purchase or through eminent domain, and a more abundant and purer supply should be brought from elsewhere."[141] Blin Page was treasurer of one of several private water companies which had served Skowhegan since 1833, first as the Eastern Aqueduct Co. and from 1853 on as the Central Aqueduct Co.[142] Thus, Clyde's call for a public water system which would entitle "those living on the plains and on the south of the river . . . to proper and efficient fire protection, and all of us to pure and wholesome water" was likely to deepen the chasm between them.[143]

Especially disquieting to Blin and his circle were Clyde's views on taxation. "The application of the law too often favors moneyed interests," Clyde argued, and he proposed to tax "timber lands and water powers proportionately with our homes and farms . . . levying . . . our tax burdens more equally between the rich and the poor."[144] Blin Page, whose timber holdings were sizable enough that the town newspaper often referred to him not as a banker, but as someone "engaged in the lumbering business," would feel any such adjustment with special force.[145]

As Clyde supported a moderate redistribution of wealth, he also advocated a broadening of power through female suffrage. The preceding year, Clyde and the rest of Maine had witnessed an intense campaign by women to gain the vote. In August, Carrie Chapman Catt, president of the National American Woman Suffrage Association and "as much of a public figure as [William Jennings] Bryan, [Theodore] Roosevelt, or [William Howard] Taft" had come to Skowhegan to speak at the opera house during a tour of Maine. In early fall Governor Miliken had asked Maine to vote "yes" in the upcoming September referendum and so to "lead on this issue so far as New England is concerned."[146] Years before, in 1884, Thomas B. Reed had written the minority report for that body's Judiciary Committee, favoring an amendment to the federal constitution which extended the right of suffrage to women.

Like Reed and Milliken before him, Clyde championed woman suffrage in his 1918 campaign for the state legislature, even though the measure had been soundly defeated in the 1917 referendum by a majority of practically two-to-one across the state. But the array of organizations supporting the measure was impressive. In the lead was the Maine Suffrage Association, followed by the Maine Republican Party, the Women's Christian Temperance Union [WCTU], the Grange, and the other substantial middle-class organizations—all of them potentially valuable allies to a politician with statewide ambitions.

On election day, 10 September 1918, almost twice as many Skowhegan voters turned out as had voted in the suffrage referendum, and they gave Clyde a resounding victory. He beat Blin Page by a margin of 3 to 1 and a third candidate, A. A. Porter, by a margin of 5 to 1. In the general election Clyde defeated his Democratic opponent 950 to 256.[147] In January, when he left for the state House he could claim "the largest majority ever given a candidate for that office by the town of Skowhegan."[148]

As of 1919, Clyde was a man with a mission. In his first two weeks in Augusta, he introduced four important pieces of legislation, one of which created a Skowhegan Water District. His most important bill was a change in Workman's Compensation, which signalled the beginning of Clyde's ongoing involvement in labor legislation. The bill increased the percent of wages that could be collected by an injured worker from 50% to 75%, and it increased the maximum amount which could be paid per week from $10 to $20. It also provided for immediate, rather than delayed, payment.

Before the legislature adjourned in 1919, the *Independent Reporter* observed that Clyde's Workman's Compensation Act was "likely to pass without opposition." According to the article, Clyde's version of the law was more liberal than those in other states. At this same time, his road commissioners bill and anti-lobby law had been "passed to be engrossed," as had the Skowhegan Water District Act.[149]

Whenever he came home for a length of time, once again he began to call on Margaret. Clyde seemed more settled than he had when she first returned from the Pitts School. He was a shoo-in for reelection to selectman and representative, and everyone, including Margaret, sensed that his future was very bright indeed. She was glad he was back.

In the spring of 1919, the returning doughboys arrived in Skowhegan in time to see the pink flowers of the trailing arbutus, or Mayflower, soon followed by lavender, Jacks-in-the-Pulpit, violets and meadowroses. World War I, which had begun for Skowhegan in May of 1917 when Company E went marching off to France, was over. For two years, letters from local boys had appeared in the newspaper under such headlines as "WILL GET A PIECE OF KAISER'S HIDE: Skowhegan Boy Now in France Writes As Tho He Meant Business."[150] Everyone had been asked to conserve food, and liberty gardens dotted Skowhegan's back-yards. At the start of the war, the selective draft took 3,040 men from Somerset County and on 6 June 1918 bells tolled at 3:00 P.M. for Skowhegan's first lost life.[151] The following June, with the countryside in spring finery, Skowhegan prepared to welcome her boys home.

The town had supported the war effort in a manner consistent with the legacy of a community which had been founded by veterans of the Revolutionary War. Her citizens had generously purchased the Liberty Bonds by which the war was financed and added their sons to the 35,000 sent from Maine to fight, more than a thousand of whom never came home. In truth, the human price exacted by World War I was much less staggering to Maine than that of the Civil War, in which ten percent of the 73,000 men Maine sent to the Union Army were killed.[152] But as the character of grief has no care of numbers or comparisons, and joy no stake in collective pain, Skowhegan rallied to welcome back her boys with the tender affection they deserved.

For the returning veterans, Skowhegan put on "the largest and most magnificent parade ever seen" in the history of Somerset County.[153] In line of march on 5 June 1919 were 1,000 World War I veterans with all Civil and Spanish-American War veterans in a place of honor. Fifteen bands, fifty floats, along with twelve civic orders and 1,000 citizens in line completed the parade. A snapshot from the period shows Margaret in costume, riding on a float, exuding vitality and enthusiasm for the spectacle—and probably looking forward to the boxing matches, ball games, tugs of war, and novelty races which had been scheduled for the afternoon, far more than to the speeches by local dignitaries, which were to follow the 10 A.M. parade, despite the fact that Clyde, as first selectman and mayor, was to deliver the remarks of welcome.

If Clyde's words of welcome were a window on his times and the impulses which shaped them, they suggest that many of the hues of his world were purple and rose, less subtle than illustrations which can be found in the work of Maxfield Parrish. "Today with our hearts overflowing with devotion, your kind and kin for all walks in life are here to greet you boys, our own boys," he began. "Your gallantry began on that day when loved ones stood at the gate bidding you a last good-bye and you never faltered until our unshakable shores danced with joy at your return. And it would be just as impossible to single out one glorious deed from all the rest as it would be to pluck from Heaven her brightest star."

Villains and heroes were as easily distinguished in Clyde's world as they would be in Margaret's. The returning soldiers had protected American womanhood against unspeakable outrages and "prattling babes from bomb and bayonet," he told his audience as Margaret listened, swelling with pride at Clyde's mastery of the podium and well-turned phrase. The buck private was one of "our boys," a precious member of Skowhegan's tribal family. "I believe the world will decree that the fearless, unrewarded and unprotected Private, who stood on the firing lines and blazed his way from top to top will be awarded the victor's crown, and all of us who remained at home, to him who sacrificed life's necessities to aid and comfort you boys will be given the noblest reward." Consistently Clyde reserved his greatest praise for the man in the trenches, the enlisted man, the human being in whom existed an honor and order of valor so natural that neither medals nor rank was required to identify him. "Medals that adorn the uniform tell of courage and endurance that braved the worst for the cause, but the most majestic and distinguishing decoration is the commonest one of them all, the Wooden Cross, and somewhere in the mysterious future, where the flowers bloom and the birds forever sing, the spirit of justice is solving their final reward, for the star that sets must rise again."[154] Margaret's rhetoric would never achieve the fullness of Clyde's, a deficiency which bothered her greatly. But the buck private, or G. I. Joe, would remain in her rhetoric a metaphor for all that was good about Maine, the military, and this country.

With the Civil War veterans in blue and the young soldiers in khaki who stood at attention that day, Clyde and Margaret shared an understanding that in times of war, the country becomes a small community fighting for its life. Once the danger has passed, gratitude, respect, and honor must be paid to those who took up arms to defend hearth and home. The ritual, though tied to the early days of the Republic, was relevant still. Through this historic present, Clyde identified with the veterans of '61 even though he had never fought in a war. And so to a degree did Margaret. At twenty-one, she understood the confluence of Maine's present-past, despite the fact that she was not yet sure of her place in that progression.

Three months after Labor Day, when the maple leaves had just begun to resemble small bursts of flame in the hills outside of Skowhegan, Roland T. Patten, the managing editor of Clyde's former newspaper—where Clyde still had some influence—came to the telephone office and asked whether Margaret would be interested in coming to work for the *Independent Reporter*. He said they would pay sixteen dollars a week and that it would probably soon go up to twenty-eight.[155] She gave Patten's offer some thought and decided that she was ready for a change. Her pay at the telephone office was the same as when she was hired, so an increase of four dollars per week was sizable, and the possibility of doubling it to twenty-eight almost too good to be true. On 23 October 1919 a small announcement appeared in the *Independent Reporter*. "Miss Margaret Chase, who has for several years been in charge of the cashier's department in the New England Telephone office on Madison Avenue has accepted a position as stenographer at the office of the Independent Reporter Co. and will commence her duties 27 October."[156]

Belatedly, the telephone company realized that they had lost a valuable employee and wrote to her in January about a position at the commercial office. The pay listed was thirteen dollars, but the general manager was willing to raise it to sixteen, "if we could get someone with experience [presumably Margaret] in this work."[157] But it was too late. Margaret had gone to work for Clyde's newspaper, where she would stay for eight years under the tutelage of Patten. That same month, Clyde's re-election to the 1921 legislature was already being discussed. In 1920, when he stood for re-election, even the Democrats endorsed him, and he was returned to the House with an unheard of vote of 1,728 out of a possible 1,753. By 1921 Clyde was well on his way to becoming one of Maine's most powerful politicians.[158]

The fifty-five year old Patten was a perfect guide for Margaret Chase as she entered the newspaper business. He was a thin, bespectacled man whose bald head and priggish ways suggested an unmarried schoolmaster or bank clerk. But he was more formidable than he appeared. He had mastered the economic realities of the business and was in tune as well with the special role a newspaper plays in the life of a small town. He shared his neighbors' love of place, and he gave voice in his columns to their deeply-felt but often unarticulated sense of its raw beauty.

He also ran personal recollections and family histories which he solicited from residents or former residents. In addition, he introduced the agricultural page, which reported the activities of the farming community. Under his management, circulation by 1925 had climbed to 5148, "larger than any other county paper in New England."[159]

Margaret Chase worked at Patten's elbow. They were unlikely to become close personal friends, these two. But from the beginning they respected one another. And they were an effective team. Not only did Patten know how to broaden the readership base, he understood people in general, and Maine people in particular. Margaret Chase was eager to prove herself, and she absorbed all that Patten could teach her. Patten told his new stenographer-clerk: "Margaret, never refuse to take an additional responsibility . . . [and] don't miss an opportunity to assist other departments than your own."[160] She took his words to heart, reporting to later audiences his admonition that "too many young people have their eyes on their pay check when experience of the first years is far more valuable."[161] She was a stickler for detail, a quality no doubt highly valued by Patten who was the kind of man who one day picked up a piece of paper which had blown off her desk and said, "Miss Chase, there is one thing sure. When we get to heaven I will be able to recognize you because I always pick up the piece of paper you drop."[162]

After only a few months, Patten came to admire Margaret's determination and her efficiency, and she moved quickly (some said too quickly) from stenographer to subscription clerk to Gal Friday. Her belief that life presents opportunities for which one merely has to be prepared was reinforced by Patten, who channeled her drive and gave her new direction for growth. It was as if she could hear her mother's voice. "There are difficulties you cannot overcome, there are problems that will baffle you, but regardless of these circumstances you alone can determine what your future will be."[163] In 1919, Margaret's attention was especially focused on the part about the future. With Clyde again in her life, she had many more options to consider than she had before.

To Patten, her commitment to giving her best was disarming, for it was just the sort of work ethic he believed in. Perhaps for this reason, she became a favorite of the fifty-five year old widower, even to the extent that during a conference about his wife's estate with his daughters, whom he had been addressing in terms of endearment, he turned to Margaret who had been asked to take notes and said "Sweetheart, get that information together so that each of us may have a copy."[164] Though his slip seemed innocent enough, it embarrassed Margaret, and similar behavior convinced her family and many of the employees that Patten was "sweet on her."[165] Someone wishing to make this point added a caption to a photo of Patten dated 1920, his right arm raised as if taking an oath which read: "I swear that if she ever comes back, I'll never let her go again." Presumably the same person altered a newspaper photo of Clyde, also dated 1920, to show tears coming out of his eyes. Printed in the white space next to the photo was the word "tears," with an arrow.[166] Both photos appear in Margaret's scrapbook from the period.

Some years later, a letter written by Patten to Clyde thus has special meaning in light of the 1920 photos: "I shall not soon forget the eight years that Miss Chase and I worked together in the *Independent Reporter* office" Patten wrote Clyde in 1930. "We were too busy almost to have the necessary conversations on business matters, and rarely, or never, exchanged a word otherwise. Yet I felt greatly favored to know that she was at her desk, but a little ways apart, and that we were able to work so long a period without a serious difference of opinion."[167]

Whatever Patten's true feelings for his employee, he seemed genuinely impressed by the quality of Margaret's work, and, as he did with the other twenty-five members of his staff, he encouraged her to grow in all kinds of ways. For her part, Margaret took full advantage of the opportunity. Patten urged Margaret toward a greater appreciation for the classics and challenged her to read. He marked passages from well-known writers and insisted that his staff memorize the words of the great poets. Once he even gave Margaret a four-line verse to memorize and called upon her to recite it daily.[168] But he also encouraged her pursuit of an interest in civic and cultural activities of the community, and it was on this road that Margaret was carried back to the jubilant sense of accomplishment she had first experienced on the Skowhegan girls' basketball team.

8. *Building A Power Base*

SOROSIS MET on Tuesday evenings for the purpose of "mutual improvement of its members in literature, art, science, and the vital interests of the day."[169] It was a literary and social group with restrictive membership, similar to the Woman's Club and attractive to younger women.[170] When the wife of one of Clyde's friends, Adelaide Ordway (Mrs. Walter P.)—who had been instrumental in getting Margaret into the Eunice Farnsworth Chapter of the Daughters of the American Revolution (DAR), based on the Revolutionary War record of her ancestor David Emery—proposed her for membership in Sorosis, Margaret gladly accepted.

Almost immediately Margaret threw herself into Sorosis' activities, the most important of which was the establishment of a Skowhegan Community Nursing Service, inaugurated by Sorosis in conjunction with the Metropolitan Life Insurance Company. Sorosis contributions and support for the nursing service lasted until 1930 when the club became inactive. In 1923, Mrs. Ordway nominated Margaret for the presidency, and in November Margaret took office along with Mildred Beale, who became secretary.[171] Roland Patten, who felt that such contacts and activity brought credit to his newspaper, couldn't have been more pleased.[172]

But Roland Patten's approval was less important than that of the man in whose company Margaret was most often seen, the Honorable Clyde Smith. In the beginning, they were seldom alone and were most often accompanied by George and Carrie, or Clyde's brother Myron and his wife. Such precautions were prudent for an ambitious legislator whose behavior might appear not to conform to the Victorian sensibilities of some small town people, and even more appropriate for a girl like Margaret, whose good name was her only dowry.

But despite Carrie's early watchfulness, and Clyde's and Margaret's later circumspection, the couple became from time to time the subject of ugly gossip. One particularly disturbing episode occurred in 1920. A woman whom Clyde had known named Lena Dyer wrote a letter on 21 December 1920, possibly to George and Carrie Chase, in which she impugned Margaret's virtue and questioned Clyde's intentions. Clyde responded on December 23: "Your reference to Miss Chase's contamination exists only in your own evil eye. How thankful you could be," he wrote, "if your own life had been as clean and as far above reproach, as has hers. Let him who is without sin cast the first stone."

"Friends and foes alike," he continued, "give you credit for being able to spread more gossip than the scandalous tongues of a whole community. I [cannot] imagine how Mr. and Mrs. Chase will treat your charges of contamination relative to their daughter, but I can give you fair warning that should you ever attempt the same with me that no time will be lost in placing you in your true light."

In one section he tantalizingly addressed the question of marriage to Miss Chase, a subject which must have been raised in the December 21st letter. "I have never stated to you or any other human being that I did not care for Miss Chase," he asserted, "or that I would or was not going to marry her and neither do I consider this any of your affair or do either of us need your advice in the matter, although as I understand it you have freely offered the same."[173]

By October 1921, perhaps because of the viciousness of Lena Dyer's attack, the couple was no longer taking pains to keep their relationship low-key. In fact, perhaps sensing that full disclosure was the best way to mute gossip, Clyde and Margaret began to announce their comings and goings in the newspaper. Thus interested parties could pick up their 6 October 1921 issue of the *Independent Reporter* and learn that "Clyde H. Smith with a party of eight friends including . . . Miss Margaret M. Chase made a weekend trip to the mountains last Sunday in his Studebaker Six." They made it to the summit of Mt. Washington, a round trip journey of sixteen miles, in two hours, a climb of about 5,780 feet.[174] Though the piece unabashedly extolled the virtues of the Studebaker, the real story here was not the automobile's climb but the politics of the climb. Among the passengers were Mildred Beale and Anne Caswell, each of whom would shortly become pivotal in fostering Margaret's ascent in the Maine Federation of Business and Professional Women [BPW]. From 1922 on, the three of them would work together both on the local and the state level. When Margaret was elected president of the Skowhegan club, Mildred became treasurer and Anne Caswell became secretary. When the State Federation met in Bangor in 1923, Margaret and Mildred were two of the five delegates from Skowhegan. And when Margaret became Maine BPW president in 1926, Mildred joined her on the executive board as corresponding secretary, while Anne took over the editorship of *The Pine Cone*, the state paper whose editorship had launched Margaret's candidacy for Maine president the year before.[175] As early as 1921, with Clyde's help Margaret had begun to build her own power base.

In October, 1923 "Banker" died. He left Carrie an estate of $12,000, which included his savings and the home he had built in which the Chase family still lived, a rather impressive achievement for a man who had worked his whole life in the sash and blind factory. Though he had been ill and his death was not unexpected, his passing left a hole in Margaret's life, and she was grateful that she was too busy to dwell on it.

9. *The Business and Professional Women*

EVERY OTHER Tuesday night, Margaret and the BPW women of Skowhegan met for the purpose of promoting "good fellowship and the feeling of unity," creating "a deeper sense of the dignity of the professions and of business," and advocating and maintaining "a higher standard of workmanship and of business ethics among women."[176] Margaret was first elected president in 1923 and again in 1924.

The growth of the National Federation of Business and Professional Women was a by-product of World War I, and it came into being when the need for "coordinated woman power as well as manpower became evident."[177] When the secretary of war, Newton Baker, sent out a call to make this womanpower available for the war effort, what became clear, upon investigation, was the fact that women were already organized, except for the business and professional women. This led to a survey of the status of business and professional women by the War Work Council, a group composed of personnel and department executives of the YWCA, which operated under government authorization. To the Council was allocated federal money which "might be used to create, maintain, and sustain women power for use in the war effort." As a step toward mobilization, the War Work Council issued invitations to two representative business and professional women from each state east of the Rocky Mountains to meet for a two-day conference in New York, on 11 and 12 May 1918. They were to set up a plan. The women who attended were a varied group: lawyers, physicians, educators, and librarians, as well as saleswomen, statisticians and secretaries. Heads of filing departments, publicity directors, editors, social workers, a factory superintendent and a chief yeoman in the Navy rounded out the number. "There were executives, accustomed to giving directions," observed the authors of *The History of the BPW*, [and] "there were women accustomed to taking orders and efficiently following out the plans of other people."[178]

The topic was how women might best be mobilized on behalf of the war effort. Several months passed, and before a clear plan evolved, the war ended, along with the national need for mobilization of women. But the individual needs such an idea uncovered, and the steady flow of women into jobs as stenographers, typists, cashiers and bookkeepers guaranteed its survival. These working women kept the project alive, and in 1919 the national BPW was established on a permanent basis.

The new organization was a magnet to Margaret Chase. It was open to any working woman, and it was devoid of the class consciousness of other women's groups such as the DAR [Daughters of the American Revolution]. It was also non-partisan, non-sectarian and essentially upbeat. The spiritual center of the organization was level-headed idealism. An editorial which was distributed at the first convention said: "We are about to embody an *Ideal*. We must be sure that this thing we are creating is always kept worthy of the spiritual idea that has inspired it. There are five things on which it must depend. We must be *Sound*, we must be *Sincere*, we must be *Sane*, we must be *Steady*, we must be *Efficient*."[179]

In the organization's hierarchy of goals, sisterhood, rather than political clout, was the primary objective. These "new women" were a limited edition. Most of their working friends were domestics or factory workers. Office workers were a growing minority among the ranks of laboring women. They were interlopers in a workplace dominated by men, and the only sensible thing to do was to organize for the common good, a path which had already been blazed for them by earlier pioneers. The impulse for women to organize had already taken hold through the Women's Christian Temperance Union (WCTU), founded in 1874, and the Anti-Saloon League, founded in 1893, as well as the Women's Trade Union League founded in 1903 and the Ladies Garment Union. But the BPW was different from these groups. Though morality shaped the assumptions of its membership, as it did in the WCTU and the Anti-Saloon League, the goals of the BPW were practical and straightforward: "to come to a better understanding of the needs and conditions of self-supporting women in different sections of the country; . . . to obtain better conditions . . . through training: [and] . . . to gather and disseminate information relative to vocational opportunities in order to bring about greater solidarity of feeling among many women throughout the nation and . . . world."[180]

The BPW was a self-help and women's solidarity group without the overt political agenda of organizations like the League of Women Voters. In its earliest years, the need for an organization dedicated to women helping one another and contributing to the common welfare temporarily overshadowed the BPW's impulse to become a strong political voice on the national level.

Gradually, however, its focus on the "needs and conditions of self-supporting women" drew it inevitably into national politics. Such involvement had been foreshadowed even at its first convention in 1919, in St.

Louis, Missouri, when the Federation urged the opening of all Civil Service Examinations to women. The Federation also asked that official rank be given to all nurses who had served in the World War. And it endorsed in principle both a federal and state employment service with the specific recommendation that "the Federation tabulate all possible information regarding working conditions for women."[181]

By the second convention in 1920, which was held in St. Paul, the Federation took stands on several pieces of legislation which related to the interests of women, lending its support to the Nineteenth Amendment, which guaranteed suffrage to women. By now, the BPW boasted a membership of 26,000 with 217 actively affiliated clubs. Within four years, the number of clubs had more than doubled to reach a level of 568, and the number of women responding to a felt need for affiliation reached 37,970.

Maine was experiencing the same enthusiasm for the BPW as were the other 47 states. In 1920, new members were coming into the Portland (Maine) Club at the rate of thirty-five to fifty at a meeting and by 1922, Portland boasted a membership of 685.[182] The club in Skowhegan had 125 paid members by the end of 1923.

During Margaret's years as president of the Skowhegan BPW, clubrooms were opened in the McClellan block on the second floor. There was a large meeting room, and a cloak room, and the members made the third room into a kitchen so that luncheons and suppers could be prepared. Some of the members used the facilities at lunch time instead of going home at noon.[183] It was an adult version of Sunrise Hill, and it provided an outlet for many of the same sororital impulses which had first led to the formation of the Campfire Girls.

Regular meetings every other Tuesday night featured speakers, card playing, and, occasionally, suppers. One year, Margaret worked out a plan which would require the members to speak about their own work and interests. She believed this would give the members confidence in themselves, as well as a better idea what was going on in Skowhegan.

In 1924, the group voted to send her to the national convention in West Baden, Indiana, and many of them went to the station to see her off. Other than the senior class trip to Washington, D.C., Margaret had never been out of the state, so this was an exciting event, one she remembered primarily for its glamour: the sleeping car to Indiana, the luxurious resort where the convention was held, the beautiful print dress she wore on the train—red, beige and touches of black—only to see the identical dress on another woman on the same train.

Her report to the Skowhegan Club dutifully covered the convention's agenda and the business which was transacted, but the real importance of the West Baden convention for Margaret seems to have been the second window it provided on a world which rewarded charm and a sense of style, a world in which achieving women moved effortlessly, swans on a lake, a world in which she sensed intuitively that she would thrive.

10. Who Is that Man in the Flying Machine?

THE YEAR 1924 is significant for several reasons. Walter E. Cleveland flew into town. He was manager of the Cleveland Air Service in Coventry, Vermont, and an intrepid aviator whose passion—apart from flying—was the theatre. He came to direct summer theatre at nearby Lakewood, and in so doing he became the catalyst for Margaret to develop both a fascination with flying and an interest in the theatre which had only been hinted at earlier by her fondness for costumes, which she donned without hesitation whether she was performing in her back yard, going fishing or riding on a parade float.

As an aviator, Cleveland was a remote and romantic figure, and he capitalized on his image. Most of the photographs taken of him during this period show him attired in a leather flying jacket, aviator's skull cap and goggles, and jodhpurs—a metaphor for all that lay beyond Skowhegan and for all that danced romantically beyond Margaret's reach.

After Cleveland's arrival in 1924, Margaret spent much of her time at Lakewood, where he was staging *The Rose Girl*. She had always loved the lake and the area surrounding it and she was especially fond of the architecture and ambiance of the summer colony. Small rustic cottages and the theatre itself—all white columned and green shuttered—a glen of serenity hugging a tranquil lake. People from all over Maine came to see productions there, some staying the week in cabins which dotted the grounds. Hollywood stars like Ed Wynn and Milton Berle came to relax and "headline" in a single production, supported by unknowns who were making their way in summer stock. Maine's beautiful people, as well as summer people from away—vacationers—would come in their silk and organza dresses, their gabardines and flannel blazers, to enjoy the theatre. This was a magical world which Margaret had only read about while growing up, and it was a world from which she may have learned much about the construction of appearances.

Clyde, it must be imagined, was not delighted with Cleveland's intrusion, though it doubtless focused his attention on the advantages of a more permanent relationship. Even less welcome was the description written by Margaret about her first flight with Cleveland, which was published by the *Independent Reporter* on 19 July 1925 and entitled: "Up Above The World So High." One Friday afternoon, just before sunset, "we sailed over my own home that I might wave to the family," she wrote. "We . . . rode over the town, straight sailing, as calmly as though we were out on the lake with a sail and no breeze." Then feeling a bit disappointed at the calmness of it all, she signaled the pilot to try a nose dive. "At this suggestion, the plane was headed straight down, almost into my own door yard. . . . We then took a turn, first to the left, then to the right, called a tight spiral, after which I shook my head and indicated that I was ready for plain sailing again."[184]

Whether the occasion of the plane ride and the article resulting from it were precipitating events cannot be known with certainty, but nine days afterward, Margaret attended a luncheon and auction party at the home of the Fred J. Poolers, friends of Clyde's, which—possibly to her surprise—"proved to be a pre-nuptial event" in honor of the approaching marriage of Miss Margaret M. Chase to Senator Clyde H. Smith. As reported by the *Independent Reporter*, "the first intimation that Miss Chase had of the nature of the affair was when she was showered with confetti."[185] Though several news stories referred to the couple's "approaching" marriage and the *Lewiston Evening Journal*'s headline read: "*Shower and Auction Party for Miss Chase Whose Marriage to Senator Clyde H. Smith Soon Takes Place at Skowhegan*," no wedding date was made public.[186] And in fact, the couple would not marry for another five years.

11. *The Climb*

MEANWHILE, Margaret had made quite an impression on the BPW. In 1923, Margaret had been elected to a three-year term of the executive board of the Federation and in 1924 she was named state publicity chairman. Soon, all of the active women in the Federation knew Margaret, and she had endeared herself to the Federation's movers and shakers. By 1925, she had caught the attention of Miss Flora Weed, of Veazie, Maine, a tall, thin, sculpted woman who was president of the Maine Federation from 1924-1926 and a Democrat.

Margaret's gifts for conciliation and organization impressed Flora Weed, as did her willingness to work hard. Of particular interest to President Weed was Margaret's role in producing *The Pine Cone*, a magazine suggested by Margaret and first issued under her editorship. The magazine came out in January 1925, just six months before the national convention was to be held in Portland, Maine.

In anticipation that many of the women who would attend the upcoming 1925 national convention might want to spend part of their vacation after or before the convention in Maine, a copy was sent to each of the 236 clubs in the U.S., Canada, and Hawaii, to every member of the Maine Federation, and to all officers of the national Federation. The magazine gave information on various vacation spots in Maine and included a map of the state with locations of local clubs. The magazine was a brilliant way to promote Maine and the State Federation. And it was a coup for Miss Weed's presidency, showcasing the Maine Federation impressively, before, during and after a national convention. Everyone of the 3,000 attendees—a record which was not surpassed for some time—could benefit from the Maine Club's efforts.

Margaret, of course, was the greatest single beneficiary. For not only was her name now recognizable to the entire membership as editor of *The Pine Cone*, but Flora Weed, whose presidency she had strengthened, was in her debt. Margaret had emerged as someone truly able, as one newspaper put it, "to write and talk right into the hearts of her hearers," a statement more apt than the author of the article knew, as Margaret had become, in Flora Weed's view, the most likely person to succeed her as president in 1926.[187]

The woman in line for the position who would have to be deposed was Republican Jennie Flood Kreger, of Fairfield, a woman very active on the state level in Republican politics and a strong supporter of Governor Owen Brewster. Margaret later claimed that Miss Weed's suggestion came as "a surprise," as she had "never thought of continuing in Club activities,"[188] but given the way in which Margaret had ascended to the presidency in Skowhegan and had risen quickly to the top in the State Federation, such assertions are disingenuous. "I used every argument that I could think of against such a move as I did not think that I was qualified or ready for such a position." Margaret recalled, "but she [Miss Weed] continued to insist, finally saying that the Federation was moving along so very well that she feared what would happen if a politician like Jennie Flood got into that office."[189] Subsequently, after Miss Weed "sent several groups to her," Margaret "finally weakened, not wanting to run against Mrs. Kreger but knowing that someone was going to do so and perhaps I should respond to Miss Weed's appeal since she had been such a fine friend of mine."[190] A more likely scenario is that by this time, Margaret's ambition was firmly propelling her toward the presidency.

Already Margaret had learned the ploy used so effectively by Clyde and which was a staple of American politics: the reluctant candidate is always the more attractive one. Certainly the newspapers treated her "reluctance" in the most positive light. "Miss Chase has repeatedly declined to seek this honor," they wrote, but of late there has been such persistent appeal from her Club associates throughout Maine that she has finally consented to have her name presented."[191]

She had also begun to learn the ropes of party politics. In 1926 Margaret and Mildred Beale were named to serve with Clyde on the Skowhegan Republican Committee. Clyde was unopposed in the Republican primaries for re-nomination to the state senate in 1926, and in the fall election, he defeated his Democratic opponent five-to-one. Within two years, Margaret had become secretary of the Town Committee and delegate to the district Republican convention in Bangor.[192] Though in these early years, she may have been more comfortable with the process of achieving success than she was with success itself—for to Margaret success was still an object without a name—her version of how she became president still stretches credulity. By the time she was twenty-eight, Flora Weed's ambitions for her could not begin to compare with her ambitions for herself. She had not exactly mapped out her future, but she certainly knew how and when to take advantage of opportunity when it came knocking.

Margaret was nominated, as was Jennie Kreger, at the 1926 BPW State Convention. And Flora Weed, good as her word, saw to it that Margaret won by a sizable majority. Margaret's ascendancy to the state presidency the following year at the age of twenty-eight became the college degree she had never otherwise had the chance to earn. She was called upon to speak, to preside over meetings, to adjudicate disputes, and to articulate the group's aspirations. Margaret devoted the full play of her intellect and energy to the job. Only on the basketball court had she given as much of herself.

One of her duties as president of the state federation was to visit clubs across the state. In fact, one of the accomplishments of her presidency was that she visited every club, from Rockland to Presque Isle, from Saco to Bangor, from Belfast to Portland. When she spoke at these meetings, Margaret's themes were tried and true—friendship, the value of associations, and the strength which comes from organized effort.[193] Rather than originality of theme, however, Margaret's genius lay "in doing even little things uncommonly well," as Clyde used to say.[194] She was attentive to every detail, using any scrap of information that would make a member feel special. "Something of Westbrook's thrift was heard yesterday by requests for dimes for a quilt scheme. Nella Hale, President, will tell us about her club." Or, "Rumford sounds a bit distant from here but you will find it worth visiting if you wish to meet more girls like Sara McCafferey."[195]

She left little to chance and was a master of preparation and organization. In anticipation of having to use someone's name in a meeting, for example, she made sure the name was in her notes, along with the exact words she wanted to use in introducing that person. She scripted even the most mechanical remarks: "The BPW will please come to order and listen to Mrs. Nichols give the invocation." Or, "We will now listen to the reading of the minutes of the last meetings, Miss Coyne. Are there any corrections? If not they stand approved. It is so ordered. (That correction will be made Miss _____.)"[196] The young woman who had been a mediocre student seemed determined to excel in this new milieu. Thus the precision and careful preparation that would become the signature of her public persona was beginning to become visible.

In May of 1927, BPW State Convention was held in Skowhegan, a tribute to the outgoing president, Margaret Chase, who had announced that she did not plan to seek a second term. She had been a popular president and the membership was proud of her. There is no doubt that she could have had a second term if she had wanted it.

Margaret was younger than many of the Federation's members. In fact, she was one of the youngest presidents in the country, but her behavior suggested fidelity to the genteel standards of a generation older than her flapper contemporaries. In Margaret, the Federation women perceived a "pleasant voiced, very quiet young woman," a tireless worker who "endeared herself to every club woman in Maine by just being herself." Said one admirer, "her youth, her personality, her ability, tact, and common sense have been the great factors of her success."[197]

While a ready smile, a direct and modest gaze, even a flash of wit, and grace under pressure caused her to be called "charming" by the Federation women, fleeting glimpses of the same determination and iron will which she had displayed as a child could also be seen. Also increasingly evident was the political reality that Clyde and Margaret were a team.

As plans were being formulated for the 1927 convention, Margaret prepared a list of distinguished speakers which included the governor of the state, the Honorable Ralph (Owen) Brewster, and state senator Clyde Smith. Her friend, mentor, and former BPW President, Flora Weed, objected, raising questions consistent with her earlier fears regarding the candidacy of Jennie Flood Kreger—that the Federation would become politicized. Mentor or not, Margaret's resolve was unshakable. Both men would speak. When Flora Weed persisted, Margaret, certain that she had the votes, called for a vote of the convention committee to settle the matter.[198] Of course, Margaret prevailed, and Governor Brewster and Senator Smith both spoke at the convention.

At Margaret's last meeting as president of the State Business and Professional Women in May 1927, the romantic interest which existed between Margaret and Clyde was called to the attention of the state federation by the doughty Dot Partridge, executive secretary of the national federation, who made sure that everyone enjoyed fully the romance which was occurring under their very noses. To make her point, she told the following anecdote: "Not long ago, one of the neighbors of the place where he [Clyde] frequents heard this conversation, 'Well, Senator,' as the window was thrown up with a bang, 'I don't object to your sitting up half the night with Margaret. I don't object to your talking for two hours on the front doorsteps; but for the sake of the household, take your elbow off the bell-push.'"[199]

In those final days of her presidency, reminiscent of moments of glory just after winning a basketball game, Margaret was at her best. Tributes to her brilliance as a president flowed through the meeting room, receptions were held in her honor, and special gifts were presented. Even a song was composed, to be sung to the tune "In The Gloaming." The third stanza reads:

> Well we know your zeal and ardor
>   For the clubs you love so well,
> Loyal to and faithful ever
>   All your praise no tongue can tell;
> Calm and gentle, staunch and true blue
>   With your sweet and graceful way
> You have won all BPW
>   O'er our hearts you'll e'er hold sway.

The song was entitled "Our Margaret."[200]

During the three days of the convention, archival information details Margaret's early, nearly obsessive attention to detail which was to pay rich dividends. Everything went better than even Margaret had anticipated. The Inn at Lakewood, which had rushed to open early for the convention, was glistening with fresh paint and polished floors, its reception room enhanced by antiques loaned for the occasion by one of Margaret's friends at the *Independent Reporter*. Though the weather was stormy, there were roaring fires in the Inn's large fireplaces, and on tables and sideboards were bouquets of sweet peas and tulips.

Even the town of Skowhegan had dressed for the occasion. Many of the store windows bore signs of welcome and displayed big cards with pictures and speakers. In the drugstore window, the Club's big trophy, a replica of the Winged Victory, was displayed. The most memorable display, by common consent, was the one in the Bowman Hardware store. There someone had filled the window with little sailboats, drawn by tiny ribbons toward a goal. Each boat bore the name of one club in the state and as the sails moved to the breeze of an electric fan, they appeared to be sailing.[201]

The whimsy of the window was appealing and the mood upbeat, much like the federation itself. After all, federation members were not downtrodden, nor were they spokeswomen for the downtrodden. While settlement workers and social reformers labored to improve the plight of the poor, the BPW was singularly interested in improving the lot of a relatively privileged membership, which had little in common with factory workers like Margaret's mother or those who worked in sweatshops. Stripped of the rhetoric of idealism, the BPW was propelled essentially by enlightened self-interest, leavened by emphasis on a spirit of cooperation and friendship. BPW women were looking inward, and trying to survive in a domain which seemed far removed from hearth and home.

Yet the members' allusions to the federation as the embodiment of an ideal bore a relation in form, if not substance, to the social gospel which was abroad in the land, where its voice was heard most distinctly in settlement houses like Hull House. Through their emphasis on "fellowship," their secular goals were linked to a Judeo-Christian tradition and cemented by an overlay of idealism.

Without this appearance of idealism, there is no way to assess how attractive the organization would have been to Margaret Chase's contemporaries. For Margaret, the federation's expressions of idealism released longings to become involved with something larger than herself, the organization itself ultimately becoming the means by which she could achieve such an end. At the vortex, of course, was Margaret's quest for selfhood, a tiny sailboat pointed toward an elusive goal, seemingly unable to be as certain of the wind as one could be of the breeze from an electric fan. There was an evanescent quality to her passage, as there was to her triumphs as president, and as there had been on the basketball court, similar to what one observes when one turns from the bow to the stern of a moving boat, and all that can be seen is a disappearing wake and a fading shoreline.

Yet the moment that had been her presidency and the convention was fixed in time, a snapshot of a boat in full sail, heading toward an unseen point on the horizon. Federation minutes and news articles, gifts and testimonials, all attested to her ability to harness her ambition and accomplish a political coup, an event witnessed, if not fully comprehended by a range of admirers. There was her mother, who came as guest of honor to the president's supper on the first night of the convention; there was Governor Brewster, who certified to Margaret's achievements and the inspiration of her leadership; and there was Clyde, who brought to her current triumph certain knowledge of her earlier victories. This was a man whose political acumen her term as president had uniquely prepared her to appreciate, whose ease on the public platform was more than she thought she could ever attain, a man who had been her first and would remain her most important mentor.

12. *Turbulence and Calm*

IN SEPTEMBER, following the BPW state meeting at Lakewood, Clyde was named to the state highway commission by Governor Brewster and in February, 1928 he became its chairman. Five years earlier, he had won statewide visibility for his efforts to reduce the work week from fifty-four to forty-eight for women and children in Maine's shops, mechanical establishments and laundries. Though the measure was defeated, Clyde so distinguished himself as he tirelessly crisscrossed the state that he won the lasting respect of the opposition, along with the enduring gratitude of supporters of the bill. If Clyde had ever before even fleetingly considered a run at the gubernatorial seat, the campaign for a forty-eight hour work week was the sort which could instantly bring such a goal into focus. The governor's chair was not his for the taking at the end of the campaign, but neither was it beyond his reach. It seemed just a matter of time. With his appointment as chairman of the highway commission, he gained control over twelve million dollars in highway funds and 7,000 jobs. In terms of capital and political patronage, by 1928 he had become the most powerful man in the state.

And he was in a unique position to expand his statewide presence. Several times he traversed the state, east to west, north to south, speaking at Rotary and Kiwanis Clubs, Chambers of Commerce and Granges, often with Margaret and another couple in tow. He told his audience that cement roads paid for themselves. Over gravel roads, a gallon of gasoline gave fourteen miles performance; over concrete, thirty-one miles. The life of a car on common roads was five years, while on cement, service increased to seven and one-half years. Road improvements also brought hundreds of thousands of tourists into the state who left behind millions of dollars. In short, improved roads were a good investment.

He carried this message east to the dowager city of Portland and north to the county of Aroostook, where stories of pine trees so tall that "the clouds were torn as they passed over them" had drawn many adventurous souls to try their fortunes in this area which was now Maine's potato capital.[202] In June he went to Calais, a city on the Canadian border, paused in the state's mid-section and spoke at Lewiston, Auburn, and the capitol city of Augusta.[203] At the height of winter, he travelled west to Farmington—entrance to the mountains of the Rangely Lake district, its chilly sky at dusk the color of chimney smoke and craggy mauve. With him were Margaret and two other couples.[204]

When Margaret accompanied Clyde to cities where he had business, she was struck by how many people he knew, and how many of them genuinely liked him. People pleaded with him to stay in their homes, to dine with them or just drop in to say hello. Very quickly, the invitations were extended to Margaret.

One can easily imagine that on such trips, in the mornings when Margaret awoke, she had a vague recollection of a recurring dream. *There she stood on a narrow street with tall houses built close together, each bearing a fresh coat of white paint. Their wide lacquered doors stood open, and in each house, there was a light on in the hall. Just as Margaret selected the one she wanted to enter, she always woke up. White houses lingered like gossamer in the early morning light and then disappeared. Dreaming or waking, the choices would come again. One of the doorways beckoned more than the others, but Margaret could not make herself go beyond the threshold.*

Two years later in the midst of a town scandal in which Clyde was a principal, and after his departure from the highway commission due to a state scandal in which he was blameless, the date of the future marriage of Margaret Chase and Clyde Smith was announced. Nine days after a close re-election race for selectman which Clyde won, but with fewer votes than in the past, the couple set 15 May 1930 as the date for their wedding.

Standard wisdom in 1930 still proclaimed that "marriage has in it less of beauty, but more of safety, than a single life; it hath no more ease, but less danger; it is more merry and more sad; it is fuller of sorrows and fuller of joys; it lies under more burdens, but is supported by all its strengths of love and charity, and those burdens are delightful. Marriage is the mother of the world, and preserves kingdoms, and fills cities and churches, and heaven itself."[205] Never had these verities seemed so filled with wisdom as now. Clyde would have some peace and order in a life that had begun to go off track.[206] The marital mishaps of the early years with Edna Page would be expunged. With Margaret by his side, he would begin again to position himself for a run at the governor's seat.

On 15 May Margaret Chase, daughter of Mr. and Mrs. George Emery Chase of North Avenue, and Clyde Smith, son of the late Mr. and Mrs. Willard Franklin Smith, were married at four o'clock in the afternoon at the home of the bride's parents. The bride was attended by her sisters Evelyn and Laura. The bride's niece was flower girl and a nephew was ring bearer. Only the two families were present.

At eight o'clock in the evening, Clyde and Margaret, now Mr. and Mrs. Smith, entertained nearly three hundred guests at the Smith home on Fairview Avenue, described by the *Daily Kennebec Journal* as "one of the most beautiful residences of this section."[207] There, guests were received at one of the house's two entrances by Mrs. Albra C. Smith, Clyde's stepmother, who resided with him at Fairview Avenue.[208]

The event was elegant but understated, appropriate for a second marriage which had long been a matter of "when," not "if." In the dining room, which had been lavishly decorated with spring flowers, the guests were tempted with fancy cakes, ices, punch, mints and nuts. Upstairs on the third floor, the large number of gifts, sent from all over the state, were displayed in the billiards room.

When the last guest said goodnight, slipped into the darkness and set off down Baptist Hill, a backward glance would have revealed a sweeping monument of a house, its roofs rising well above the other houses, its thirty-two rooms ablaze with light. The house resembled an ocean liner suspended magically on a Maine spring night, its mansard roof hiding smokestacks, its portico a ship's bow cutting fearlessly into the waves.

After Evelyn and Laura had left Margaret's new home, Carrie bid the couple, who would wait until the next morning to leave for their wedding trip to Augusta House, goodnight. She had seen her daughter wedded to the best-known man in town, possibly the next governor of the state, and she had helped Albra look after the last of the guests. Now it was time to return to North Avenue and the rest of her family.

As Carrie Murray Chase crossed the grand, sweeping lawn she may have hesitated for just a moment to take in again the house's handsome facade—its scale, even in darkness, impressive, *its massive lacquered door standing slightly ajar, the light in the hall behind it flickering every so slightly in the soft night air. In room after room, lights were going out, as Albra Smith closed up the house and prepared to go to bed. Swiftly the house blended with the night, its bulk, rather than its shape, discernible. At last only the hall light remained, until with a sudden breeze the front door began to slowly close, as if pulled by its own weight, and Carrie was left alone in the darkness.*

PART II
A FEMALE ADVENTURE STORY

1. *Hail and Farewell*

I have learned that if you must leave a place that you have lived in
and loved and where all your yesterdays are buried deep—leave it
any way except a slow way, leave it the fastest way you can. Never
turn back and never believe that an hour you remember is a better
hour because it is dead. Passed years seem safe ones, vanquished
ones, while the future lives in a cloud, formidable from a distance.
The cloud clears as you enter it. I have learned this, but like everyone, I learned it late.

Beryl Markham, *West with the Night,* 1942[1]

THE EIGHTH OF APRIL 1940 was the day Clyde died and she began to fly
solo. A decade had passed since they had married, a decade which carried
her from young woman to mature matron. At forty-two, her hair was long
past "prematurely gray" and her eyes had lost some of their softness, though
none of their liveliness. The children she had not yet borne would never be.
And yet, there were signs that she felt younger than she had for years.

She had travelled everywhere with him, driven the automobile and
drawn the maps, taken notes for him, packed his suitcase and kept his
calendar. She waited in the corridor in Augusta while he attended meetings and did needlepoint as she absorbed the political culture of that
capitol city—the hallway deals, the backslapping, the enmity and camaraderie. She even took pains not to interfere with Clyde and his cronies.
The night he had "the boys" to their room at the Augusta Hotel to play
poker, she stayed in the lobby with friends until late, spoke to them all,
took a book into the bathroom and read until 4:30 A.M. when one of them
said, "What became of Margaret?" By breakfast, Augusta widely acknowl-
edged that Clyde was the luckiest man alive to have the kind of wife who
accepted a late night poker game.[2]

And then there was that afternoon in Augusta when she had a
headache and decided to stay in the hotel room while Clyde met with

the Governor's Council. She had just stretched out to take a nap when she heard a man's voice. Something about Clyde and his candidacy for governor. Next door, several women and men, including one of Clyde's opponents for the nomination, were planning to expose Clyde's extra-marital affairs in a whispering campaign.

Those words, "Clyde's affairs," coming from the other side of the door—from people she hardly knew—stunned her, even though Carrie had warned her of it when she first met Clyde, and Clyde had given her ample reason to doubt him during the courtship. Soon after they were married, she knew that he would never change. From that day on, it was as if she carried a stony resolve to let nothing interfere with their political partnership. And it never did.

Now at forty-two, she had the chance to pilot her own plane. She was a less flamboyant adventurer than the statuesque Beryl Markham, who had recently flown solo across the Atlantic, but no less daring.

The 8 April 1940 notation in the campaign diary read simply: "Clyde gone, 12:30 a.m.." Nothing in that cryptic entry indicated that she had decided to succeed him, no musings, no reflections on their ten years together. Nor was there any pain—just a stony, stenographic note. On 11 April, the day of the services in Skowhegan, her entry was a capsule of what others had expressed: "He tried."[3]

On Sunday, 7 April, the day before Clyde's death, the newspapers knew that Margaret was to be his successor.[4] From his sickbed, Clyde released a statement to the press, "My physician informs me that I am a seriously ill man, and that in his opinion even though I survive I may be physically unable to take an active part in congressional affairs for an indefinite time. All that I can ask of my friends and supporters is that in the coming primary and general election, if unable to enter the campaign, they support the candidacy of my wife and partner in public life."[5]

The message and style had Margaret's, rather than Clyde's, imprint. To Clyde she had been an asset, especially when it came to constituents, but they had not been *full* partners. From the beginning he wanted to keep her off the payroll, ostensibly because of a concern about nepotism. And when he grudgingly hired her as a secretary at $3000 per year, he also hired Roland Patten, who became his de facto chief of staff and chief confidante. Clyde and Patten fashioned an easy relationship, informal, and comfortably male.[6] Patten picked Clyde up in the morning and the two men worked together all day, often past dark. Patten served as a clipping service, and he used his newspaperman skills to ferret out capitol news. He and Clyde were an effective team on the Hill. Margaret's job was the mail. Clyde's reference to her as "my wife and partner in public life," which suggests that he thought of her as his political successor, was a leap he had never before made, not even after two of his three heart attacks.

When news of Clyde's death broke, it struck Washington with considerable force. Clyde's reputation for hard work, coupled with the fact that he was the twenty-fourth Member of the 76th Congress to die in office of a heart attack, struck a nerve among his congressional colleagues.[7] Both houses of Congress adjourned. Numerous colleagues from both sides of the aisle, including Owen Brewster, who as Governor had first appointed Clyde to the Highway Commission in 1927, offered testimony on the floor of the House to Clyde's life in public service.

Reaction in Maine was a combination of shock and sorrow, though some were no doubt mindful of the opportunity suddenly created by Clyde's first defeat. Republican Attorney General Franz Burkett said that "in the death of Clyde Smith we have lost a man intensely interested in Maine and the Maine people, especially in the working classes. It was in their service that he undoubtedly wore himself out." To others, Clyde was a "pillar of strength" for Maine's labor groups."[8] Said state Senator Robert Coney, who hoped to be Clyde's successor, "he battled hard for everything he gained. For several years he battled ill health and died as he would have wished—'in the harness.'"[9] Coney's remark was the only mention made of Clyde's long-time battle with health problems.

But Margaret, eyes already on the target ahead, paid closest attention to the measured words of the powerful House Minority Leader, Joe Martin [R-Mass.]. Clyde was "one of the most valuable members of the House, . . . devoted to social and human problems." He "had a broad sympathy for the common man, [and] his close devotion to congressional work and his fine personality won for him the respect of all his colleagues."[10] The day before Clyde died, the same day he had issued his statement urging his friends and supporters to support "his wife and partner in public life," Margaret had talked with Martin.[11] He had been "helpful at that difficult time."[12]

On Tuesday, 9 April, a simple funeral service for Clyde was held at the Smiths' Newark Street home. Later that day, Margaret announced her candidacy for her husband's seat, and by 4 o'clock in the afternoon, she and her close friend and current housekeeper Blanche Bernier were on a train bound for Skowhegan by way of Waterville. With them were Maine's Senator Wallace White and Representative Brewster, who had been named to the official congressional funeral escort by the Speaker of the House. The rest of the Republican escort would join them Wednesday and accompany them to Skowhegan for a Thursday service.

More than one hundred mourners met the train carrying Clyde's body when it arrived at the Waterville station. The Maine State Police formed an honor guard as the body was transferred to a hearse, and then the funeral cortege formed, pulled away from the station, and slowly began the twenty-one-mile journey to Skowhegan.

Clyde had returned to a place he had never wanted to leave. He came home to the grandest house in Skowhegan. Its bold, figured wall paper and dark wood paneling, its hardwood floors and oriental rugs were just as he left them. The large center hall with his simple desk and swivel chair was ready for the usual stream of visitors. The massive grandfather clock was still faithfully keeping track of the time.

Quickly the cavernous house filled with old friends and political cronies. Pall bearers from the Carabassett Lodge of Odd Fellows stood ready for Thursday services, along with two governors who would serve as honorary bearers.

In Clyde's last year, time was spinning out of control, the hands of a case clock racing backward before they stopped still. He had written with increasing tenderness of his youth, of his boyhood on that back-road farm among the Somerset county hills, of the Maine he used to know. In what seemed like a metaphor for his own life, he described the Maine woods-man whose journey began long before sun up in freezing temperatures. In the darkness, "the snow, dry and crystallized in that mountain air, would squeal, not unmusically, under the sleigh runners, a sound to which few of this generation have ever listened," he wrote, as if he could hear the sound still. "It was an invitation to whistle or sing, but in that vast solitude with the stars overhead, the command to meditation must have been stronger."[13]

The day of his funeral dawned bright and cold. After a service by three clergymen, in a moment that Clyde would have enjoyed, the congressional delegation and honorary bearers stood at the entrance to his home as the large crowd filed out from the short service. Throughout the town, flags stood at half-mast, and schools and businesses were closed. More than 400 people attended the funeral services, while hundreds more lined the streets through which the funeral procession passed.[14] Slowly the cortege rolled out of Skowhegan for Hartland, toward the Somerset hills and the site of the austere cape of Clyde's boyhood—the house in which his mother had died, and in which he had raised his brother Myron, the house from whose second-story windows he had caught a glimpse of distant mountains and wondered what lay beyond. Slowly the cortege rolled along the narrow road to Pine Grove Cemetery.

Toward the end of his career, Clyde said one election night, "There'll be an end to this sometime. One of these days, a combination of circumstances, outside my control, will catch up with me and return me to private life."[15] All things considered, however, not even this last combination of circumstances dealt him a defeat, not with everyone who was anyone in Maine politics paying him homage, and small children lining the streets to watch as he was carried home. Maine and a simpler time had acted as a magnet on him all the while he was in Congress. Washington mirrored a world that was changing too fast, hurtling in the direction of "slickness," an affront to the tribal ways he had learned as a boy and the truths he embraced as a man. In this way, his homecoming was a return to a past that had encircled him always, in a season that though capricious, was likely to be kind. Soon April would turn to May, and Pickering's tree frogs would be heard throughout the land, sounding the notes of spring. The eastern bluebird and red-winged blackbird would return, devil's paintbrush would brighten the fields, the scent of pine would fill the air, and people would begin to put in their gardens. April was a good month to come home.

* * * * * *

The season for grieving after Clyde's death was short. In Maine, congressional vacancies are filled by popular election rather than appointment.

So, unseemly or not, if Margaret intended to fill Clyde's unexpired term, she would have to run in a special election which consisted of both a special primary and state election. The date of the primary, 13 May, would come barely a month after the funeral, the state election three weeks later. Since she was not introspective, but a "doer," Margaret was relieved to throw herself into the next phase of her life.

When it was announced that Clyde's wife, who had been his "political helpmate" and secretary, would run for his seat, Edward J. Beauchamp, Androscoggin County prosecutor and unopposed candidate for the Democratic nomination to the *full term*, suggested that Clyde's widow be elected to the *short term* without opposition.[16] The gesture was both gallant and shrewd. Gallant because it granted Margaret a prerogative of widowhood, and shrewd because it allowed the Democrat Beauchamp to conserve resources for the regularly scheduled general election in September. In conceding to Margaret the few months of Clyde's term and the primary race for the full term, Beauchamp would face an incumbent in the general election whose hold on the office was short-lived and tenuous, and who would be easy to defeat. But Beauchamp underestimated the widow Smith.

Republican Frederick P. Bonney ignored Beauchamp's suggestion. As expected, when the primary vote for the special election was tallied on 13 May, Margaret easily defeated him. Out of 8000 votes cast in the Second District, Margaret received 7,361 to Bonney's 671.[17] Even in the Democratic primary, where there was no candidate, Margaret received a scattering of votes. In Margaret's assessment, the vote "indicated that I had maintained the friendships of my husband."[18]

The day she won, she attended funeral services for Clyde's brother's wife, Frances, who had died the previous Friday after a prolonged illness. In less than one month Myron, now a semi-invalid, had lost the older brother who had raised him and the woman he had married before Margaret and Clyde began courting. Both events were recorded in the campaign diary much as Margaret had recorded Clyde's death:

> May 10 Frances died.
> [May] 13 Election Frances funeral [19]

The following day, 14 May, was her wedding anniversary, the day on which Clyde and Margaret would have completed a decade as man and wife, and two decades as political partners. Not even a stark stenographic entry marks the occasion. Perhaps in the end, she knew how profoundly Clyde had betrayed her. Dr. Dickens had said that Clyde died of "the Congressional disease," meaning heart disease, which was the great killer of members of Congress. His colleagues in the House believed that his work on labor legislation and the long hours it necessitated "speeded his death."[20] Two earlier coronary attacks, the second one serious enough to keep him away from Congress, heightened the impression.

The real killer, however, was a condition which had been diagnosed after his announcement at Lakewood in 1937 that he would run for reelection to Congress in June 1938 and, if successful, for Governor in 1940. In a letter dated 21 December 1938, from the Research Institute of Cutaneous Medicine in Philadelphia to a Portland, Maine physician who had sent Clyde for a second opinion, Clyde's condition was diagnosed as "an arrested case of tabes dorsalis or taboparesis," with symptoms which included a "somewhat ataxic stanch [*sic*] and gait, absence of patellar reflexes, argyll-Robertson pupils and slightly ataxic bladder, as well as ataxic sphincter ani, definitely indicate spinal cord infection."[21] In other words, Clyde had a central nervous system disease caused by an advanced case of syphilis.

The physician's diagnosis was doubtless a shock to Clyde. And it was probably not information he possessed when he publicly declared himself a candidate for governor. It was also likely, since Clyde could be secretive, that he did not tell Margaret the true source of his illness. As Clyde and Margaret didn't become husband and wife until after the disease had reached its dormant state and was no longer contagious, it would have been no kindness to tell her. And why humiliate himself?

Thus he died, most likely keeping to himself any guilt he may have felt over a misspent manhood, salving his conscience, perhaps, by this last point of honor. Whether she knew, or would allow herself to know cannot be determined, for that vulnerable part of Margaret that had so often been betrayed by Clyde was carefully hidden. After Clyde's death, she remained the picture of composure. If the charm was forced, no one noticed. And not for a few years did anyone penetrate to the steeliness which lay underneath.

2. An Expanded Vision

THE LEAP from secretary to congresswoman seemed to occur overnight, but it was one for which the Smith partnership had been preparing her for more than a decade. As early as 1928, she had emerged as a person of influence in Republican state politics. With Clyde's help, in 1928 she had been elected a delegate to the Republican District Convention, as well as secretary of both the town and county Republican committees. In 1930, when incumbent Jeannie Flood Kreger declined to seek another term as Republican State Committeewoman from Somerset County, Margaret declared herself a candidate. By the time the Somerset County delegates assembled in Bangor for their annual convention, Kreger — whom Margaret had earlier defeated for the Maine BPW presidency — surprised everyone by changing her mind and declaring her candidacy. The announcement was a bombshell "which reminded old timers of those . . . days when conventions were more than cut and dry affairs."22

The election, which the *Independent Reporter* characterized as "bitterly contested," proved Margaret's mettle and signified her growing influence even before she married Clyde. She defeated Kreger 43 to 12 and on 30 March 1930, Margaret became the Republican State Committeewoman from Somerset County.

Within five years, she caught the eye of a reporter for the *Lewiston Evening Journal* who described her as "one of the cleverest women political workers of Maine. She is a member of the State Committee and she is working for her husband's [gubernatorial] nomination. Add to this fact that she has for many years been prominent in BPW work and is very popular and you have a combination which is helpful."23 The Lewiston political observer suffered no illusions that she was simply the wife of a prominent man, or merely a woman who had married well. He saw Margaret as a first-rate partner and a wife whose skills as a political worker might make the necessary margin of difference in her husband's campaign for governor. But that assessment only came after a dramatic adjustment in Margaret's perception of her role as Mrs. Clyde Smith.

Originally, the house on Fairview Avenue in Skowhegan had belonged to Governor Coburn's younger brother, Samuel, and his wife, Sarah, before it passed to their daughter, Mary Ella, and her husband,

Manley Pooler. Manley had the old house torn down in 1882, and then he built a bigger one, suitable to changing tastes. Those who liked it saw in it echoes of a French country house; those who didn't saw only ostentation and a florid style. Clyde liked it.

Margaret was overwhelmed by it, or at least by the running of it. Even with Clyde's stepmother Albra's considerable skill, one couldn't keep up with the cleaning. And it was impossible to heat in the winter. The polished wood floors had to be mopped every few days to keep them shining, and the rugs beaten regularly because of all the traffic in the center hall from people coming to see Clyde on business. The house on Fairview Avenue was both their home and Clyde's office, and from the time Clyde no longer served on the highway commission, it was Clyde's sanctuary as well.

He set up his office in the large center hall, the high ceilings and ornate arches dwarfing his rather simple desk and chair. When Clyde wasn't seeing people face-to-face, he was talking to them on the phone. And when he wasn't handling state business, he was handling his own. At times the line between them disappeared. For Clyde, work and politics were always intertwined. Early in his career, when he was elected first selectman of Skowhegan, he was made president of the board of trustees of the Shoe Factory Fund, a municipal effort to attract industry to Skowhegan and a tenant to the newly-renovated shoe factory building.[24] Subsequently, after the Northeastern Shoe Company took over from the original tenant, Rowan and Moore, he became Northeastern's treasurer. By 1930 he had accumulated extensive holdings in commercial and residential real estate and was also a salesman for the Portland Tractor Company and the Auto Sales and Service Company of Portland, the latter probably an outgrowth of his work as a highway commissioner. In addition, he was director and sales manager for the New England Culvert Company, through which he stayed in close contact with all of the township road commissioners, many of whom came often to the Fairview Avenue house to talk with Clyde. When he wasn't at home, Margaret would "take notes of what they wanted." Later in 1940 when she made her bid for Clyde's seat, she noted that many of these same officials led the way for her campaign.[25] Whether Clyde was working for a company or working the halls of the legislature, he was always engaged in politics.[26]

Some would say that Clyde was captured by fiction and driven by dreams. And if that was the case, the first year of his marriage to Margaret, when he had scant hope of realizing his political ambitions, was a test most trying. But if waiting had to be done, then something worthwhile would be done as he waited. And so he had put in a garden. In the early days of summer, one could find him outside until noon, hoeing or pulling weeds in a long-sleeved shirt, his open collar the only sign that he was not at work in his office.

Margaret, in the meantime, was very busy. She had left the *Independent Reporter* in 1927 to become office manager for Willard H. Cummings, a prominent Republican who owned the Daniel E. Cummings woolen mill, at a salary of $50 per week, almost twice her pay at the *Independent Reporter* after eight years. Six months after her wedding, she resigned from the woolen mill to "work harder" than she had ever before worked in her life—as Clyde's full-time wife.

In many ways, the choice was similar to that of Claire Callahan, who wrote an article for the *Ladies' Home Journal* in 1930, entitled "A Woman With Two Jobs." "I know without any hesitation that [my husband's job] must come first . . . ," she wrote. "I am like the invaluable secretary to a big executive. He produces but I make it possible for him to produce efficiently. And once I had the right slant on my work . . . I would begin to see my job as a real job . . . I would work toward an executive position in my home."[27]

Clyde had become her work. And her job as his wife offered a brighter future and more variety than any office manager's job ever could. She would preside as mistress of Fairview Avenue and provide domestic, secretarial and emotional support for Clyde in his quest to become governor. His part of the bargain was to be successful, to take care of her and keep her safe. Of the two of them, only Margaret truly kept her part of the bargain.

Though Margaret was prepared to work hard, she was not prepared for all the snide remarks, sniggers and sneers about class difference and age difference and motive—snatches of which could be heard even on the breeze which moved the curtains of her open kitchen window.[28] Clyde could not protect her from such viciousness, any more than he could transform her from Margaret Chase of North Avenue to Mrs. Clyde

Smith, mistress of one of the largest and grandest homes in town. For that to happen, Margaret's internal landscape had to change, her vulnerability diminish, her "charm" increase. That was a road she would have to travel alone, and it was a journey that would take the next decade.

In this quest, Clyde was at first of little help. Her impulse was to please him, and so she was seduced at first into rituals of domesticity which he did not value but took for granted. What he had perhaps treasured most about her was his glimpse of the self she had now to regain — the self-possessed and confident young woman in whose realm the world danced at her feet, the young woman who could turn heads and win people over with her easy charm, the young woman who could have organized Caesar's legions, the young woman for whom becoming mistress of the manor would be no harder than learning to play center in basketball.

But Margaret's transition to housewife was not an easy one. At thirty-three, she did not know anything about cooking or housework, because she "had always worked outside."[29] And living at home with Carrie and George with no domestic responsibilities had certainly not prepared her to take over the "big house" on Fairview Avenue. She was disadvantaged by the value placed by her rural Maine culture on good home-cooked food and a well-run home, an ideology reinforced by magazines such as *Ladies Home Journal* and *McCall's*, which likened domesticity to the building of a beautiful cathedral and claiming that "it exercises an even more profound influence on human destiny than the heroism of war or the prosperity of peace."[30] And she was hampered by her inexperience in entertaining. As she later recalled, "I had to learn [to run the house] because people who were opposed to me marrying Clyde said 'what was he going to do with that young woman?' They said, 'he was in public life and did a lot of entertaining, what's she know about it?' There were awful things said about me," she reflected, "so I set out to show 'em."[31]

Albra Smith, "an old-fashioned wonderful cook," got Margaret off on the right foot. "She was too old and frail to do much around the house," Margaret recalled, "but she did help me in learning to cook." From her, Margaret learned to make baked beans and brown bread, yeast bread, muffins and rolls, and cookies, sheet after sheet of cookies, to please Clyde's sweet tooth. One day, when Albra went "over town," Margaret decided to surprise her and show her what she had learned. "I got my apples out . . ." she recalled. "I didn't take good measure to do it but it looked like I did. I cut them so evenly. I placed them so evenly around in circles, all around the plate and put the crust down, and I patted it down. I slit it and I put the milk over it." Then the doorbell rang and it was Albra Smith wanting to get in. She had come home early. "I closed the kitchen door, and I could smell my pie [as] I knew she would. Just as she came through the door, I said, 'what did I put in that pie except apples? I didn't put a thing in that pie.' I was so intent on arranging. When Albra came into the kitchen, she said, 'smells like you're cooking.' And I said, 'yes,' and I began to cry. 'I was trying to surprise you by making an apple pie.' That little old lady . . . was so nice to me, she took it out of the oven and ripped that top crust off and she put all the things that were necessary in it and put the crust back on, and then put it back in the oven. It was a beautiful pie. No one ever knew it at the dinner table that night that it was not Margaret's pie."[32]

Not quite disguised beneath the aroma of an apple pie baking, however, were growing tensions. Albra had been the mistress of the house since 1928 and housekeeping came easy to her. Even though her physical strength was ebbing, the knowledge which Albra had accumulated over decades gave her enormous power, and her expertise insured that guests would be entertained properly and dinner served on time. Success or failure were hers to bestow or withhold, an arrangement which, however convenient, soon became intolerable for Margaret.

On dark, gloomy days, Margaret must have wondered if she had gotten more than she bargained for in taking on the Fairview Avenue house. Then she would redouble her efforts, and all would go well for a while. She even cleaned the hard wood floors with a cloth on her hands and knees.[33] On Saturday nights the Smiths frequently entertained, and Margaret served anywhere from six to sixteen by herself, cleaning up afterwards when everyone had left. Those Saturday night dinners most often consisted of baked beans, brown bread, ice cream and coffee. Margaret later recalled enjoying such entertainment. "I was fortunate that I did," she said, "also that I was well and strong physically, as Clyde was of no help other than looking after the guests."[34]

Twenty years hence, Margaret would cooperate with various womens' magazines to promote the hard-won domestic skills acquired during her first few years of marriage. Readers who were themselves experiencing what *Life* in 1947 called the "American Woman's Dilemma" were curious to know how women like Margaret balanced traditional ideas on woman's place and "involvement in activities outside the home."[35] Hence, splashy photos of Margaret's Skowhegan kitchen, her recipe for halibut loaf with lobster sauce, and a photo of Margaret herself, happily "doing a bit on her needlepoint," appeared in articles like, "Kitchen for a Lady Senator," which ran in a 1956 edition of *Ladies Home Journal*.[36] Though in fact by the fifties Margaret was what many feared most—a completely independent woman who had freed herself from the restraints of gender—such articles would help to preserve the impression that she was a traditionalist who still found significance and worth in woman's conventional role, even as she functioned outside the boundaries of convention. Throughout much of her career, she would rely on the vocabulary of the private sphere, saying there was "too little of the home in Government," and telling women: "Get out your political broom and sweep clean."[37] Between 1930 and 1932, however, as she was struggling to become the mistress of Fairview Avenue, she had more house and many more brooms than she could handle. And any idea that the domestic skills of these years would someday be used to her advantage in politics was too far-fetched to deserve consideration.

For no matter how hard she tried, she somehow couldn't make it come out right in those early years. Something was missing. Later on, when she reflected on the fever pitch of her first few years of marriage, she said that she took on all that she did in order to keep busy. She was struggling to overcome the problems inevitable when a man and a wife have a relationship "more on the basis of a team," with both people more "interested in people and doing for them than for each other."[38] Clyde's chronic health problems, in the meantime, were a constant worry to him, and they probably took a toll on the quality of their intimacy.

After eighteen months of marriage, the matter came to a head one day at lunch. Clyde had spent the morning working in the garden. Margaret spent the morning in the kitchen, peeling, chopping, and sautéing as she prepared one of Clyde's favorite dishes—fish chowder. At twelve o'clock sharp, she called Clyde. He liked his meals on time. Promptly she put the steaming bowls on the table. At twelve-fifteen, there was still no Clyde. Finally he came in, washed up, and came to the table. She watched anxiously as he ate the chowder. He said nothing. He talked about the garden and the chores that needed to be done around the place, but on the subject of the chowder, he was mute. Finally, unable to stand it, she asked how he liked it.

"Like what?"

"The fish chowder," she said.

"It's all right," he replied.

"I spent the whole before noon making that fish chowder," she exploded.

Then Clyde, who always called her "Sis," looked straight at her, and said: "Sis, you could spend your time to better advantage. I would suggest you not do that again."39

He was wisely saving "the best living girl" for the more important journey which lay ahead.40 He did not need a housewife. Instead, he had chosen for his mate a woman who was a thoroughgoing political asset. From that moment, Margaret's duties expanded, and she became a political wife and junior partner. On 14 December 1931, Clyde conveyed one-half of the Fairview Avenue house to Margaret.

With the new year, Clyde's political ambitions found their way into print. As the *Lewiston Evening Journal* described the situation: "Although the election does not come until January 1933, there is a lot of interest developing in the choice of a member of the Executive Council. Clyde H. Smith, for many years chairman of the board of selectman of Skowhegan, who has served in both branches of the legislature . . .is an avowed candidate for the place."41Whether 1932 would bring Clyde success would not be clear until the end of the year. In the meantime, 1932 would bring with it sweeping changes in Maine and elsewhere.

In Germany, for example, President Hindenburg managed to hold on to his presidency, defeating Adolph Hitler by seven million votes, though Hitler's Nazi party would claim 230 seats in the Reichstag elections, to the Socialists' 133, the Center Party's 97, and the Communists' 89 seats. In India, the Indian Congress was declared illegal and Ghandi arrested. In the U.S.S.R., the population endured a serious famine. Two events in the U.S. particularly captured people's interest: the kidnapping of the Lindbergh baby and the daring of Amelia Earhart, first woman to fly solo across the

Atlantic. Against this backdrop and with one of the year's popular songs ringing in their ears, "Brother, Can You Spare a Dime," the electorate swept a Democrat named Franklin Roosevelt into the presidency in a landslide victory over the Republican incumbent, Herbert Hoover.

Buried on the back pages of the newspapers was a news event unlikely to have come to Clyde, or even Margaret's, notice. In its own way, however, its implications were fully as important as the election of Franklin Roosevelt. In Arkansas, Hattie Caraway, "a mother whose life largely was concerned with domestic affairs" was elected in a special election to fill out her dead husband's unexpired term in the U.S. Senate. Heavy rains kept the voters away, but the results purportedly fulfilled the "fondest hopes of suffragettes who but a little more than a decade ago picketed the White House for 'equal rights.'"[42]

In December 1933, Clyde went on the road. He was gone about ten days, during which time he and Margaret wrote to each other daily. Though he mentions "culverts" in one of his letters, the precise purpose of the trip is not discussed, though it seems likely that financial exigence played a part in prompting him to take it.[43] "I would rather live on crackers," he wrote from Middletown, Ohio, "than to exist in this way . . . Only the fates of the everlasting will tempt [me] to leave you. Not a day has passed without shedding tears [over] this thing I am doing." In a second letter from Middletown, he assured Margaret: "Now then little girl, don't worry anymore. If you could look at my heart tonight you would plainly see you need not worry." No matter what financial benefits the trip might have produced, emotionally it exacted an enormous toll from Clyde. His absence from Margaret and all that he loved on Fairview Avenue produced in him unbearable loneliness. "Dear little girl," he wrote from Springfield, Mass. at the beginning of his trip, "As per wire we arrived here this evening after driving about two hundred and fifty miles. I feel both tired and lonesome. Having resolved that we will not separate again with my permission until the last parting makes it final." From his next stop, in Geneva, New York, he wrote: "Never again will I go away without you if I can have my way. It seems so strange and unnecessary to be separated." By the last leg of the trip, he had become quite homesick. "Never again little girl will we separate," he wrote, "if I can have my way that is so long as earthly ties are concerned. We live together so closely that we did not appreciate the comfort we were enjoying. I am trying to keep my grip [suitcase] just as you so nicely packed it. Tears come to my eyes every time I look into it. If you could see this moment—you would know [how] much I would like to be at home. . . . I would like to [see] Betty, Peggie and the ducks, too."[44] The dashing Clyde Smith of earlier days had become a gentle and avuncular Clyde. Not exactly a man spent, but certainly not a young man whose passion could not be contained.

Soon Clyde's travail was over. By mid-month he was home and by the end of the month (22 December 1932) he was nominated to serve on the Governor's Council. The legislature elected him on 4 January 1933, one day before Louis J. Brann took office as the first Democratic governor in sixteen years. He would represent Somerset and Kennebec Counties, and his pay would be $600 during the legislative season (the same as the legislators), plus $20 per day for each day the Council met when the Legislature was not in session. In wages and expenses during 1933, Clyde would be paid $1924 by the state.[45] His financial ship had righted itself.

The change from a Republican to a Democratic chief executive in Maine in 1933 mirrored a national shift in power which culminated in the inauguration of Franklin D. Roosevelt as president of the United States. In his 4 March inaugural address, he outlined an aggressive policy to deal with America's economic collapse and uttered what has become one of America's most memorable oratorical phrases: "The only thing we have to fear is fear itself." Soon after the inaugural, on 12 March, he delivered his first fireside chat—on the reopening of the banks—and by the end of the month, three-quarters were operating again.

Meanwhile, Clyde and Margaret were enjoying the social side of state politics, both in Skowhegan and Augusta. From the time Governor Brann was inaugurated in January, their calendar resembled one long, continuous house party. By spring, the Branns had "discovered" Skowhegan. On 2 June Governor Brann spoke to the Skowhegan post of the American Legion, and the Governor and Mrs. Brann were being entertained at the Smith home.[46] July found Governor Brann and the Governor's Council at a luncheon meeting of the Skowhegan Rotary Club, where Governor Brann discussed the existing banking situation. That afternoon, a Council meeting was held at the Smith home and in the evening the party travelled to Lakewood for dinner and a theatre party.

Following the performance, the group returned to Augusta. The event was a political coup, good for all concerned: for Governor Brann, for Skowhegan, and, of course, for Clyde himself. As the local newspaper reported: "The occasion is unique in the fact that it will possibly mark the first Council meeting ever held in the County and possibly the first visit here of a Governor and his entire council."[47]

Central to all of these activities with the Branns and the Council was Margaret. She entertained Mrs. Brann and oversaw all of the arrangements for visitors. She decided whom they would meet, who would serve at tea with her, what dishes would be prepared for the luncheons and dinners, who would stay in which rooms and what fresh flowers would be used to decorate them. When the Council met, Margaret's job was to entertain the wives. And she did her job very well indeed.

By 1934, the year in which the popular governor announced that he would seek a second term, the Branns and the Smiths had become close friends. On 1 February, Governor Brann nominated Margaret Chase Smith to be a member of the Board of Visitors to the State Reformatory for Women, and in spring Clyde and Margaret attended the wedding of Governor Brann's daughter at the Blaine Mansion.[48] Margaret also accompanied the Branns to Boston in May, where they were guests at a banquet and meeting of the Maine Hotel Men's Association at the Copley Plaza Hotel. Uncharacteristically, Clyde was unable to join the party for the trip, "due to other business engagements."[49]

A divided Republican Party failed in its efforts to unseat Brann in 1934, and he was returned to office by a margin of 23,000 votes over his closest competitor. Two days after the election, Blin Page, who had lost his first bid for the Republican nomination for governor in 1934, became the first to announce his intention to run in 1936.[50] The next day Clyde H. Smith became the second. "My record," Clyde said, "for introducing and supporting legislative acts calling for a more liberal workman's compensation act; a shorter work day; child labor restrictions and an old age pension may appeal to those who elect the next Governor of Maine."[51] With that, Clyde confirmed what had long been known—that he would never be satisfied until he had reached the governor's mansion in Augusta, a city once thought to be a "consecrated place" by the Abnaki, now a sprawling, bustling state capitol which he had first seen at the age of twenty-one when he arrived from the village of Hartland to take his seat in the state legislature. The city then was as exotic to Clyde as the lutes and arid desert of Arabia, and as seductive as all of Babylon. And so it remained.

Throughout the months following his announcement, Clyde was a man in love with what he was doing. His mood was expansive, even when he was told that Governor Percival P. Baxter might enter the race for governor, which he and Blin still had to themselves. Clyde welcomed the announcement of Baxter's candidacy, and proclaimed that Baxter was "a million times more entitled to become a candidate for governor than the man [Blin Page] who had never done a single, solitary thing for his town, county or state."[52]

From the start, both Page and Smith had strong organizations to carry them through the election. Page began the race with an array of 500 workers from all over the state who had supported him in his unsuccessful bid the year before, a head-start which led one supporter to characterize him as "a candidate to be reckoned with."[53] Clyde, on the other hand, was a natural politician, "one of those men who couldn't keep out of politics if he wanted to and doesn't want to." Pundits believed that Clyde's stands on labor issues would bring him votes, though whether or not it would be enough for a win in June 1936 was another matter. "So far in Maine politics," observed one writer, "those men who have placed great reliance on any one group, whether the Grange, labor or anything else have learned it was a mistake. No one," he continued, "has ever been able to deliver sizeable groups of Maine voters in blocks. This may be the time when it can be done and Smith may capture the entire labor vote . . . in the primary. There is always a first time for everything."[54]

By late summer, according to the *Waterville Sentinel*, Clyde believed that everything "looked rosy" for his campaign. After months of personal appearances from one end of the state to the other, the fifty-nine year-old's campaign had met its first test: the re-enrollment of large numbers of voters from the Democratic Party to the Republican Party. By the deadline, Clyde's workers from five cities and towns reported over 3,000 changes in registration and new enrollments.[55]

Suddenly, in November 1935, Clyde's level of activity came abruptly to a halt. On 15 November the state's attorney general filed a bill in equity to permanently restrain the state from purchasing $85,000 worth of trucks and snowplows from two Portland companies, the Portland Tractor Co., and the Autocar Sales and Service Co. In the bill it was charged that Councilor Clyde H. Smith was "an officer, agent or stockholder" of the defendant companies and was "pecuniarily interested directly or indirectly in the contracts."[56]

Within eleven days, a hearing on the charges was convened and the first witness sworn. Charles Scribner, a selectman from the small village of Athens, less than twelve miles from Skowhegan, told the court that on 12 September Smith had come to his home in Athens to discuss the town's purchase of a tractor. Scribner alleged that Clyde had threatened to revoke $1,000 in state monies that had been allotted the town to aid in bridge construction unless the tractor was purchased from the firm he represented, the Portland Tractor Company. "To _____ [expletive deleted] with the $1,000 if we have got to do what you say all the time," responded Scribner to Clyde's threat. Clyde had countered with an offer to waive his "$200 commission" if the town bought a tractor through him, allegedly telling Scribner, "I am going to be the next governor of Maine."

Corroborating Scribner's story was another Athens Selectman, Oliver French, who testified that Clyde had said that he had already stopped the $1,000 bridge payment but "would gladly give my commission to reduce the price of the tractor from $6,300 to $6,100." French then claimed that Clyde had asked: "What will the people of your town say when they learn I have taken away $1,000 from your bridge?" French added that Smith had said: "I have been a _____ [expletive deleted] fool all my life and I've just begun to find it out."[57]

Clyde denied pressuring the Athens selectmen, and he was backed up by his partner, Harold O. Pelley, of Smith-Pelley Motors. Pelley corroborated Clyde's story that he had only stopped off in Athens for a few minutes to ask why he had not been given a chance to demonstrate the tractor. Strengthening Clyde's case was Edgar Fox, yet another selectman from Athens, who testified that he had never heard of any threat by Clyde to withhold funds.[58] Clyde's final defense was that the $1000 of Athens funds he supposedly threatened to withhold had already been received and expended by the town of Athens.

In practical terms, what was going on was what Margaret would later call a "smear." What was at stake was Clyde's character. Rising out of his past like an evil specter were the town and highway commission scandals of earlier years, compounded by continuing gossip about Clyde's extra-martial and pre-marital activities. His uncertain past—magnified in impor-tance by his present predicament—raised serious questions of ethics, pro-bity, and judgement that could cripple his gubernatorial campaign and boost the strong Page candidacy. Nor could the damage be contained to a local venue, for implicated with Clyde was one of his poker partners, state treasurer George Foster, who had to approve state contracts. Even Governor Brann (who had first appointed Clyde in 1933 to head the Governor's Council Committee on State Highways) was drawn in as he testified at the hearing that the choice of trucks and other road equipment was left to the highway commission, not the Governor's Council.59

Immediately, Clyde went on the offensive, boldly asserting that "the attack against him by Charles Scribner" was "cheap politics." Not "a scintilla of evidence [had been] presented to connect [him] directly or indirectly with the purchase of state trucks," he said, while "hundreds of letters, telegrams have reached me from all sections of the State."60

Six weeks after the trouble began, the bill was dismissed without costs because in the words of Supreme Court Justice James H. Hudson "all matters in dispute between all parties to the proceeding have been satis-factorily adjusted," a statement which suggests that the matter was settled out of court. Henceforth, orders for trucks and snow removal equipment would be divided among the Eastern Tractor Co., the Four Wheel Drive Co., and the Portland Tractor Co., a plan satisfactory to all parties.61 But after the dismissal of the bill in equity, the fire went out of Clyde's cam-paign. After faltering for months, and despite his apparent lead over Blin Page and a campaign that exploded off the starting block, on 1 April Clyde withdrew from the race for the Republican nomination for governor.

"Several months ago I became a tentative candidate for governor, my only opponent being Mr. Page of the same county," he told the voters. "Recently, Mr. Barrows and Benjamin Bubar unexpectedly came into the field. While I would like to be governor . . . , these unforeseen con-ditions invite far reaching contingencies. Rather than embarrass the party, so many times honoring me, with a bitter contest, I withdrew as a candidate for governor."62 Paradoxically, when official announcement of withdrawal from the governor's race appeared in the Skowhegan news-paper, it ran under the headline: "SMITH EXPECTED TO RUN FOR CONGRESS; OUT OF GOV. RACE."[63]

The decision had been made at the Maine Republican Convention. Clyde's vulnerability had become the Party's opportunity. They had used Clyde's misstep to solve one of their major problems: a destructive con-gressional race in the Second District. The contest had already been described by one reporter as a race "where seven Republican candidates are sawing one another's heads off, with a dangerous prospect that the vote will be so badly split up that Moran [the Democratic nominee] may run away with the prize." By entering that race, however, Clyde could "con-solidate the Republican strength in the Second District, win the nomina-tion at the polls," and beat the Democratic nominee in September.[64] The Party would throw its considerable support to Clyde in the congressional election, while ensuring the victory of Lewis Barrows for governor, the clear choice of the Old Guard.[65] The $200 or $300 Clyde had already spent on his gubernatorial campaign would also be reimbursed.

Clyde took the deal, though its psychic cost was steep. A photo taken at the convention shows the couple smiling, Clyde thinly, Margaret more broadly. In his customary way, Clyde was looking directly at the camera and though smiling, his face lacked its usual vitality. Gone was his rapport of earlier years with the camera, its lens an adoring witness to his high spir-its and ebullience. The 1936 photo reveals only a tired, if genial fifty-nine year old. With Margaret, too, something was amiss. Perhaps it was the hat. In the photo, Margaret wore a short-brimmed hat, set on her head in such a way that the strong, angular lines of her face were emphasized. At the same time, her open coat, with its wide, flared lapels, suggested intense girth. Margaret looked at least a decade older than her thirty-eight years.

As the boy in Clyde cried foul, and the politician in him weighed the alternatives, Margaret internalized the experience and distilled it down to three axioms: the Party always looks out for itself, innuendo is the quickest way to derail a career, and politics are dirty. Comments like "Clyde Smith himself ought to know enough to pull out before he is knocked out" and "there is evidence available, evidence that is pretty likely to get thoroughly advertised, that Clyde Smith is utterly unworthy of any elective office" began to appear in print, smacking of the threats she had heard Blin Page and his crowd making at Augusta House.[66] These attacks stung her and frightened her as well, for she had seen enough of the mercurial world of politics to understand how vulnerable she and Clyde had become. Sown at this time were the seeds of what would become in later years Margaret's paranoid political style.

Within a few weeks of the convention, the Smiths became too busy to dwell on might-have-beens. Clyde's announcement that he would be a candidate for the Republican nomination to Congress required the couple to swing immediately into action, for only three months remained until the primary. As had been her custom for several years, Margaret drove the car, handled the mail, took dictation for—though never wrote—Clyde's speeches, and in her words, "served as a consultant, some said campaign manager."[67]

She and Clyde visited almost every town, village, hamlet and crossroads in the Second District. For information, they relied on a three-ring notebook—a campaign diary—which was the sum total of Clyde's years in office. The notebook measured eight inches by six inches and contained the names of everyone in each town that Clyde and Margaret had knowledge of, with any relevant information about them, such as "wants farm loan," or "regent, D.A.R.," or "American Legion." The names of those who had not signed primary papers, or who had not proven to be supporters, or who had simply moved to a different town, were crossed out, with a brief notation of the reason.[68]

For three months, Clyde and Margaret feverishly covered every inch of seven counties, even missing the now-traditional theatre party with Governor and Mrs. Brann in May. Meanwhile, their hometown newspaper began to predict victory, both for Blin Page in the gubernatorial race and for Clyde in the congressional race. "It will be no surprise . . . to receive the report on the evening of June 15th following the primary election that Page is the Republican Party's gubernatorial candidate and Smith is the same party's choice for U.S. Representative," the newspaper predicted. "It is pretty general opinion throughout the state that these nominations spell certain election in the fall."[69] The newspaper was almost wrong on both counts. Blin Page never made it to the general election in the fall. He was defeated in the primary by a margin of about 18,000 votes, a triumph of organization over individuality, explained *Independent Reporter*.[70]

Clyde, on the other hand, did win by a margin of 2,072 votes, a narrow victory which nonetheless the *Independent Reporter* described as "truly substantial" and saw as a natural outcome of a field of six candidates, with "anyone of four of the group likely to gather in first honors."[71] In fact, though Skowhegan itself gave Clyde 1107 votes, only 360 fewer than they had given Blin Page in a much less crowded race, the county as a whole gave Clyde only 1520 votes more than they gave his closest opponent. In other words, without the votes from the town of Skowhegan, Clyde would have won his home county by a mere 413 votes. Rumors about his character and his attempt to trade bridge construction for a tractor purchase in Athens had cost Clyde the rural vote.

In September, in the general election, a similar pattern emerged. In a record turnout, Skowhegan gave Clyde approximately 900 votes more than it gave to former Mayor Ernest McLean of Augusta, Clyde's Democratic opponent, enough to offset the votes from rural towns like Fairfield and Athens, where Clyde's Democratic opponent actually received the majority of votes.[72] When the polls closed and all seven counties had reported, Clyde had won the Second District congressional seat by a margin of some 20,000 votes.

In October a torchlight parade was held in his honor in Skowhegan, to celebrate his victory. More than three thousand people attended (approximately 10% of the entire county), including bands, Boy Scouts, Girl Scouts and Campfire Girls, as well as officials from various Somerset towns. Most of the local officials offered brief remarks, while the recently successful county candidates joined the parade as an escort to Clyde and Margaret. Blin Page took no part.

When Clyde delivered what in effect was his farewell speech to the large crowd, he promised that when he went to Washington he would advocate old age pensions "large enough for the old people to live in comfort," and a higher tariff on agricultural products and industrial goods. Before he closed, he extended an invitation to all of his friends to visit him and Margaret whenever they were in Washington, almost as though he were homesick for Maine already.[73]

In late December 1936, he and Margaret left for Washington accompanied by Norma Turcotte, who had recently been employed as a housekeeper at their Fairview Avenue home and who for the next year would take care of the small red brick house on Raymond Street, near the Chevy Chase Country Club, which they had leased.74 The fourth occupant of the car was Betty, the Smiths' Mexican hairless Chihuahua. She went everywhere with Margaret and Clyde, including the campaign trail, and had even "written a letter" to the newspaper while Clyde was on the Governor's Council, in which she described the social doings of Augusta. The *Independent Reporter* ran the letter along with her picture. By the time the Smiths left for Washington on 27 December, Betty, at thirteen years of age and four pounds, was at least as well-known in Maine as were her owners.

The prospect of moving to Washington was not one which Clyde welcomed. He could not seem to forget that the congressional seat was a sop, with the real prize having gone to Barrows, and the real action and power remaining in Augusta. Moreover, both he and Margaret were weary. The year had been so topsy-turvy that they were emotionally exhausted and physically spent. So, once they had repacked, at Margaret's urging they decided to drive south—possibly to Florida—for some sunshine and rest.75 But even this excursion proved less than satisfactory. Rather than the respite the couple badly needed, the trip created additional stress. When they reached Savannah, they found extremely cold weather. The only sunshine and warmth to be had was in Miami, approximately five hundred miles farther south, too far for Clyde, who "felt we had had enough travelling so we turned around to go back North."76 In North Carolina, they stopped in Fayetteville, where they stayed for two or three days before returning to Washington. At least in Fayetteville, Clyde could see at first hand some of the working conditions which had been so much discussed in Augusta as Maine's textile mills closed and moved south.77

Back in Washington, a sullen January signalled the approach of Franklin Delano Roosevelt's Second Inaugural and Clyde's swearing-in ceremony. The day itself, 20 January 1937, dawned cold, dreary and wet, the gray and somber sky casting a mood of heightened solemnity over the ceremony. By the day's end, Clyde H. Smith had become a member of the United States House of Representatives, and Margaret had been promoted from the wife of a state politician to a congressman's wife. But Washington's stately grandeur was no cure for Clyde's mood, which approximated the gray and darkened skyline.

In contrast, Margaret, was in her element. Soon after her arrival in

Washington, Margaret was "discovered," or in this case "rediscovered," by the socially prominent Mrs. Owen (Dorothy) Brewster, who had first met her years ago when she and her husband, then the governor of Maine, attended the state BPW meeting in Skowhegan. Now the wife of a congressman, Dorothy Brewster moved as a swan on Washington's glacial, social surface. Within reach of her protective wing was Margaret. In a day when calling on other women of the same social set was required of wives, especially in Washington's diplomatic and military circles, and was still expected in political circles, Dorothy Brewster's tutelage in the fine art of making calls was invaluable to Margaret's growing mastery of the social graces.

Dorothy had a large car and chauffeur, and on the day of the week designated for wives of Representatives—Monday—she and Margaret would set out, calling first at the White House and then on the vice president's wife. Seldom was anyone home, so it was largely a matter of leaving engraved cards with the right corners of the cards turned down to indicate to the hostess that the call had been made in person.[78] On the appointed day and during the accepted calling hours, Margaret and Dorothy would appear at the door and ask for the hostess. More often, the servant who came to the door would indicate that she was not at home, which often meant merely that she wasn't receiving any visitors, a necessary social device not intended to offend. The callers would then leave their cards on a convenient table, usually in a card tray. The purported benefit of this ritual was that official calls were "always answered by an invitation to some social function," so it was up to Margaret to decide how much of a social career she wished to enjoy.[79] The real benefit was that it provided a finishing school polish to Margaret's emerging public self.

With encouragement from Dorothy, she elected to officially enter the glittering world of Washington society through the door of the Congressional Club, a club for wives, daughters, and official hostesses of members of Congress.[80] The club owned a large clubhouse on 16th and New Hampshire Avenue, N.W. where they hosted teas, dinners and dances. Eventually, Margaret succeeded Dorothy as treasurer of the club, an office which required her attendance at board meetings and gave her enormous visibility, especially since she took office in the middle of a fund-raising drive which had been launched to refurnish, redecorate and change the clubhouse at the cost of nearly $200,000 a sizable amount of money in those post-depression days. The first official function of the 1937 season was a tea honoring Mrs. Franklin D. Roosevelt, to be followed later by events honoring Mrs. William B. Bankhead, wife of the Speaker of the House, and Mrs. Garner, wife of the vice president.

Perhaps spurred by the public ease of the women around her, 27 December 1938 found Margaret enrolled with Alice Keith, director of the National Academy of Broadcasting, who coached her in public speaking and radio delivery. A picture of Margaret wearing a simple, fitted dress, dark in color, with a V-neckline which flattered her once-again slender figure, and a hat which added height to her small stature appeared in the *Washington Times*. Around her neck was a double strand of costume pearls, and in her right hand, the ring finger of which displayed a ring with a stone of modest size was a microphone. Standing next to her was Alice Keith. According to the caption under the picture, Margaret, "who works closely with her husband in his office here, and during his campaigns at home, appreciates the *"importance of preparedness."*[81] She was one of several wives of congressmen who were coached by Keith, though it may be imagined few were probably doing it with more single-minded dedication.

In addition to creating social opportunities, the Congressional Club was also an important source of information for and about Margaret, and she was later to credit the warm reception she received from her colleagues in the House of Representatives in 1940 to the years of association with their wives through the Congressional Club. When she shared this insight with a female colleague in the House, Judge Jessie Sumner (R-Illinois), a graduate of Smith College and the University of Chicago Law School, the judge replied (somewhat icily it may be supposed), "I don't want them to be good to me because their wives tell them to be." Margaret, more unreceptive to Sumner's style than to the ideology which underlay her indignation, noted that she was "grateful for whatever reason."[82] Common ground between women like the tart-tongued feminist Sumner, who never married and who was often quoted as saying that "if a woman has neither husband nor children, she wants to do something for her generation," and the centrist Smith, who assiduously avoided strident feminism, was established with great difficulty — and almost never sustained. Their divergent understandings of what women *should be able to* expect from society created too deep a chasm for either to cross.

A burgeoning source of public power for women in 1937 was the Women's Press Corps. When Eleanor Roosevelt took the unprecedented step of holding press conferences once a week for women reporters in the Treaty Room on the second floor of the White House, women journalists gained an opportunity they had not previously enjoyed—regular access to the First Lady, as well as press conferences restricted to women journalists. In addition, she dispensed hard news at these conferences "so that newspapers and syndicates had to add women to their staffs," though she was also careful to avoid what she called "my husband's side of the news." In short, the First Lady made women journalists "part of what was going on."[83] Among the best known members of the Washington Press Corps was (Elizabeth) May Craig, a staunch advocate for women and a reporter for the Gannett newspapers of Maine. Because May's columns were so readable, they were politically potent. May was a good storyteller, chatty but credible. And she was a master of nuance, able with ease to make a conscientious congressman, who stayed in Washington more than he visited his district, seem either hard-working and dedicated, or plodding and slow-witted. The spin of the story would depend on how much she liked him. Thus, the Smiths had every reason to want to win over this small, energetic woman. And by 1 March 1937, Margaret had managed to do so.

May, like the other members of the Women's Press Club, was entitled to take four guests to the Annual Women's Press Capitol Dinner, the equivalent of the exclusive Gridiron meeting for men. It was one of the most important political events for Washington women, and it was an occasion to which May invited Margaret Smith. At the event, which was held at the dowager Willard Hotel, Margaret rubbed elbows with Eleanor Roosevelt, Senator Hattie Caraway [D-Ark.], Cornelia Otis Skinner, the well-known actress, Margaret Bourke-White, internationally known photographer, and Dorothy Thompson, columnist and foreign correspondent.[84]

In contrast to Margaret's adaptation to social Washington, Clyde attended a White House reception once only and counted the minutes until he could leave. He despised the large dinners and large cocktail parties that were the backbone of the city's social life, preferring instead the pattern he and Margaret had established on Fairview Avenue—entertaining a few people at home. For a man who had used charm all of his life to successfully create a world in which he was central, Washington's sheer size—not to mention its indifference to him—was off-putting. Simply stated, by the time he entered Congress, Clyde was sixty years of age and well-established in his home state. In Washington he was a freshman congressman forced by the seniority system by which he himself had benefitted when he was a member of the Maine legislature, to start over again. Worse than that, few of the issues taken up by Congress—except those assigned to the Labor Committee where he excelled—had much relevance or significance for the small towns and villages of his home district, and so he spent much of his time in Washington turning his back on that alien environment and longing for the cool, pine-scented air of Maine and heady atmosphere of Augusta.

Because he could make little sense of this new, larger, world in light of the values of the Maine villages he both knew and understood, he embraced his old "small, familiar environment" with growing fervor, while changes that he believed signalled the erosion of bedrock American values especially exercised him.[85] "If changes are to be made, we propose to do the changing in the good old New England way, deliberately and in accordance with well-considered popular will," he would assert, railing against what he called "foreign-isms" and their sponsors "who come here, or choose to remain with us because they like American institutions better than those of the lands from which they came . . . and yet choose to assail, rather than defend those institutions."[86]

Increasingly during his Washington years, rural Maine became for Clyde something like the embodiment of a pastoral ideal, modified only by his impulse for progressivism. "It was a glorious feeling—to fully trust your neighbors," he used to tell Margaret, "not some of them but every one . . . Even in this hard-boiled generation, standards of conduct in the sparsely settled districts, cannot after all have changed so much."[87] As in Jefferson's agrarian landscape and Frost's "Two Tramps in Mudtime," rural virtue remained for Clyde "the moral center of a democratic society," the only constant in a world grown impersonal and unfamiliar.[88]

Years later, when Margaret was on the stump in Maine, echoes of the pastoral ideal would shape the character of Margaret's appeal, though in her hands it would become an idealized rank-and-file at whose core was eternal, immutable, enduring Maine. As she invoked the magic of the "noble democrat" in virtually undiluted form among friends and neighbors in her campaigns, she would herself become the paradigm, and in her, contemporaries would see qualities as vital and compelling as intellectual superiority had once been for their ancestors.[89] In essence, what she would restore was balance between past and present, the husbandman and the factory worker, the idealized and the real selves of rural Maine.[90] Though her vision was intuitive, rather than intellectual, it did not emerge full-blown until she ran for the Senate, and its genesis can be traced to the early days with Clyde.

3. Victory

WHEN ON 13 MAY 1940 Margaret was elected to the eight months remaining in Clyde's term, the regular primary for the full term loomed just a month away.[91] Soon Margaret and four other Republican candidates would square off in the June primaries for the full-term nomination, with the winner facing Democrat Edward Beauchamp in September, who had been unopposed for his party's nomination.[92] In the meantime, Margaret left for Washington to hear President Roosevelt deliver his national defense message.

Chivalry and old ties fused when Margaret was seated on the floor of the House in defiance of a House regulation limiting the floor to members and former members only. Speaker William Bankhead, a Democrat from Alabama and husband of one of Margaret's fellow members of the Congressional Club, had arranged it by calling Margaret a "representative delegate." Representative Owen Brewster escorted her to her seat.

President Roosevelt's speech was stirring, the mood of Congress somber. War was coming. Two years earlier, Germany had swallowed up Austria and the year before had invaded Poland. Already Britain and France were at war with Germany, and recently Hitler had warned that he was ready to "protect" Holland against their aggression. Dunkirk, from which 340,000 British troops would be evacuated, was looming on the horizon, with the Battle of Britain only three months away.

Roosevelt's text resonated with the cadence of war. As Margaret listened, the President told Congress that the crisis in Europe demanded an "impregnable America." He asked support for a national budget that would help produce 30,000 airplanes and prepare thirty-five destroyers from World War I for active duty. He also sketched out plans for an army of 750,000 regulars by 30 June 1941. The day after his speech, the *New York Times* ran the following headline: NAZIS PIERCE FRENCH LINES ON 62-MILE FRONT; TAKE BRUSSELS, LOUVAIN, MALINES AND NAMUR; WASHINGTON SPEEDS ITS BIG DEFENSE PROGRAM.[93]

Intractable isolationists, many of them Republicans, were upset by his defense message, but Margaret was not. If anything, it validated the view she had expressed about the importance of the Navy on 27 October 1938 (Navy Day) when she had substituted for Clyde at a Republican Women's Club. The women, expecting a talk about social life in Washington, were no doubt surprised and perhaps disappointed when instead she trumpeted the Navy's importance to Maine. "Those who oppose Naval protection fail to perceive that the real attack, if any, will be by way of the sea," she had said. "Development of our Navy is necessary self-preservation."[94] The founders of the Republic had advocated preparedness when months were required to cross the Atlantic. Now "when barely hours are required, preparedness is doubly imperative."[95] Substituting Naval preparedness for society-page gossip demonstrated a certain amount of prescience, as well as courage. Margaret's choice also suggested an intuitive grasp of naval historian Alfred Thayer Mahon's metaphor that the sea was almost "all open plain" and that any nation whose armed fleets controlled this plain would flourish in war and peace, cornering strategic points on the seas (Gibraltar, Panama, Singapore) and dominating markets.[96]

Still more significant was its sharp departure from the script of distaff and its suggestion of discomfort, perhaps even rebelliousness, at the constraints which limited congressmen's wives to the discussion of inconsequential social matters and gossip. More than anything, Margaret's Navy Day Speech revealed a woman prepared to ignore gender-related boundaries and to challenge conventional ideas of woman's place. Muted by style, however, her "rebellion" went unnoticed.

In May 1940 even though she knew that she was in agreement with Roosevelt, the already politically astute Margaret at first decided to keep her distance as he outlined his request for strengthening America's defenses. "Contrary to the President's statement, that ways and means of financing [defense] are a mere detail," she said in a June 1940 radio address, "I emphasize that this is the time to decide upon the source of revenue and if it is to come from taxation, the kind and amount shall be specified." Earlier in the week she had warned against sending American boys "into battle on foreign soil."[97] After all, although 93.6% of Americans currently favored building up the armed forces, more than 64% wanted America to stay out of the European war, at least according to the relatively new "science" of polling that was rapidly gaining influence.[98] Her caution proved prudent, as former Governor Brann's identification with the New Deal would cost him the upcoming U.S. Senate race.[99]

With the approach of the 17 June regular primary, Margaret leveraged her Navy Day speech into support from Guy Gannett and his Maine newspaper chain. When he asked how she stood on national defense, particularly the Navy (which he wanted to see strengthened), she sent him "a clipping from the *Waterville Sentinel* and *Kennebec Journal* (Gannett's papers) of [her] public stand two years ago on Navy Day," and it did the trick. Gannett gave her his "enthusiastic" support.[100]

Unresolved, however, was the extent to which Margaret's gender would be a liability in the election. Although Maine had elected more women to the state legislature than practically any other state in the union, sending a woman to Congress from Maine was unprecedented. As for Margaret's succeeding Clyde, detractors believed that the district had met its obligation to him when they elected his widow to fill his seat for the interim term.[101] In fact, the *Lewiston Evening Journal* reported "definite opposition to Mrs. Smith among women voters . . . based not on a personal matter but . . . from a very pronounced sentiment that the congressional place is a man's job, not a woman's."[102]

Such sentiments might have prevailed had the Kennebec County "Mrs. Smith Goes to Washington Club" not been formed on the 11th of June, one week before the primary. Gender was the first issue discussed by Herbert Carlyle Libby, one of the principal speakers of the evening, and Mrs. C. E. Towne, who became president of the organization.[103] Mrs. Towne's opening remarks set the tone. "I am not a feminist," she began. "I would not vote for Mrs. Smith simply because she is a woman, though there are some who will. Nor will I vote against her for the same reason—though she may lose a few votes on that account." Instead her support flowed to Margaret because of "her heritage," "her experience in Washington," and her charm.[104] To Mrs. Towne, lack of charm was the last barrier to full equality, though a charming woman deserved to be judged as any other candidate was judged. Gender alone, she argued, should not be held against Margaret, who was clearly the better candidate.

Then Herbert C. Libby, a Harvard-educated professor of Oratory at Colby, former editor of the *Waterville Mail*, and an old friend of Clyde's, strode to the platform. His ties with Clyde were of long duration, going back to the early days of the *Independent Reporter* when Clyde was president of the newspaper and Libby wrote editorials. On the eve of the primary election, the ever-articulate and frequently eloquent Libby—a familiar figure in various church pulpits throughout the state—addressed the issue of Margaret's fitness, and women's fitness in general, to be elected to Congress. His argument, which stressed competency and equity, would serve Margaret well for the next two decades.

"The thought has been expressed that the people of our district have fulfilled their personal obligations to the late Congressman Clyde H. Smith in heeding his last public request, when they elected his wife to congress this month . . . ," he said. "The thought is based upon the assumption that when he made the request that his wife succeed him it was based upon sentiment only. I want to say," he asserted, "that the request, while it may have been prompted by sentiment, was based upon the fitness of Mrs. Smith to hold a position in congress." Just a few months earlier Clyde had told Libby "that he was the most fortunate man among all the congressmen in having a wife who was far better versed in the conduct of his office than was he himself."[105]

Not only was Margaret competent, but she knew the important figures in Congress and understood the issues connected with Clyde's membership on the Labor Committee. Nor was the idea of sending a woman to Congress shocking, even though "now and then" he had "met with voters who . . . expressed the conviction that congress is no place for a woman." These voters, he said, "hark back to the days when women held no political rights and were classed with idiots, paupers, and criminals." And while "I respect the judgment of those who maintain that congress is a place for men only . . . I am frank to confess that I find no facts to support it and no reasoning to substantiate it." He pointed out that women were being elected to most public offices in growing numbers, including Congress itself which had seven women in its membership. Thus, it was "unthinkable, that our leading women educators and philanthropists, and social workers, and writers . . . should not find places in political life."

With the very center of the enemy line in his sights, he drew upon the argument he had saved for last. Similar to the one used by Louise Coburn and Mary Low Carver in 1890 at Colby, and derivative of the one used by moderate suffragists after 1888, the argument conceded that conservatives were correct.[106] Women were indeed the spiritual creatures they were thought to be and possessed "certain attributes of character, mental and moral, that many men do not possess . . . [especially] an amazing sense of intuition that seems entirely foreign to men." Because of their spiritual superiority, he argued, women's participation in government could not help but serve to raise the moral level of that sphere. His "spin" on Margaret's candidacy was quite important. Libby had explained her in such a way that she threatened no one and yet was more than just a grieving widow who hoped to return to Washington for one term. Moreover, Margaret's candidacy was not only viable, but highly desirable. On the battlefield of "conventional ideas of woman's place," Libby helped to weight the scales in Margaret's favor, purify her persona, and secure her future. A quarter of a century later, she would publically give credit to the pivotal role Libby played in her first congressional campaign. "He was one of the early political liberals in Maine, although in his later years he grew more conservative. He was the manager of my very first campaign back in 1940 when I first ran for the House of Representatives. To him I owed so very much." [107]

After the Waterville rally, Margaret increasingly punctuated her speeches with statements like "of course, we women do not want to take over the government, but we do want to be more active now than ever before," and, "being a woman, I am interested in what women can do through their ideals and their courage at this time of crisis."[108] She was no feminist, she would tell her audiences, but she could bring "special" sensibilities to the act of governing. For women like Mrs. Towne, "feminism" was a category reserved for members of the militant National Women's Party, and any identification by Margaret with feminism would have courted, or even ensured, defeat.[109] Margaret's style, however, greatly reduced the chances of that happening. The *Independent Reporter* described her campaign as "quiet and unobtrusive . . . typical of the type of womanhood which she represents."[110] The *Bangor Daily News* noted the way she "bolstered her political fences by quiet reorganization."[111] From the beginning Margaret successfully became identified with the established order.

A similar pattern had been set in 1923 when the arrival of the newly elected (Mrs.) Dora Pinkham rippled the calm surface of the 81st Maine legistlature. Pinkham was a product of the nineteenth amendment, which had passed two and one-half years earlier on 26 August 1920, the legacy of a cause which had consumed "fifty-two years of pauseless campaigns . . . fifty-six campaigns of referenda to male voters; 480 campaigns to get Legislatures to submit suffrage amendments to voters; 47 campaigns to get State constitutional conventions to write woman suffrage into State constitutions; 277 campaigns to get State party conventions to include woman suffrage planks; 30 campaigns to get Presidential party conventions to adopt woman suffrage planks in party platforms, and 19 campaigns with 19 successive congresses."[112] With unintended irony, when she was asked after her election why she had decided to run for office, Mrs. Pinkham said it was "because the men . . . thought they could not spare the time from their livings."[113] Such lack of stridency, or modesty, suggested to some that she was not interested in the cause of suffrage. "On the contrary," she protested, "I was never more interested in any cause as anybody who knew me personally would testify." Interested perhaps, but not publicly identified with it any more than Margaret Chase Smith would be with women's liberation. While both women furthered the goals of female activists and helped clear the path to full sexual equality, neither chose to present herself as a "feminist," or "suffragist," primarily because of the political liability such labels were thought to impose.

In 1940, Margaret stood poised on a tightrope stretched between a new social order, which sought to erase boundaries to public life for women, and conventional ideas which located women in the home For the next thirty years, through countless boundary-breaking campaigns, the voices of Pinkham, Libby and Towne would co-mingle in Margaret's public persona, fortifying her against attacks that she was indeed an agent of social change. Throughout the forties and fifties, the paradox of her position would remain unchallenged until a new generation of feminist activists, who had little time or patience with the Dora Pinkhams of the world, rooted it out and used it to unseat Margaret. But that would not happen until she had grown old. For now, her strategy worked, a canny accommodation to the constraints to which she and other women were heir.

On 17 June, the Republicans in the Second District made the forty-two year old widow their standard-bearer. She had campaigned for old age assistance and military preparedness, Clyde's initiatives.[114] And she had vowed to be in attendance for congressional sessions, a pledge that would later translate into a highly publicized string of unbroken roll call votes.[115] She won with a total of 27,000 votes, four times more than her closest rival, and in her home county of Somerset, she captured 1450 votes, nearly three times the number Clyde had received in his 1938 race against only one other candidate. Other victors in the 17 June primary included Owen Brewster, who became the Republican nominee for the U.S. Senate, and Sumner Sewall, World War I ace and descendant of the Bath shipbuilding family, who became at 44 the Republican nominee for governor. Within seven years, all three of them would face each other as political opponents.[116]

Almost immediately Margaret kicked off her campaign for the general election—her fourth campaign in three months—though she paused briefly to go to Philadelphia to observe, though not participate as a delegate, in the Republican National Convention of 1940. What she saw there would put her in the company of a whole new generation of Republican leaders. And it would expose her to the sweetness of victory snatched in a stunning upset. Whether she went to the convention supporting one of the front-runners—Thomas E. Dewey or Robert Taft—or the dark horse, Wendell Willkie, is not clear. But when she returned to Maine, "We Want Willkie" was ringing in her ears, and Margaret, along with the rest of the convention, was rallying to this ambling, genial progressive as the hope of the party. On 9 September, she would take to the hustings for Willkie.

When she returned to Maine she campaigned in the general election as if she were an underdog, even though "real" political contests in Maine in 1940 were still confined to the Republican primary. Speeches to the Maine D.A.R., suppers with the BPW, Republican rallies, radio addresses, and dinners with old supporters like Inez Wing—the woman who had first proposed Margaret's name for president of the Maine BPW—filled her weekends, while weekdays were spent in Washington.[117] The same pattern of high energy, combined with the same attention to detail which had characterized her Maine BPW presidency, was used to ensure a win in September. One weekend in August, she gave speeches all day Saturday and on Sunday arrived in Searsport harbor at 4:00 A.M. to visit points of commercial interest before climbing to the top of Mt. Waldo in Frankfort at sunrise with a group of young Republicans.[118] Over Labor Day weekend, less than a week before the general election, she spoke on Saturday at Mechanic Falls and Boothbay, on Sunday at Fairfield, and on Monday travelled to Lewiston to attend American Legion ceremonies in that city.[119] The pace was like Clyde's congressional campaigns and so was the style—from glad-handing on street corners to 'politickin' on village greens. When the votes were counted on 9 September Margaret was the clear winner, with 57,000 votes to Beauchamp's 31,000, a margin of two to one.[120] Her campaign was "energetic in the extreme," and yet, observed the *Independent Reporter*, "she has found time to act as the gracious hostess, which she always is, at intervals during her hasty visits to her Fairview Avenue home."[121]

Clyde himself would have enjoyed Margaret's campaign. He would have applauded her chasing down votes in every hamlet and village and her caution in avoiding the feminist label. He would not have been surprised by Margaret's enthusiasm for "pressing the flesh" or her love for the *adventure* of politics, but what would have most amused the man who called her "Sis" was Margaret's impressive resiliency and adaptability in adjusting to change. Swiftly she had launched her campaign, and just as swiftly installed herself behind Clyde's desk in Room 231 of the old House Building. Blanche Bernier—who had come from Skowhegan to keep house for Clyde and Margaret after the departure of Norma Turcotte, and whose brother Joseph ("Spike") had married Margaret's sister Laura—now occupied the receptionist's desk. The loyal Bernier, who

made many of Margaret's clothes, also shopped for her, and even sham-
pooed and set Margaret's hair.[122] In many ways, she was an adult version
of Margaret's first friend, Agnes Lamore. Sharing the front office with
Bernier were Roland Patten, who would stay on until Margaret moved to
the Senate, and Lena Haskell from Mechanic Falls, who was Margaret's
secretary. In the second office of the two-room suite, Margaret's imprint
was as yet only faintly visible—primarily in the addition of fresh flowers,
a radio, and several photographs of Clyde. But Clyde's red velvet drapes
still covered the windows and his large state of Maine flag still dominated the room. Clyde, knowing full well Margaret's wide streak of frugality, would have been amused that, except for a few touches, she had left
the room as she had found it. Not as a tribute to him—but because she
could see no point in getting rid of perfectly good drapes.

4. The Willkie Boomlet

A FEW WEEKS after her election to Congress for a full term, Margaret hit
the campaign trail for Wendell Willkie. Her first stop was a luncheon for
1800 Republicans in Detroit at the biennial meeting of the National
Federation of Women's Republican Clubs.[123] The Federation meeting,
which drew 20,000 for the evening session, provided the kind of visibility that could launch Margaret's national career.[124]

Some voters in Maine "were not quite ready to send a woman to the
House of Representatives," she told a luncheon audience of 1800. But an
old man who pumped gas in Sidney, Maine had given her hope. "I'm
getting sick of having men run things," he said. "Women ought to take
over the government and straighten things out." The story would become
standard fare for Margaret's audiences, as would themes of women's dis-
tinctiveness. "The thing that concerns women more than anything else
is the betterment of social conditions of the masses. Women are needed
in government for the very traits of character that some people claim disqualify them."[125] It was as though Libby were writing her speeches.

Seated at the head table with her were Mrs. Willkie and Mrs. McNary
(wife of the vice presidential candidate). Margaret, who was eager to
learn what she could from such women, jotted notes about Mrs. Willkie:
"pretty, intelligent, dresses well. Exhibit A. Called for everywhere. Goes

everywhere. All like her"—high praise from one who used popularity and attractiveness as benchmarks for her own success.[126]

After Detroit, the Republican National Committee asked her to speak for Willkie in several states. She was to support national defense without disavowing isolationism, damn Roosevelt's New Deal, and spread the word that women could control the 1940 race, unlike 1936, when 13 million had stayed home on election day. Different cities called for slight modifications, but standard fare was criticism of the national debt of nearly sixty billion dollars and the inflation, waste and extravagance of the New Deal. Margaret frequently accused the Administration of neglecting defense "when money was appropriated for adequate defense," and she urged women to go to the polls.[127]

When Margaret jumped aboard the Willkie train, she joined an impressive group of young hopefuls. Collectively they would not only shape the future of the Republican Party, but one of their number, Richard Nixon, would alter the character of the presidency itself. Margaret's old confidante and future mentor, Joe Martin, who steered the Willkie campaign after the convention, would be elected Speaker of the House in 1947 and again in 1953-1954 at the outset of the Eisenhower administration. He would also serve as permanent chairman of the next five Republican conventions. Clare Boothe Luce, the actress-wife of the publisher of *Life* and *Time*, who entered Congress in 1942 and later became Eisenhower's Ambassador to Italy, made her first public speech at a "Work for Willkie" rally on 15 October 1940. Eventually she made more than forty appearances on his behalf.[128]

In Southern California, Richard Nixon was making his political debut. Though Nixon "favored some of Roosevelt's domestic programs, particularly social security," he made the rounds to service clubs in Southern California, attacking Roosevelt on his defiance of the two-term tradition and his 1937 court packing plan, and speaking on Willkie's behalf.[129] In 1946, after war-time service in the Navy, he would enter Congress as an avowed foe of Roosevelt's policies, at which time Margaret would come to know the freshman congressman only slightly. Later the two would cross swords.

Margaret would, however, grow close to the Maine woman who had organized the Detroit meeting. Her name was Marion Martin, and she was from Bangor. Though Margaret and Clyde had known Marion socially, the two women became much closer as a result of the Willkie campaign.

An early interest in politics, kindled by her father, along with a need to excel, had led Marion in 1937 to accept the position as head of the Women's Division of the Republican National Committee. Her early years had been a boy's odyssey, punctuated by horseback riding, mucking stalls and hiking. Then came summer camps, boarding school and finally Wellesley, where at chapel the school's founder, Henry Fowle Durant, used to tell young women: "The higher Education of Women is one of the great world battle-cries for freedom: for right against might. It is the cry of the oppressed slave. It is the assertion of absolute equality."[130] Unlike Vassar, which heeded a call for "reform" in 1924 and altered its curriculum so that its young women could be trained to be "gracious and intelligent wives and mothers," Wellesley had remained through Marion's enrollment true to the course its founder had charted for it, despite the already "surging . . . disillusion" of some of its older female faculty.[131] Where Wellesley left off and Marion's natural bent began cannot be known, but her life choices did incorporate many of the themes of post-suffrage feminism: financial independence, personal accomplishment, equality and a decision not to marry. Much like a heroine from the Campfire Girl series, when Marion left Wellesley she travelled with a party of Wellesley girls around the world and spent the following summer in Europe. Afterwards she came home to Maine to pour herself into summer camps for girls, work as a riding instructor and spend most of her time at Abena Camp in the Belgrade Lakes. Later, like Margaret, Martin's sororital needs were met by the BPW, as her need to excel found an outlet in politics. In 1930, when Margaret married Clyde, Marion was one of four women in Maine's House of Representatives. After two terms, she moved to the Maine Senate, completed her undergraduate degree at the University of Maine and was inducted into Phi Beta Kappa. After being outmaneuvered by legislators with law degrees, she went to law school. And when she was offered the number two spot on the staff of the Republican National Committee in Washington, she accepted without hesitation. When Margaret met her, she was fresh-faced and sturdy, and though in later years she became stout, she possessed great presence.

People who knew her described her as a woman of "decided tastes and individuality" and a "frank, direct and friendly manner."[132] In a man's world she moved with good-natured ease, with no concessions asked or given because of gender. To Margaret, she seemed sure-footed, resourceful, popular, and courageous.

Even more important, the two shared a vision of what was possible for women. Their belief that women could succeed in politics and that "seasoned women"—those who had paid their dues at the lower levels—could rise to the top, was a direct outgrowth of their experiences in Maine, where in 1940 nearly 2,400 women held public office. Dozens served on Democratic and Republican state committees and on numerous other state committees.[133] Maine was electing women to public office, particularly in small towns, and keeping them in office at a higher rate than any other state in the union.[134] Politics thus represented a promising outlet for womens' individual yearnings to excel and a likely source of adventure. Or so at least it seemed to Margaret and Marion when they joined forces to carry the Republican message to "all classes of women" and show them that Willkie was *for* the social legislation "that all women approved of."

Once again, however, in November the GOP was disappointed. Though Willkie made a good showing (22 million votes to Roosevelt's 27 million) the rumpled, engaging contender could not dislodge Roosevelt from a third term. In an effort to snatch some kind of victory from defeat, Marion Martin looked to the women's vote for bright spots. North Dakota, she said, would not have gone Republican had it not been for the women, as even the men in North Dakota admitted. Moreover, only four states in the Union had not increased their percentage of Republican votes over the preceding four years. And although Maine was one of the four, it was the "splendid work of the Maine women" which kept Maine in the Republican column. After the close of the campaign, she was told the Women's Division would be maintained.[135]

Like Marion, Margaret emerged from Willkie's campaign a winner. By the time she joined seven other women in Congress on 6 January 1941, she had won her spurs and was a seasoned veteran, despite her freshman status.[136] She had made appearances and speeches in seven states and ten cities outside of Maine and had become known to thousands of Republicans across the country, had received a generous amount of credit from Marion Martin for Willkie's 7,373 vote edge in Maine, and had established a favorable balance of favors given and good will dispensed. In short, she was ready for Washington.

5. *The Land of the Lotus-eaters*

To MARGARET, the city on the Potomac was never just a city of marble, but a city of dreams. Everything about it fascinated her—its grace, its sense of style, its Southern charm, its architecture. From the capital's massive bronze doors to the frescoes in the dome where gods and mortals mingled, Washington was a setting which expanded political adventure to mythic proportions. In this city she felt herself and her acts to be important. Her most ordinary choices took on added meaning, even the matter of what she should call herself.

The decision was necessary for the official plate for the frank (mailing privileges) and for consistency in signing daily correspondence. The "rules" of etiquette which governed such matters were quite specific. A widow was expected to show respect for her husband by using his name socially in every way. In Margaret's case, the correct choice was "Mrs. Clyde Smith," not "Mrs. Margaret Smith," no matter how long she survived Clyde. In business matters, on documents and checks, she was allowed to be "Margaret Smith," but not "Mrs. Margaret Smith." If it was necessary to show the prefix, she was to sign "Mrs. Clyde Smith" in parenthesis under her signature. If she wanted a career, she was advised to use her first name and her maiden name, so that she would be "Miss" in business and "Mrs." socially. So declared Amy Vanderbilt.[137]

For the first two years she was in Washington, Margaret's letters carried the typed name "Mrs. Clyde Smith" under the signature "Margaret Chase Smith." The decision was one she weighed carefully and which generally conformed to Vanderbilt's advice. She wanted to capitalize on the name she had made for herself as Margaret Chase when she was president of Maine's BPW, and she wanted to keep the name "Clyde Smith" active, as it was of enormous value in political circles across the state. So she contrived a way to accomplish both objectives.

After her first term, she dropped the typed signature and used only

"Margaret Chase Smith," explaining that when she used "Margaret Smith," people didn't recognize her. One evening she called a man in Washington County, Maine on an official matter and told him: "This is Margaret Smith." "Who?" he said. When she repeated her name, using "Margaret Chase Smith," his reply was: "Why in the Hell didn't you say so?" The swing of the three names and their uniqueness convinced her that from now on she would be Margaret Chase Smith.[138]

And yet, in giving herself a name, she had done more than attend to a bureaucratic detail. She had in a real sense recognized the existence of another person.[139] "Chase" was the name of a fine basketball player—a name to be proud of, a name which showed English antecedents, while "Smith," was a name ubiquitous throughout New England, proudly borne by numerous descendants of families more distinguished than Clyde's. The two names were rooted in the soil of Maine itself. Margaret Chase Smith was a name with presence and power, recognition of which would come fittingly and dramatically from Margaret's opponents when she ran for the Senate in 1948. In the midst of that bitterly-fought campaign, they spread the word that Margaret had been an illegitimate child by the name of "Chasse," brought to Skowhegan from the Fort Kent-Madawaska Canadian border. The story claimed that Margaret had been adopted by Carrie and George Chase, who legally changed her name to "Chase."[140] Though the ruse was unsuccessful, her enemies' ploy of "unnaming her" was itself telling.

The name had an upper-class resonance. It echoed with the voices of her culture far better than the less prepossessing and more alien (to her) "Mrs. Clyde Smith." It suggested Maine blue-bloods in drawing rooms, who murmured over teacups as they chose selectmen and governors, who went to Wellesley or Colby if they were female, Bowdoin if they were male. "Margaret Chase Smith" had the ring of Sunday churchbells and the sweep of broad green lawns and white porticos. It was the name of someone who mattered and someone who belonged. Her name would stand her in good stead in a city as socially attuned as Washington, D.C. "Margaret Chase Smith" she had in actuality already become.

6. *The View from Jenkins Hill*

FROM THE OPENING SESSION of the 77th Congress, Margaret and her colleagues faced one of the defining events of the century: the threat of German conquest of two continents. War had come to Europe even before Clyde went to Washington for his first term. And when Margaret took her seat in January 1941, Washington was abuzz with talk of war and the possibility of American entry. The war would provide Margaret with her first important political test.

On the evening of one of Britain's worst fire bombings, 29 December, President Roosevelt described his Lend-Lease plan to the nation in a fire-side chat. The "chat" was among the best that Franklin Delano Roosevelt ever gave. He made a compelling case that the fall of free Britain would mean Axis control of Europe, Africa, Asia, Australia and the high seas, with America living "at the point of a gun." There are some who "would like to believe that even if Britain falls, we are still safe, because of the broad expanse of the Atlantic and of the Pacific. But," he continued, "the width of those oceans is not what it was in the days of the clipper ships." Calling America "the great arsenal of democracy," he asked that America provide the implements of war, "the planes, the tanks, the guns and the freighters," to enable the people of Europe "to fight for their liberty and our security."[141]

Public response was immediate and enthusiastic. Polls reported that 71 percent of the public agreed with the president; 54 percent wanted Lend-Lease to start immediately.[142] Numbered among those who agreed with him was Maine's new congresswoman, Margaret Chase Smith. And on Lend-Lease—in contrast to her coolness toward Roosevelt's defense policy in 1940—she declined to play politics.

"We should help Great Britain in her fight against dictators," Margaret told her Maine readers in the 2 January newspaper column she wrote for her constituents called "Washington and You," for so "long as British resistance is successful, we have little to fear." Echoing statements made in her campaign, she opposed "getting into the war with either men or credit," though "it may be that we will have to help Britain financially, if her resources run short."[143] Eight days later, on 10 January, H.R. 1776, the Lend-Lease bill, was introduced in the House. For the next month until Lend-Lease was passed, Margaret's support for the measure was unwavering.

In February, when the bill passed the House 260-165, Margaret alone among Maine's three Representatives voted for it. One of her Maine colleagues so strongly opposed it that he predicted "war for American youth on foreign soil, and military dictatorship here."[144] In contrast, Margaret's explanation for supporting the Democratic administration was that "even though there is only a chance of attack, I dare not risk the menace." She told her constituents, "I would not have a clear conscience . . . if I had failed to support a single proposal that might save us from war, or from having to live in the kind of world the dictators will make if Britain fails."[145] Though she later claimed that her mail was largely against Lend-Lease, she had learned during her eight months in office that a strong stance for defense would not cost her many votes in patriotic Maine.[146] Its more likely toll would be her standing with the isolationist wing of the Republican Party. Perhaps as a gesture to them, she dutifully promised to scrutinize each defense item which came before her, judge whether it was really necessary for defense, and "seek to prevent unnecessary delegation of power to the President." But she also announced that she would not "take a partisan attitude toward the administration's suggestions for defense, nor . . . sacrifice efficient defense progress by refusing necessary powers to the Executive."[147] Soon, she was to make good on that promise.

Within six months, Margaret again voted with the Democrats on an important measure—this time to extend the draft for eighteen months. The issue was hotly argued, with opponents claiming that an extension was a breach of faith with the soldier. The measure barely passed, with the final vote in the House 203-202. House Democrats were divided in favor of the bill, while House Republicans solidly opposed it. Out of 154 Republican votes in the House, only 21 were cast in favor of the bill. Margaret and Frank Fellows (from Maine's Third District) were among the 21.

In mid-October 1941 America experienced the first casualties of World War II. The U.S.S. destroyer "Kearny," took a torpedo in the side trying to rescue a British convoy from a German "wolf pack." Two men were wounded and eleven missing, presumed dead.[148] In her column "Washington and You," published on 16 October, the day after the attack, Margaret reaffirmed that the "administration must be given every power necessary for defense production," though she made no mention of the incident.[149]

Even before the "Kearny" incident, President Roosevelt had asked Congress on 9 October to repeal Section VI of the Neutrality Act of 1939, forbidding the arming of merchant ships. He also requested language rescinding the prohibition on travel by ships into combat zones or the ports of belligerent nations. On the 17th, by a vote of 259 to 138, the House repealed Section VI. When the bill went to the Senate, the President asked them to include his other repeal requests. Though the Senate complied, their vote of 50 to 37 gave the administration its narrowest victory in the Senate on a foreign policy issue since the beginning of the war in Europe. When the bill was returned to the House on the question of concurring in the Senate amendment, Margaret's bipartisanship was again put to a dramatic test.

Debate raged for eight hours. Supporters of the Administration argued that the Neutrality Act was a hindrance in seeking the downfall of Hitler. Opponents replied that cargo ships in combat zones could only result in "all out war for the United States." Finally, the question was called and the vote taken. By a slender, eighteen-vote-margin the Democrats prevailed, avoiding what the *Bangor Daily News* predicted would have been "a prestige-shattering defeat."[150] The final vote was 212 to 194, with the Democrats supporting the measure 189 to 53, the Republicans opposing it 137 to 22. Once again, unlike her fellow Representatives from Maine, Margaret voted with the administration.

After only eleven months in office Margaret's voting record was much more independent than Clyde's. And it was likely to attract the kind of attention from Republican leaders which would make permanent her disappointing committee assignments of the first year: Education and Post Offices. So far she had not cut the kind of congressional figure that would help a freshman rise quickly through the ranks.

The voters, however, loved it. No less than the influential President of the all-male Bowdoin College wrote to applaud her votes on defense, a letter she referred to with pride in her November column. That same month, the Maine Young Republicans raised their voices in a chorus of support. They urged that in matters of foreign policy, "political considerations be put aside . . . and whole-hearted support of this country [be lent] to a foreign policy designed to destroy and defeat totalitarianism."[151] They also criticized "Republican members of congress who are digging the grave of their party by consistent, blind, unconstructive opposition to the administration's policies."[152]

One source of their enthusiasm, and part of the explanation for Margaret's willingness to pioneer a departure from the Republican's traditional embrace of isolationism, was Maine's deeply-embedded patriotism. Despite the fact that several Maine congressmen voted with Republican isolationists in the House and Senate in 1939, Maine was the only state to surpass her quota in the army's nation-wide recruiting drive. And when the Selective Service Act of 1940 became law, Maine's 120,000 young men signed up to serve their country with the quiet enthusiasm that had been their habit in all of America's wars.[153]

Also allowing her some latitude was Maine's wide vein of contrarianism and respect for political independence. For years Margaret had watched Clyde juggle a progressive agenda the Party cared nothing about, while in election after election the voters returned him to office by resounding margins. These grandchildren of pioneer's children revealed a perceptible tendency to "you-be-damnedness," as though they saw the best part of themselves in representatives who maintained independence.[154]

Finally, the defense industry was vital to Maine's economy, bringing with it prosperity that was nothing less than astounding. In December 1940 Maine learned that the Bath Iron Works would receive a $400,000 federal grant for plant expansion, the largest single expansion in the corporation's fifty years of shipbuilding at that site. That same month, the shipyard in Portland received a contract to build 30 merchant ships for Britain, necessitating the construction of a new yard in South Portland. The new yard would employ five thousand workers and carry an annual payroll of $6 million.[155]

Margaret wasted no time exploiting the opportunity the impending war presented. By the time she wrote the second newspaper column of her term (on 9 January 1941), she had already met with Navy officials to discuss the expansion of small shipbuilding in the Second District. "All along the coast," she told them, "there are shipyards, companies capable of building submarine chasers, mine sweepers, torpedo boats, mosquito boats, of lengths from 65 feet to 300 feet."[156] She talked to the Coast Guard and Maritime Commission, along with the Navy, and spread the word to available yards that Maine would not be disadvantaged by having a woman represent them.

By April 1941 defense monies had been allocated for an airport project in Pittsfield and contracts had been awarded to yards in Rockland and Camden for eight mine sweepers at a cost of $1 million. Eight small shipyards received contracts in the amount of $5.1 million for 26 vessels, and the Bath shipyards were optimistic about landing a contract to build 20 to 30 cargo ships for the British out of the new $1 billion Lend-Lease appropriation.[157]

By year's end, the need for a strong defense, which Margaret had consistently supported, was tragically demonstrated. On Sunday morning, 7 December 1941, the Japanese launched a surprise air attack on the U.S. Navy base at Pearl Harbor, knocking out eight battleships and three cruisers, along with several destroyers. Since U.S. planes were destroyed on the ground, no effective counter-attack could be launched. When the attack ended, except for the aircraft carriers which were at sea at the time, the Pacific fleet had been destroyed.[158] Margaret, like the rest of the country, was taken completely by surprise.

7. *Florida*

IN FACT, she was in Florida. No diary entry for 7 December 1941 reveals Margaret's feelings about the attack on Pearl Harbor. She had long since abandoned the habit of jotting down dates or thoughts in the campaign diary. Besides, she was taking a holiday with a group of young congressmen, which probably included Albert C. Vreeland [R-N.J.], an East Orange attorney with whom Margaret was becoming good friends.[159]

What remains from 7 December comes from Margaret's scrapbook. There can be found a candid snapshot, taken by an unknown photographer of a slender woman framed against horizon and sea. She is smiling, her features pleasant, but not "arranged," and her hair windblown. Even though she is squinting slightly as she looks into the camera, and the bright light in which she is bathed is unkind, she looks far younger than her 44 years.

Margaret was enjoying an unaccustomed respite in Florida, its balmy weather and wide white beaches the stuff of mid-winter Maine fantasy, its sunsets and the smell of the sea sources of gratuitous delight. This was indeed the sybaritic paradise she and Clyde had set out for after his congressional race but never reached.

Without warning, news of the attack on Pearl Harbor came, a tidal wave on an evanescent, tropical day. Margaret and her friends scattered. "Home" was where they ought to be. Margaret, especially, wanted to get "home" to Washington. She left immediately, already uneasy about the reaction in Maine should she appear to have been "on vacation" as the country went to war.[160]

8. Washington in Wartime

WASHINGTON'S ENERGY, always intense, teetered on the keen edge of frenzy by the time she returned. All military personnel who were on leave had been recalled. All leaves were canceled. Army and Navy officers, who had not typically worn their uniforms when going to work in the huge Army and Navy buildings, could now be seen everywhere, sporting shoulder straps, gold braid, and "brass hats." The White House, which had been closely guarded for some time, was now barricaded, its blue-coated guards reinforced by men in khaki, their bayonets fixed. Faces were set and talk grim. Words like "treachery" and "duplicity" filled the air, and rumors of FBI agents rounding up Japanese aliens began to circulate. On Wednesday the president announced that he would address a joint session of Congress and people began to scramble to gain access to the House, where the speech would be given. Over the radio came the announcement that only those holding special cards would be admitted, but thousands came just the same.[161]

They lined the sidewalks to catch a glimpse of the president and crowded the corridors of the House building to try to catch snatches of the deliberations. In the chamber itself, Supreme Court justices, the cabinet, and the diplomatic corps joined members of the Senate and House. Those lucky enough to have special cards packed the galleries.

The president "plainly much moved," delivered his message from the Speaker's desk, stating simply that the action of the Japanese had made war inevitable. The hall rang with cheers. When he asked for a declaration of war, everyone jumped to his feet, those in the gallery and those on the floor, and shouted agreement. At the end of his speech he was cheered again. And when he turned to leave, the audience again applauded him.[162]

Everyone in the chamber watched and listened intently. A few congressmen spoke. Finally the roll call was taken, and vote after vote was cast in support of a declaration of war. "Aye, aye, aye, aye . . . no." A gasp rippled through the crowd. Jeannette Rankin (R-Montana), the first woman to be elected to the U.S. Congress and an ardent pacifist, the only member of Congress to vote against America's entry into World War I, once again cast the lone vote against entering a war. It was said that when she tried to speak before the voting began, a congressman close to her called: "Sit down sister!"[163] Afterwards, when she left for her office in the Cannon Building, she needed the protection of the capitol police.[164]

Margaret's comments on the president's message to Congress were "brief and to the point," the same words she used to describe his message. "I am satisfied that I have done right in following the Administration's foreign policy and voting for all defense measures," she said. "To the vicious attack on us by Japan and their declaration of war there could be only one answer—a recognition that a state of war exists between us. I voted today for a declaration of war against the Japanese Empire."[165]

No immediate crowing about the fact that history had proved her correct, no finger-pointing at fellow Republicans who had taken a different path on Lend-Lease or repeal of the Neutrality Act. For the most part, Margaret was content to let others brag for her—like syndicated columnist Imogene Clarke, whose tribute appeared in the Skowhegan paper on December 18. "It should be a matter of great satisfaction of all of us," she wrote, "that our Representative in congress has voted consistently for preparedness, putting aside party prejudice and placing the National good above politics, not an easy road to choose. Hats off to Margaret Smith!"[166]

Privately, of course, Margaret savored the wisdom of her votes. And among her friends, like women from the Maine BPW, she found ways to remind them that "it wasn't too many months [following her vote on Lend-Lease] before we found out how essential it had been to help England carry on while we continued to prepare." She was also fond of telling the story of a "good, younger friend, . . . a lawyer from one of the coastal towns and his wife," who took a stand against the bill and tried to convince her to vote against it. When she didn't, the lawyer sent her a "very, very critical telegram" saying that he had read about her vote in the newspaper, and he was certain the paper had not recorded the vote correctly. Margaret sent him a note. The newspaper was correct, she had voted for the bill. A few years later Margaret saw the couple at the Army-Navy Country Club. The young lawyer asked her to dance, and after the second time around the floor, he apologized for his "mean telegram" and said: "Thank God we had a representative . . . who knew what she was doing and voted right. You were right and I was wrong." Over the years, Margaret frequently worked that story into conversations.[167]

The weeks following Roosevelt's war message were consumed by the needs of constituents who were already feeling the effects of war. Shortly after Pearl Harbor, a Waterville woman wrote for help in locating her husband and daughter in Greece. Margaret put her in touch with the Red Cross, which confirmed that her family was well but needed money. Margaret suggested that they send funds by American Express, which could still make remittances through Rome to American citizens in Greece. It was a first, slight trickle of the torrent which was to follow. Ahead lay problems which would not be so easily solved.

Soon Maine would experience scarcity of sugar in a rural economy which depended on canning to survive the long winters; shortages of rubber, tires, and gasoline in an economy driven by tourism and sustained by the export of produce, milk and dairy products to lower New England.[168] As price controls were imposed and "doing without" became an article of faith, all that Margaret could do was remind her readers that civilian sacrifices were bearable when one considered "how much more our fighting men are giving up."[169]

The war granted immunity to no one. From Maine to California, thousands of military families were learning that the struggle in which their country was involved was a bloody one. Helplessly they watched as the British lost Hong Kong on Christmas Day 1941, and the Allies were defeated in the Battle of Java Sea, with only four American destroyers escaping. In March, the Japanese took control of the Dutch East Indies, as well as Celebes, New Britain, the Solomons, Borneo, and part of New Guinea. Two small islands in the northern Pacific, Wake and Guam, fell to the Japanese before December ended, and American and Filipino troops retreated to the island fortress of Corregidor and to a small peninsula which formed part of Manila Bay named Bataan. There, one hundred and twenty-thousand men, deprived of food and supplies and doomed from the start, fought in vain to defend the Philippines.

Two days after Pearl Harbor, Margaret's friend Albert Vreeland announced that he would leave Congress. Vreeland would enter the army as a captain, the rank he had held in the Military Intelligence Reserve. Rising in the House on 9 December he asked for unanimous consent for a leave of absence. "Is there any objection?" the Speaker asked. Hearing none, the Speaker declared: "So be it."[170] For four months he would remain in Washington before travelling to Ft. Benning, Georgia, for training.[171] Several other congressmen joined the armed services as well, even though members were eligible for deferment. By April, six Representatives and one Senator had gone on active duty, and Congress as a body had agreed to curtail travel, a more dramatic decision than at first it appears, as the life-blood of congressmen flowed from their home districts.[172] In Margaret's case, curtailment of travel legitimized what appears to have been a growing desire to stay close to Vreeland.

Because Margaret knew that Maine expected its Representatives to come home, and often, she took special pains to explain why she was staying in Washington. "Congress expected to have a brief Easter vacation so that Members could go home," she wrote in her column in April, "but as this is written the recess seems doubtful." While "it would be good to get home and talk things over with the people of my District, my principle has always been that my job is in Washington, that was what I was elected for, and . . . trips home must be subject to congressional activities."[173]

By mid-July, pressure on Margaret to remain in Washington may have been somewhat lessened when Vreeland was ordered to complete the last six months of his congressional term. Not until December, when he entered the Army as a major, would he have to say his final good-byes.[174] By that time, Margaret had been handily re-elected by a 3818-vote margin in Somerset County, in what the *Independent Reporter* characterized as a display of appreciation "for her conscientious endeavor to be alert to the interests of her Maine folks."[175] Likewise in 1944 and 1946, she would face no primary opposition and would effortlessly defeat her Democratic opponents.

One source of Margaret's electoral strength was her attention to constituents. She made them feel welcome when they visited Washington, answered mail the day it was received, and resourcefully used the small, rather than the grand, gesture to remind them how hard she was working on their behalf. During World War II, for example, it was her practice to send copies of Maine newspapers to the Lounge of Union Station, a room traditionally reserved for the president and distinguished guests, but recently fixed up "for the convenience and amusement of service men passing through Washington, including a file of home-town papers from everywhere."[176] Sending her own newspapers left "a pretty slim pile on the table in [her] office which [she] kept for constituents," so she asked newspaper editors in her District whether they might like to provide subscriptions so service men could have fresh news from home. The suggestion worked, and at least six editors made sure that "fresh" newspapers from Maine were available in the Lounge of Union Station, which Margaret noted "leaves these papers on my office table." It reflected Yankee ingenuity, frugality, and attention to detail on a very small but memorable canvas.

Although gifted with constituents, Margaret was much less sure-footed with House colleagues. Compounding the problem was her appointment to Education and Post Offices, two committees whose very narrowness offered her little opportunity to make a name for herself. So, she had "to decide which [other] street corner [she was] going to fight on" in order to establish a reputation with colleagues and leave a mark on legislation.[177]

Of the senior Republican women in the House, the activities of one especially caught Margaret's eye. In January 1941, soon after Margaret was sworn in for her first full term, she and Edith Nourse Rogers were part of a "small group" invited to the White House for a radio broadcast which urged everyone to work for the "Fight Infantile Paralysis" Drive.[178] Over the next year the two became well acquainted, and by October 1941, Margaret was providing a sketch of Rogers' seventeen-year career in her "Washington and You" column and highlighting Rogers' 28 May 1941 bill to establish the WAAC.[179] The following year, she expressed her preference that the Woman's Corps be "a regular part of the Army in every way, excepting, of course, actual combat."[180] On 2 April 1942, in response to a letter from a constituent who wanted to know how older women might contribute to the war effort, Margaret suggested enlistment in the WAAC.

All women between the ages of twenty-one and forty-five were eligible or this "full-time, uniformed, live-in-barracks, in-for-the-duration service," according to Margaret.[181]

Her enthusiasm for women in the service extended beyond the WAAC, however. Citing a demand for women in a variety of professional activities and observing that "women are being employed as draftsmen, engineers, and many other skilled professions," she told the Maine BPW meeting in Skowhegan in June there has "never been a time when women have been more physically fit, more thoroughly trained and ready for service than today." Although "a war is generally fought by men, and women have been expected to replace them on the home front," she continued, "women will be taken into combat as necessary."[182]

Women in combat?

The search for a vehicle with which to build a congressional career had suddenly carried Margaret well beyond ambition. In what almost seems a Freudian slip, Margaret was applauding a thoroughgoing military role for women. Though women in combat were favored by the BPW, the image was in sharp contrast to the mood of the country and to the persona Margaret had carefully created, a model of gentility and decorum. Coexisting with the ladylike and quite feminine Margaret Chase Smith were several selves—including one whose goals and desires ran headlong into the social realities of women's role. Had her more androgynous self emerged initially, with its forbidden striving and focused goals, Margaret's political career might never have been successfully launched. Without the presence of that self, however, she might never have embarked on the journey or stayed the course. Both her (initially) well-concealed strengths and her traditional "femininity" were central to the public woman, and usually they were kept in balance. Tipping the scales in 1942 was the war. In a period in which heroism was expected from all quarters, Margaret's more daring side took over, shedding temporarily any attempt at disguise. Increasingly as she grew older, this aggressive side would frequently emerge with unresponsive generals and cabinet members, its sharpness a dramatic contrast to Margaret's signature ladylike elegance. In tribute to the effectiveness of this balancing act, contemporary Democratic Senator John Stennis of Mississippi said of Margaret: "You didn't take Mrs. Smith for granted. No one controlled her. We tended to treat her as a man, without ceasing to treat her as a woman." Most often the tension between Margaret's selves was an oscillating current, so well held in check that she was almost always described in one word—a "lady."[183]

9. *Expanding the Adventure*

MARGARET INAUGURATED her third term with a dinner at the Congressional Club in honor of the Maine Delegation. The Owen Brewsters and the Wallace Whites along with the rest of the Maine delegation were there, as was Maine newspaper mogul Guy Gannett, Marion Martin, newspaper columnist Elizabeth May Craig, Republican floor leader Joe Martin, and Rep. Edith Nourse Rogers.[184] Although the Democrats controlled both the House and the Senate in 1943, Margaret was doing what she could to strengthen political ties and nurture political friendships. The freshman member from Maine's Second District did not intend to remain a back-bencher, even though that was traditional for third-termers.

At the start of the 78th Congress, an amendment to the Constitution which would give men and women equal rights throughout the United States and which had first been proposed in 1923 by the ultra-feminist National Women's Party [NWP], was again introduced in the House and Senate.[185] Though the measure had long divided social feminists—who felt women needed special protection—from anti-protectionists, Margaret's support for the measure in 1943, even though it had been framed by the militantly feminist NWP, was unambiguous. "I believe this to be a principle which should be placed in the Constitution and expect to vote for a bill to that effect," Margaret told her constituents.[186]

As early as 1920, the BPW—which Margaret saw as the cornerstone of her political support—under the leadership of its first national president and Maine native, Gail Laughlin, had opposed all legislation based on sex. Even protective legislation, argued Laughlin, who was also an officer of the NWP, was undesirable unless it was applied equally to men and women.[187] Influenced by the strong stand of the BPW, Margaret early established a pattern of support for the Equal Rights Amendment, cosponsoring it in 1945 with Edith Nourse Rogers and in 1949 with Iowa Senator Guy Gilette.

During the war, however, domestic matters took a back seat. For almost a year, the Pacific campaign had gone badly for the allies. The previous May, Corregidor had surrendered after almost five months of half-rations and heavy casualties. From Australia, General Douglas MacArthur had written, "Corregidor needs no comment from me. But through the bloody haze of its last reverberating shot I shall always seem to see the vision of its grim, gaunt and ghostly men, still unafraid."[188] One month earlier, on 9 April, Bataan had fallen, and the Japanese had marched 72,000 survivors—sick, hungry, wounded—55 miles to prisoner-of-war camps. Ten thousand failed to survive the trip. They had literally been "marched to death."[189]

Civilians had few parallels to help them deal with the enormity of the unfolding tragedy. A mother whose son had been "slightly wounded" in the first month of fighting in the Philippines wrote to Margaret in September 1942. She had received no information about her son since December 1941. Could Margaret help? Margaret's response, which provided the best information available, was intended to comfort the boy's mother. "The Japanese Government," Margaret wrote in 1942, "has indicated its intention to conform to the terms of the Geneva Convention regarding treatment of prisoners of war."[190] By early 1944, she would find herself sick at heart and forced to admit that "the awful story of what the Japanese have done to our captured soldiers casts a shadow over Washington. . . . I have the deepest feeling for all, and will do what little I can as time goes on to get as much information as possible about their fate."[191] For the present, however, noncombatants were spared the details of what "missing in action," especially in the Pacific, meant for thousands of men.

Despite the equal parts of detail and tragedy by which the lives of those who govern during a war are defined, Margaret was busy, and thus happy. Moreover, when her third term began in January 1943, a door had opened on a shortcut to power and a way to expand her adventure. On 21 January her new committee appointment was announced on the front page of her hometown newspaper: CONG. SMITH ON NAVAL AFFAIRS COMMITTEE. Quoting the associated press, the article referred to Margaret as "the gracious and attractive Representative of Maine's "Second District," and observed that Margaret would be the "second woman ever named on this committee."[192]

The assignment was a plum. With the country at war and much of America's effort firmly concentrated in the Pacific, the Committee on Naval Affairs was assured a busy schedule and high visibility. Margaret had broken through a congressional "glass ceiling," never again to be placed on a committee like the Post Office, which was usually dominated by newcomers.[193]

Publicly at least, congressional opinion about her appointment was very favorable. Columnist May Craig, still her cheerleader, quoted the response of the committee's powerful chairman, Carl Vinson (D-Ga.): "It is a fine selection—tops. Mrs. Smith will be an asset to the Naval Affairs Committee [and] . . . is one of the outstanding Members of the House."[194] Joe Martin, who as Republican floor leader had a hand in her selection, waxed equally enthusiastic and attributed Margaret's appointment—along with the appointment of newcomer Clare Booth Luce to Military Affairs—as the fact "that the women in the country take an active part in the war effort."[195]

At the same time that Margaret was rising from the congressional back-benches, her old friend Albert Vreeland was preparing to leave Washington for his next posting with the Army. No notes or letters exist from the period, no musings by Margaret or Vreeland. Two small snapshots of Vreeland, dated 24 February 1943, can be found in her scrapbook, each a quiet portrait of a man in uniform at work in a smallish office, a man removed from the limelight for the moment, a very private man, taking care of business.

But for the added presence of two 8 x 12 photos of a more public Vreeland, these two small snapshots would be easily overlooked. But the inscription on one of the two large photos invites speculation. The man in the picture is the public Vreeland, open-faced, genial, likable. He is wearing the rank of major and is posed in front of a map of the world. In his hands is a sheaf of papers. Inscribed in his handwriting on the front of the portrait is the message: "Margaret Chase Smith, a charming colleague and a fine friend." On the back, he wrote: "To the dearest, sweetest morale booster a soldier ever had." At some point during his stint in the armed services, he also gave Margaret a locket. On its face was a corps insignia, and inside, two pictures—one of Vreeland and one of Margaret. The date of the gift cannot be verified. Despite the romance implied by such leavings, there was never any public scandal attached to their friendship, nor even any public notice taken. Circumspection, personal ambition, and even honor may have protected them, along with a war that made their friendship more evanescent, more precious, and of less interest to the outside world than it might otherwise have been. Of special note is the fact that even with the emergence of a hidden, adolescent self that defied a conventional female role, Margaret did not abandon the romantic imagination of a more traditional femininity.

10. *Naval Affairs*

OVERNIGHT Margaret became engrossed in the Naval Affairs Committee. The Committee convened in the morning at ten, or earlier, met until noon, and sometimes all day, usually in secret session. Early in March, the chairman announced that they would begin evening sessions.[196]

That same month, Margaret was appointed to a subcommittee "to investigate living conditions in congested areas where the Navy had an interest." Travelling by rail, the committee visited Norfolk and Newport on the East Coast, then sped West to Portland, San Francisco, and San Diego to investigate schools, sanitation, fuel and the needs of children of working mothers[197] Chairing the subcommittee was a handsome World War I hero, a man of slight build and greying hair, Edouard V. Izac [D-Calif.]. Other members were James Mott [R-Wash.], Melvin Maas [R-Minn.], a reserve colonel in the Marine Corps who participated in the capture of Guadalcanal; George Bates [R-Mass.], John Fogarty [D-R.I.], John Z. Anderson [R-Calif.], and Winder Harris [D-Va.]. Special counsel to the Committee and Naval aide was Lieutenant (jg) William Chesley Lewis, Jr., on loan from the office of the undersecretary of the Navy.

Lt. Lewis, a personable and friendly thirty-one year old Naval reservist, quickly won the confidence of Chairman Izac by his unrelenting attention to detail and his gift for public relations. Though nominally and legally he owed his first allegiance to the chair, Lewis earned the gratitude of the whole committee by his even-handed solicitousness and his unswerving efforts to make them all look good.[198] He was praised for "the thoroughness and excellence of his work, . . . his vigorous and painstaking assistance to the Committee, [and his] exceptional service."

Within three years the Committee would recommend him for the Navy's prestigious Legion of Merit."[199]

Indeed, Margaret's praise of Lt. Lewis would have been no less glowing. Though fifteen years separated them, the young bachelor and the older woman formed a bond immediately. During the hearings, he often slipped a timely and well phrased question to Margaret, often gaining her publicity in the press and attention from the Navy.[200] In almost every group photo of the subcommittee from that period, the two could be seen in close proximity to one another.

Several informal photos of them can be found in Margaret's personal scrapbook. In the foreground of each is a plaid stadium blanket with a picnic basket to one side. The trees in the background are in full bloom, the weather is fair, though perhaps a bit breezy, as both of them are wearing light jackets. The mood of the subjects is carefree. Each is smiling as the other snaps the photograph. The date is 1943.

Born in Wilburton, Oklahoma on 29 October 1912, Bill Lewis began his career at West Point as a cadet in 1929. Sight problems, it was said, forced him to leave, and he enrolled at the University of Oklahoma, where in 1934 he took a degree in geology and in 1935 a Bachelor of Laws, after which he passed the Oklahoma bar. In 1937, he earned a Master's degree in Business Administration from Harvard and then returned to Oklahoma City to practice law until April 1938, when he joined the legal staff of the Securities and Exchange Commission [SEC] in Washington, D.C. In May 1942, he was called back to active duty as a member of the U.S. Naval Reserve.[201]

Raised in a striving, success-oriented family, Bill had early been taught duty and loyalty. The only son of then-Col. William C. Lewis, Sr. (U.S. Air Force retired)—a former U.S. District Attorney for the Western District of Oklahoma—and Nelle Wyrick Lewis, also a member of the Oklahoma bar, a great beauty, and a natural politician, Bill Lewis had first-hand knowledge of what was required for success.[202] No detail could be overlooked; no superior disappointed; no decision made lightly. Wrote Edgar B. Naught, one of his bosses at the SEC, "He has common sense, is thorough in his preparation and very efficient in his work."[203] In the words of the SEC General Counsel, Bill displayed "discretion, tact, and ingenuity" throughout his four-year stint at SEC, along with "imagination and energy."[204] Thus, what this dark-haired, lanky, young man brought to Naval Affairs besides competence was sagacity and seasoning. Despite the fresh-faced charm he exuded, he was, in actuality, quite knowing in the ways of the world. For this reason, it was not surprising that he quickly gained the confidence of the members of the subcommittee and attracted the attention of the formidable chairman himself, Carl Vinson, who became one of his most important mentors.

In a sense, Margaret's House career began with her work on the subcommittee. Not only did the committee carry her to "The Great West" for the first time, but it expanded her psychic boundaries as well. In the San Francisco Bay Area, she was shocked by crowded housing conditions spawned by the war and wrote of "a downtown store with stalls fitted up where there were cots, rented for a dollar a night, [with] twenty-eight families on the first floor, fourteen on the second, with one toilet for all. . . . Many of these people are receiving good wages and could afford a more livable place."[205]

She also noted with horror "the mounting venereal disease among young girls who are not professionals," and was disturbed by prevalence of under-age drinking. In May, when she returned to Washington, she told her readers "it was good to get home," though it "looked like a steady grind" in Congress "now until summer."[206]

On or just before 2 June 1943, Margaret was asked to introduce her first major bill in the House—a measure which would allow WAVES to go overseas.[207] Originally, the bill had been introduced by committee member Melvin Mass, but it had become deadlocked following the bitter objections of Rep. Beverly M. Vincent, a Democrat from Kentucky. According to *The Washington Post*, he had read a newspaper account of WAACS living in convents in North Africa and had mistakenly inferred that these women were doing so to protect themselves from the men in the area. Once the error was corrected, he "continued to complain of women in the service," shifting his ground to contend "they should not have pension and disability rights 'just for pushing civil servants out of their jobs.'"[208]

Whether the Kentucky congressman's real concern was escalating costs, or the virtue of American women, he agreed to support the WAVES bill if a few changes were made in it and Margaret Chase Smith sponsored it. Accordingly, the bill was revised to say that no WAVES would be sent overseas until all U.S. billets were filled; WAVES would get all benefits for dependents (except husbands) that other servicemen got; the top ranking WAVES officer would be captain and the number of officers would be limited; WAVES would "not be assigned to duty on board vessels or in combat aircraft."[209] In other words, they would not be sent into combat, nor placed in units with combat missions. On 3 June Margaret introduced the bill and it was promptly passed by the House. When it arrived at the Senate, it foundered, due to the opposition of the chairman of Naval Affairs, Democrat David Walsh of Massachusetts, who balked at service by WAVES overseas. Finally, as a compromise, Margaret agreed that the WAVES (as well as the SPARS and the Marines) would be limited to what was called the "American arena" of North and South America, Hawaii, Alaska, Canal Zone and the Caribbean."[210] To gain final passage of her bill, Margaret was forced to ask Admiral Nimitz, the Commander of the Pacific fleet, to make public his immediate need for 5,000 WAVES, 1,535 Marine women, and 150 SPARs to release men in Hawaii for combat duty.[211]

Finally, though limited in scope, the bill passed, signalling an advance for women for which Margaret would receive a generous share of credit. As a direct result in December 1943, Louise Coburn's alma mater—Colby College in Waterville, Maine—awarded a Master of Arts to Margaret as a "Member of the House of Representatives in the 78th Congress . . . and of the important Naval Affairs Committee in that body; known for your ability to envisage in a statesmanlike way the needs of the entire country without forgetting your responsibilities to your own constituency in Maine."[212] Thus, relatively soon after her work on Naval Affairs had begun, George Chase's little girl acquired the college degree that had so long eluded her, and with it a form of approval from an institution whose graduates often bore the rank and pedigree of Maine's most prominent families. In large part due to her assignment to Naval Affairs, she had been given the means to embark on an adventure of much wider scope than she could ever have imagined. On 14 December 1944 the *Independent Reporter* dubbed Margaret the "mother of the WAVES," and from then on the "'mother' of the WAVES" she became, though later, in 1972, she expressed the fear that her efforts on behalf of women in the

Armed Services had "left the impression . . . that I was a feminist concentrating on legislation for women. And if there is any one thing I have attempted to avoid it is being a feminist."[213]

11. *Growth*

FOR THE REMAINDER of her House years, Naval Affairs continued to shape and expand Margaret's world. In Margaret's visit to the West Coast she had been captivated by the sight of women working in the plants. "To prevent accidents, slacks are worn and their hair protected by kerchiefs tied around their heads," she wrote to her constituents. "I was proud to see how women are turning to the war work, doing anything needed."[214] With these women she shared a new female adventure, a story with a new plot and an unfinished script. "Since the Government asks women to work in war plants to fill the work benches of their men who are in combat service, we must take care of the children the women must leave. All of us want the women to stay at home and take care of their own children . . . but this is a war need."[215] New forms would have to be constructed and new models found. She soon became an advocate for child care facilities for children of the women factory workers, and after four years in the House was stirred to deliver her maiden speech on this issue.

In March 1944 when the women of the House, who seldom functioned as a voting bloc, joined forces on child care for working mothers, Margaret became a key speaker. Representatives Mary Norton, Frances Bolton, Edith Nourse Rogers, Clare Booth Luce, Winifred Stanley [R-N.Y.], and Margaret Chase Smith all appeared before the House Appropriations Committee to request that funds for child care centers (under the Lanham Act) be increased. A debate ensued, in the course of which an amendment was proposed by Representative John Taber of New York which would have cut funds for community services by one-half. The women were outraged.

"Mr. Chairman," said Margaret. "I rise in opposition to the amendment." Citing her work as a member of the Congested Areas subcommittee of the House Naval Affairs Committee, she described the scenes she had witnessed. "My committee visited industries, housing projects, schools, and nurseries and child-care centers. We talked with men and with women workers. . . . [and] found many women standing in line waiting for medical care, for themselves and for their children. We found them waiting hours after work to get their groceries and other necessities. We found children roaming the streets and some even locked in automobiles, not only because their war-working parents were absent from home but also because of the lack of child-care facilities and schools. This is an emergency."[216] The Taber amendment was defeated by five votes.

In the months following the congressional debates, Margaret spent several column inches on the problem of child care. And she took up the question of maternity care with Martha Eliot, acting chief of the Children's Bureau—an umbrella organization for child welfare policy in the United States and a bastion of female progressives. The Children's Bureau was "a female dominion in policy making," and a dynasty of which Secretary of Labor Frances Perkins was herself a product—having come through the ranks of social work by way of Hull House, the Consumer's League, and the New York State Factory Investigating Commission.[217]

In part because of Margaret's identification with the Children's Bureau, in April 1944 she became Perkins' choice (the only House member and the only Republican) to attend an International Labor Meeting in Philadelphia. She was one of fourteen U.S. delegates—only three of them women.[218] The honor was one she listed in her campaign material for the 1944 election. Indirectly, her work on the Naval Affairs Committee had helped her to forge an alliance with the New Deal's best known female appointee.

Just before her fourth term was to begin—after a better-than-2-1 margin of votes in the general election—Margaret received word that the Naval Affairs Committee was to leave immediately on a twenty-five-thousand mile, three-week Pacific tour. Before she left, she dictated a letter to her constituents, telling them that she would try to send home bits of news, assuring them "I shall spend every moment in the hospitals looking for boys from Maine, talking over their problems, hoping to take them a word from their folks many of whom contacted me today by wire and letter."[219] She was as good as her word and took the names of Maine men, promising to call their parents on Christmas Day with their messages "as her Christmas gift."[220]

Decked out in a WAVES uniform, Margaret left with the committee for Kwajalein, Manus, Guam, Saipan, Australia, and the Johnston Islands.

The trip was what she later described as "the nearest to a junket of any trip that I made during my entire House service,"[221] but she made good use of her time, stressing to her constituents the importance of mail from home and urging them "to write, and write, and write. Mail from home is what they want more than you will ever know."[222]

At forty-six, she cut a spare and tidy figure. Her prematurely gray hair and lean body signalled a distaste for sloth and self-indulgence. Her quick steps and boundless energy were the marks of a woman with a mission who was not easily distracted. She worked nearly all of the time, never drank in public and did not smoke. Photographers seldom caught her in casual clothes, except when she was clambering about an aircraft carrier or a submarine. Against the sweeping panorama of a war that seemed to destroy everything in its path, she represented a link with traditional values, even as she continued to break ground for women simply by her presence. Her muted sexuality was in sharp contrast to the full-lipped voluptuousness of pin-ups like Jane Russell, whose torso enlivened the lockers of many a G.I. And her carefully ordered femininity dispelled the spectre of masculinized women in uniform. To Maine G.I.s (part of her extended family), she displayed interest, offered compassion, and provided a link to mom, dad and sweetheart.

One day at sea aboard an aircraft carrier, she watched as the carrier engaged in battle practice. The spar-target, which the carrier was towing, was "not larger than a huge fish and bobbing up and down and weaving from side to side like a fighting barracuda. Soon it would be set upon by the carrier's fighters and dive bombers, while the carrier's torpedo planes made mimic dead runs at the ship itself." She described the great roar of propellers as the Hellcat fighters "wheeled overhead at a great height and started to 'peel off.' Down they came at the end of the towed surface target. Their tracers hit with deadly accuracy at the target and all around it. Then, as the fighters zoomed for a long turn and another 'run' at the target, the dive bombers came screaming down almost perpendicularly."[223]

With a sense of wonder reminiscent of the description of her first airplane flight with Walter Cleveland which she had described in the *Independent Reporter* more than twenty years earlier, she recreated the beauty of the killing exercises. "We were intrigued by the fantasy of color which enlivens the flight deck as the planes come aboard, and again as they take off. Blue, green, white, red and yellow jacketed and helmeted men seemed to spring out of nowhere and take on their perspective duties. Some of the planes were spotted for catapult take-off from the bow. With motors running, they were literally shot into the air, gaining their flying speed of nearly 100 miles an hour in less than the length of the average houselot."

Her prose was uncharacteristically lively, suggesting that she was caught up in the drama of the moment and well versed in what was unfolding before her eyes. Both the spirit of adventure and the presence of danger were conveyed, along with respect for mastery of the sea and dominance over a human enemy; bravery and discipline in the face of death, balanced against the vision of men doing well a job they never sought—the cost to them in their future years unknown and troubling. The beauty of the game was balanced with words like "deadly," which she used several times, and "lethal." She even wondered, as she watched the boys, how they would fit back into civilian life after the war. "So recently from farms and factories, city and county districts," she wrote, "they seem to have mastered in a few months the deadly trade they are now called upon to follow."[224] Hers was indeed a complex and uncommon female vision.

With April came the sudden death of President Franklin Delano Roosevelt. "The atmosphere around the capitol is no different than it is everywhere," Margaret told her readers. "It has been one of stunned silence." Yet the new President, Harry S. Truman, "instilled much confidence in this hour of crisis . . . with his sincere determination and admirable humility—he was most convincing in his evident determination to carry on for his Chief."[225] Privately Margaret already missed F.D.R.'s grin and his laughter, the tilted cigarette holder and the familiar wave. More than that, she missed the friendship of Eleanor Roosevelt, "a friendship which crossed Party lines, [and] was based . . . upon mutual respect."[226] Until 1945, she had not known Washington without a Roosevelt in the White House.

On 8 May 1945 victory in Europe (V-E Day) finally came to the Allies. In contrast to Margaret's prose when she described mock combat, her comments on this important day seemed flat and colorless. "Instead of declaring time off on this day," she said, "everybody should work a few hours longer and make these few added work hours on this V-E Day a symbol of

our determination to carry on to the end in the Pacific. Time saved by staying on the job today will save thousands of lives [and] mean that many more
days, hours, minutes and seconds nearer final victory throughout the world
and the day when all the boys will be back with us. . . . Let's wait until we
can all take time off for V-J Day—Victory over Japan."[227]

Even with victory in sight, the Naval Affairs Committee continued to
keep Margaret very busy. On 14 June, accompanied by the recently-pro-
moted Commander William Lewis, they travelled to Quincey, Mass. for
the launching of the new ship, "Oregon City." From Quincey, Bill and
Margaret went to Maine. There they inspected the activities at the Bath
Iron Works with subcommittee member Rep. Jim Mott of Oregon, and
travelled to Skowhegan to visit with Margaret's parents. On Sunday the
committee inspected the Naval Air base at Brunswick and "toured the
Maine coast by air, . . . lunching with Governor Hildreth in Augusta."[228]

In other years, Clyde would have hosted the delegation in his house
on Fairview Avenue, entertained and charmed them. But the Fairview
Avenue house had been sold the previous fall by Margaret, its large,
proud rooms converted to sick quarters, its sweeping lawns the site of the
Clyde Smith Memorial Hospital. In October 1944 she also sold a North
Avenue apartment house she had received as part of her inheritance from
Clyde, and by November 1945 she would sell Clyde's most prized investments: the two business blocks on Water Street which housed the A&P
on the ground floor, with the Townsend Hall on the second story, along
with a second, adjacent building, referred to around town as the Smith
block.[229] For the next five years, until Christmas of 1949, Margaret's headquarters in Skowhegan would be 81 North Avenue, the house "Banker"
had built and in which her parents still lived.

In October 1945 Margaret received her second honorary degree, this
time from Wilson College, a small school in Chambersburg,
Pennsylvania. In conferring the degree, Wilson's President noted her "contributions to the war effort and particularly your interest in women in the
armed forces, and the promotion of their welfare, indefatigable in the
search for facts and energetic in championing constructive legislation."[230]

Again Margaret's work on Naval Affairs had been the basis for this
award, though the specific catalyst may well have been Margaret's recent
efforts to provide benefits for Navy nurses, which she had initiated after her

tour of hospitals in the Pacific earlier in the year. Not only had she found conditions for the nurses there "appalling, but worse was their insecurity; if they got sick or hurt as a result of such duty, they were simply sent home."[231] Three years would be required to achieve regular status for nurses, though as she reported in her column of 15 November 1945, "At least [at present] the Navy nurses are on the same basis as Army nurses, WAVES, WACS, and other commissioned officers. Up to this date," she continued, "as long as the Navy nurses were on active duty, they received the same pay as others, but when retired because of injury of disability, they received considerably less than officers of the same rank." She did not consider her bill a reward for the nurses, but a correction of an inequity.[232]

When the Republicans met in Bangor on 11 April 1946 there were no signs that anyone would challenge Margaret's pursuit of a fifth term. Citing "continuity of service" as the "most effective element of individual strength in a legislator," she declared her candidacy just two days short of the convention, but few attending the Republican love-fest probably gave the matter any thought.[233] The outcome for Margaret Chase Smith was not in doubt.

Nor was it for most of the GOP candidates. Maine was still solidly in the Republican column. As expected, in Maine's first post-war election in September 1946, all of the major GOP candidates were winners by big votes. Horace A. Hildreth defeated his Democratic opponent by nearly 40,000 votes in the gubernatorial race, while Robert Hale was returned to Congress with a margin of 12,000 votes and Frank Fellows by a margin of 20,000 votes. In the Second District, Margaret defeated her old opponent, Edward J. Beauchamp, the Democrat from Lewiston, 39,217 to 25,416 and nearly beat him in his home county of Androscoggin, managing to pull within 2,000 of his lead.[234]

Some observers were moved to ask: What next? No sooner were the results in than election rumors about 1948 began to fly. She would run for Senator White's seat when he retired, they said. As early as 1944, the most perspicacious observers speculated about Margaret's entry into the 1948 Senate race. Edward D. Talberth, political columnist for the *Portland Sunday Telegram* told his readers that "within recent weeks talk has developed, and reliable sources say with accompanying evidence . . . that Mrs. Smith may have some designs on Wallace White's office. It was pointed out that . . . Mrs. Smith has been making Portland [Maine's most populous city] her headquarters and more often than not Republicans in the First District . . . made requests of her for service in Washington rather than from their elected representative Robert Hale."[235]

In 1946, in light of her continued voter appeal and the national visibility which Naval Affairs had provided, even the cautious L. A. Lemieux of the *Lewiston Evening Journal* saw her as a potential dark horse for the Senate. "The contest [for the U.S. Senate] has been regarded as being chiefly between Sumner Sewall . . . and Governor Horace Hildreth. Now, with Mrs. Smith reportedly casting longing glances at the upper House of Congress, matters really can get complicated. A closely fought battle between the two Governors might well open a side door for a third candidate to slip in. A split-up of primary votes could turn the tables on both Sewall and Hildreth, and leave them on the sidelines while the 'dark horse' rode across the line."[236] The column was written on 28 September 1946.

Had Talberth or Lemieux observed Margaret closely over her six years of campaigning, they would have been even bolder in predicting Margaret's future. A campaign trip in August 1942, just prior to the general election, is instructive.

After numerous rallies and visits to small towns throughout the Second District, her campaign swing culminated at the Sunday morning service of the Skowhegan Centenary Methodist Church in the heart of Canaan. The church was crowded. Members of other congregations slid into the pews next to the regular members of Centenary, and together they filled the large church to hear Margaret speak. Summer had arrived in Maine two months earlier. Dark suits and dresses had given way to beiges, cocoas and whites with a sprinkling of navy blue and bright prints. Women wore straw hats and white gloves; ushers sported carnations in their lapels. The robed choir sang, accompanied by organist Mrs. Matthew Greene. The chancel, where Margaret spoke, was banked with flowers. Sgt. Merwin Gordon, home on furlough, unveiled an honor roll which bore the names of other men from Centenary serving in the Armed Forces.

In a quiet voice, Margaret spoke of the boys in the service and pledged to mothers that every effort would be made to help their sons. The war was a crusade to restore the Ten Commandments, she said, a conflict between Christian civilization and scientific barbarism. However great

the reward may be, we only seek to live as we have lived," she added.[237]
And she asked for the improvement of the home, church and town, for
the morale of the boys in the service lay with the folks at home.

Then she explored the tribal ties she had with these people. Her
grandfather Murray "was for many years a citizen of Skowhegan." John
Wesley Chase was a "minister of the Methodist denomination" whose
farm lay just outside of town along the banks of the Kennebec River. The
farm had been lost by the family for taxes after the Civil War and in 1889
had become the site of a residential school for boys and girls.

Many in the congregation remembered that homestead, how it left
the family's hands after John Chase's untimely death, how it sat just
above the Kennebec River on the Waterville road and was now the
Hinckley School. As they listened to one of their own, they drew out the
names of other children of pioneers, the Atwoods and the Getchells,
whose farms had also once nestled along the Kennebec before falling
into disrepair in the decades after the Civil War. Not a few who listened
had barely saved their own family farm. They understood what the Chase
family, along with countless others, had endured. Time and a seamless
web of memories enveloped them all, kinfolk and neighbors alike,
bound them to each other, as to the land which sustained them and the
past which nurtured them. In Margaret on that bright August morning,
they saw what the struggle had produced. What time had yielded.

A little girl in braids who grew up and married a local politician. A
flimflam man, some said. A man not hard to like, said others. Off to that
big, drafty house, to drive him everywhere, tend to his needs. Clyde sure
had a way with women. Not an easy man, Clyde, for all his charm. A
widow at forty-two, not one to quit living, she ran for office and went off to
Washington. Plucky she was and smart, too. Not afraid of anyone or anything, people said. And not just a politician, either. That Sunday she never
even mentioned that she was up for reelection. Still, Rev. Hubbard was
right when he said she was someone you have learned to love.[238] All in all,
the Chases had turned out pretty darned well, for all their troubles.

On that day at the Centenary Methodist Church, Margaret wove
political magic. It was the same magic that would characterize most of
her career. It was the magic passed on to her from Clyde. It was the
magic that would send her to the United States Senate.

Carrie Murray Chase, Margaret Chase Smith's mother. *Nineteenth century portrait.*

Margaret Madeline Chase, age 6

After a family outing, Wesserunsett Lake, Maine, *circa* 1910

Margaret Chase at the capitol on her senior class trip to Washington, D.C., 1916

Skowhegan High School basketball champs. *Left to right:* Corinne Sally, Gladys Pennell, Nell Gifford, Beatrice Smiley, Margaret Chase, Helen White, 1916

Mamie Haydenn and Clyde H. Smith, *circa* 1916

Margaret Chase in front of Pitts School, Skowhegan,
where she taught school for seven months, 1916-17

A nineteen-year-old Margaret Chase in front of Red Cross Headquarters, Skowhegan, 1917

Margaret Chase (*second from right*) with staff of the *Independent Reporter*, May 1925

MCS in her wedding dress, 14 May 1930

Margaret and Clyde Smith in their yard, Fairview Avenue, Skowhegan, July 1932

Our Home
Fairview Avenue, Skowhegan — 1939

The "Big House," Fairview Avenue, Skowhegan, 1939

Newly-sworn-in Representative MCS at her office desk, 10 June 1940

House Naval Affairs Committee, Congested Area Sub-Comm. *Left to right*: Rep. John
Anderson, Rep John Fogarty, Rep. Edward Iac, Rep. MCS, Lt. William C. Lewis Jr, 1943

MCS and William Lewis, Jr., Skowhegan, 1943

MCS with her dog, Minnix, Fairview Avenue, Skowhegan, 13 September 1944

MCS aboard the USS Saratoga during Pacific Inspection Trip as a member of the
House Naval Affairs Committee, December 1944

MCS and Republican National Committee woman, Inez Wing,
Pittsfield, Maine, 27 August 1947

Meeting of the United Nations Educational, Scientific and Cultural Organization
(UNESCO) in Florence, Italy, 27 May—17 June 1950. MCS attended this meeting just
after her Declaration of Conscience speech.

MCS in her Skowhegan living room where she and Bill Lewis wrote the Declaration of Conscience speech, 1950

Maine Congressional Delegation, January 1952. *Left to right*: Sen. Owen Brewster, Rep. Charles P. Nelson, Rep. Robert Hale, Sen. Margaret Chase Smith, Rep. Clifford G. McIntire

MCS with Richard M. Nixon,Republican Rally,
Belgrade Lakes, Maine, 2 September 1952

MCS meets villagers in Machhgar, India with host Faridabad Block, March 1955

Danny Kaye, MCS and Jimmie Stewart meet in 1955 at an Overseas Press Club dinner,

Appearance on *Face the Nation* with Eleanor Roosevelt, 4 November 1956, two days
before the 1956 election

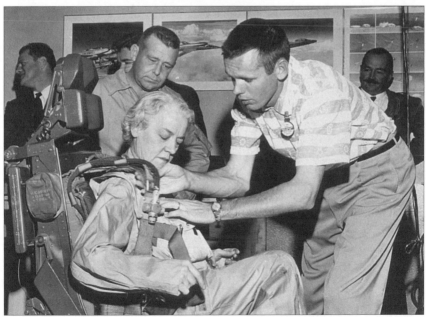

Major Clyde Good assists MCS, preparatory to flying in a F-100 Fighter while breaking
the sound barrier, 1957

MCS campaigning at St. Croix Paper Company, Woodland, Maine, 28 September 1960

MCS and Lt. Betty J. Hill discuss details of her trip to Guantanamo Bay U. S. Naval
Air Station, Cuba, 1 December 1962

King Savang Vatthana of Laos greets MCS at a State Department dinner given
by vice president Lyndon Johnson, Washington, 25 February 1963

Run for the presidency. Republican National Convention, San Francisco, July 1964

MCS at her Quaint Acres home, following her defeat in the 1972 election. Silver Springs, Maryland, 3 February 1973

Last formal portrait of MCS, summer, 1993,
Photograph by Benjamin Magro

PART III
DO IT WITH THY MIGHT

"Whatsoever thy hand findeth to do, do it with thy might."
Ecclesiastes 9:10

1. *A Return to "Normalcy"*

MARGARET'S FIFTH-TERM VICTORY on 10 September 1946 came with the world at ebb tide. Thirty five million people, including 322,000 Americans, had died in World War II.[1] On 8 May 1945 when President Roosevelt broadcast his V-E Day Proclamation, Europe was a dead land where no lilacs bloomed, nor seemed likely to bloom again. Following Allied victory, relief turned to horror as Americans watched grainy newsreels of concentration camp atrocities. Even after the Nazis trekked to the gallows, some observers remained uneasy with the face of evil that had been revealed. Nagging at them was the fear that nothing, anywhere, was likely ever to be quite the same again, despite the world's jubilant return to an already uneasy peace.

Margaret's public reaction to the war's moral ambiguities was to embrace what Warren Harding once called "normalcy." Within two months of V-E Day, she turned her attention to reuniting military wives with husbands who had served overseas. Unlike columnist Dorothy Thompson, who lost hope that the family was a protection from barbarism when she toured Dachau and saw that the Nazi exterminators had been family men—devoted to their wives and children—Margaret threw her support to the institutions of marriage and the family with new-found enthusiasm after the war.[2]

In this vein she proposed that "the Army permit wives of men assigned to duty in occupied countries for one year or an indefinite time to join them." The proposal was prompted by what she described as "my desire to prevent further disintegration of the American home and the American family life. The absence of these men has already placed a severe strain upon the preservation of domestic ideals."[3]

The suggestion precipitated her first run-in with General Eisenhower. Food shortages and inadequate living quarters abroad made the idea impractical, said the Supreme Commander of the Allied Forces. Like his own wife, wives of servicemen would simply have to be patient and stay at home. But the idea struck a chord with the public and continued to receive wide coverage by the press. Thus, at the very outset of the country's return to traditional gender roles, Margaret—who most often appeared in public in a hat and gloves—seemed to cast her lot with traditional values, even as she co-sponsored an Equal Rights Amendment with Edith Nourse Rogers, the first time two female House members had done so. Thus, as the country re-affirmed the institution of marriage and a conventional role for women after the war, Margaret was publicly well-positioned to become a part of America's return to the past, despite the fact she had been keeping company with a man fifteen years her junior since 1943.

William E. Lewis, Jr., was a composite of Margaret's first uniformed hero, the pilot Walter Cleveland, and the politically-absorbed Clyde Smith. At the outset, there was a hint of romance in the relationship between the then-forty-five-year old woman and the fresh faced thirty-one-year old. But the shimmering evanescence of those first months had become by 1946 something more permanent, if less intense. The spark of romance so strongly suggested by 1943 snapshots had smoldered into a friendship which entwined their personal and political lives.

During these years, Margaret had been virtually adopted by the senior Lewises who were—she was convinced—far more impressed with her accomplishments than was her own family.[4] By spring of 1947 Army Air Reserve Colonel and Mrs. William C. (Nelle) Lewis, Sr. were in her words, "old friends."[5]

The political alliance which began in 1943 was similar to the one Margaret and Clyde had shared, although this time around, Margaret was in charge, with Bill eventually overseeing not only the administration of the office but the "housekeeping" side of things as well. Like most successful public figures, Margaret understood the importance of a partner, if not a "wife," and Bill Lewis had become for her that person. She was to describe herself and Bill as "one person," with Bill devoted to her career.[6] He would, she recalled "do everything to please me."[7]

Until 1946 Bill had continued to work for the powerful chairman of

Naval Affairs, Carl Vinson, and he had become adept at helping Vinson navigate through the shark-infested waters of Congress. But he especially distinguished himself by helping to erect for Vinson a persona which projected the kind of heroic vision which usually flourishes only in one's imaginings about oneself. Bill not only perceived the depth of Vinson's ambitions, but understood with uncanny acuity the craters and canyons of the congressional psyche, an insight that was perhaps a legacy of a lonely childhood spent observing two strong adults whose whims and weaknesses had to be manipulated in order to gain some psychic space. He also knew that despite constant compromises and 'days of long knives,' most congressmen believed that at heart they were selfless patriots. The image Bill reflected back to Vinson took full account of all of these impulses.

Vinson, a Georgia Democrat and great-uncle of Senator Sam Nunn, had won his chairmanship "by living long and getting re-elected regularly."[8] He was an able politician, "an effective conservative regular, but he was no Thomas Jefferson, or Lyndon Johnson, either, for that matter."[9] Yet Bill not only cast him as "'Father of the United States Navy'—the greatest Navy in the world," he characterized Vinson's career as "statesmanship in action," an enterprise of high moral purpose, a battle-station of great moment.[10] As Bill wrote to Vinson on 29 December 1946 after Vinson lost the post of chairman, Naval Affairs Committee, in the Republican congressional sweep of that year, "You know that despite the termination of our official relations on 3 January 1947, I shall always be at your command."[11] The man Vinson saw in the mirror which Bill held up was all that he had hoped to be—and more.

On a par with Bill's image-making skills was his capacity for solicitousness and flattery, two qualities which would carry him far. "It is my fervent hope," Bill wrote to Vinson, "that some day I will have sufficiently distinguished myself and reflected sufficient credit upon you that you will point to me and say he is my protege. Surely then I will feel that I have won my 'place in the sun'—that the stimulating inspiration of my service with you has partially repaid you . . . by reflecting additional, however limited, credit upon you." The sentiment may have been somewhat standard issue, but Bill's unique spin is worthy of consideration. "My continued affiliation with the Committee *at a financial sacrifice* was more than offset by the pleasantness and interesting character of the work," he told Vinson. "The anonymity of my work for you and the Committee prevented prestige and publicity. Although I, like any normal man of ambition, aspire to a 'place in the sun,' yet I have been deeply satisfied with that anonymity for I knew that it was what you wanted."[12]

In light of his rapid rise in military rank and his increasing access to one of the most influential men in the House, Bill's allusions to the 'anonymity of his work' and the 'absence of prestige and publicity' were ludicrous. Moreover, his purported 'financial sacrifice,' based on his affiliation with the committee, bordered on untruth in light of his former position with the SEC. He did not leave a highly lucrative law practice for the relative austerity of the public sphere as he implies; rather he chose to exchange one kind of public service for another. But in his words was the drumbeat of patriotism, and a sense of *his own* high moral purpose. The timbre of Bill's service as well as Vinson's patronage were thereby raised rhetorically to an almost heroic level.

Especially in his relationships, Bill Lewis was a man of very different parts than was Clyde Smith. And the Smith-Lewis partnership differed accordingly. Clyde was a charmer and even a deceiver, but he did not dissemble and he did not count on the patronage of anyone else to move him forward, though he never turned down the help of powerful friends. He submitted his fate to the vote of the electorate and by their judgement stood or fell. In contrast, Bill tied his fate to one person, to the relationship he could create with that person, and to the interpersonal skills he could employ on his own behalf. Thus, unlike the Roman emperor who had a slave at his side to remind him that he was mortal, Margaret thus grew dependent on the voice of a man whose first impulse was to please, rather than demur, and whose devotion and loyalty often deprived her of healthy criticism and balance. While such support bolstered Margaret's confidence and created a sense of well-being, it also tended to constrict her personal and political growth, even as it increased Bill's importance to the partnership and furthered his career.

A similar pattern had caused Bill to flourish during his four years with Carl Vinson. After serving less than a year as a staff member for Naval Affairs, he received a promotion to full lieutenant. Four months later, members of the Congested Areas subcommittee were already expressing "the highest commendation of, and . . . most sincere esteem for, Lieutenant Lewis," and gave him their "unqualified backing."[13] By the following Spring, Bill's third promotion (to lieutenant commander) had been proposed by Carl Vinson. When the Navy failed to respond as Vinson hoped, he wrote a forceful letter to the chief of Navy personnel and repeated his request. The Navy responded with their reasons for denying it. There was the relative unimportance of Lewis' work, the unfairness of such a promotion to those on sea duty, and insufficient time of service in grade. Each of these was countered by Vinson with considerable skill, though he and the letter's recipient doubtless shared an awareness that Vinson's position as chairman of the Naval Affairs Committee was probably his strongest argument. "As you are aware," he said at the close of his letter to the chief of Navy personnel, "I have scrupulously avoided asking favors from the Bureau. On the other hand, I have no hesitancy to express my frank convictions in deserving cases. The facts in this case speak for themselves and it is my deep conviction that Lieutenant Lewis should be promoted to Lieutenant Commander."[14] The Navy complied.

Bill's ambitions, however, were not so easily quenched. Soon Vinson began a campaign to see that Bill was awarded the prestigious Legion of Merit, one of the service's most coveted service awards. After writing to the secretary of the Navy and the recorder of the Navy Department of Decorations and Medals, Vinson finally contacted Artemus Gates, the undersecretary of the Navy, on 28 November 1945. "Yesterday, I was informed that the Board had approved and endorsed my recommendation," Vinson wrote, "but that you had reversed and overruled the Board's decision and action and stated very vigorously that you were opposed to any award to Lieutenant Commander Lewis. . . . To the reported reason that you had not even heard of Lieutenant Commander Lewis, I can only comment with the question: 'Are the awards made exclusively on the basis of notoriety and only to celebrities or those known to you?' . . . Is an award dependent upon rank?" he asked. The letter's intensity escalated. "I should like to point out that if your reported reasoning is followed through, it would mean that before Lieutenant Commander Lewis could be decorated, all of the officers up the line superior in command to him would have to be decorated also . . . even though they were in no way connected with what he had done to merit the award. If you have the slightest doubt of the character of the service of Lieutenant Commander Lewis, I would be most happy to clear it up. As I have said in four letters in the past three months, he deserves at least the Legion of Merit."15

On 11 April 1946 Bill Lewis was promoted to the rank of commander, and on 29 May a letter was sent to Vinson from the Bureau of Naval Personnel. "In accordance with your request of 22 May 1946, there is forwarded herewith for presentation to Commander William E. Lewis, Jr., U.S. Naval Reserve, the Legion of Merit and permanent citation awarded for service during the war."16

The vehemence with which Vinson fought for his assistant suggests the expertness with which Bill forged bonds of loyalty which went well beyond the usual employee-employer relationship. Bill's four promotions in as many years, along with a coveted service award and a permanent citation for his service during the war, are testimony to that, especially since Bill's record showed no sea duty during that time.17

From 1947 on, after Bill officially became Margaret's Administrative Assistant, her loyalty would match and even exceed Vinson's. Soon he became known as the power behind the throne, someone who had to be reckoned with in any dealings with Margaret, a "prime minister" of sorts. Theirs would become a political marriage held together by a mutuality of need, solidified by vows to protect and defend.

Apart from Bill's charm and attentiveness, Margaret probably saw him as a means by which to scale the impenetrable wall of her next objective, the Senate. In that body, more than in the House, she would be an outsider, a foreigner in much the same way that her French-Canadian grandfather had been an alien in Yankee Maine. Not only would she be the lone woman among men, but a lay person among attorneys, a public high school product amidst the flower of the Ivy League. Bill, with his Harvard degree, his lawyer's mind and his veneer of sophistication seemed to supply just the strong arm she needed. He could take Margaret the rest of the way down the road, helping to ensure her election to the Senate and securing her success once she got there. Her assessment, like Vinson's, however, was shaped by the combination of distortion and truth in the mirror Bill was holding before her.

But on the evening of 21 March 1946, an event occurred which could

only have heightened the value of his constancy and devotion and cemented Margaret's need for his presence. At 6:00 p.m., George Emery Chase
died at the home of his daughter Evelyn and her husband Rex St. Ledger,
with whom he and Carrie had been spending the winter. After many years
as a barber, during which time it was rumored that his fondness for drink
began regularly to exceed his capacity to handle it, George Chase had
taken a job as a caretaker at the Maine Spinning Company. In 1942 at the
age of sixty-eight, he retired. The last four years of his life were spent at the
family home on North Avenue. "Mr. Chase was born June 9, 1874, the son
of Rev. and Mrs. John Wesley Chase at Hinckley. His birthplace is now
known as the Good Will cottage purchased in his boyhood by Dr. George
Hinckley."[18] According to the remainder of the press release from
Margaret's office, she would spend the week following her father's funeral
at home in Maine. No personal notes or musing are extant from this period, nor any public expression of emotion. Characteristically, she avoided
the deeper meanings of events almost as though they were too frightening,
or as if giving into them was self-indulgent and weak, a legacy of the strong
and stoic Carrie perhaps, or in this case possibly a reminder of the pain of
emotional abandonment by her father in favor of her brother Wilbur. In
any event, George Chase's death provoked an external response that can
only be described as controlled and matter-of-fact, a style as flat as Clyde's
had been florid. On a deeper level, even though for Margaret her father
may have died much earlier, his passing could not help but remind her
how very much on her own she was. And Bill's presence provided reassurance that she was not alone. But it was the April death of President
Roosevelt, and the jumbled events which followed in its wake in
Washington, D. C., that made someone like Bill—someone who always
seemed to have her best interests at heart—a strategic necessity.

2. *Women in Washington*

No LESS A MASTER of the art of acquiring power than Clare Boothe
Luce once observed that "America understands almost nothing about
women and ambition. America, in terms of power transferred to women,
is the most backward of Western countries."[19] During the years historians
call the Cold War, that assessment became especially apt, though at the

end of World War II, the future for Luce and Smith—as Republicans and women—looked bright.

Optimism among Republicans ran especially high in 1946. The war had left price controls, inflation and shortages of every kind in its wake. A series of nation-wide strikes for higher wages had decreased production and increased the scarcity of certain consumer goods, making them obtainable only on the black market at exorbitant prices. Especially acute was the housing shortage, a crisis created by six years of reduced construction, compounded by the return of more than fifteen million veterans, many of whom needed housing. Reports from Chicago described veterans living in their cars, washing up in the rest room of the public library, and cooking over a fire in the park. In New York, a Marine captain who had spent most of his terminal leave searching for an apartment in Manhattan summed up the feelings of many when he declared: "Peace is sure hell."[20] Such exasperation spelled good news for Republicans. Since they had not set foot in the White House since 1932, Republicans had nothing for which to answer. On 12 April 1946, when President Roosevelt died in Warm Springs, Georgia, the Democratic giant who had heretofore been able to quell all criticism was no longer able to do so. At last, the Republicans had a chance to break the Democrat's stranglehold on the White House. Never again, wrote historian William Manchester, "would the Grand Old Party be daunted by that wicked grin, that maniacal laughter, that tilted cigarette holder and flashing pince-nez."[21]

As they had anticipated, in November 1946, in the "off-year" elections, the GOP won its greatest victory in fifteen years. They gained control both of the Senate, where they increased their number from 39 to 51, and the House where their membership climbed from 188 to 246. Their sweeping victory was the first for the GOP since they lost control of Congress in the early thirties.[22]

In the division of spoils following the November sweep, several of Margaret's friends were elevated to top party ranks. Her old friend Joe Martin became Speaker of the House, while Wallace White of Auburn, Maine became President Pro Tem of the Senate. But the bitter struggle behind the scenes between the liberal, northeastern wing of the party which backed Thomas Dewey and the midwestern and southern wing which backed Robert Taft was to have a more far-reaching impact on Margaret. Just as Martin's ascension to Speaker and Indiana Rep. Charlie Halleck's rise to House Majority Leader signalled rising Dewey influence in the lower House, the appointment of Brazilla Carrol Reece—a conservative from Tennessee who denounced Communists and Truman's Civil Rights Program with equal fervor—to chairman of the Republican National Committee signalled a takeover of the party by Taft forces. More than that, Reece's appointment sounded a death knell for Margaret's friend, Marion Martin. Almost immediately, Reece moved to remove Dewey loyalists like Marion from the staff of the National Committee and bring that body into line with the conservative wing of the GOP

For six years in the shifting landscape of politics, Marion and Margaret had remained for each other fixed points, sounding boards, sources of support and solace—maternal figures in an otherwise male world. Enlightened self-interest had certainly played a part, but at the core of their friendship was a deeper bond. The awareness that they were fellow pilgrims in pursuit of the same kind of adventure had created the sort of comradeship often identified with men but anticipatory of the concept of sisterhood that would flourish in the 60s.

For a while they occupied apartments in the same end of Washington, a lovely shaded area west of Wardman Park, near the Shoreham Hotel. An October 1946 letter from Marion to Margaret, who had left Washington for a brief visit to Skowhegan, suggests the nature of their regard. "I have noticed every night when I come in that your apartment is still dark, so I am hoping you are getting a bit of rest, but will be coming back soon," Marion wrote. "Do take care of yourself because you will have a tremendously busy session ahead of you and we don't want our Margaret getting worn out."[23] In a similar vein, Margaret closed her 12 September 1946 letter, "Do hope your mother is on the road to recovery and that I shall see you before long and talk this all over." Frequently, they talked politics: "I thought I would call and talk the election over with you but haven't stopped a minute since it was over," wrote Margaret to Marion after the fall general election. "On arrival home in August I joined the Republican tour and continued through the seven [Maine] counties. . . . But really, Marion, with the apathy and lack of contests in the Republican counties—Waldo, Knox, Lincoln and Franklin, and the activity . . . of the Democrats in their strongholds like Waterville and Lewiston, I feel pretty pleased that I should even get through."²⁴ Margaret then noted with obvious pride that she had topped the Republican ticket in her bid for her fifth term in Congress.

In the same letter, Margaret gave her friend at the National Committee ammunition with which to fend off criticism by the Republican Right. "Although the press continues to say that I was CIO-PAC endorsed, such an endorsement has never come to me. The CIO in Maine is largely Democratic [as Marion surely knew] and although I must have received the votes of individual workers, I could not have had the solid support that is reported or I would have carried Waterville at least. Actually the only endorsement which came to me through the entire year has come from the Railroad Brotherhood groups. This is not for publication but thought you would be interested in the story as I know you will be in other stories which I can tell you."

Embedded at the end of the letter was a coded reference to the upcoming 1948 Senate race which Margaret would enter as a dark horse. Her remark, which speculated on the prospects of the two front-runners, indicates that Marion was one of a handful of intimates with whom she discussed the possibility of her candidacy at least a year before her announcement. "The Hildreth campaign," referring to Hildreth's recent re-election to governor, "appeared to be carried on with 1948 in view. I hear he and Sewall have many pledged in Aroostook County."²⁵

Similar fires burned within them, and within other women ten to fifteen years their senior. But following the death of Roosevelt, theirs had become a generation in the process of being displaced.²⁶

Twelve years earlier, the cover of the 8 October 1934 *Time Magazine* had carried a photo of five distinguished-looking women who were channelling their impulses for self-expression into educational, social welfare, and political activities. First Lady Eleanor Roosevelt was seated between Dean Virginia Crocheran Gildersleeve of Barnard College and Helen Rogers Reid, Vice President of the *Herald Tribune* and wife of its owner, Ogden Reid. Behind them stood Mrs. Ordway Tead of the Katherine Gibbs School and Miss Valentine Chandor of Manhattan's Spence School. The issue highlighted a conference for women which had recently been held at the Waldorf-Astoria in New York City under the auspices of Reid. Eleanor Roosevelt delivered the opening address and the President spoke at the close.

Though *Time* characterized the attendees as "large and small, handsome and unlovely, most of them middle-aged, many of them buxom and not a few of them with funny hats," the magazine was anything but condescending about the conference's extraordinary speakers, or its success. No fewer than 38,000 women had applied to the *Herald Tribune* for tickets, with 25,000 actually registering for the five sessions. The ballroom could provide seats for only 2,500.[27]

Of special interest to *Time* was a session called "The Changing Status of Women." Speakers who appeared at this session were women with whom Reid had a personal and professional kinship, and who held down jobs in a man's world "with no concessions asked or given because of their sex."[28] They included Mary Elizabeth Dillon, president of the $12,000,000 Brooklyn Borough Gas Co.; Mrs. Charles B. Knox, President of the Knox Gelatin Co.; Eleanor Medill Patterson, editor, Hearst's *Washington Herald*; and May Greer, cashier of Firestone Tire and Rubber Co., reputed to be the highest salaried woman in the United States. Speaking by transatlantic radio to the group was British suffragist Viscountess Rhondda, who, at 51, was chair of seven companies and director of 24 others, with interests ranging from coal, iron, and steel to newspapers and shipping. She had gone to jail and hungerstruck in the Pankhurst campaign, fought for the right of peeresses to sit in the House of Lords, and — probably to no one's great surprise — survived the sinking of the Lusitania when it was torpedoed. In *Time*'s idiom, these speakers were "big women in big jobs."[29] In fact, they were women who had changed the rules and pursued their own dreams, much as Marion and Margaret would do in the forties. They had carved out their own adventure stories and had expanded the boundaries of the possible for women. The age of Earhart had nurtured both female friendship and female heroism. When the newspapers reported that Earhart had disappeared on 2 July 1937 on the last leg of her trip from New Guinea to the Howland Islands, First Lady Eleanor Roosevelt told readers of her weekly column: "I have scanned the paper with great anxiety since Friday evening, when I first heard over the radio that Amelia Earhart and her navigator were missing. . . . I am hanging on the telephone hoping to hear good news of her. I feel sure that if she comes through safely, she will feel that what she had learned has made it all worth while. But her friends will wish science could be served without quite so much risk to a fine person, whom many people love as a person and not as a pilot or adventurer."[30]

By the late forties, however, the celebration of individual female achievement had run its course. Though the thirties had, in the words of historian Nancy Wolock, "brought a rise of women in Democratic ranks, an influx of women into New Deal posts, and a brief revival of female 'influence,'" the political strength of women quickly flagged following the death of President Roosevelt in the forties.[31] Almost immediately there was an exodus of high-ranking New Deal women from the upper reaches of the executive branch, one of whom noted a "kind of panic hitting women in Washington after Roosevelt died" and a form of "petty persecution of women." They "were denied access to phones, they were pulled off inter-departmental committees, they were denied promotions."[32]

Between 1937 and 1946 Marion Martin had used advances for Democratic women as leverage, warning that unless the Republicans took steps, the other party would win the race for women voters. For a time, and especially in 1940 during Willkie's campaign, the strategy worked. When the chase for "the woman vote" was abandoned by the Democrats in the late forties, however, the Republican National Committee wasted little time following suit. Within seven years of Roosevelt's death, the Women's Divisions of both parties were abolished, both in "economic moves." The Republicans abolished theirs in 1952, shortly after Eisenhower's inauguration, and the Democrats followed suit in 1953.[33]

For Margaret and Marion, and for many other professional women, Roosevelt's death and the Republican sweep signalled the end of an era. As Secretary Frances Perkins prepared to leave office, she wrote on 26 June 1945 to fellow New Englander, Margaret Chase Smith. "We have had, I think, a common objective in which we felt a moral purpose, and the cooperative effort has therefore been of constructive benefit to the wage earners of America and, through them to all the people of the United States."[34] Though on the surface Perkins' words resemble a stan-dard-issue message from a departing cabinet official to a member of Congress, her reference to a "common objective" and "moral purpose" suggests that she, along with Margaret and Marion, had also shared a journey.[35]

On 16 December 1946 Margaret wrote an impassioned letter to Carroll Reece on behalf of Marion. "Her resignation under most questionable circumstances is a great disappointment to all women irrespective of party. . . . and your "action is so far reaching that it demands an explanation . . . [with] no delay if anything is to be salvaged from the irreparable damage caused." In fact, she wrote, "your action is interpreted by many as the adoption of a policy by the National Committee of slamming the door on women in the Republican party. The reason it is being interpreted by many in this manner is because Marion Martin is not only the widely-acknowledged champion woman organizer but more so because she had become the vigorous crusader for greater participation and recognition of women in public service, both in Government and in the acceptance of political responsibilities." Her termination "will subject the Republican party to the risk of a tremendous defection of women voters—who as the greatest single voting bloc in 1946 elections made the sweeping Republican victory possible."[36]

But Margaret was unable to dissuade Reece. After a polite but unproductive meeting, Reece wrote Margaret a brief note. "I was very glad indeed that we had the opportunity for a visit yesterday so that we could discuss the various angles of Miss Martin's resignation," he wrote. "I certainly do not want anyone who I think of as much as I do of you to be under any misapprehension."[37]

Writing as she did suggests that Margaret felt Marion's loss with uncommon force. The letter not only courted disapproval from the National Committee, it attracted criticism from Herbert Libby. Having read her letter to Reece in the Waterville Sentinel on 18 December, Libby immediately composed a cautionary letter which was dated the same day. "I am very deeply concerned over your public criticism of the possible part taken by Chairman Reece in dropping Mrs. Martin from the National Committee," he told her. "I know nothing about the matter except what appears in the press, but the regrettable part of public criticism of the national Chairman is that it plays directly into the hands of our political opponents, and makes the work of Chairman Reece extremely difficult." After reminding Margaret that a new chairman "should be given the right to have much to say about persons associated with him on the Committee," he speculated that it was "entirely possible that Mrs. Martin may not be the best suited to work with him."

Then he spoke to Margaret sternly about her references to the Party's treatment of women. "It seems most unfortunate, also, for you to suggest in your public statement that the head of our committee is 'slamming the door on women,' [for] that statement will find lodgment in the minds of many people and will be taken full advantage of in the national election. Offhand," he concluded, "I would say that would be the last thing a Chairman would think of doing."

In closing, he said: "Please forgive me for writing so frankly; but you have always been most kind asking for my judgments, and I have always tried to say and do what would be to your best good."[38] Best good indeed, at least where Margaret's political fortunes were concerned. But Libby with his narrow pragmatism had failed to appreciate Margaret's noble act of defending a friend and her capacity to put principle above politics. In fact, he had overlooked almost all of her best qualities, a wry foreshadowing of what Margaret could expect in her dealings with the National Republican Party.

Because she valued Libby's support, and the harshness of Libby's criticism frightened her, ultimately Margaret struck a chord more politic than heroic. "I feel that anything you write or say to me is sincere," she wrote. Then, agreeing that the chairman was within his rights to replace Marion, Margaret covered her own vulnerability by taking exception to "the way he brought it about," presumably referring to the peremptory nature of the firing. After reminding Libby that Senator White and Congressman Hale had also written on Marion's behalf, and that Margaret would have done the same for a Maine man in a similar position, she took up the lingering issue of feminism. "I am sure you will agree that I have never been a feminist, or in any way demanded or expected, recognition because I am a woman," she reassured Libby. "Instead, I have taken my position as a representative of the people and carried on that way—sometimes to the extent of criticism because I have not been active in strictly women's activities." At the same time, she continued, "Marion Martin [has] struggled through the years to organize and interest women in government and Republican politics. It seems a pity that, right at a time when Republicans are coming into power . . . we have to be confronted by a fight among our-selves—all because of the Presidential election of 1948."[39]

Clearly struggling not to fall victim to the same fate as Marion, Margaret's tone became conciliatory and affectionate. "I am most happy to hear from you," she said, "and although I have not had a chance to see you and Mrs. Libby for a long time, I think of you often and wish I could benefit by occasional conferences." After soliciting Libby's comments on a proposed reorganization of Congress, she closed "with very good wish-es and much appreciation for your friendship through the years." Whether she knew that the battle to save Marion was lost, or whether she was simply acting out of fear that she would lose Libby's support is not clear. What does seem apparent is that Margaret's willingness to fight competed with an equally compelling impulse for self-preservation. There is no extant correspondence on behalf of Marion Martin until some years later. For now, Margaret had done all that she could, or was willing, to do. She was, after all, a pragmatist.

Meanwhile Owen Brewster, who saw himself as a defender and pro-moter of women—contrary to Margaret's assessment of him—rallied to Marion's cause, using his ties with the Truman Administration to try to pro-cure for her an appointment to the Federal Communications Commission. But his efforts were to no avail.[40] Finally, Gov. Horace A. Hildreth found a spot for her in his administration, and on 1 April 1947, she was sworn in as Maine's first woman commissioner of labor and industry.[41] Public response in Maine to Marion's appointment gave weight to Libby's cautions to Margaret to avoid being seen as a feminist, and it foreshadowed what lay ahead for women. Although hometown supporters who had fol-lowed Martin's career in public life (faithfully reported by her hometown newspaper the *Bangor Daily News*) were convinced that she would "dis-tinguish herself as Maine's labor and industry commissioner," the "anti-feminists," who referred to Marion as "another Madame Perkins," attract-ed greater publicity.[42] Over their objections, Marion Martin presided as Maine's commissioner of labor for a quarter of a century.

Not only were Libby's cautions about feminism as apt in 1946 as they had been in 1940, but he gave Margaret another piece of advice in his 18 December 1946 letter which proved to be similarly prophetic. "We have lived far too many years under the rule of our political rivals," he told

Margaret. "Now that we are at least getting out from under it and standing a fair chance of electing a Republican President, it would seem to me
extremely wise to keep our internal troubles very much to ourselves."[43]
Increasingly after World War II, the Republican Party would view mavericks within their ranks as a threat, for much the same reason as the one
given by Libby. They had been denied power for too long. The mood of
the Republican Party toward mavericks, and the mood of both parties
toward women, thus made someone like Bill Lewis absolutely essential
to an ambitious woman's survival. In 1946, possibly in anticipation of the
upcoming senate race, Bill established legal residence in Skowhegan at
the home of Margaret's youngest sister, Laura, and her husband, Joseph
"Spike" Bernier. Soon thereafter, Bill purchased land on the shore near
Portland where he planned to build. By this date, he had truly become a
part of Margaret's family.

3. Regular Status for the WAVES

WHEN THE EIGHTIETH CONGRESS lumbered into action in early
February 1947, Margaret became chairman of the subcommittee on
Hospitalization and Medicine, House Armed Services Committee, a committee which had been merged with Naval Affairs in January 1947 when
the Republicans took control of the House. She announced that she
expected all witnesses "to come prepared with sufficient copies of their
statements for committeemen and the press" and that statements were to
be held to a minimum. Moreover, no witness was to be "interrupted by
questions until completing a statement, when committee members will be
given an opportunity in turn and uninterrupted to ask questions."[44]
    One of the earliest bills considered by the subcommittee was H.R.
1943, a measure giving Army and Navy nurses permanent regular status.
Margaret had become convinced of the importance of nurses to a peacetime military during the war, and she took it upon herself to shepherd
the measure through her sub-committee. Because of well-publicized
nursing shortages in the Army and Navy, the bill met little resistance and
passed both Houses in April 1947. Margaret's role in its success was
described by a journalist who watched from the House gallery as
Margaret parried an attempt to jeopardize the bill with an amendment.

"Her straightforward statesmanlike handling of the issue averted the threatened controversy. She refused to be tripped by an issue that wasn't there, and the measure was passed promptly and overwhelmingly without amendment. It was," concluded the reporter, "the gentle persuasion of the Lady from Maine that accomplished that."[45]

But gentle persuasion was not a viable strategy three months hence when Senate Bill 1641, which granted virtually all military women reserve and permanent status, passed from the Senate, where it had met little opposition, to the House, where it was assigned to the House Armed Services Committee.[46] Though the earlier bill for nurses (widely perceived as angels of mercy, operating within a female role) had raised few hackles, WAVES and WAC—213,000 strong at peak wartime enrollment—comprised well over half of women in uniform. They were widely considered by rank-and-file servicemen and officers as promiscuous, or as women assuming unnatural male roles.[47] Observed Virginia Gildersleeve of Barnard College, "If the Navy could possibly have used dogs or ducks or monkeys, certain of the older admirals would probably have greatly preferred them to women."[48]

But the problem was broader than chauvinism. If they became regulars, the women in the women's corps would be subtracted from the military's allowable strength; reservists would not. Or at least that is what proponents of the military like Carl Vinson feared. Moreover, argued Vinson and others, putting women in the regular navy "would be a nice way for women to get killed." The permanent reserves, where they could be used as needed, was a "happy solution."[49] These views were to translate into stubborn resistance by key members of the House Armed Services Committee to S. 1641.

Despite entrenched hostility, women had carved out an important niche during the war years by processing the massive paperwork demanded by a bureaucracy, thereby releasing men to fight. When the war ended and women began to leave the service for better civilian jobs, the "brass" quickly became alarmed. Who would process the mountain of paperwork? In July 1947 Defense Secretary James Forrestal and General Eisenhower, Fleet Admiral Chester Nimitz, Major General W. S. Paul, director of Personnel and Administration, and Chief of Navy Personnel, Rear Admiral T. L. Sprague appeared before the Senate Armed Services

Committee to attest to the military's critical need for women.⁵⁰ In response, S. 1641, the Women's Armed Services Integration Act, which gave co-equal status to women in the armed services, was proposed. In short order, on 23 July 1947, S. 1641 passed the Senate and was sent on to the House where the bill was to travel a rocky road and Margaret would use up valuable political capital in trying to see that it was passed.

When the bill reached the Armed Services Committee it was referred to the Policy subcommittee, where it languished for seven months. Finally it was sent for hearing and action to the Organization subcommittee, the chairman of which, W. G. "Ham" Andrews, a Republican from upstate New York, also chaired the full Armed Services Committee. Serving with him on the Organization subcommittee were the four top-ranking Republicans and three top-ranking Democrats in the House, including Carl Vinson. Until this time, Andrews was someone about whom Margaret had expressed positive feelings.⁵¹ Soon, however, Margaret learned that the bill had made it out of Policy only at Andrews' "urgent personal intervention" and only on the strict condition that the bill be amended to "prevent women from being given Regular status in the Armed Services [thus] keeping them on active duty indefinitely." In sum, a deal had been made in off-the-record executive session with representatives of the Navy Department to give women reserve status only.⁵² When Margaret learned of this, she decided to engage in the first major battle of her congressional career, in spite of "hourly communiques" from the leaders of the WAVES, WAC, and WAF who were willing to accept the loss of permanent, regular status for fear of losing reserve status if they made a fight of it. Margaret disagreed. The year before in May 1946, she had offered an amendment to Carl Vinson's proposal to establish the WAVES reserves on a permanent basis. Her amendment passed the Naval Affairs Committee 10-2 but was effectively bottled up by Vinson until the 79th Congress adjourned. A WAC bill in the same Congress received similar treatment. To Margaret, the issue was one of fairness. Without permanent *and* regular status, women were treated as temporary help and discarded when the need passed. "The issue is simple," she wrote to "Ham" Andrews, "either the Armed Services have a *permanent* need of women officers and enlisted women or they don't," she said. "If they do, then the women must be given a Permanent status."⁵³

Andrews, who favored the idea of a Woman's Reserve Corps in which women were to be on hold until they were needed, was unmoved by her logic. Nor was he persuaded by the testimony of the brass, all of whom reaffirmed to the House the value of women to the military and the necessity for being able to offer them a career track in order to keep them. Thus the bill which emerged from the subcommittee provided reserve status only. When the full Armed Services Committee voted, Margaret was not present. Her vote was cast by a member to whom she had given her proxy. The final tally on the Armed Services Committee was 26 ayes, one present, and one no. Margaret was the no.[54]

Had Margaret dropped the matter there, her identification with women in the military would have been less intense, but her standing with fellow Republicans more secure. She would not, however, stay out of the fray. She knew that women were being pushed around. In early spring, 1948, when the bill finally reached the floor of the House, Andrews placed the bill on the consent calendar, implying that it was an uncontroversial measure and therefore not open to debate or amendments. Not only was his maneuver an attempt to steamroll Margaret's opposition, but it ignored the basic difference between the bill passed by the Senate and the House committee's version. Margaret, however, was not to be outflanked. When the clerk called the bill and asked whether there were any objections, Margaret spoke up: "Mr. Speaker, I object," a tactic that forced Andrews to bring the bill up under the regular rules of the House and possibly disclose the "deals" that had been made. In essence, she was taking on her own committee, and that day she inserted into the *Congressional Record* her reasons. Essentially, the committee version was flawed because it gave women a temporary one-year reserve bill and unwise because it would not attract "women of desirable calibre for the Armed Services."[55] It was also a radical departure from the Senate's bill, S. 1641.

The heat subsequently generated on the floor, for which Margaret could properly take credit, created an opportunity for her to propose three amendments which would restore to the bill permanent, regular status. The debate also produced the kind of candor by opponents that cooler heads would have preferred remain unstated. Dewey Short [R-Mo.], especially, let the cat out of the bag.[56] He told the House that all officers from majors on down, as well as enlisted men, were opposed to giving women permanent status and that "there are several aspects to this bill that I do not care to discuss here publicly. We discussed them in detail and rather intimately in our committee. . . . We were told that 8 percent of all the women while they were in the service became pregnant [and] that when they reach the age of menopause or go through the change of life . . . the cost of the program would be stupendous if not prohibitive."[57]

Now that was some cat. And to a large degree it suggests both the level of threat posed by women in the armed services and the extremes to which Margaret had pushed her fellow Republicans. As the full House participated in the debate, Margaret thought that "it looked as though a majority of the House Armed Services Committee would reverse themselves and vote for the Smith Amendment." She noted that "the debate was going so badly against them . . . a frantic call went out from the Republican leadership to get the Andrews-Shafer-Short followers on the floor."[58] Though ultimately the only amendment to prevail was a change in name from the "Women's Armed Services Integration Act" to the "Women's Armed Services Reserve Act," Margaret won at least a tactical victory. She had both drawn her opponents into the open and strengthened the hand of the Senate conferees who would be resolving the differences between the House and Senate versions.

Not content with this outcome, however, Margaret wrote to Secretary of Defense Forrestal, whom she and Bill had come to know socially, to urge his support and demand that he look into the report that "behind closed doors and in executive session" the Navy had been involved in opposing permanent status.[59] Forrestal complied, stressing to members of the joint conference that the military establishment felt strongly about granting women permanent regular status.[60] When the conferees' compromise bill, giving regular status (though with some limitations), was voted on in the House on 2 July 1948, it passed 206 to 133, with 91 not voting.[61] On 12 July 1948 President Truman signed the Women's Armed Services Integration Act into law.[62]

Though Margaret's fight for co-equal status of women in the military was courageous—requiring her to abandon her carefully cultivated feminine persona—and although it brought her more recognition than any other issue during her years in the House, it was not a complete triumph.

Not only were many issues for women in the armed services still unresolved after the June 1948 vote, but the potential damage inflicted by the battle on Margaret's standing with her colleagues mitigated many of the short-term legislative gains. In her willingness to embarrass fellow Republicans over permanent, regular status—especially when the women themselves indicated they were ready to settle for reserve status alone—she created an impression of party disloyalty and grandstanding. Not only had she fought a measure on the floor of the House which came out of a Republican-dominated committee, but she had backed fellow Republicans into a corner.

Whatever else the battle for regular status symbolized for Margaret, at least two components were especially significant—one personal and the other political. Traditionally the military had offered young men from poor families a way to better themselves, not through a temporary job but in a career track. Had such an option been available to the young Margaret Chase, it is likely she would have preferred it to a year in a country school, especially if a real career could be launched. Moreover, the issue touched directly on the question of woman's place and her right to choose a non-traditional career path. As Margaret would argue for the next twenty-five years in a much-used speech entitled "A Woman's Place," a woman's place was "everywhere"—in the military as well as Congress.[63] On the political side, several prominent women and many of the major womens' organizations testified on behalf of S. 1641, including the American Association of University Women, the DAR, the General Federation of Women's Clubs, and her core support group, the BPW.[64] In addition, Bill Lewis, who admired Margaret's combative streak, most likely assessed the fight as an opportunity to position Margaret on center stage.

Bill had been trained to fight, and he functioned as a loner. Unlike Clyde, who had stood for public office before he was twenty-one, Bill was never elected to any public office, and he saw politics through the lens of an early life that had been a lonely and difficult battle. Politics were a laboratory within which to apply the tactics taught in the military, a game to be won by the best player. He understood that force can often be met only with counter-force and that in the game of power politics, the timid are often brushed aside. He seemed to believe that for Margaret to be taken seriously, she had to demonstrate a capacity to wield power—

in today's idiom, to play hardball—so he encouraged the emergence of a more forceful persona, a part which Margaret relished. Thus in May 1947 (two months before her fight for women in the military began), with no great principle at stake and no political ground to be gained, she had followed Bill into the "wrenching, bitter struggle" for military unification which pitted "army and air corps advocates of military 'unification' . . . against navy defenders of the . . . status quo."[65] It was a battle which breathed new life into Bill's military career and gave Margaret the opportunity to become more closely identified with her primary area of interest—defense. More than that, it once again revealed that Margaret was a woman of many different parts. And the part of her that was conventionally feminine did not prevent her from doing battle.

4. An Emerging Air Force

THE STRUGGLE HAD BEGUN in 1944, even before the war's end when the House appointed a Select Committee on Post-War Military Policy and held hearings on a "Proposal to Establish a Single Department of Armed Forces." Historically, the Army and the Navy had operated independently, but the war had demonstrated to many the need for unity of command. Proponents of the measure favored the creation of a single Department of Armed Forces, with a cabinet-level secretary to oversee the Army, Navy, and a newly-formed Air Force. Naval loyalists, especially, fearing a diminution of the Navy's power, passionately insisted on retention of the status quo. The fierce interservice struggle which ensued—primarily between the Navy and the Air Corps—became in the words of Forrestal's biographers, "a mortal struggle between the destiny of the one and the survival of the other."[66]

Three years later, in February 1947, the secretaries of Navy and War announced that they had reached agreement. S. 748 was introduced in the Senate on behalf of the administration and a similar bill, H.R. 4214, was introduced in the House. Both established a Department of Defense, headed by a single cabinet officer, and parity among the army, navy and air force.

In January 1947, a Republican had replaced Democrat Carl Vinson as chairman of the newly-formed Armed Services Committee. When no staff position was made available for Bill Lewis, he went to work for the Air Reserve Association [ARA], a group headed by Bill's father and committed to Unification and the establishment of a separate Air Force. After four months with the ARA, in a move designed to save a stalled military career and in something of a fit of pique, he resigned as a commander in the Naval Reserve and accepted a commission as a lt. colonel in the Army Air Corps Reserve.[67] From December 1946 through July 1947, Bill served as ARA treasurer and general counsel, as well as editor of the publication, *ARA Contact*.[68] At the close of the campaign for the Unification, Bill was credited by the ARA with much of the success for its passage, both because of his "quarterbacking," and because of his influence with Vinson. Concluded one ARA supporter: "As Vinson's continued authority on Unification, Lewis advised Vinson to drop his fight. . . . Vinson was completely silent on Unification, offered no opposition to the bill, and even did not vote against the bill."[69] Whether Bill deserved credit for Vinson's silence is difficult to gauge, especially since the author of the memo quoted above is not identified. But Vinson's new-found support for the Air Force after December 1946 was noted by Hoopes and Brinkley, who observed that by 1948, "the long-time champion of navy autonomy and supremacy was jumping on the air-power bandwagon."[70] Indisputably, such behavior was in sharp contrast to his intense opposition to Unification between 1944 and 1946 when he relentlessly attacked the measure as a diminution of the Navy.

Early in May 1947, Margaret and Bill were visiting with Bill's parents in Oklahoma City when a call came from Washington for Bill Lewis, Sr. about Unification. He was asked to come to Washington immediately to "see what he could do to resurrect the Unification Bill." According to Margaret, "the two of us [Bill and Margaret] went to bat immediately."[71]

While the fight for Unification dragged on through four months of hearings in the House, Margaret worked hard behind the scenes. She consulted friends on the Executive Expenditures Committee to which the bill had been referred, and learned that Navy and Marine Corps advocates were working hard to weaken the authority of the proposed secretary of Defense and "nail down absolute guarantees in law for navy autonomy in general and/or naval aviation and the Marine Corps in particular."[72] She also learned that the only way for the bill to be forced out of committee was for Speaker Joe Martin to tell its chairman that the bill must be reported out. In the Senate, Robert Taft, chairman of the Republican Policy Committee, would have to "say the word before the Senate committee would report the bill out."[73] This information, relayed to Bill and his father, sparked a letter-writing campaign by ARA members. They reminded the Republicans that they had won in 1946 on the promise of passing the Unification Bill, and if they failed to do so, it would be "nothing less than a betrayal of the electorate which would not be forgotten."[74]

Public awareness of Margaret's involvement with the bill, beyond brief references in her weekly columns, did not come until 8 July, eleven days before the bill passed the House. She and Lt. General Jimmie Doolittle, the famed Air Force leader of the bombing of Tokyo, teamed up to advocate passage of H.R. 4214 in a radio debate on the "American Forum of the Air."[75] On the negative side was Melvin Maas, current president of the Marine Reserve Officers Association and former congressman who had served with Margaret on Naval Affairs, and Congressman Harry Sheppard, past chairman of the House Naval Appropriations Subcommittee. In response to a "request" from Margaret, Bill began immediately to coach her "in every detail of the subject" and help her to prepare an opening and a closing statement.[76] Two questions were sure to be brought up by opponents of Unification, and to answer them, she needed the help of the Air Force. How much would it cost? Why was it called "Unification" when functions such as procurement, transportation, etc. were not going to be unified?

In an interesting twist, the Air Force claimed that there weren't any answers to such questions and refused to help her. On the day of the debate, when the questions came as expected, General Doolittle, who had spent the afternoon with the Air Force public relations office, was fully prepared. He presented a detailed financial cost analysis of what Unification would cost, as well as what would be saved. The change would cost an additional two million dollars annually but would save one hundred million annually.[77] Had the Air Force withheld information from her because she was a woman, or because she was a civilian? Probably both. During this period "it was standard practice in the Air Staff to delay or stonewall a reply or to provide an arbitrary, uncooperative answer," even to requests from Secretary of Defense Jim Forrestal, presumably because he was both a civilian and a former secretary of the Navy, write Hoopes and Brinkley.[78] Such insularity was for Margaret and the Air Force, however, a hint of things to come. In any event, Doolittle stole the show, though Margaret's performance received good reviews.

A benefit of her involvement was the notice she received from the National Commander of the American Legion, an organization which at war's end boasted 2,000,000 members. So impressed was Commander Paul Griffith that he departed from his prepared statement to the Armed Services Committee on Universal Military Training to "congratulate the lady of the committee for her fine presentation on the subject of Unification on the air last night. It was a very intelligent presentation," he continued, "and as National Commander . . . I am very happy to know that she is serving as a member of this committee."[79] She was also praised by the *Portland Press Herald* in an editorial on 11 July 1947.

On 9 July 1947, the day after the debate, the Senate passed its own Unification Bill by voice vote. On 16 July the House Expenditures Committee finally reported out its bill, and the House passed it on 19 July by a voice vote. A Senate-House Conference Committee ironed out the differences, and on 26 July, one day before Congress adjourned, President Truman signed the National Security Act of 1947 into law.

On the same day the president signed the bill, Bill Lewis, Sr. was already writing to friends and colleagues to ask a favor for his son. "Several members of congress on both sides of the Capitol," he wrote, "as well as both the Republican and Democratic parties are supporting Bill, Jr. for a position of Assistant Secretary of the Air Force . . . in recognition of services he rendered with the passage of the Unification Bill. . . . Both he and I would appreciate it if you would write . . . the President a letter of indorsement [sic]. . . . Please be assured that we shall be deeply indebted to both the senator and you for any help you may give in this matter."[80] Over fifty pieces of correspondence making similar requests or responding to such requests, written between 26 July and 30 August 1947, are extant. Margaret herself wrote to John R. Steelman, assistant to the president, and David Niles, also on the White House staff, as well as to the president himself.[81]

The appointment would have been a coup for the thirty-five year old

lawyer and a source of pride to his family. Despite the best efforts of
Nelle, Bill Lewis, Sr., and Margaret, however, Bill Lewis' just reward for
helping to establish the Air Force as a separate branch of the service was
to be delayed for some years, though not ultimately denied him. Four
years after passage of Unification, Bill Lewis—who had resigned his
Naval commission on 28 April 1947—was promoted to a full colonel in
the Air Reserve, and by 1966 he held the rank of major general in the
USAF (Reserve).

While the event's importance to Bill's career is evident, its psychic
benefits can be inferred from Bill's heightened fondness for being photographed in uniform after he won his two stars. More photos of Major
General Lewis are extant than of Bill at lower rank. Moreover, by the
time of his death, his professional resume bore the title, "Major General
William C. Lewis, Jr.," an interesting choice for a man whose professional career had been made in Congress. Bill's father became a
brigadier general (USAF, Res) on 19 February 1948. When Bill Jr.
became a major general, however, he surpassed his dashing and handsome father and laid claim to his own manhood. The victory for
Unification ultimately brought Bill rich rewards indeed.

Margaret's benefits were less obvious, though two years after
Unification passed, she received a commission in the U.S. Air Force
Reserve. The move was instigated by a Maine man, George S. Robinson,
who was legal advisor and special assistant to the director of Air Force
Legislative Liaison. In gratitude for Margaret's help with the creation of
a separate Air Force, he proposed that "the Air Force get her before the
Navy" snatched her up, and in 1949 she became a lt. colonel.[82] Her commission placed her in the company of extraordinary women like Mildred
McAfee, captain in the Women's Naval Reserve and (in civilian life)
president of Wellesley College, with whom she had become friendly in
1944. But it also made public the existence of the buried self that
Margaret had rediscovered during the war years. Unlike Bill, however,
she was seldom photographed in uniform, other than in official Air Force
photographs. The uniform and the trappings of command would have
made palpable that part of Margaret which defied a conventional female
role. Her choice was the decision of someone who did not quite trust
public sentiment on the issue of women and the military, and who did

not care to be identified as a symbol of defiance in the ongoing debate on woman's place.

Nonetheless, as she had earlier named herself, so during her seven years in Congress she had made a place for herself. She had not come to Washington to do congressional housework or attend exclusively to women's issues. Her support of a strong defense policy was the place on the canvas from which she had begun to paint her picture, even before she ran for Congress, and it ultimately became the source of an enduring identity. In the early forties, it had caused her to break with her own party and expand the part of herself which was non-traditional. Though she was not again to lead a major fight for military women, the military itself would continue to attract her for the next twenty-five years, both as a pathway to the most powerful committees in Congress where Bill's knowledge and connections would be invaluable, and as an end in itself. Consistently throughout the years of the Cold War, Margaret would devote her attention to a strong Reserve and military preparedness. In the male domain of conquest and courage, in which infrequently a lone woman has risen to prominence, Margaret would make a place for herself.

More than anything else, Margaret's involvement with the military and her willingness to do battle freed her from the constraints of gender. Though she appeared impeccably "feminine" in appearance and demeanor, a rose always on her lapel, the journey she was making had little to do with twentieth century femininity. Her need—perhaps heightened by the disappearance of women at the highest levels of the Party—had impelled her to find her own small door beneath the wall. And once she had passed through it to deal with what had always been thought to be a male concern, she entered a new orbit, one with epic sweep, but one for which she had been preparing from her earliest days on the basketball court.

5. *The 1948 Senate Race*

ON 1 JUNE 1947, Margaret became a candidate for the seat of U.S. Senator Wallace H. White, a decision which she made "strictly contingent" on Senator White's decision to retire.[83] Finally she confirmed what the pundits had suspected for some time—that she was Senate-bound.

Contrary to the myth which Margaret herself helped to perpetuate, however, her eye had been on the Senate well in advance of Senator White's announcement.[84] Not only had White's impending retirement been forecast by Maine newspapers for over a year, making his decision anticlimactic, but Margaret had first publicly—albeit obliquely—indicated her interest in running as early 19 November 1946. In a letter to a constituent, after claiming to have "'no career plans' except to carry on successfully as the representative of the people of the Second District," Margaret ended the letter with a tantalizing quote. "Doris Fleeson," she wrote, "says 'Margaret Smith, Representative of Maine, a Capitol favorite, is building an excellent record which may put her into the Senate to succeed aging Wallace White.' Sincerely yours, Margaret Chase Smith."[85] Though Clyde's practice of remaining aloof from the zealous pursuit of office was by 1947 part of her political arsenal, so was a high degree of readiness. When a Senate seat became available, greatness would not have to be forced upon her. She was more than ready.

In early July, with Congress still in session, she announced that she would cover the entire state of Maine during the next six to eight months and would spend considerable time there in late summer and early fall. She also announced that she would make a European inspection trip with the House Armed Services Committee.[86] By the end of the month, the 80th Congress adjourned with its "usual hoopla, back-slapping, cloakroom quaffing and singing." Though columnist Drew Pearson complained that there was little for the general public "to get up and wave the flag about," Margaret, whose natural strengths did not propel her toward crafting legislation, had nonetheless managed to keep herself busy even in the "do-nothing" Congress.[87]

In addition to the WAVES bill, Unification, and the Reserves, she championed the establishment of a Jewish homeland in Palestine and became one of twenty-nine House members to introduce such a resolution. She also supported universal military training, though not enthusiastically, and urged congressional decisiveness on the issue so that young people could plan their lives. On 15 July she was asked by Speaker Martin to preside over the House, an honor accorded earlier in the year to Massachusetts Republican Edith Nourse Rogers, author of several bills to secure a place for women in the military. While Margaret presided, the

House discussed a bill aimed at discharging disloyal persons from federal jobs, a measure for which Margaret subsequently voted and which passed the House 319 to 61.[88] Both measures were supported by the Truman administration.[89]

During the summer of 1947, questions of Party loyalty which had bubbled just below the surface ever since she entered Congress were carefully assessed through an "independent survey" conducted in Washington and reported in Maine newspapers. In contrast to Senators White and Brewster, who had voted with the Party 95 percent of the time, Margaret voted only 77 percent of the time with the GOP. She voted against the Smith-Connally anti-strike bill, and against cutting OPA funds, freezing the Social Security tax at its current levels, and punishing absenteeism from war work.[90] Even though she mollified conservatives by voting for the Taft-Hartley Bill, her continued habit of independence increasingly frustrated the Party, even as it endeared her to the large segment of Maine voters who were themselves iconoclastic.

By far the most important event occurred at the end of the summer — Margaret's six-week tour with eight other congressmen from the House Armed Services Committee of American occupation zones in sixteen nations in Europe, North Africa, and the Middle East. The trip was especially newsworthy because of the debate over the Marshall Plan's aid for war-torn countries.

"It's a pretty sad, sick world," she said when she returned home. She had seen hunger and destruction on a scale unimaginable. And for the first time, she understood the despair that characterized many of the war's survivors. She reported in her column on the Yugoslav troops who were massed along the borders of Trieste, an area in northeastern Italy which was administered as the Free Territory of Trieste by the United Nations from 1947 to 1954. The troops, she said, were well trained "but brutal." And she told of an incident of an American soldier's mascot dog which wandered into the six-foot No-Man's land dividing American and Yugoslav forces and was stoned to death by the Yugoslavs. It was as though she had seen evil for the first time in her life.[91]

But it was Germany which overshadowed all other stops in the tour. Berlin was one of the most desolate cities in Europe, with 75 per cent of it destroyed and its citizens allowed only 1550 calories a day, provided, of course, that they could afford to buy food at all. Germany was "a country of old men and little boys" she said. Everywhere, odors and ashes still lingered from the fires. On people's faces she saw desperation, in the streets, destruction. The only solution seemed to be operating the coal mines of Germany at peak production. They were the key to the reconstruction of Germany and to Europe as a whole. Hence the coal miners, she believed, should be given preferential treatment for food rations. "Something along this line is already being done—the men being fed in the mines," she said, "but their little children loiter around the mine entrances hoping for a bit of soup or some meager crumbs. That doesn't make for production from men when they know their families are hungry."

She feared that the outcome of such despair would be a victory for Communism. It would take "very little in some spots for people to go Communistic—even promises sound good to people in their circumstances. . . . I don't think the Germans want Communism," she said, "but Communism breeds on despair and hunger, and their faces are drawn and taut—the personification of despair."[92]

When she returned from Europe, service clubs all over Maine listened to her message. "Let's be realistic," she told them, "our motive is self-preservation. But in building up Germany as a buffer between Russia there is a danger of making the same mistake we made after the last war. The Germans deserve little sympathy because they brought their present plight on themselves. We shouldn't forget the boys that were killed and maimed fighting Germans. We can't be so overzealous as to let it happen again." Nonetheless, Germany should be permitted to rebuild "only to a point of relative self-sufficiency." We must "keep enough control to prevent any action against the United States."

"Are we at Peace?" she asked. "If we are honest we will say no. Not real peace. With Berlin and Vienna surrounded by Russia and with Yugoslavia ready to push into Trieste and the Po Valley, we have much to think about." Margaret's solution was to keep the U.S. military strong.[93]

Though her rhetoric remained understated and even flat, the Yankee logic and practicality of her analysis resonated with her audience. War crime stories were still appearing in the newspapers, mothers and wives were still mourning men who had come home wounded, or not at all. The war for them was not over. Neither sentimentality nor images of world brotherhood clouded her vision. The Germans should be fed so that Russia could be held at bay. But they should be kept on a short leash. The talk and her conclusions were as tough as those of any male, cold-war politician.

The trip to Europe put her in great demand as a speaker. Everyone at home wanted to know more about the conditions "over there." She had thus come home "to find her engagement book filled" with "speaking engagements every day and on some days two and three up to December 2," as reported by the *Bangor Daily News*.[94] Her campaign for the United States Senate had truly begun in Europe.

Sumner Sewall of Bath, a former governor of Maine, and sitting Governor Horace A. Hildreth, chairman of the National Governor's Conference, both announced their candidacies before the year's end. To the Maine Republican establishment, either would have been preferable to Margaret. The last to join the field of Republican candidates was the Reverend Albion Beverage, a Congregationalist minister known for his impassioned oratory and his antipathy to internationalism. He could cut into Margaret's support among rural voters, but he had little chance to win.

Wealthy and from an old Bath shipbuilding family, Sumner Sewall had entered Harvard College in 1916 and as a freshman volunteered to go overseas with the American Ambulance Field Service. After six months at the front, he enlisted in the American Air Service, where he was commissioned as a first lieutenant. Before World War I ended, he became an air ace, shooting down nine German airplanes and surveillance balloons. After several terms in the Maine House and the Maine Senate he was elected governor for two terms. In 1946, he accepted assignment with the military government in Germany and eventually became military governor of Württemburg Baden, one of the three states in the American zone.

In his early years, he had worked on a rigging crew in the oil fields of Mexico, as a clerk in a bank in Spain, on a sugar plantation in Cuba and a ranch in Wyoming. But his heart belonged to aviation, and it was in the field of commercial aviation that he made a name for himself. He had helped to organize and operate Colonial Air Transport and was a director of the United Airlines from 1934-1945. In 1945 he became president of American Overseas Airlines, which operated transatlantic service to Europe.[95]

Governor Horace Hildreth's career, though less colorful, was similarly impressive. He was graduated from Bowdoin College in 1925, where he lettered in football, basketball and track. In 1928 he received a law degree from Harvard and was admitted to the Maine and Massachusetts bars that same year. Soon he married Katherine C. Wing of Brookline, Massachusetts, whose family was identified with the First National Bank of Boston. He moved back to his home state of Maine at the suggestion of Speaker Joe Martin for the express purpose of getting into national politics, and in 1945 he was elected governor. For much of the 1948 Senate race, Hildreth was widely believed to be the choice of the party machine, due to the open support given to him by the Chairman of the Republican State Committee, Alan L. Bird of Rockland.[96]

Albion Beverage, the last to enter, was a true dark horse. Beverage was a Congregationalist minister and a skilled speaker whose primary claim to fame "was that he had worked for Nebraska Senator Kenneth Wherry and Indiana Senator William Jenner, each of whom he gave credit for reciting his speeches on the Senate floor under their own names."[97]

Of Hildreth and Sewall, Margaret said they were very decent people. She could say no less, for they seemed the very models of what leadership had traditionally meant in New England. But the prize of Wallace White's Senate seat was not to bring out their best. As the campaign gathered momentum, they tried whispering that her morals were not what they seemed and the Senate was no place for a woman, anyhow. In the long-run, such tactics were to prove their undoing. By the 21 June primary election, they had so damaged their own characters that Margaret, with the help of her cadre of volunteer campaign workers, was able to sweep past them into Wallace White's seat. In the final analysis, it was she, not they, who demonstrated the "greatness of soul" expected of leaders in a state whose roots went back to the Massachusetts Bay Colony.[98]

As Libby had observed a decade before, gender remained Margaret's greatest area of vulnerability. As early as 6 December 1947, a "girls vs the boys" theme was being played out in the newspapers. Lorin Arnold, a seventeen-year veteran political reporter and newly-appointed state editor of the *Bangor Daily News* made that topic the focus of his very first column for the paper. "Mrs. Smith will leave no stone unturned," he wrote, "to keep intact the large woman's vote she had received in the Second District in her several campaigns and to reach out for the women's support in all other sections of the state," a claim that was not so much incorrect, as misleading.99 While Arnold's assertion that large numbers of women had previously voted for Margaret was certainly true, her victories had been won by such wide margins that one could also claim that a majority of men had voted for her as well. Hence, the impression Arnold created—that Margaret's political strength came from "the woman vote"—was wide of the mark. The only hard data available to him were the number of women registered (estimated at 64%) and the final vote tallies. As fragments from an internal male world which perceived women as having the potential to "take over," a threat which had certainly not materialized after the passage of the 19th Amendment, Arnold's assertions are interesting. But they were not an accurate analysis of who would win the election and why.

A columnist for the *Portland Press Herald* wrote more accurately: "The advent of U.S. Representative Margaret Chase Smith . . . into the Republican senatorial contest against three male opponents doubtless is the underlying reason behind this feverish activity by the women because the appearance of a woman in the senatorial race for the first time in Maine history has drawn both the approval and disapproval of voters, be they men or women." For the first time since the victory for women's suffrage, the women's vote in Maine was both feared and courted—a contradiction captured by the headline: "WOMEN STEAL MAINE POLITICAL SHOW!"100

The "woman vote" did more than make good copy. Margaret was later to claim that the 1948 race changed the style of campaigning in Maine. Candidates' wives, who had traditionally remained at home, became visible virtually overnight and integral to their husband's campaigns, even taking to the stump as the need arose. Both Mrs. Hildreth and Mrs. Sewall were "out in full strength to snatch that women's vote for their husbands." In addition, Sewall added the state's lone woman state senator, Miss Ruth Thorndike Clough, a top-notch vote getter in Penobscot County, to his staff. Then too, noted Arnold, "there are those women's votes controlled by Miss Marion Martin of Bangor, former National GOP Committeewoman from Maine, who less than a year ago was appointed the first woman State Labor Commissioner by Governor Hildreth. Certainly another interesting picture!"101

From the start, the Smith camp was aware of the volatility, the danger,

and the positive potential of the gender issue. As one of Margaret's supporters wrote to her on 11 November 1947 after speaking with Don
Larrabee, a columnist for the *Bangor Daily News*, he (Larrabee) "still
thinks the one thing you have to contend with is the one we talked about
the other day—that you are a woman—and you have already faced that
from the start and knowingly."[102]

Margaret's way of contending with the gender question was to exploit
it to the fullest. When the fierce Maine winter set in, her opponents grew
vicious, attacking her character and her political judgement. But the nas-
tier the attacks, the more stubbornly Margaret sought high ground. She
refused to mention her opponents by name—a decision she claimed
would keep attention focused on issues, rather than personalities—but
depended on the swelling ranks of supporters who called her "our
Margaret" to defend her. Through it all, in sharp contrast to the behavior of her opponents, Margaret remained "that nice Mrs. Smith."

Underneath her genteel exterior, of course, was a will of iron. On
Friday morning, 13 February 1948, Margaret fell on the ice and fractured
her right arm. She was rushed to the hospital in Bangor where her arm
was set and put in a cast. At noon on the same day, as if nothing had happened, she arrived in Rockland, 60 miles away, to speak to a joint meeting of five mens' service clubs. The sub-text was that she could take the
rigors of the campaign trail, physical as well as mental, as well as any
man. Gauging accurately the strength of her will, a friend and admirer
wrote to her after the accident, "I am awfully sorry to hear that you broke
your arm. I hope you did not do it deliberately for political reasons but I
think the sympathy always helps."[103]

Drawn to her candidacy, either by her strength of spirit or her daz-
zling charm, were numerous acquaintances and casual friends who
became missionaries on her behalf early in the campaign. They were
central to her eventual success. One such friend, Lydia [Mrs. Claude]
Gillette, was a conduit to many of the informal opinion leaders in her
shipbuilding hometown of Bath, and an invaluable source of information about what people in the community were thinking and saying. In
one letter she described to Margaret a party she had attended where "the
prize statement was made by Wadleigh Drummond's wife (who is for you
by the way) who said to the assembled multitude that she would NOT

vote for Hildreth because of his rotten appointments . . . whereupon Judge Tirrell spoke up and said . . . yes, Mrs. Drummond, you are looking at one of them!" The correspondent also reported that she had heard from some Lisbon Falls people that Margaret was not popular in that county and "that there is a man by the name of Beverage who has that area hypnotized and if he announces his candidacy all labor will vote for him . . and so it goes . . endless rumors and stuff."[104]

In an earlier note to Margaret, she had offered to hold a reception so that people in Bath could meet and get to know Margaret, even though Bath was regarded as Sewall territory.[105] After that reception, Mrs. Gillette wrote to Margaret, "I thought I'd send this clipping and suggest you drop a note to Mr. Edward True, 352 Front St., Bath . . and congratulate him on his appointment . . you met him and his wife at my house and I know they are 'for you' and she is a Lioness, and gets around. Also a note to Mr. Charles Savage, 1270 432 Washington St., Bath . . When I took your [primary] paper to him to sign, he asked me if I could spare it, for he would like to take it himself . . he owns a filling station and comes in contact with a lot of people . . a note from you would tickle him to death." Over both addresses were large checkmarks, indicating that Margaret had followed through.[106] Those few details which escaped Margaret's attention did not long remain unattended by volunteers as committed and socially astute as Mrs. Gillette. Their dedication and single-mindedness would have been almost impossible to duplicate among campaign workers who worked merely for a salary.

Thus the real news was not the way in which womens' votes were being courted, but the way in which women were central to the inner workings of Margaret's campaign. Women dominated the informal network which was its backbone. Women who were friends, or who belonged to the BPW, women who had barely met her, and women whose glimpse of her revealed a person they would like to know—a woman who adhered to the same social conventions which they had been taught to observe—all joined in a common, grass-roots effort to help get Margaret elected. They promoted her candidacy in the butcher shop, at the bridge table, at the dinner table, and at meetings of the various groups to which they belonged. They were unpaid volunteers, and they were Margaret's greatest asset in a campaign which was being run on a shoestring, with funds coming primarily from Margaret's own pocket and small donations of ten dollars or less.

The women arranged for Margaret to "drop-in" at upcoming church socials and Kiwanis meetings, and they distributed her literature. Some, like Mrs. Gillette, supplied names and addresses of potential supporters, as well as tidbits about the latest goings on, in and around their communities. Others supplied Margaret with the names of those whose support could not be counted on. Wrote a male supporter from Farmington, home of Farmington State Teacher's College, "At the Holman reception the Dean of Home economics at the Teacher's College—Helen Lockwood—who is retiring this year—said to Kay and me 'Isn't it a shame that the Governor cannot be two persons so that he can continue as our Governor and also go to Washington—he is such a fine man.'" Noted the correspondent, "we smiled."[107] Around Helen Lockwood's name, Margaret, or someone on her staff, drew a circle. By the 1948 campaign, Margaret's world was clearly divided between supporters and non-supporters.

One of the womens' most important contributions was as an antidote to the whispering campaign that was being used against Margaret. The onset of such a campaign was noted in a letter from Mrs. Gillette to Margaret. "Now here is some scuttlebutt I've 'heard' here and there," she wrote. "Uncle Percy was down yesterday and said that two intelligent men from York County were in his office the day before . . and were sounding him out as to what he knew about your views on labor. . . Uncle Percy said he didn't know much about it . . but he did say that he thought you should itemize different bills, what they were, and how you voted . . and clearly state how you do stand on labor . . and *it would stop the 'whispering campaign' which was already started*."[108]

Margaret responded immediately. Following "Uncle Percy's" advice, she sent copies of the labor bills she had introduced to her supporters for use in countering misinformation. As for other aspects of the "whispering campaign," she waited for more information. It was not long in coming. On 2 March 1948 a friend from Auburn, in the industrial heart of Maine, wrote to Margaret. "What do you suppose I heard today about you?" she asked. "That you are a Communist. Believe me," she said, "I went right into the air and made quick work of contradicting that."[109]

The rumors about Margaret's Communism and her leftist leanings

were not, however, easy to dispel. During the eight years that Margaret
represented Maine's Second Congressional District, she had cast more
than 1500 recorded votes. From the beginning, as her vote in favor of
Lend-Lease accurately telegraphed, she had a mind of her own. When
she agreed with the Democrats, she voted with them, though most of the
Maine delegation more faithfully followed the Republican Party line.
Especially in the area of appropriation and expenditure of public funds
was Margaret likely to vote with the Democrats. On 20 February 1948, for
example, when only one Republican vote was cast in the House to stop
a $6 billion cut in the Truman budget, that lone vote was Margaret's.

She also voted against her own Party on labor legislation and in the
early years, especially, stayed in close contact with the Maine Federation
of Labor. A notable exception was her vote for the Taft-Hartley Bill. She,
like many Americans in 1947, had come to believe that as management
had once been unchecked and arrogant in dealing with employees, labor
had reached a similar plateau. Thus, in the spring of 1947, over the
protests of President Truman, Margaret and 307 other Representatives,
including the majority of Democrats, passed a measure intended to control and circumscribe the union's right to strike.[110]

A third area in which Margaret displayed unusual independence from
her party was in the investigation of un-Americanism. Although Margaret
supported inquiry into Communist influence in the State Department
and elsewhere, she was uncomfortable with the methods and style of the
House Un-American Activities Committee [HUAC]. Her vote to prevent
HUAC from becoming a standing committee on 3 January 1945 and to
deny HUAC increased funding on 17 May 1946, as well as two other similar votes, stemmed from such misgivings. But their impact was to create
doubt as to her party loyalty. To some of the conservatives who still ran
the Maine Republican party, her votes put her on a par with "New
Dealers," though she voted for HUAC measures 80 per cent of the time.
Even to her mildest critics, she was a "progressive Republican"—that
subspecies who refused to make a fight against the Democrats, "New
Dealerism," or "Trumanism."[111] In any case, Margaret was not the
machine's choice to succeed Wallace White.

Two months before the June primary, anonymous circulars, purporting
to present a factual analysis of Margaret's voting record, appeared across

the state. Their import was that she was a traitor to the GOP, a "tool of the C.I.O.," and a fellow traveller of left-wing Democrat, Rep. Vito Marcantonio, who belonged to the American Labor Party of New York and was a prominent pro-Communist. Two years later in the 1950 California Senate race in which Richard Nixon defeated Helen Gahagan Douglas, Nixon depended on a variety of similar pamphlets to establish that Douglas was pro-Communist. The most famous was his "Pink Sheet," which revealed that Douglas had voted "342 times with Marcantonio."[112] In Maine's 1948 Senate race, smear sheets charged that Margaret had voted 107 times with Marcantonio and "was with him 44.2 per cent."[113]

Attacks were not limited to gossip and anonymous smear sheets, however. The opposition even mounted a letter-writing campaign which questioned the basis of Margaret's support from women. Signed letters claiming that clubwomen were voting for Margaret just because she was a woman began to appear across the state early in 1948. Their argument was that if her record were examined and she were held to the same standards as a man, her limitations would become obvious to all. In style, these letters seemed more like the work of neighbors than political operatives, though Margaret suspected they were generated by Carroll Reece's Republican National Committee and sent to Maine for signature.[114]

Gender was a constant of the campaign, though as the June primary approached, the tide began turning against misogynistic arguments. On 28 April one of Margaret's supporters wrote to her of a dinner which had been hosted by Governor Hildreth and attended by about sixty men. During the meal, "a P.I. [Presque Isle] man got up and said right out loud 'This is no office for a woman.'" The speaker was then "greeted with an instant CHILL which probably indicates that his remark might make a martyr out of you and may help more than it hurts." In closing, the correspondent asked, "Don't you think you should bring this charge out in the open and answer it?"[115]

"Yes," would have been Margaret's answer, had it not been for her unofficial campaign manager and the "largest money contributor to [her] campaign," Bill Lewis. Ever the tactician, he counseled her to wait and "let them misinterpret your silence as confirmation that you can't and dare not try to answer the charges." Once they get out on a limb, "saw it off at a time of your own choosing and place and manner."[116] Margaret followed Bill's advice and held her fire on both the pro-Communist charge and the gender assaults until late May.

The most vicious aspect of the attack on Margaret's gender was an attack on her morals. In the long, cold, dark days of the Maine winter, the rumor mill was running at full speed. Nasty stories continued to be spread all over Maine, many of them traceable to a "man on the [Hildreth] payroll that spends his time travelling around and starting nasty scandal about you," according to one of Margaret's supporters.[117] At one point, it was suggested that Margaret was "'carrying' on in Washington with men," though that rumor could not be traced directly to the Hildreth camp. At another point, it was claimed that Margaret's origins were actually French—a tale that was capable of inflicting serious damage among more insular Mainers. Tongues wagged that her name was not Chase, but rather that she was an illegitimate child by the name of Chasse, brought to Skowhegan from the Fort Kent-Madawaska Canadian border and adopted by Carrie Murray and George Emery Chase who changed her name from Chasse to the solid New England name, Chase.[118]

But the most damaging rumor and the one most difficult for Margaret to refute was the allegation that she had destroyed Clyde's and Edna's marriage.[119] Word also spread that Margaret had been supporting an illegitimate child of Clyde's for years, a rumor persisting to this day in Skowhegan, though it has never been confirmed. Although Margaret was able to ignore the rumor about the illegitimate child, her role in the break-up of Clyde's marriage was not so easily brushed aside.

At first she tried handling it matter-of-factly. On 9 March, she wrote to a friend and supporter, "I may have told you that the story was going around that I broke up Edna and Clyde's marriage. I asked Butler [Clyde's attorney] to give me some information about their marriage and learned that they were married in 1908 and divorced in 1924. Guess I was a little young to be involved. It shows how ridiculous some of the stories are getting to be." Then, she added "they haven't anything that amounts to much or they wouldn't be using it."[120] Ordinarily, Margaret's use of the grapevine as a method of containment was an effective counterpoint to gossip. But in the matter of Clyde's divorce, the ploy almost backfired. Her chronology was wildly inaccurate. Clyde and Edna did marry in April 1908, but divorce proceedings were begun in mid-1913 and a divorce was granted on 27 January 1914. Although Margaret would have been a "little young" in 1914, she would not have been *too* young, for she had just turned sixteen. Moreover, as of 1924, the year she had mistakenly identified as the date of Clyde's divorce, Clyde and Margaret had been seeing each other for six to eight years.

Margaret's inaccurate chronology was uncharacteristic of a woman whose mind ran to the concrete, rather than the abstract, and whose capacity for absorbing detail was one of her greatest assets. Subsequently, she set the record straight and released a letter from the law office of Butler and Butler which correctly identified the date of Clyde's divorce as 1914. Though suspicion lingered for some that there was more here than met the eye, doubt did not run high enough to overshadow the entire campaign.

What served to refute the issue best was the simple fact that Margaret neither looked nor acted like a homewrecker. She was easy to perceive as someone who was just too much of a lady to have done something like that. In a state still regulated by rural Victorian impulses, that assessment was essential. One supporter, Anne Dudley, stated it plainly when she wrote to Margaret on 28 April. "I think you are conducting yourself in a very ladylike and dignified way."[121] Said another woman who first heard the rumor that Margaret was a homewrecker and then heard her speak, Margaret was "the most charming lady she ever saw and a most interesting speaker," said a new convert. "She was convinced right then," reported one of Margaret's informers, "that you surely would not be the type that would cause Clyde's divorce."[122]

On 21 May just one month before the primary, Margaret spoke at an anniversary meeting of the Somerset County Women's Republican Club, the only organized women's group besides the Maine BPW which worked on Margaret's campaign.[123] The moment had arrived to saw off her opponent's limb. Her reply was intended to be as complete as possible, leaving no questions unanswered and no doubt that she could hold her own with the men. In Bill's view, "A home county audience will love to hear their daughter defend herself and rip into the smearers." He was convinced that the situation was "tailor made" for a devastating rebuttal.[124]

She began by answering the accusation that she was a puppet of the CIO. After reminding her listeners that she voted for the Taft-Hartley Act, she informed them that the latest CIO scoresheet on congressional voting revealed that in 1947 she had voted against the CIO ten out of twelve times.[125]

As for the Marcantonio issue, she showed that not only was the information in the smear sheet factually inaccurate, but in those instances when she *had* voted with Marcantonio, so did Republican leaders like John Taber, chairman of the House Appropriations Committee; Charles Eaton, chairman of the House Foreign Affairs Committee; "Ham" Andrews, chairman of the House Armed Services Committee; Joe Martin, Speaker of the House; Carroll Reece, Chairman of the National Republican Committee; Clare Boothe Luce and Wallace White. She was neither leftist, nor a traitor to the Republican Party.

Having thus dispensed with the pro-Communist charge, she turned her attention to the more delicate issue of the whispering campaign that the Senate was no place for a woman. "I have avoided making an issue of being a woman in this campaign, for I truly believe that one's sex should not be a determinant in this election of public officials," she said. "But my opponents have raised the issue—and the challenge to the women of Maine—and I believe that they will accept the challenge on June 21."[126]

The challenge was arguably to become Hildreth's biggest blunder of the campaign. He had given Margaret and the women a cause from which to mount a crusade. "The issue that the Senate is no place for a woman is a direct challenge to every woman," said Margaret on 21 May. "I am confident that the women will accept that challenge, for certainly if they are good enough to campaign as wives of the candidates of the United States Senate, then they are not without the necessary qualifications for the Senate."[127]

Not only had the opposition handed Margaret's troops a rallying cry, but they enabled her to use it without forcing her to assume the mantle of a feminist. As was the case when she first ran for office in 1940, Margaret again avoided the trap of asking voters to vote for her as part of a sexual revolution. None was in progress, she seemed to say as she appeared on the platform immaculately groomed, asking for votes on the basis of her record. That her message on gender "got through" was suggested in a letter to the editor which appeared the *Portland Press Herald*: "The time has come to forget whether a candidate wears skirts or trousers and to judge him or her solely on the record of achievements," penned the author. "If some men and a few misguided women are out to knife a sincere, experienced public servant because of her sex, it is time for the rest of the women to rally to her support."[128]

The day after her speech, "Margaret Smith's Answer" became part of an organizational kit that was sent out to every city, town and village Smith-for-Senate Committee. In addition, over the next four weeks, penny postcards—an idea which had originated with Nelle Lewis—were sent to targeted groups like the Grange, railroad workers, nurses and teachers. Many were prepared in Washington by Bill Lewis' father and mother and then mailed back to Skowhegan for posting.

In the final weeks of the campaign, Margaret carefully exploited her "underdog" status. She was opposed by men who were better financed and who had behind them strong, political machines, her ads reminded the voters. Margaret, on the other hand, had very little money and no formal machine. In response to an editorial by Lorin Arnold which suggested that the well-financed campaigns of Margaret's opponents would swamp her, Margaret reprinted his words and followed them up in a paid political announcement with her own question: "Was he right when he said she would 'slip back' when her opponents start writing checks and throwing in a lot of 'Folding money'? Answer 'NO' by voting for Margaret Chase Smith." A more explicit attack on money politics was contemplated but discarded by Margaret. Some of the rejected drafts of the advertisement were: "Is the U.S. Senator's Seat for sale? Will Maine Sell Its Votes? Don't Sell your Vote."[129] One note from the same period to her campaign workers said: "She does not have the money and professional paid workers that her opponents do. That is why we volunteers must help her." Not until 1980 would Margaret reveal that Bill Lewis had been the largest money contributor to her 1948 campaign.[130]

By the end of May, the outcome of the election was portended by several occurrences. All across the state, "small fires of organized support for Smith started lighting up all over the state," from the Canadian border to the New Hampshire line.[131] The groundwork laid by Margaret's friends and supporters was beginning to pay off. Further, there was evidence that the anti-woman line (which probably originated in the Hildreth camp) had backfired. In the 31 May edition of the *Press Herald* was a letter to the editor entitled "Boomerang." Its author, Wallace A. Ripley, from the mid-coast town of Damariscotta wrote, "a good many Maine voters received in their mail Wednesday, a letter from Mrs. Winslow, Rock Gardens Inn, Sebasco Estates . . . denouncing Margaret Chase Smith. . . . Mrs. Winslow, or someone behind her, must be a woman-hater, interested only in the defeat of Mrs. Smith because she is a woman. I have no patience with the silly notion that a woman is not equal to a man in many, if not most of the important positions requiring great responsibility. . . . Letters like the Winslow letter can become a boomerang, and I hope every State of Mainer who received it will make it hit back at those who sent it out."[132]

Perhaps most telling was that as election eve approached, neither platforms nor stands on issues dominated talk at the grocer's, or in political columns, or at the barber shop. All three of the leading candidates supported the Marshall Plan, the Mundt-Nixon anti-Communist bill, the Taft-Hartley Act, revival of Maine's Quoddy Tidal Project, federal aid to education and housing. What held people's interest was how ladylike Margaret had been. How, despite the smear sheets and the whispering campaign, she had brought propriety to the podium. More than that, she had continued to display real character, in sharp contrast to her male opponents. "Maine people who have sensibilities at all cannot help but be ashamed of the way in which the men candidates are attempting to smear a notable record and even personal character," wrote one Smith sympathizer. "Maine folks just don't do things that way."[133]

And she worked hard at it, too. After spending the week in Washington, on weekends she flew to Portland, where she faced a one hundred mile drive to Skowhegan over roads often clogged with snow and treacherous with ice. As Bill ran the campaign from Carrie's house on North Avenue, Margaret courted votes door to door, turned up at every baked bean supper and Grange meeting she could find, and spoke no ill of her opponents, even though she was "overmatched." It was a fetching picture, and not an unreasonably sentimental one. Over the course of eight months, her good manners and charm attracted those who valued propriety, spunk, and determination. And though she seemed to be the very embodiment of the middle class voters who were increasingly drawn to that 'nice Mrs. Smith,' she was a great deal more.

She knew the delicate balance between resolution and moderation, control and vulnerability, what Maine expected in its leaders, whether male
or female, and she was able to deliver it.

On the Sunday evening before the Monday election, at 10:49 p.m.,
Margaret gave a radio address to the people of Maine. It was an elaborate
thank-you to her supporters, thousands of them, "friends and supporters
that money can't buy"—and a rhetorical tour de force.

Margaret said that she had received several phone calls from supporters reporting the reappearance of the same smear sheets she had refuted
in detail weeks ago. "I believe they will mean hundreds of more votes for
me," she said, "because, as they have incensed the fair-minded people of
Maine before, they will rally many fair-minded people to go to the polls
and register their repudiation of such methods by voting for me."

The fundamental issue of the campaign, she said, was in what each
of the candidates for United States Senate symbolized. "Each of us symbolizes something to Maine voters. My supporters say that I am a symbol
of a 'grass roots' protest against political machines, money politics, and
smears. They say that the issue is simple and clear. . . . And with respectful humility, I must say that they are right."

It was an old populist script, a legacy of travels with Clyde through the
small towns of rural Maine. She told them she wanted to win for "the
sake of those things that people say I symbolize. . . . Because the victory
will not be a personal one for me—it will be a victory for them and their
ideals. It will be a victory for the rank-and-file of the people of Maine. It
will be a 'grass roots' victory that springs from the people themselves
rather than from professional politicians." She wanted to win for the
Worumbo Mill worker of Lisbon Falls who risked her job because she
supported Margaret, and she wanted to win for the Spanish War veteran
of Norway (Maine) who contributed some of his life's savings to her campaign and "who has assured old people throughout the state that I am
their real friend." She wanted to win for the World War II veteran of
Bangor, "who refused the money of one of my opponents to switch to his
side," and she wanted to win for the courthouse workers in Knox County
who supported her "in defiance of the Sheriff's machine."[134]

George Chase's little girl was both reminiscing aloud and making
political magic. She was pursuing the vote of the rural towns of which

she was a product and which accounted for 60 percent of Maine's 847,000 population.[135] Her concern for "the rank-and-file" could be translated into votes from lumbermen (a group with a potential vote of 25,000), farmers (39,000), those involved in sea and shore fisheries and related businesses (more than 70,000), and countless businessmen who helped to form the backbone of Maine's economy.

In them, Margaret's rhetoric—its very flatness enhancing its authenticity—touched something old and deep and proud. In her was mirrored what Whitman loved best about his native land—a "native elegance of soul," a shared disdain for "anything indecorous or soft or mean," a shared "susceptibility to a slight" and an air of someone "who never knew how it felt to stand in the presence of . . . [her] superiors."[136] Much was conveyed by Margaret's sketches of supporters, especially her sketch of an eighteen-year-old girl in Portland who sent her a one-dollar contribution and wrote, "I regret only two things: that this must be merely a token contribution to your senatorial campaign, and that I am not yet old enough to vote." Buried somewhere in that story was a younger Margaret, a girl to whom one dollar would have seemed like a very large sum and who wanted very much to believe in something or someone. For that brief moment Margaret both recreated herself and echoed the daily choices of people whose support she sought. For one instant, the line between actor and agent, candidate and voter was gone. In both her bearing and her embrace of their shared experience, it was as though the best of them was in front of the microphone. "God willing," she said in closing, "we will win because we have given the people of Maine an inspiring cause to fight for."[137] And that's just what she had done. She had given them themselves.

Margaret and Bill listened to the election results on Carrie's radio. As Margaret took the lead and held it, visitors started arriving and the phone started ringing. Over two hundred people crammed into Banker's small house to listen to the final tally.[138] With all of Maine's sixteen counties reporting, Margaret won all but two of them—63,786 votes to her nearest competitor's 30,949. In urban areas, Margaret won sixteen of twenty-one Maine cities—twice as many votes as her nearest opponent and more than the other three candidates combined.[139] "I'm happy, I'm honored, I'm humble," Margaret told the press.

From the coast to Maine's interior, Margaret's victory was a romp. She was good. Astonishingly so, and she had gained a glorious slam-bang fireworks and harbor-hooting victory. An ascendance even Clyde could not have imagined. Nor Carrie. Nor Margaret herself. A victory so overwhelming, so dramatic, and so clearly without the help of the conservative, male Republican Establishment that opposition to her in camps as divergent as Taft's and Dewey's was inevitable. But that would come later. For now, she was the toast of the Republicans nationwide.

When the *New York Times* tried to make sense of Margaret's victory, they attributed it to "the support of women's groups." Margaret set them straight, saying that although Maine women "contributed greatly to her victory," she "wouldn't know" whether the women supported her "wholeheartedly." "My way of campaigning and my many personal friends contributed a great deal to my nomination."[140] The *New York Times* never did figure out what she meant.

May Craig came closer to the truth when she pointed out in her column that Margaret's eight years in the House had been marked by attention to even the smallest problems of her constituents. The most recent beneficiaries of this attention were returning veterans, many of whom she knew by name. She had visited them on her trips to Europe and to the Pacific, and she had brought word back to wives and mothers as to their welfare. They never forgot her. Moreover, to the farmers, and fishermen and lumbermen of Maine, she was in her own way a female version of "give-'em Hell Harry," a woman fully capable of holding her own, with an independence that made them proud. No one owned Margaret Smith, though on economic matters which affected Maine—tariffs on foreign imports, defense spending, and the use of the sacred Maine potato by the Defense Department to feed the troops—Margaret was always politically correct.

But the real source of her strength was inseparable from a people and a region. In her bearing and style were the hallmarks of a proud people, softened by the veneer of pleasantries she had first heard as a young girl when she worked in the homes of the town elite and later as Clyde's wife—a style now burnished to a fine hue. Beneath the words was a spiritual toughness that asked for no special favors, and gave none. Her gentility pleased them, reassured them in its dignity and grace. But it was neither soft, nor decadent. It was civility masking strength. It was upper class manners with the flintiness of a farmer wrenching his living from the soil. As roses in large silver bowls could be imagined when she spoke, so could the whine of boat engines, heading out to check lobster traps, or the stuttering explosion of a pick-up truck starting out for market before first light, a combination which engendered fierce loyalty and even love.

Her voice carried the intonations of a region and the past memory of a tribe. It cut directly to the internal landscape of a people wedded to land and villages, where "the native air is pure and sweet, and the trees o'ershadow each well-known street, as they balance up and down . . . And Deering's Woods are fresh and fair, and with joy that is almost pain, my heart goes back to wander there" to "find my lost youth again."[141] But it connoted as well a shared past that was born in struggle and baptized by tragedy. In her clipped speech the audience could hear their mothers' voices, women who cooked over wood stoves and chopped wood to help the family survive the winter. And in its sharp edges was the memory of April river-drives, when spring freshets from the mountains turned rivers into leaping chasms, crushing men beneath huge, felled, limbless trees as they broke apart from a jam, carrying men forever away from their native towns—rivers like the Saco, which had once seen mighty schooners under tow and the Kennebec, which took the life of her father's brother, though he was not a logger. Behind her restraint and emotional economy lingered the fleeting memory of two baby brothers who died of curable childhood illnesses for lack of medical treatment and their older sister who, perforce, turned her back on childhood. The immense jams at the falls and the deafening roar when the logs broke loose were as much a part of her speech as Maine's lush greenness and the glories of its rural scene. In her tribal cadence and clarity of tone, she challenged the notion that all of the good ones had left, and she reminded them of why they had stayed.

Neither the urbane Sumner Sewall, nor the wealthy Horace Hildreth, was close enough to the struggle to understand or embrace it. Margaret, who was able to do both, also possessed the ability to know a good thing when she found it. For the next twenty-five years, Margaret's constituents, their hearts firmly planted in an earlier Maine, loyally turned out at the polls every six years to cast their vote for a way of life that was slowly vanishing. For them, Margaret seemed able to make even the hands of time stand still, to deliver prosperity without polluted air or water, to locate meaning and value in the Maine husbandman.

No more dramatic proof of the source of Margaret's appeal can be found than in the primary election results in the beautiful little lobster fishing village of Mantincus. There, at land's end, where actions are driven by the sound of the wind and the movement of tides, where neighbors depend on each other for survival, almost all of Mantincus voted, men and women alike. The final tally was Hildreth 0, Sewall 0, Beverage 0, Margaret Chase Smith 61.[142] The result forecast a quarter of a century of electoral strength.

PART IV   THE SENATE YEARS

1. *Out of Step*

NINETEEN FORTY-EIGHT was a great year for mistakes. The presidential race would be a shoo-in for Thomas Dewey. All the pollsters said so, and the radio commentators and columnists and reporters who covered the race agreed. Certain that Dewey would win, the *Chicago Daily Tribune* put the newspaper to bed on election day with the headline DEWEY DEFEATS TRUMAN. But Harry Truman fooled them all. Not only did he score "the biggest upset victory in American history," but the Democrats won 263 House seats to the Republicans' 171, and 54 Senate seats to the Republicans' 42. When Truman declared, Republicans are "gluttons of privilege" and "deaf to the voices of the people," the "little people" listened and voted for him.[1] Deposed as Speaker by the November upset, Joe Martin blamed the loss on the Republican Party.[2] His assessment that they had "digressed" too far from the people was a danger Margaret had foreseen six months before the November election and Dewey's defeat when she spoke in Philadelphia at the twenty-fourth Republican National convention, just two days after her Maine primary victory.

Already Margaret was a celebrity. Though officially she had won only the GOP primary, the Republican Party's domination of Maine for the last thirty-two years meant that her primary victory was tantamount to election. And though she was not the first woman to be elected to the Senate (six had preceded her), she was the first elected completely on her own.[3] Dazzled by her success, the *Washington Post* and the *New York Times* ran several stories on her victory, and Eleanor Roosevelt congratulated her in her newspaper column "My Day."[4] To the BPW, who had much to crow about, Margaret's victory inspired "thousands of potential women office seekers," demonstrating that "women can compete with men on an equal basis with men."[5] Both *Time*, which put her age at forty-nine instead of fifty, and *Newsweek* carried photos and articles about her on their National Affairs pages.[6] Overnight she had come to embody sincerity, trustworthiness, and an appealing package of old-fashioned virtues, the latter attested to by a voter whose description "Margaret is straight as a yard of pump water" appeared in *Time*.7

On Wednesday, 23 June, a campaign-weary Margaret arrived in a city reveling in late spring. Sculls were knifing through the still-chilly waters of the Schuylkill. Tulips and crocuses had yielded to roses and honey suckle Debutante photos vied with bridal portraits for space on the society pages on the *Inquirer* and the *Bulletin*—Philadelphia's primary sources of news—and the Belleview-Stratford Hotel hummed with the activity of conventioneers. A few blocks away from the hotel in the heart of the city, pigeons roosted on Ben Franklin's hat, while along the "main line" at the Merion Cricket Club, women in crisply laundered white skirts and sleeveless tops and men in vanilla-colored sharkskin shorts and cable-knit sweaters dotted the grass courts, their white silhouettes and their muted sounds a tribute to what was thought to be a gentleman's game.

At Philadelphia's southwest airport, Margaret was met at 4 P.M. by a large delegation of Maine women who had only politics on their minds—among them Mrs. Dorothy Brewster, Mrs. Selma Wagg, vice chairman of Maine's Republican State Committee, and Mrs. Inez Wing, a national committeewoman from town of Kingfield in the western part of Margaret's Second District. After Mrs. Wing presented her with a large bouquet of orchids and a blue handbag on behalf of the Maine delegation and alternates, Margaret was whisked away, accompanied by a motorcycle escort, to Philadelphia's Municipal Auditorium, where she was ushered through a private entrance to avoid the "huge throngs" who hoped to see her.

After a five-minute breather, she walked briskly to the press conference room "where she was greeted by scores of newsmen, including veteran Washington correspondents, many of whom she greeted by name." Throughout the conference they asked different versions of the same question. How had she won the nomination? "By hard work and on my record" came the reply. From the back of the room an "old timer" was heard by some to say, "If we have to have a woman senator it's a good thing it will be a pretty one."8 Asserting that she had been "her own campaign manager," Margaret said, "I believe the people of Maine want candidates who will stand on their own feet."9 She estimated her campaign expenditures to total about $16,000, "or about $1,000 for each county" and expressed the belief that her weekly column, "Washington and You," which appeared in several Maine newspapers and in the *Philadelphia Inquirer,* had "been helpful" to her.

Asked by a newspaper woman whether she believed there should be a woman vice president, Margaret gave no direct answer but said, "I think it is well to have more women in all our higher offices all along the way."[10] Before Margaret's arrival William S. Linnell of Portland, retiring national committeeman from Maine, had received a telegram from Milford A. Payson of Camden. The message asked simply: "How about a token nomination for Margaret Smith as a favorite daughter for President or vice president?"[11]

A reception attended by about two hundred well-wishers preceded the evening's activities and what might have been for Margaret the most important evening of her life. "Now Margaret," said Joe Martin, "this is your evening. The platform is yours. I am going to introduce you. You can say anything you want to, as brief or as lengthy as you want."[12]

But Joe Martin's kind words were in stark contrast to what happened behind the scenes. When Martin gave Margaret a blank check to say anything she wanted and take as long as she needed, national committee members Owen Brewster and Carroll Reece—both conservatives and backers of Horace Hildreth in the Maine race—"just exploded right before me and would have no part of it. They would have nothing to do with me," Margaret said later. "The program was all set up . . . and there was no place for me there. And they made a big issue of it." Behind the scenes in Maine, Margaret believed that Brewster had fought her "every inch of the way" and Reece had "done everything he could against me" from Washington.[13] At the convention, they closed ranks. They were not willing to lose any more ground to the progressive, internationalist wing of the party, or to women, either, for that matter. Martin, however, got his way. Margaret would speak to the convention.

The audience she faced on the other side of the klieg lights were veterans of several days and had already responded enthusiastically to the wittiest Republican to come along for some time, the stunningly beautiful Clare Boothe Luce. On Monday her attacks on President Truman as a "gone goose" and on the Democrats as a decaying party held together only by "bosses, boodle, buncombe and blarney" had all been captured on television in the first Republican convention to be televised. Her shorthand for the New Deal as the Tower of Babel and her prediction that "they cannot win elections except in the climate of crisis," had amused and charmed her audience. Her characterization of Democratic presidents as "troubadours of trouble, crooners of catastrophe" had delighted them. When Luce finished the 7-page, 25-minute speech, she received "a tremendous ovation. . . ., [with] delegates, alternates and visitors rising and applauding while she bowed and smiled in appreciation."[14] It was a tour de force.

Although Clare Boothe Luce had come to the convention prepared to make magic, Margaret had not. In fact, she was barely prepared at all. As a precaution, Bill had typed up a statement and tucked it in her suit pocket—"one of the few times that he really wrote a statement without me bothering him," reflected Margaret. "Now if you get caught," he told her, "don't worry about it, take it out and use it." And that is exactly what she did.[15]

Wednesday night was "Maine night." As delegates from across the United States joined the Pine Tree State in honoring Margaret, and the band played Maine's "Stein Song," Margaret was escorted to the stage by the Maine delegation and two national committee members. After she was introduced by Martin and Congresswoman Frances Bolton, with newsreels clicking and cameras rolling, she delivered a short—3-minute, 249-word—speech. In it was no mention of the new metaphors which had come to replace the populism of Wendell Willkie and which now dominated much of the party's rhetoric: cynical betrayal at Yalta, subversives on the federal payroll, Potsdam compromise with evil, radicals and Communists in the New Deal.[16] Instead, 157 words were allocated to the importance of women and to the Republican Party, and the remainder to what she termed "a greater aspect to my victory in Maine"—the role of the rank-and-file in the Republican Party.

Its impact was much like a box-step on a dance-floor of two-steppers, a fox-trot to ragtime. The only time Margaret was in step was when she said "I know that 'as Maine goes, so will the nation go' this fall." That statement was interrupted by applause. Otherwise, especially in contrast to Clare Boothe Luce's glittering Cold War performance, Margaret's effort seemed pokey, slow, and old-fashioned. By 1948, Republicans had lost interest in the women vote and had lost touch with the "rank-and-file," a term which smacked unpleasantly of labor unions and strikes. The GOP's disconnection from the "little people" and Margaret's isolation from the Party's psyche were astutely noted by Maine's Democratic party chief, Harold Dubord. "Not one word was said to indicate the Republican Party even recognized the existence of such an American element as the rank-and-file," he told fellow Democrats. Except for Margaret's speech, "the proceedings, including the acceptance speech of the presidential nominee, . . . [were] devoid of anything to indicate that the Republican Party will legislate for the welfare of the common people of this nation."[17]

Her moment on the national stage had not established her as a politician of rare vision and foresight. Instead, her continued proclivity for the populism she had learned from Clyde and relied on in her own Senate campaign pulled her ever closer to the Republican progresssives of the past, and away from the party of the future. In September, as expected, Margaret won in Maine's general election, defeating Dr. Adrian Scolten, a Portland skin specialist, 167,624 to 62,723, a 72.8 percent win that set new records. Said Wallace White, who had remained above the fray in the primary campaign, her election to the Senate was "the outstanding political event of a generation."[18]

But what was revealed in Philadelphia foreshadowed Margaret's Senate career. Her psychic terrain was still dominated by the cadences of Sousa, the sound of children on the green near the bandstand, and the voices of men like Clyde who had never fought in a war. In the Senate she was about to enter, however, men like Clyde and Wallace White were gone, replaced by young and restless veterans who had come to manhood during World War II.[19] Men like 33-year-old Richard Nixon, a dark and eager nominal Quaker attorney from Whittier, California, who watched the 1948 Republican Convention from the bleachers; John F. Kennedy, the lank and lean Harvard-bred son of former Ambassador Joseph P. Kennedy; and Joseph McCarthy, a darkly-bearded Wisconsin native whose campaign attacks on the shy and progressive Robert M. LaFollette, Jr. as a man who "sat out the war . . . [and] lived on his Virginia plantation while 15,000,000 Americans were fighting the war" provided just a hint of what lay ahead.[20] The territory inhabited by these men was unfamiliar to Margaret, the terrain inhospitable. With them, as with the post-war Republican Party, she had little in common. Her alienation and her continuing identification with a genteel past rather than a bare-knuckles future could be glimpsed at the convention in Philadelphia. But not even the most astute observer would have guessed that looking backward would become the central theme of her Senate years.

2. The "First" Woman Senator

ON MONDAY, 3 January 1949 a poised Margaret Chase Smith took her place in the all-male Senate. The gallery was packed. Women had come from all over the country to see "their" senator sworn-in. Many who arrived by special train could not squeeze into the gallery and had to settle for meeting her later at a tea hosted by the Women-for-Public-Office Committee, an umbrella group of 36 national organizations.[21] The gallery rippled with excitement as the gavel rang down to open the morning session.

For this moment in history, Margaret had chosen black. Her long-sleeved dress of black crepe was fitted and flattering to her trim figure. Around her neck was a three-strand string of pearls and on her left shoulder was her signature red rose bud in a small vial. In an age dominated by Dior, Schiaparelli, and Fath—all of whom were commuting to New York to design for the masses—Margaret displayed both fashion sense and an understanding of the relation of costume to power. With her prematurely gray hair pulled back from her face, she was the picture of elegance, dignity and authority.

When Margaret appeared, applause burst from the gallery in defiance of Senate rules. Later, when Senator Brewster escorted her down the red-carpeted center aisle to the front to be sworn in with three others, applause again broke out. She was the only senator to receive applause that day, despite the swearing-in of senators-elect Lyndon Johnson and Estes Kefauver.[22]

"Do you solemnly swear that you will support and defend the Constitution of the United States . . . ," intoned the president pro tem of the Senate.

She had first heard those words more than a decade ago on a gray January afternoon during Clyde's swearing-in and Roosevelt's second inaugural. And she had heard them again on 10 June 1940 when she took Clyde's seat in the House. Then she had felt strangely disoriented and unsure, with no idea what to wear and no one to advise her. Tentatively she had selected a checked dress and a silver fox coat, choices which, from the moment she entered the House chamber, she knew were all wrong. The mistake was not to be repeated. Over the next eight years, she built a wardrobe around simple dressmaker suits and dresses with matching jackets in pastel shades of blue and green and shocking pink—suitable for the House floor but which could be worn to a reception or tea by removing the jacket and adding pearls and a fresh rose. They were often the handiwork of Blanche Bernier, and their understated elegance contributed mightily to making her "the darling of womens clubs."[23] In her office closet, in addition to at least one evening dress, she kept an iron and ironing board which contributed to an "immaculate [and] neatly pressed" appearance.[24]

"Do you solemnly swear that you will support and defend the Constitution of the United States . . . ?" "I do," answered the four senators in unison. Then the senator in black crepe turned and walked back to her temporary seat next to Owen Brewster, to the left of the presiding officer where the Republicans traditionally sat. There she and conservative Senate leader Bob Taft conferred, a cameo which suggested that Margaret had already gained favor. Her support on Sunday for Taft as chairman of the Republican Policy Committee in the face of a rebellion by party liberals had been an auspicious beginning.[25] In this spirit of conciliation with party conservatives were her Senate years launched.

At one-thirty sharp, Senator Margaret Chase Smith arrived at the Statler Hilton to deliver the keynote address to a huge luncheon of BPW women from 15 states. It was covered by most major newspapers and beamed by radio signal to BPW clubs all over the country. Later in the day she would make the first "Voice of America" broadcast from the State Department's new Washington studios.

Seated with Margaret at the head table was Carrie Murray Chase. She sat very straight in her chair as her daughter called upon Queen Juliana of Holland to stop the Dutch-Indonesian fighting and to support world peace and domestic security.[26] No doubt with some surprise she heard Margaret remark that she had been "repeatedly warned" that unofficially she was the "Senator-at-large for women all over the nation." Though her first duty was "to the people of Maine," she was willing to accept "the unofficial responsibility of being Senator-at-large for America's women to the extent that the women desired." Others in the room, especially the BPW women who had called for "new women in a new world" throughout the forties, listened nearly as intently as Carrie.[27] But any impression that Margaret perceived women as a special category or class quickly evaporated. Almost immediately she asked whether there were "any subjects in which women have exclusive interests?" Answering, she returned to the themes of world peace and domestic security. "Men are just as interested in these subjects as women," she said, "men and women are no different on this point."[28]

On the subject of new roles for women, apart from her sustained support for the ERA, by 1949 she had publicly done as much as she was willing to do, even though she continued in private her lifelong quest to carve out a separate sphere for herself. "Yes, we women have come a long way in the last hundred years, but we must remain ever alert to our civic responsibilities from the standpoint of equality—not from perpetuated feminine privileges," she warned.[29] Her belief that women needed equity but not special consideration would remain in place in public and in private for the rest of her life—a principle which put her in step with women who had recently served in the armed forces, or who had gone to work during the war and had found a life of breadwinning and independence rewarding, but who had also discovered "the powerful forces which put checks on women's aspirations and options."[30] For the time being, she was in step even with feminists like Mary Wooley of Mount Holyoke, who argued that it was "time sex be forgotten and men and women become co-workers in all that concerns the destiny of the human race."[31] On 13 January Margaret once again co-sponsored a constitutional amendment which would give equal rights to women. At the same time, however, she cooperated with womens' magazines which portrayed her in a conventional role. In fact, on the very eve of her election to the Senate, a *Saturday Evening Post* photo essay appeared which featured an apron-clad Margaret in her kitchen, her hands busy with a mixing bowl and batter.[32]

Beneath the headlines which trumpeted Margaret's victory and now chronicled her ascendance were buried other matters which in a different way forged the shape of her life and career. In the first weeks of her term, as she waited for Senator Fulbright to move to his more commodious office—a benefit of the seniority system—and vacate suite 329, she established headquarters in a tiny room just off the main entrance to the Senate Office Building. The day she was sworn in, the small room was filled with bouquets of flowers. There were flowers from the National Woman's party and the Federation of New York State Republican Women's Clubs. And there were flowers from individuals. One of the bouquets was from Marion Martin. "I'm so proud of your glorious success," she had written to Margaret after the general election.[33] But from Margaret came no reciprocal warmth. The 1948 Senate race had abruptly ended their friendship, its epitaph typed in a note to the file, written by Bill Lewis, which alluded to Marion's "nerve" in so "hypocritically" writing.[34]

By now, a file identifying supporters and detractors had replaced the black campaign book of the Clyde Smith era. And Marion had found her way into that file as someone who "not only supported Hildreth against Margaret Smith, but went out and talked viciously and maliciously against Senator Smith."[35] Quite simply, Margaret had been led to believe that Marion helped to write the smear sheet which compared Margaret's voting record to Marcantonio's. Such a breach of loyalty could not be forgiven. Because Hildreth appointed her Labor Commissioner, Marion owed him support, but she didn't have to ruin Margaret.[36] That Marion may have been unjustly accused seems not to have crossed Margaret's mind, though no extant evidence confirms Marion's complicity.

Moving with her to the Senate Office Building was Blanche Bernier, who had learned typewriting and shorthand since arriving in Washington to keep house for the Smiths, and some of Senator White's old staff. Bill Lewis, now referred to in the *Bangor Daily News* as "a citizen of Skowhegan," officially joined "Mrs. Smith's All-Maine Staff" as her administrative assistant. His salary of $10,000, was nearly half of her office allowance of $23,880.[37] But Margaret desperately needed help of a different sort than Bill could provide. In her campaign, no visions of reform had guided her, no legislative agenda had defined her candidacy. She had arrived at her destination with nothing but her destination in mind, and she had given her all to get there. Now, in order to distinguish herself, she needed a post-election staff that could provide not only efficiency but new initiatives and ideas. The man she had selected as her Administrative Assistant could fill only one of these two needs. His primary strength derived from his crisp sense of organization and his willingness to be Margaret's "no" man. He was a survivor, rather than a dreamer, a master of recall with few ideas—despite Margaret's assessment of him as the one with "the brains and the judgement and the know-all" and herself as the one with "courage and popularity."[38] His invention of a persona which he believed would transform Margaret from a regional politician to a senator with broad, national appeal is instructive.

The metaphor he settled on was Joan of Arc, a comparison first made publicly by Taft (at Bill's suggestion) during a January 1949 party given by the Brewsters to celebrate Margaret's victory. Offsetting its heroic quality was the figure's prophecy of defeat and its rejection of compromise. The choice reflected the limits of Bill's inventional powers and his insensitivity to the mood of the times. Under no circumstances would the wily Clyde have chosen such a metaphor. He was too seasoned a politician to think it fitting for a body in which there prevailed "great pressure for conformity," much like living in a small town.[39] And time would prove that assessment correct. Contrary to her opinion, Margaret did not have by her side a man of soaring imagination and intellectual depth. The fact was, his vision of the quest myth for women was limited to a paradigm which delivered salvation (success) only in the shadow of death (defeat). Though Lewis's aspirations for Margaret were boundless—at least as suggested by his appropriation of the Joan of Arc metaphor—the quality of his imagination could only lead them both to political disillusionment.

3. Days of Peril

THE FIRST TWELVE MONTHS were the best. In Margaret's very first week as a freshman senator she was named to Taft's Policy Committee, the group responsible for determining party strategy and legislative priorities, and the most important Republican body in the Senate. The appointment was both a reward for her earlier support for Taft and recognition of her stunning win in Maine. Since Owen Brewster relinquished his claim to a seat in favor of Margaret, chivalry at first appeared to play a part, too, though it was noted by Frank Graham in *Woman of Courage* that the letter Brewster wrote urging party leaders to place Margaret on the committee was written and made public long after Taft had already decided to do just that.[40]

Throughout 1949 there were signs of her growing prominence. On 22 February as the nation observed the 217th anniversary of Washington's birthday, she was selected to read his Farewell Address at a joint meeting of the House and Senate. In March she was asked to substitute for Republican Ken Wherry of Nebraska as the Senate Minority Leader. Later that month, her quip on the occasion of Vice President Alvin Barkley's 36th year in Congress suggested the self-possession of an insider. "I want to join . . . in . . . [the] tributes to Vice President Barkley," she told her colleagues. "I am sure that no Democratic vice president has ever attained the place in the hearts of Republican Senators that Vice President Barkley has."[41]

In the meantime, speculation was growing that she was a front-runner for the number 2 spot on the Republican ticket in 1952. The possibility had first been raised when she was interviewed in Philadelphia and the newspapers had run with the story. In September 1949 a report that she had been tagged the Party's candidate appeared in a syndicated column by Jack Lait, who was substituting for Walter Winchell. Lait's story, which was reported in the *Bangor Daily News*, described a meeting which was attended by Joe Martin, Robert Taft, GOP National Chairman Guy Gabrielson (who had replaced Carroll Reece), Edgar Queeny of St. Louis, and Margaret Chase Smith. Margaret denied that she knew anything about such a meeting, though she said "it's most flattering to be mentioned in connection with the party strategists."[42]

Eleven days after Lait's story appeared, Margaret was quoted as saying that women should "fight for either spot on the ticket—president or vice president." Asked if she were in a fighting mood she said "I certainly am. But before you jump to conclusions, I mean that I am in a fighting mood for women on both tickets in either the presidential or vice presidential nomination." She also said that she would "make no effort" to get either nomination for herself.[43] The story was picked up by *Time* and given wide play.[44] Speculated a Maine political writer, the Republican Party, eager to acquire the reins of power in 1952 was "likely to discard its hidebound traditionalism and place a woman on its presidential ballot for the first time in American history. That woman MAY be the senator from Maine Margaret Smith."[45] In December, when for the second year in a row Margaret was named political Woman of the Year, she did indeed seem the obvious candidate should the Republicans decide to run a woman.

Though she was regarded as a moderate, her stands on domestic and foreign issues were close enough to the party's platform not to be a handicap. At home she favored more low-cost rental housing, federal aid to education, national health measures, a broadening of social security and old age assistance, developing the nation's water power resources, and revisiting its labor laws. In foreign policy she favored the United Nations and a strong military. On the latter issue, she believed that it was "impossible to stop Communism from spreading in a highly unstable world without a military force-in-being."[46] She also retained her interest in the reserves, thereby tapping into a broad reservoir of support among voters for the military. With the "cold war" in its fourth year, a 20 February 1949 Gallup Poll showed that 56 percent of those questioned on national defense supported an increase in the size of the Army, 57 percent an increase in the size of the Navy, and 70 percent an increase in the size of the Air Force.[47] In almost every respect, she seemed a viable possibility for 1952.

But even as Margaret's candidacy gained momentum, a back-bencher from Wisconsin was searching for a way "to be a major political figure in the nation's capital." Although "he wasn't sure for a time how to reach the top . . . he knew the right avenue would present itself sooner or later. It always had."[48]

Since World War II, Americans had grown increasingly fearful of a world-wide Communist conspiracy. In 1949 alone, fifteen states passed anti-subversive laws, and the United States Chamber of Commerce suggested the establishment of sub-committees on the local level to expose Communists and "Commie sympathizers."[49] Had America been "sold out" at Yalta? Was the state department riddled with Communists? The stage was set for a Red scare and for the rise of a Republican who would convert "public fear about Communism into a winning issue against the Democrats."[50] The man who would do just that was the junior Senator from Wisconsin, Joseph R. McCarthy.

In February 1950, he agreed to make five Lincoln Day appearances for the GOP on the rubber-chicken circuit. "The scheduling," observes one

of his biographers, "was drab, fit only for the least conspicuous of senators: the tour was to begin in Wheeling, West Virginia, and end in
Huron, South Dakota. The only bright spots were stopovers in Reno and
Las Vegas, where Joe could exercise his passion for gambling." The brief
address McCarthy delivered in Wheeling on 9 February 1950 was not out
of the ordinary. He used the familiar theme of Communists in high
places and the Russian threat, echoing statistics Nixon had given two
weeks earlier and language "almost identical to that employed by Nixon
in a speech before the House on January 26" condemning Hiss.[51]

But McCarthy added a sentence that would alter the face of
American politics for almost a decade. He claimed to hold in his hand a
list of 205 names "that were known to the Secretary of State [Dean
Acheson] as being members of the Communist Party and who nevertheless are still working and shaping policy in the State Department."[52]

In Denver, and then in Salt Lake City, McCarthy was asked by
reporters about the list. He bluffed. In a radio interview in Salt Lake City,
the number became 57 "card-carrying Communists." During the next
few days, McCarthy used "57" and "205" almost at will, as though they
were interchangeable.[53] By 13 February the State Department made its
third departmental response to McCarthy in four days.[54] The issue was
generating bold headlines. An obscure Wisconsin Senator had shot
overnight from the back bench of the Senate to dinner and breakfast
tables all over America. No one who was both sentient and literate in
America at this mid-point of the twentieth century would henceforth be
unfamiliar with the name Joe McCarthy.

Margaret's own attitude toward Communism was formed when Clyde
was in the House of Representatives and a Democrat from Texas, Martin
Dies, chaired the Special House Committee on un-American Activities
[HUAC], the group which became the model for Joe's subsequent
Investigation Committee. Clyde had voted for the Hatch Act of 1939, a
measure which eliminated from federal employment any political party
or group advocating the overthrow of the U.S. government. When
Margaret became a congresswoman she followed much the same pattern
as her husband. In 1947 her views hardened as a result of her trip to
Europe, where she became convinced of the need for a U.S. presence in
the Middle East (particularly Saudi Arabia) and the importance of the

Marshall Plan as a means for containing Communism in Europe. Though she predicted in 1948 that "Communism will ultimately fail," she also predicted that it would take a long time before Russia would "join the rest of the world and at last will we have one world and peace."[55]

When Joe returned to Washington after his Wheeling speech, he called a press conference on Monday morning and announced that he would provide the Senate "detailed information" about Communism in the State Department in an address later that evening. He also urged a bipartisan investigation of Communists in government.[56]

As the Democrats scrambled to appoint a sub-committee to begin hearings, the Republicans had to make a decision as to whether they would follow the lead of the junior Senator from Wisconsin. From the oracle Bob Taft came support for the course McCarthy was pursuing; Maine's Owen Brewster, New Hampshire's Styles Bridges, California's William F. Knowland, South Dakota's Karl Mundt, Nebraska's Kenneth Wherry, and Indiana's Homer Capehart also rallied to his cause.[57] By the time the Tydings Committee began its hearings, the conservative wing of the Republican Party had committed itself to McCarthy's program.

Meanwhile, Margaret "made it a point to go to the Senate floor repeatedly to listen to his speeches." His claim to "'hold in my hand a photostatic copy,' had a most impressive tone and ring of authenticity," she said. "It looked as though Joe was on to something disturbing and frightening."[58] One day, she asked to look at the photostatic copy. At first glance it was "impressive" and "appeared to be authentic," though she did not clearly see its relevance to Joe's charges, a reservation she discounted, however, because she was not a lawyer.[59]

Over the next few months her misgivings increased. The more familiar she became with the papers he had in his hand, "the less [she] could understand what he was up to." Increasingly she began to "wonder whether she was as stupid as [she] thought," and she began to question the "validity, accuracy, credibility and fairness of Joe McCarthy's charges." She told Joe "in a friendly manner" that she "was concerned because he couldn't produce evidence to back up his serious charges against people." When he protested that he had shown her the photostatic copies, she answered, "Perhaps I'm stupid, Joe. But they don't prove a thing to me that backs up your charge." Finally, she told him she wanted to see the proof. "I have been waiting a long time now," she said, "for the proof."[60]

From the outset, Joe McCarthy had been a likely candidate for Margaret's disapproval. The only time she was in his company socially was at a dinner given by columnist May Craig. May often gave dinners for newcomers or people who were up and coming, and Margaret's name often appeared on the list of invitees. Once she invited Margaret to meet someone she called "a most charming, coming young man," and she sat them next to each other at the dinner. Margaret "was not charmed," even though "the girls were really chasing him a good deal." She simply didn't see "anything of particular interest or attraction to him."[61]

By the time they met, Margaret was 52. She had preceded Joe into Congress by six years, though he beat her into the Senate by two, making him the more senior. He had worked his way through Marquette University, then a school of 500 students in Milwaukee, by washing dishes, doing yard work, odd jobs and construction, and managing two service stations. For fun, he boxed. Though it was said he was slow and not a particularly good puncher, he was "strong and absolutely fearless," a "slugger more than a boxer."[62] Even with a law degree, a judgeship, and a stint in the Marines, the persona of a boxer was the one he brought with him to the Senate, and this was the side of Joe McCarthy that was bound to clash with the hard-won gentility of Margaret Chase Smith.

Actually, as is often the case with people who repel each other, the two had much in common. Like Margaret, Joe had gained his niche by hard work and grit and was as tireless in the pursuit of a goal and as hard to dissuade once a path had been chosen. Like her, he had pulled off a remarkable upset to reach the Senate, with part of his success attributable to his commitment to send a "personalized" McCarthy post card to every voter in Wisconsin, the same strategy Margaret had employed when Bill Lewis, Sr. sent penny postcards to 63,000 petition signers in Maine's primary.[63] Also like Margaret, Joe McCarthy had considerable charm and ambition, although he never felt the need to camouflage the latter as she did.

On the second day after his arrival in Washington as Senator-elect, he called a news conference, a brief account of which appeared in the *New York Times*. Quickly he began to make friends with newsmen, a pattern followed earlier by Margaret and which had resulted for her in important ties with Doris Fleeson and May Craig.

Though the similarities between Margaret and Joe were striking, their differences, of course, set the stage for their inevitable enmity. In contrast to the well-groomed, gray-haired Margaret, Joe McCarthy was rumpled and slovenly, a boxer in a business suit. But he was a man with a mission.

Between February and June 1950, even in places as remote as Maine, despite Joe's continuing problem of jumbling numbers, he was attracting headlines on a weekly basis and averaging ten major news stories a month. At the start of his anti-Communist campaign, Joe announced that he would "tell this story over and over until the public gets so tired of it the administration will have to clean up the mess." It was one promise Joe McCarthy would keep.[64]

But Joe was careless. The number of Communists he cited changed from 205, to 57 to 81. Old anti-Communist hands saw through him, recognized his bluffing for what it was, and accurately assessed him as a "reckless novice" who might, if exposed by the Democrats, cripple or destroy "the Red Scare that had been building since the 1948 elections" and on which the Republicans were counting to unseat Truman.[65] Meanwhile the right-wingers, including FBI Director J. Edgar Hoover, continued to rally to his cause, while reporters such as Jack Anderson dug out information for him.

Margaret watched as the Tydings Committee, appointed to investigate "whether persons who are disloyal to the United States are or have been employed by the Department of State," met on 8 March 1950 in the Senate Caucus Room.[66] Their first witness (after Joe) was Dorothy Kenyon, a sixty-two-year-old attorney and former municipal judge who was currently "in a high State Department position" and belonged to "28 organizations cited by the Attorney General and House and Senate Committees 'as subversive or disloyal.'"[67] But Kenyon was not and had never been a Communist, and when she heard Joe's charges, she told reporters: "Senator McCarthy is a liar." Then she herself asked to appear before the Tydings Committee.

During her presentation, she spoke out forcefully against guilt by association and loss of due process. [68] Applause broke out in the middle of her testimony, and Tydings warned the audience not to interrupt the hearing again. In the judgment of the *Washington Post*, Dorothy Kenyon [Case No. 1] "turned out to be not only an outraged and innocent American, but a woman of spirit.[69] Her "successful" defiance of Joe, and the audience's widely-reported response may have strengthened Margaret's growing belief that she should speak out against McCarthy's tactics.

Meanwhile, McCarthy continued to grab headlines. On 21 March he announced that he had given Tydings "the name of the man—connected with the State Department—whom I consider the top Russian espionage agent in this country.[70] For the next eight weeks, Owen Lattimore, McCarthy's "top spy," a bespectacled 49-year-old Johns Hopkins University professor whose area of expertise was Far East policy, and who had advised the State Department to stop its support of Chiang Kai-shek and withdraw from "entanglements in South Korea," was unsuccessfully attacked by Joe. By early May, when Lattimore made his final appearance before the committee, the members agreed that McCarthy's charges of treason had not been substantiated.[71]

In May newspaper articles began to report that Senate Republicans were split by a move "among some of their members to seek an early end to the inquiry into Senator McCarthy's Communist-in-government charges.[72] Reports leaked out that Senator Bourke Hickenlooper [R-Iowa] and Henry Cabot Lodge [R-Mass.], members of the Tydings Committee, might walk out, while "two G.O.P. senators who asked not to be quoted by name told a reporter they are looking around for some method of winding up an affair they said they don't think is ever going to bring a clear cut decision one way or the other on McCarthy's charges."[73] Many Republicans, like the public itself, felt that while McCarthy's allegations were not literally true, he could be on to something too big to ignore. Besides, McCarthy's ability to capitalize on the Communist threat and bludgeon both the New Deal and the Fair Deal were exactly what was called for if the Republicans were to capture the White House in 1952.

Even before the Kenyon incident, Margaret was out of patience with Joe. "You can't stop Communism merely by calling it names," she said, pointing out "the injury that was done by the increasing political trick of calling your opponent a Communist when you couldn't find anything else to smear him with." Then, without mentioning McCarthy by name, she recommended an alternative to his methods. Infiltration, "going right in to the Communist cells and learning their secrets, getting their names and exposing them," as the FBI was doing quietly and without sensationalism, was "the most effective deterrent we have to Communism, not the congressional committees."[74] She also advocated student exchange between the countries of the world "as a way of planting the idea of democratic freedom in the minds of other peoples."[75]

By May, with most of the Democrats silenced and the Republicans presenting a solid front of support for McCarthy's crusade to root out Communists from the Truman State Department and the Executive branch, Margaret knew she wanted to *do* something. In a fundamental way, Joe McCarthy was to Margaret a shadow on the wall. A moving object, perhaps no bigger than a night moth magnified by the trick of light and shadow, blown up in size to be more fearsome than it really was, a sight to inspire terror in the innocent as well as the guilty.

But neither her Maine-generated resistance to bullies, nor her personal dislike for the man and his style fully explains why she would choose to publicly oppose a man so powerful that no one else in the Republican Party was willing to cross him. Certainly she was not blind to the potential price she might have to pay. Bill Lewis himself warned her about the danger of taking on McCarthy. "You want to think this thing through," he told her. "I think you are on the right track. I think you should do it, but you must remember that this can kill you politically."[76]

But even without Bill's advice, Margaret should have been well aware of the political risks to anyone who spoke out. During her year on the Republican Policy Committee she had observed that "top echelon of the Senate" leadership embraced McCarthyism as "an issue that Republicans could win on."[77] McCarthy may have been the pit bull of the Senate, but he was the Republican's pit bull, and on him their hopes were pinned. Margaret understood well the stakes for which she was playing. And that was the point.[78]

For Margaret the contest had irresistible allure, quite apart from Bill's motif of an isolated warrior, which in its own way certainly acted as a spur. It guaranteed a national platform, it pitted truth against duplicity, drama against melodrama. And it could wrest the nation's attention away from its desperate fascination with McCarthyism. It suited her temperament and her enthusiasms, but most of all, it cast her in the role of hero, battling the forces of darkness, a script which had all but vanished for women with V-E day. Her crusade was, in William James' idiom, the "moral equivalent of war," a means by which she could display the courage and larger vision of a hero.[79] Simply voting for a strong military and battling for women's place in the military in a post-war economy were thin substitutes for real battle. But in tackling McCarthy, she could attempt what no one else seemed willing or able to do. She could demystify him and by her example restore to the political fabric the right to dissent, to speak out, to be tried by a jury of one's peers and presumed innocent until a verdict could be fairly rendered.[80] It was an extension of her search for a larger life, and the natural outcome of decades spent in pursuit of a quest plot.

The clearest signal to her constituents that Margaret had finally 'had enough' came on 12 May in her "Washington and You" column. "Communists here and in Russia and throughout the world undoubtedly are getting great comfort out of the confusion coming out of the current congressional investigation," she wrote. "Clearly, the biggest loser from failure of an investigation to prove or disprove charges, to distinguish between facts and smears, to expose the accused or discredit the accuser, will be the American public." She demanded "incontrovertible written evidence in black and white instead of conflicting oral outbursts in nebulous hues of red and pink."[81]

Bill urged her to test the political waters and talk with the highly regarded columnist and political commentator Walter Lippmann. On 23 May 1950, Margaret met with him at his Washington home and told him she was thinking about taking on McCarthy in a speech on the Senate floor. "Lippmann," she remembered, "expressed strong approval, but he did not suggest any theme or wording for my potential speech."[82]

On Friday, 26 May Margaret and Bill left Washington for Maine. Margaret had three speeches to deliver, one in each of the three congressional districts. As she and Bill drove, they talked "very, very frankly" about the dangers of what she was about to do.[83] Though the speech involved great risk, it was a calculated risk, with some chance of a successful outcome. Margaret believed that she was somewhat untouchable. If the party were to win in 1952 they needed the woman vote, and her perceived influence with women would work to her advantage. Moreover, her upset victory in Maine with a 104,901 majority and 72.8 voter percentage had set new records and established her as a winner in a party desperate for a win. She also believed that she had the backing of the liberal establishment. Urging her on were Doris Fleeson, her longtime supporter and a liberal columnist who had "stood McCarthy as long as she could," and Ed Hart, radio commentator and manager of Drew Pearson's syndicated radio program. She saw herself as freer to be "independent" than most of her colleagues, who had "left their law practice, moved to Washington," and who tended to "forget back home."[84]

After her speeches, Margaret and Bill sat at the dining room table in Skowhegan and framed a five-point declaration. "We are Republicans. But we are Americans first" it began. It assailed the ineffectiveness of the Democratic Administration and the selfish exploitation of fear and bigotry, ignorance and intolerance by the Republicans. It claimed that "Democrats and Republicans alike have . . . played directly into the Communist design of 'confuse, divide and conquer.'" And it ended with the admonition: "It is high time that we stopped thinking politically . . . and started thinking patriotically about national security based on individual freedom. It is high time that we stopped being tools and victims of totalitarian techniques [which] . . . if continued here unchecked will surely end what we have come to cherish."[85] Its five points were straightforward and bipartisan, and they fit on less than a full page.

On Tuesday morning, when they left Skowhegan and headed south to Washington, among their papers was a document which would alter the course of Margaret's career. All day long they drove—through New Hampshire and Connecticut, skirting Hartford and Boston as best they could, stopping for meals only when they were sure they were ahead of traffic. It was evening by the time they reached the lush, rolling pastures of southern Pennsylvania and crossed the Mason-Dixon line into Maryland. By the time they reached Washington the day was gone. Darkness had eclipsed the evening sky, and no faint afterglow of the sun remained.

That week Margaret called six other senators personally and invited them to join in the statement. Margaret's friend and Vermont moderate George Aiken was the senior member, Robert Hendrickson of New Jersey, the newest Senator. Other signers were Charles Toby from New

Hampshire who was "very sincere" and "on the liberal side"; freshman Senator Irving Ives of New York, a leader of the rebellion against Taft; Edward Thye from Minnesota, a "good man"; and Wayne Morse, Oregon, also a good friend of Margaret's, a liberal maverick, and at the time, a Republican.[86] Of others who were considered, some were "ruled out because of the tendency to nit-pick on language—some because it was doubtful that they would keep the matter in strict confidence—some because they might go to the influential Senator Taft for advice, which could result in pressure against the statement."[87]

Margaret didn't mention anything about a speech, but she read each man the statement she and Bill had framed, and they "jumped on it . . . immediately and said it was time somebody did something and they would be glad to go all the way . . . and keep it confidential." The only one who suggested a change was Ives, who asked for a word change from "tactics" to "techniques," a request agreeable to Margaret. After circulating the statement, Bill said, "Now I think you should give a little speech along with it." They talked it over. "I made some notes, and he made a good many notes," she recalled, "and, as he always did, he refined it for me." Then Bill "took that speech and typed it and made the stencil himself and took it down and mimeographed it himself." Nothing could leak out. "The people in the office didn't know what we were up to."[88] After lunch, Bill and Margaret left the office and headed for the Senate floor. No one had made a slip or breached a confidence. The two hundred mimeographed copies tucked under Bill's arm would not be released until Margaret had actually begun to speak.

As Margaret and Bill approached the senate tram, they met McCarthy. "Margaret," he said, "you look very serious. Are you going to make a speech?" "Yes," said Margaret, "and you will not like it." When he asked whether it was to be about him, and Margaret told him, "Yes, but I'm not going to mention your name." Then he frowned. "Remember, Margaret, I control Wisconsin's twenty-seven convention votes," a not-so-veiled reference to the vice presidential slot. Finally, they arrived at their destination.[89]

Margaret's Declaration of Conscience was her maiden speech, as well as the first significant challenge to Joe McCarthy. For the occasion she wore an aquamarine silk suit with a single red rose on her lapel. With her gray and silver hair, her erect posture, and her still youthful figure, she was a strikingly feminine, as well as a commanding figure.

Inwardly, doubts were rising. She turned to Bill, who had stayed by her side when they entered the chamber, and said that she didn't think she could go through with it. "This is awful," she said. "I'm new here, not only a new member of the Senate but a woman. And I'm getting up and telling that Republican crowd. . . . "

"You came in with a whale of a vote from Maine," he told her. "They have great confidence in you. Of course, you're going to be able to do it."[90]

Margaret took her seat at her desk on the Senate floor and waited her turn to speak. Bill stood near the desk next to the wall, holding the mimeographed sheets. Two rows behind Margaret sat a quiet Joe McCarthy. When Margaret stood and was recognized, Bill handed the mimeographed copies of the speech to a page, who delivered them to the press gallery. Reporters turned to May Craig, believing her to be Margaret's mentor, and asked her what was going on. Probably much to her embarrassment, May had no idea.[91] Their friendship, which had grown shaky with May's strong support for Joe McCarthy, would be virtually ended by Margaret's speech. May, along with others in the press gallery, leaned forward to hear what Margaret was going to say.

"I would like to speak briefly and simply about a serious national condition," Margaret began softly. "I think that it is high time for the United States Senate and its members to do some soul searching," and remember "that the Constitution, as amended, speaks not only of the freedom of speech but also of trial by jury instead of trial by accusation. . . . Those of us who shout the loudest about Americanism in making character assassinations are all too frequently those who, by our own words and acts, ignore some of the basic principles of Americanism—the right to criticize; the right to hold unpopular beliefs; the right to protest; the right to independent thought. The exercise of these rights," she continued, "should not cost one single American citizen his reputation or his right to his livelihood nor should he be in danger of losing his reputation merely because he happens to know some one who holds unpopular beliefs. Who of us doesn't? Otherwise none of us could call our souls our own."[92]

The American people "are sick and tired of being afraid to speak their

minds lest they be politically smeared as 'Communists' or 'Fascists.' . . .
Freedom of speech is not what it used to be in America. It has been so
abused by some that it is not exercised by others."93

This "nation needs a Republican victory. But I don't want to see the
Republican Party ride to political victory on the Four Horsemen of
Calumny—Fear, Ignorance, Bigotry and Smear. . . . I am not proud of
the way in which the Senate has been made a rendezvous for vilification,
for selfish political gain at the sacrifice of individual reputations and
national unity. . . . As an American, I want to see our nation recapture
the strength and unity it once had when we fought the enemy instead of
ourselves."94

Margaret followed her speech with a reading of the five-point statement which had been signed by her six colleagues, while Joe McCarthy
sat "white and silent, hardly three feet behind her."95

Her speech assailed Democrats and Republicans alike. The
Democrats for their lack of "effective leadership" and "daily contradicto-
ry grave warnings and optimistic assurances" as well as their "compla-
cency to the threat of Communism here at home" and the Republicans
for allowing innocent people to be smeared "and guilty people white-
washed."96 It was all over in a flash. The Senate, and especially the
Republicans, were stunned. McCarthy heard her out and then left as she
was "being congratulated by several colleagues," reported the *New York
Times*.97 Other than immediate congratulations from fellow signers
Smith and Hendrickson and from Millard Tydings of Maryland and
Herbert H. Lehman of New York, whom the *Washington Post* quoted as
saying that Margaret had said "things that should have been said long
ago," reaction from her colleagues was much less enthusiastic than
Margaret imagined it would be.98 They, better than she, understood that
she had just committed political suicide.99

Public reaction was varied. Her mail, which was the heaviest of her
career, ran eight to one in favor.100 Portions of the press lauded the
speech—the *Washington Post*, the *New York Times*, the *New York Post* the
New York Herald Tribune, and the conservative *Washington Star*, which
observed that "not in a long time, in either House of congress had there
been a finer, or more pertinent address."101 Others, like the *Chicago
Tribune*, called Margaret and her six signers "hypocritical Republicans."102

Joe himself, ever careless with numbers, labeled Margaret and her co-signers "Snow White and the Seven Dwarfs."[103]

Of the periodicals, Newsweek's coverage was the most favorable, though Harold Ickes ran a glowing full-page article in the New Republic.[104] Newsweek's 12 June cover carried Margaret's picture and devoted three pages to an assessment of her career with an eye to her vice presidential hopes for 1952. The writer predicted that although Margaret's "touch of the maverick" would hold little attraction for Presidential front-runner Bob Taft, her best bet in 1952 would be an Eisenhower-Smith ticket.[105] In hindsight, it is the article's conclusion, however, that strikes the current reader with peculiar force. "In an equal-rights world, such as Mrs. Smith hopes to achieve, with women equal to men, she might well sink into the background—a nice gray liberal but not particularly outstanding senator. What gives her special distinction is the man's world she vows to change."[106] Embodied in that view was uncanny prescience. Just three weeks after her speech, hostilities in Korea seemed to confirm the warnings from McCarthy that the State Department was not doing its job, an event historian Gregory Gallant suggests further diminished "the importance of the June 1 Declaration of Conscience, pushing her even more into the background, rather than the foreground of the Senate."[107]

In the short run, there was little doubt that Margaret had just overdrawn the account created by her Senate win, her gender, and her personality. But perhaps it had been a worthwhile sacrifice. On that vain hope, the editor of the Lewiston Evening Journal provided an interesting perspective. In a 3 June 1950 editorial he reported a conversation with Mrs. Joseph B. Farrington, president of the National Federation of Women's Republican Clubs. When he asked Mrs. Farrington to comment on Margaret's speech, President Farrington told him that she hadn't "read it."[108]

Except for a handful of public individuals who praised her speech—among them columnists Dorothy Thompson, Walter Lippmann, Doris Fleeson, and economic advisor Bernard Baruch—Margaret had led a charge that no one followed. Eventually, as David Oshinsky in A Conspiracy So Immense points out, even Margaret's original co-signers, with the exception of Wayne Morse, drifted away, in the end decrying their own actions and applauding McCarthy.[109] Her effort did little to stop

McCarthy or demystify the man behind the movement. Like Truman and Eisenhower, nearly everyone was held captive by him.[110]

Slim as Margaret's chances for the vice presidency may have been prior to 1 June 1950, on that date they all but vanished. Despite heavy fan mail and a flattering article in *Collier's* on 29 July which characterized Margaret as the "spokesman for a group of Republican 'Moderates' now openly challenging the party leadership in the Senate" and "an obvious choice for the national ticket," Margaret's vice presidential ambitions were dashed.[111]

Despite Margaret and Bill's immediate attempt at damage-control—specifically by referring in the *Collier's* article to her party regularity and the speech as "her only real disaffection" from the party—Margaret's attack on Joe McCarthy had forced the Party's hand.[112] And that breach of loyalty was not likely to be forgiven for something as unpredictable as the woman vote. She had challenged the GOP to choose between Party discipline and independence, conservative and liberal, male and female, McCarthy and Smith. Given the Party's faith that McCarthy could deliver the White House, the outcome was never in doubt.

Retribution came almost immediately. On 29 January 1951 when the Republican National Committee announced speakers for the annual Lincoln Day Rally and radio broadcast in Washington, Margaret's name was not among them. A similar pattern occurred in Maine. As Republicans geared up for the general election three months after her speech, the state committee scheduled only two speaking engagements for Margaret, neither of which was in her stronghold in the Second District. In contrast, Senator Brewster was booked for seven Republican rallies, one of which was in the Second District.[113]

Seven months after her speech, on 27 January 1951 the *Lewiston Evening Journal* announced, "THEY DONE OUR GAL DIRT." In her first year, Margaret had been appointed to the Senate Expenditures Committee and subsequently to its Permanent Investigating sub-committee. After her *Declaration of Conscience*, she was dumped from the sub-committee by "loud-mouthed Senator Joe McCarthy of Wisconsin." As the committee's senior Republican member, McCarthy had the power to assign members to the sub-committee, and he had decided to remove her.[114] The *Lewiston Evening Journal* reported that when she learned she had been replaced by the newly-elected junior senator from California, Richard M. Nixon, she became incensed. She had entered the House in 1940 and had become a member of the Naval Affairs Investigating Committee in 1943, three years before McCarthy or Nixon arrived in Washington. McCarthy claimed that he chose Nixon, "because of his work on the House Un-American Activities Committee," which gave him more investigative experience than Margaret, but she knew that she was being punished. When she appealed to the chairman of Executive Expenditures, Democrat John B. McClellan of Arkansas, to reverse her removal, he refused, claiming that he didn't have jurisdiction in the Republican squabble.[115] Nor was the chairman of the sub-committee, Democrat Clyde R. Hoey of North Carolina, willing to do battle with McCarthy, though he later sent Margaret a note which said: "Let me say how much I miss you on the Committee. I am still greatly disappointed that my Committee has been deprived of your valuable service."[116] In a parallel move, she was also bumped from the Republican Policy Committee in what Doris Fleeson described as "a studied attempt to humiliate" her because of her "deviationism" from the Republican's embrace of McCarthyism.[117]

When at the end of 1951 George Aiken told reporters that Margaret Chase Smith was his choice for vice president and that her selection would "attract a large group of women, labor, farm and independent voters to the Republican ticket," Margaret's response less than a year and a half after her *Declaration of Conscience* was telling. "I appreciate the confidence that Senator Aiken expressed, [but] I am not a candidate. I am realistic enough to know that there is not even the remote possibility of such a thing happening."[118] She had privately conveyed doubts to Owen Brewster before her *Declaration of Conscience*, but she had never before expressed them so candidly and so unequivocally in public.[119]

It has been said that we get the heroes we deserve. When Margaret was removed from the Investigations sub-committee without a peep of protest by anyone, it foreshadowed the climate which would eventually lead to Army Counsel Joseph Welch's plaintive question of McCarthy (in 1954): "Have you left no sense of decency?" As of 1 June 1950, Margaret's days of being groomed for bigger things vanished, transforming her overnight from a maverick to a renegade, from a rising star to a knight-errant. Unlike the classic hero, she was defeated by a world where moral ambiguity was a substitute for courage and where real heroes were out of vogue.

Even so, she accomplished some of what she had set out to do from the start. If she had not stopped Joe McCarthy, at least she had called his hand and put the Republican Party on notice that not all Republicans were proud of McCarthy's means, even if they supported his ends. Secondly, as McCarthy supporters rushed to defend him, they exposed themselves and their political motivation by their fealty to him. And third, she had set the stage for national debate on the propriety of McCarthy's behavior, raising questions which would become more insistent in the years ahead.

Just as her impulse to battle grew out of her own personal sense of adventure, her words suggested the moral geography of New England — a stony field, accessible only by a narrow and steeply inclined road, an internal landscape with a clear sense of what was fitting and proper. It was as though the famous Puritan minister, Jonathan Edwards, was never so far away that she could not hear his great voice thundering, "Resolved, never to do anything which I should be afraid to do if it were the last hour of my life." In her crusade against McCarthy was an echo of that larger life. Yet especially in Maine, the crusade against McCarthy created a climate of ill will from which she was never fully to recover. She had stirred up a raw welter of feelings even among a few of her supporters, and after June 1950 their bitterness increasingly transformed her basic optimism about the human spirit into a capitulation to suspicion and doubt. Weekly doses of the following reveal a great deal about this transformation. Wrote a Portland, Maine man some time after her speech: "While he [McCarthy] ridiculed you, he was charitable enough not to embarrass you as much as he could have if he knew what your own generation of Maine people say about *Maggie Chase.*" From a Lewiston, Maine correspondent came the following: "You remind me of a snake who hiss [*sic*] at a mountain in your narrow-minded attempts to try to degrade the beloved Sen. Joseph R. McCarthy. Many of us in Maine really know you, don't we Margaret!!!"[120]

4. *Nineteen fifty-two*

ANY FLICKERING HOPE that Margaret might yet become the Republican's vice presidential nominee in November seemed to be snuffed out for good on 1 July 1952. On that date the Republican National Committee announced that Senator Joe McCarthy would address the twenty-fifth Republican National Convention to be held in Chicago the following week.[121] Reeves writes, "There were reports that Joe had 'bullied' his way into the convention program, but these were denied by A. G. Hermann, executive director of the Republican National Convention. . . . Asked why Declaration of Conscience signers Ives of New York, Thye of Minnesota, and Smith of New Jersey . . . were not included, Hermann snapped, 'They can't get on the program.' One Senator told a reporter, 'Senator Taft controls the national arrangements committee that selected the speakers. It's as simple as that'."[122]

Since Margaret had been on the list of vice presidential hopefuls for the last few years, the omission of her name from the list of speakers was not inadvertent. Speculation spread that McCarthy had kept her from a prominent spot on the program. According to one account, she had been invited by Joe Martin to be one of the main speakers at the convention and had been given twenty-five minutes to speak. Later, her time was reduced to fifteen minutes. Finally, "Martin called her back to tell her that it had been decided that she could only speak for five minutes. 'And you'll have to represent a minority,'" Martin told her.

"What do you mean a minority?" asked Margaret.

"You represent the women," he replied.

"Under the circumstances," she told him, "you can give the five minutes to someone else."[123]. Evidence suggests that Margaret was indeed asked to speak but on 20 June withdrew her name. In a telegram to Guy Gabrielson, chairman of the National Committee, she stated simply, "Called home unexpectedly on account of my mother's serious illness. Appreciate invitation to speak at National Convention but condition of my mother's health makes my presence at convention uncertain."[124]

By the summer of 1952, Margaret's life was in turmoil. Carrie, who was seventy-six, had abdominal cancer and was terminally ill. Surgery had been performed at the Thayer Medical Center in Waterville in late

June, but after a week she had a relapse and was hospitalized. The alienation Margaret felt from her Party and her state was mirrored in the greater isolation she experienced as Carrie's condition worsened. For the next two months, her mother lay in her hospital bed, suspended between life and death, and Margaret stayed by her side.

Meanwhile in early July, the twenty-fifth Republican National Convention got underway in Chicago. It promised to be a bitter one, with both Eisenhower and Taft chasing the presidency. Though the two were almost evenly matched in delegate strength, Taft came to Chicago with slightly more delegates than Eisenhower, and he controlled the convention machinery as well. The choice between them would be made by 300 delegates from California, Michigan, Pennsylvania and Minnesota who were pledged to favorite sons or were uncommitted.[125] The two men offered the Party a clear choice in many respects, but in no area were their differences so dramatic as in their personal styles. Taft drew strength from the Party organization and professional politicians, while Eisenhower had a "persistent grass-roots popularity quite apart from the synthetic enthusiasm drummed up by professionals." His "broad grin, which disarmed the hostile, reassured the nervous, and charmed the non-committal" was in sharp contrast to the more aloof and cerebral Robert Taft. The Gallup Poll of 19 June pointed out the most important effect of that difference, for it showed that while Taft would lose to the two leading Democratic aspirants, Eisenhower would easily defeat them.[126]

The titanic struggle between Eisenhower and Taft continued right up to the convention itself. While the two men fought for delegates, a handful of women quietly advanced Margaret's candidacy for vice president, despite her public ambivalence about her candidacy.

The earliest organized effort on Margaret's behalf began with Priscilla Owens, of Boston, who started a letter-writing campaign out of her home and tried to enlist the support of the New England Women's Clubs to back Margaret. When Margaret realized that Owens was incurring considerable personal expenses in duplicating costs and postage that she could ill afford, Margaret thanked her for her efforts and told her: "Since I am not a candidate, I do not share your optimism about the Vice Presidency for me. Thus, I am most reluctant to give any further expressions of future encouragement to you."[127]

In May when the New York Federation of BPW asked Margaret whether they could "propose [her] name through the proper channels" to endorse her as the Republican candidate for vice president, her handwritten note on their letter said, "I have no objection. I am a bit embarrassed to say yes and dislike saying no."[128] Subsequently, when the New York BPW endorsed her at their state meeting June 5-8, Margaret said she was "greatly honored," though she "was not seeking the nomination." When they pushed further and asked whether she would accept it, she said, "I don't know."[129] On 30 June, the New York BPW Convention submitted a resolution at their national convention which endorsed Margaret Chase Smith for the Republican ticket and the BPW's national president, federal Judge Sarah T. Hughes, for the Democratic ticket.

The resolution was immediately and enthusiastically adopted.

Point guards for Margaret's campaign at the Republican Convention were Isabella Jones of Pennsylvania, Ellen Mullaney of Maine, Geraldine Hadsell of California and Helen Irwin, incoming national president of BPW. Dorothy Titchener, a Democrat, would work from her home in Binghamton, New York on pre-convention arrangements and later manage the campaign of Judge Hughes at the Democratic Convention from a room they shared at Chicago's Conrad Hilton Hotel.

Long before 1952 the BPW had begun to set the stage for the nomination of women to national office. In 1937, they had endorsed the Equal Rights Amendment, which remained their number one legislative item. During World War II, they supported the right of women to serve in the military with the same rank, responsibilities and benefits as their male counterparts. By the end of the war, the BPW had turned its attention to the likelihood that "there would be the inevitable movement to send a large proportion of the women workers back to the home."[130] They lent their support to non-discrimination in the workplace and "equal pay for equal work" along with "vigorous exhortations to press for the election and appointment of qualified women to city, state and national office." The election theme was sounded in a 1946 article entitled "Women . . . Sleeping Beauty of Politics," which appeared in the BPW's official publication, the *Independent Woman*. "While no woman worth her salt will hesitate to step aside to make room for a returning soldier," wrote the author, "we are confronted today with evidence that the old balance of power is back. The solution, she said, was to become a part of the government and "learn to use politics for the purposes for which politics are intended. Otherwise, this will remain a world in which men are going to decide whether or not women shall have a place outside the home. Until we have a proportionate number of women in our legislative bodies instead of a handful, this is going to continue to be a man's world instead of a people's world."[131] Nowhere was the world more a man's world than in the inner circle of the Republican and Democratic Parties, as Margaret and Judge Hughes and the BPW well knew.

By the time the 1206 delegates assembled in Chicago for the opening session on 7 July the contest between Eisenhower and Taft, which reached a flash-point just before the convention, had become so bitter that everyone was in a grim mood. And the issue of the vice presidency was of little import except to the BPW women who were trying to round up delegate support and identify an appropriate person to make Margaret's nominating speech. Complicating matters was Margaret's unavailability, even by phone. She was staying by her mother's side night and day, and Bill was handling communication with the women at the convention. Bill told the women they should do whatever they wanted to do, though he asked that the nomination—if it materialized—should come from the state of Maine.[132] He explained that "Senator Smith did not want to place any of the delegates on the spot or in an embarrassing position."[133]

Despite the fact that the BPW campaign for Margaret had begun only two months before the convention, by the end of the first day of the convention—thanks largely to the skill of Isabella Jones, who was an old hand and a well-connected member of the Pennsylvania Republican establishment—the women had a delegate count of twenty-five.[134] Reported attorney James Blenn Perkins, Margaret's "man on the scene," so intense were the efforts of Margaret's supporters that one day Isabella Jones "lost her pocket book and coat in the midst of her efforts by being shut out of the hall, but she did not even pause in her stride."[135] On the second day of the convention, 8 July, when they were asked whether they were going to be successful, Jones replied, "I think there is a chance—slim, but still a chance."[136] At that point, they had brought the delegate count from 25 to 250, though that figure seemed to some an overly optimistic projection.[137]

But Margaret's absence and McCarthy's prominence would prove to be too much for the Smith-Hughes campaign to overcome.

On 9 July McCarthy delivered a nationally televised speech which brought the delegates to their feet. Wrote the *New York Times*, the GOP had "reached rock bottom."[138] But the *Times* did not find any allies for that opinion among Republican leaders. Taft could hardly be expected to criticize McCarthy, and Eisenhower was determined to keep his own counsel. Asked point-blank about McCarthy, Eisenhower refused to comment, saying that he would not "discuss personalities."[139] In contrast, McCarthy was expansive on the subject of Eisenhower's candidacy. On the evening of the nomination, McCarthy had nothing but praise for the general and told reporters "I think that Eisenhower will make a great President."[140]

On Friday morning, 11 July, after a long evening of nominating speeches, Permanent Chairman Joe Martin started the roll call. The results were more favorable to Eisenhower than his managers had anticipated. When the votes were tallied, Eisenhower had 595, Taft 500, Warren 181, Stassen 20, and McArthur 10. With Eisenhower only 9 votes shy of victory, Minnesota changed its vote to put him over the top, and a number of other states followed suit.[141]

For Taft, who had been working toward this nomination for years, the outcome was a "bitter blow." His consolation was in knowing that "many delegates who had wound up in the Eisenhower column preferred him." According to political scholar George H. Mayer, "the truth was that after twenty years in the political wilderness a majority of Republicans were not in the mood to gamble. They preferred a candidate who looked like a sure winner to their uncrowned champion who faced uncertain treatment at the hands of the voters."[142]

Though Margaret's Declaration of Conscience had already become her political obituary, the BPW women, who were consumed with the goal of putting "top flight women in office" and who were for the most part political novices, misread the situation.[143] When Eisenhower's nomination became official, Isabella Jones called Margaret's headquarters in Skowhegan and talked with Bill Lewis. The BPW had the Maine delegation pledged and had lined up Clare Booth Luce to make the nominating speech. Early in the convention they had consulted with Henry Cabot

Lodge, Eisenhower's convention manager, and "cleared Margaret's candidacy." Lodge had expressed his high regard for Margaret and said that "no deals had been made." It would be "perfectly proper . . . to proceed so far as the Eisenhower headquarters were concerned."[144]

After his nomination, however, Eisenhower sent word that Nixon was to be his choice for running mate. What were they to do? Isabella Jones asked Bill in a hurried phone call to Maine. Bill reviewed their options. They could proceed as planned, drop the matter entirely, or, in a symbolic gesture, they could place Margaret's name in nomination and then either withdraw it immediately or just before the first tally, having made the point that women should be full partners in politics. The women decided to proceed as originally planned.[145]

At first, everything went as scheduled. Clare Boothe Luce was seated with the Maine delegation, speech in hand, ready to make the nominating speech. Arrangements were in place for her to be recognized by the chairman. Then, just before the time came, Mary Donlon, a New York woman who (Margaret believed) had opposed her nomination from the beginning, approached Clare Booth Luce. Word had been sent from Eisenhower to Dewey to Donlon that "under no circumstances should Margaret Smith's name be placed in nomination for Vice President."[146] Her nomination could draw in candidates like Harold Stassen, who was just waiting for such an opening, and start a floor fight over the vice presidential spot, preventing Nixon from getting a first ballot nomination even if Margaret did not get the nomination herself.[147] Disgruntled Taft supporters could use it to strike back at Eisenhower, which, at the very least, would ensure more inter-Party fighting. Eisenhower wanted none of it.[148]

A decision had to be made quickly. Even though Governor Fine of Pennsylvania had made it clear that everyone in his delegation was to go down the line for Eisenhower, the regal and self-possessed Pittsburgh native, Isabella Jenks Jones, declared that she would vote for Margaret in any case, and she gave up the honor of seconding Eisenhower's nomination in order to help her. Clare Boothe Luce, however, declined to nominate under the circumstances, and the Smith-Hughes contingent made the decision to withdraw Margaret's name.[149]

When Luce was recognized she gave the following short announcement. "It was the desire of women delegates and millions of Republican women throughout the nation that I should put into nomination for the vice-presidency the name of Margaret Chase Smith. It seems there is to be one name placed in nomination. [Therefore] . . . it is the request of Margaret Chase Smith that her name be withdrawn. She herself does not wish to create on this floor any divisions of the loyalties which have not already existed."[150]

The lie must have seemed innocuous enough to the sophisticated and worldly Luce, who in later years told her friend and biographer Wilfred Sheed, "I don't have any warm personal enemies left. All the SOB's have died."[151] And it was so plausible that almost instantaneously the Smith-Hughes campaign was united in its belief that Margaret herself had called and withdrawn her name—which of course she had not done.

When Margaret learned how the former playwright and editor of *Vanity Fair* (who reportedly kept over her desk the motto: "Down to Gehenna or up to the throne. He travels fastest who travels alone") had handled the situation, she was furious.[152] As Margaret saw it, the purported "withdrawal" confirmed a candidacy she had not chosen to pursue and undermined the respect of the women who had worked tirelessly on her behalf. The BPW was deprived of a candidate and the chance to make a fight of it.[153] And worst of all, it created the impression that Margaret was willing to let others do the fighting for her, only to dance away when the going got tough. The decision was antithetical to her character and a slap at the BPW. And it could not be overlooked.[154] In spite of a report from Blenn Perkins, and a separate account by Isabella Jones which claimed that all three of them—Perkins, Jones, and Luce—had collaborated on the decision not to present Margaret's name for nomination, Margaret held Luce alone accountable.[155]

The following month, in August, the BPW were more successful in placing the name of Judge Sarah Hughes in nomination at the Democratic National Convention. When Judge Hughes gave her speech, however, she brought up the matter of Margaret's "withdrawal" and claimed that the Republicans had not allowed Margaret's name to be placed in nomination.

Immediately, Bertha Adkins, on of behalf the Republican National Committee, wired Margaret to ask for a press release and affirm that her nomination was withheld at her own request. Once again, Margaret was at a political crossroads. To go along might smooth relations with the National Committee, but Margaret had been made to look bad to her supporters, and she was not in the mood to curry favor. Besides, she didn't want to repudiate Sarah Hughes, especially when she was correct.

"At no time did I talk with anyone at the convention," she wrote back to Adkins. "If you desire further details I suggest you talk with my assistant Mr. Lewis in the Washington office."[156]

Steadfastly, despite requests from several quarters over the next few months, she refused to make a public statement which would exonerate the Republicans. As she explained sweetly in a letter to Luce, "I just can't bring myself to falsehood."[157]

In fact, her correspondence with Luce on the subject of the convention reveals a side of Margaret that stands in sharp contrast to the frank and honest persona she publicly projected. Two weeks after the convention ended, she sent a note to Luce which said in part: "I want you to know how much I personally appreciate what you did for me at the Convention. You were most generous and understanding. I hope some day to see you and orally express my gratitude to you."[158] On 5 August Margaret heard (through Blenn Perkins, who had spoken to Luce's secretary) that Luce was offended by Margaret's failure to write to her and express her appreciation. That same day, Margaret wrote a note to say that she had in fact written and "would be greatly grieved if I had offended you in any way." Eight days later, Luce responded and broached the issue of "withdrawal" at the convention. "As you will see from the enclosed letters," Luce wrote, "there has been some criticism of the way in which your name was presented in nomination at the Convention. Frankly, I was afraid you yourself might have felt in some respect 'let down.' So I am happy to learn that you do know that we did the very best we could, in view of the fact that we did not have you right there to take the important decisions about the 'timing' of the withdrawal, etc." Then she pushed a bit too far, even for her. "It is unfortunate . . . that the impression lingers that in some way, the men of the Convention prevented you from being put into nomination, and otherwise disparaged your candidacy. I feel it will help 'the cause' greatly if you would follow the suggestion of Mr. Jonas [a Republican Congressman from North Carolina] and make a public statement repudiating Judge Hughes' charge."[159]

The effrontery of this remark must have infuriated Margaret, but she never let it show. In private, she told people that Luce was to blame for what had happened at the convention, but she would not let herself get caught making such statements publicly. Part of the reason grew out of her knowledge that a public feud between two well-known political women could be the undoing of both of them. And the power and reach of the Luce publishing empire probably gave her pause as well. But the strongest reason for avoiding a confrontation with Luce was Clare Boothe Luce herself. She was beautiful, wealthy, smart, and (except for the writer Dorothy Parker) was as witty a woman as the country had produced. Her quip about Roosevelt — "He lied us into war" — was an effortless but incisive thrust, and Margaret knew better than to put herself at the mercy of that wit.

Thus, without specifically letting Luce know that she knew what had really happened, Margaret tantalized her with the possibility, adding demurely at one point, "My only comment is that I have absolutely no criticism of anyone and bear no ill feeling at all. To the contrary, I am highly complimented by what you and others did and I am most grateful and have the warmest feeling about you and the others." Her three-page letter ended with an offer "to stump the State of Connecticut for you if you want me to," a reference to Luce's as-yet-unannounced bid for the Senate.[160]

In much the same vein, on 25 July she wired candidate Nixon: "Maine Republicans are desirous of having you their Vice Presidential nominee of whom they are most proud to launch their campaign in August with objective of building up record majority to put nation on right track."[161] Survival in the Party required at least the appearance of team work. And Margaret was still willing to do her part, despite her basic dislike for the man.

Soon, torn by her mother's worsening condition, she nonetheless agreed to make some speeches on behalf of the Eisenhower-Nixon ticket and to write 1500 words on "Why Vote for Eisenhower." The article was to run in *Woman's Home Companion* in the November issue and would reach readers more than a week before the election. There was to be a similar article entitled "Why Vote for Stevenson."

In addition to concern for her mother, her hesitance came from a "surprising lack of definitiveness in the General's expression on vital issues" which forced her to speak in generalities in representing them. In the months which lay ahead, she reasoned, his speeches would inevitably become far more definite and perhaps inconsistent with the views she had ascribed to him. Attempting to reassure her, Eisenhower wrote on 25 August that he had "trouble finding reasons for [her] doubts and hesitancies. At least I can promise you that nothing I shall say in this campaign will knowingly violate the sense of the 'generalizations' on which you have quoted me." Moreover, he added, "I hope you and the magazine will give us permission to have reprints made for very wide circulation throughout the country during the campaign."[162]

But Margaret had more bees in her bonnet than the fear that she might misrepresent Eisenhower's views. She wanted to maneuver Eisenhower into repudiating McCarthy, and she was trying to use her endorsement as leverage. In the *Companion* article, for example, she had carefully composed a paragraph on "Communism at home and abroad" in which she made reference to her Declaration of Conscience speech and criticized "tactics of smear and character assassination." The paragraph ended with the statement, "Like General Eisenhower, I [Margaret] dealt in principles and not personalities." When the article appeared, however, the entire paragraph on Communism had been deleted.[163]

In late October, Eisenhower asked Margaret for pertinent excerpts of the Declaration of Conscience, in case he "found it necessary to repudiate McCarthy." Margaret was sure the call had been "prompted by reports that Eisenhower was losing support of liberals and women because of his expressed support for McCarthy." Aware of her electoral strength in Maine, Eisenhower asked that she appear on an election eve panel that would ask him questions on a national telecast. Specifically, she was to ask about his position on her Declaration of Conscience, and he was to say that he agreed with it. On the day of the broadcast, Margaret was advised by her mother's doctor that Carrie was in her last hours. And at 2:00 P.M., Margaret called Eisenhower's headquarters to say that she would not be able to appear. That evening, at 8:45, Carrie died. On the 10 P.M. telecast, when Eisenhower briefly paid tribute to Margaret and noted her mother's passing, it seemed for the moment as though the specter of the junior senator from Wisconsin which had bedeviled the

Eisenhower-Smith relationship might have been exorcised.[164] But for once, even Eisenhower's good will was of little significance to her.

The high-spirited woman who could not bear to hear Margaret cry—who was proud of the daughter who became a senator but was likely to respond to compliments about her famous first-born by reminding the flatterer that she "had five other children"—was gone.[165] She was 77. For Margaret at age 54, it was "the greatest sorrow, grief and tragedy of my life." She had "lost the dearest thing in life to me, my mother. Yet the memory of her and all that she did for me can never be taken away. She was always by my side when I needed her. It was with great happiness that I could share with her some of my success and good fortune in life."[166]

For four long months Carrie fought the cancer that eventually killed her. And for four long months Margaret tended to her needs, fitting even the requests of a future president around the woman who had given her life. When the battle finally ended, the services had been performed and Carrie buried, Margaret settled her affairs, put on her public face and with Bill returned to Washington, knowing that she would never again hear applause from the first person whose approval had ever really mattered.

The wonder is that Margaret did not give up in despair that fall. The last two years had been the cruellest of her life. The 1952 nomination had taken far more from Margaret's career that it had given it. Those who first made the claim that she had withdrawn to help the ticket knew otherwise, and, as a consequence, owed her nothing. Those who didn't know the circumstances of her withdrawal now had reason to doubt her capacity to abide. Sadly, the lingering possibility that had she been in Chicago herself, the impossible might have been reached, remained in the minds of some of her most loyal supporters. Even though the nomination was Eisenhower's to bestow, she might have made an impressive showing, they thought. Wrote her friend Blenn Perkins, who had worked with the Smith-Hughes forces, "It is regrettable that circumstances prevented your attendance as this might well have made a good deal of difference. You had wide-spread support over the country if the convention had been open and I think you are even more popular with the men than you are with the ladies."[167]

But Margaret, who had dazzled the Maine electorate and arrived in Washington at the head of her freshman class, knew that the road to the top of the party ticket was now marked "Detour. Do not enter." At mid-century, after thirty years of political suffrage, there was still little room for women at the national political level, and no room for mavericks. Women were highly visible at national conventions and were the backbone of both parties in precincts across the country, but they weren't present where decisions were being made. Word even got back through a Maine woman who was in Chicago that "the Republicans decided that they would not permit the BPW to take over," a message Margaret shared with Clare Boothe Luce.[168] Her best chance to thrive in spite of gender had been to become an exemplary party regular, but both her speech at the 1948 Republican Convention and her Declaration of Conscience had foreclosed such an option.

Two of the women involved in the Smith nomination, both party regulars, did in this way thrive. After Clare Boothe Luce's unsuccessful Senate bid in 1952, President Eisenhower appointed her Ambassador to Italy in 1953. She was the first woman to hold such an important post. In 1955 Mary Donlon, who was supposed to have brought word to Luce from Eisenhower not to dare place Margaret's name in nomination, was appointed a Judge in the U.S. Customs Court in New York City, the only woman on the nine-judge court and only the second women ever to be appointed to this court.[169]

The others faded into relative political obscurity. The indomitable Isabella Jones, who at the time of the 1952 Convention was Secretary of the Republican State Committee of Pennsylvania, became an assistant-to an Assistant Secretary in the U.S. Department of Health, Education and Welfare in 1956. Dorothy Titchener, who had helped to spearhead the campaign, went back to Binghamton, N.Y. and threw herself into BPW activities and volunteer work. Wistfully, and still bothered by the origin of the erroneous information that Margaret herself had requested that her name be withdrawn, she wrote to Margaret in 1970: "I don't think it can be fully solved," she said, "for no one will admit who did what to whom." Disillusioned by the continuing refusal of the national Federation office to revisit the account of Margaret's "withdrawal" and set the record straight about the 1952 convention, she confessed to Margaret: "I have received many more rewards and personal satisfaction from my Volunteer jobs than I ever have from BPW—other than N.Y.

State Federation and my local club." It was as though the world of high stakes politics had made her weary.[170] In this, she and Margaret were currently of much the same mind.

In 1952, as if to further tarnish for Margaret the optimism and high hopes of the Willkie years and dispel the belief that political friendships between women were possible, Marion Martin made her final major appearance on Margaret's personal stage. In December 1949, when Marion's reappointment as Commissioner of Labor was uncertain, Margaret received a phone. The caller reported that Marion had said: "Margaret Smith wants to run for Vice President and it would undoubtedly be much better if she, Marion, was reappointed to the Labor Commission as that would keep her out of circulation and for the best interest of Margaret Smith." Marion was re-appointed, though without Margaret's help. But the meaning of the slightly menacing message did not become clear until 1952. That April, Margaret was informed by Owen Brewster that Selma Wagg—Maine's national committeewoman—and Marion Martin were alleging that Senator Smith was a lesbian. Purportedly Marion Martin was only repeating something that Selma Wagg, former Vice Chairman of Maine's Republican State Committee, had said, but Margaret was never to feel certain that she had gotten to the bottom of the lie, even though she confronted them both. Rumors of sexual deviance, of course, had long been a cheap and easy way to slow down an ambitious woman with aspirations beyond hearth and home. But the fact that Marion was party to such a smear, even though she and Margaret had not been allies since the 1948 Senate race, was especially painful.[171] And it reinforced an impulse that needed little encouragement—that she couldn't trust anyone. Except, of course, Bill.

Other circumstances during this period heightened Bill's importance as well, most notably Margaret's estrangement from the Eisenhower White House. Even after Eisenhower had been in office for a year and a half, Margaret had not yet been invited to dinner, a situation about which she felt especially sensitive when she learned that Eva Bowring, a newly-appointed senator from Nebraska, received an invitation only a few weeks after her appointment. The fact that Margaret had been invited to the White House by Truman soon after he became president made Eisenhower's snub all the more humiliating. Behind the scenes, Bill learned from presidential assistant Earle Chesney that several insiders who had the president's ear were warning him to avoid association with Margaret lest it upset McCarthy. Only after she won a stunning primary victory over a McCarthy-sponsored opponent in June 1954 was the silence from the White House finally lifted.[172]

It was the Eisenhower sweep, however, that saved Margaret from political obscurity and heightened Bill's importance to Margaret. When in 1952 Eisenhower defeated Adlai Stevenson with 55.1 percent of the popular vote, and the Republicans took over both the House and the Senate by narrow margins, Margaret received the most important committee assignments of her career: to Government Operations, to which she had been appointed earlier, Appropriations, widely regarded as a plum, and Armed Services, by far the most important to her. Not only was defense central to the Maine economy, but it was still her primary interest. Moreover, it was on matters of defense that Bill's insider's knowledge and connections were invaluable.

But her years of exile were far from over. For the next two years, McCarthy held the GOP and much of the country captive, while the man in the White House stared with blind indifference. Increasingly, she would lean on Bill Lewis, whose predilection for polarities—friend/foe, good/evil, anti-McCarthy/pro-McCarthy—not only served to reinforce her native rigidity, but fostered the paranoia which had begun after her Declaration of Conscience and which was antithetical to the kind of vibrant political enterprise which had successfully launched Margaret's career.

5. Right Is Chiefly with the Strong

FROM 1950 to 1972, Margaret's Washington address was Quaint Acres, a Silver Spring, Maryland property owned and built by Bill Lewis where he, with his parents, resided. In her way, Margaret had announced the move in her column of 29 June 1950, saying that she had traded her efficiency apartment for a home in the suburbs. The disadvantages she said, were the longer drive to work, the wear and tear on her car, and the need to arise earlier than before to keep her daily work schedule. But these disadvantages were more than offset by the clean, fresh air of the suburbs, the cool evenings, the home-cooked dinners and after dinner relaxation "like you can't get anywhere else."[173]

What she did not say was that she had found a second family. With the Lewises, Margaret was enfolded in an energetic, fun-loving, emotionally-complex family which offered what her own family had lacked in terms of ambition, sophistication, and an exaggerated appreciation for accomplishment. In contrast to Carrie, who tried to keep Margaret's feet on the ground, the Lewises—who were "very good to her," especially in the 1948 Senate race—gave Margaret unbounded support, respect, and admiration.[174] At least part of the year, they lived upstairs with Bill, while Margaret lived alone in an efficiency apartment downstairs. Each unit respected the other's privacy, and in fact Margaret's quarters were off-limits to General Lewis, as his wife Nelle suspected that he had a wandering eye.[175] Often Margaret did not see Bill, Jr. until he came to get her in the morning to leave for work, but her solitude, which was by choice, could easily be ended just by going upstairs. She had companionship whenever she wanted it—by the pool, over dinner, or on the grounds. And it was companionship of a sort that she greatly enjoyed: extroverted, engaging and worldly. As Margaret put it: "My, did they whoop it up when they had parties."[176] The Lewises understood and supported her career, even as Bill, Jr. made it possible for her to devote the whole of her life to her job, a benefit traditionally reserved for the male partner in a marriage.

At 40, Bill was arrow-straight and slender, which made him look taller than his 5'10". He worked hard to maintain his sharp-edged profile, hardly ever eating breakfast and giving up his favorite dessert—ice cream—whenever his weight seemed to be climbing. He was meticulous in his personal habits, taking time to massage his scalp for five minutes a day and, during the winter, using the sun lamp for 10 to 15 minutes. But for the fact that he had inherited his mother's small chin, he might have been described as handsome. Bill was extraordinarily close to his captivating, politically astute mother, and Margaret once speculated that Bill "saw in me what he would like to have had his mother do."[177] Certainly his protectiveness and solicitude for Margaret was not unlike that of a son for his mother. He especially enjoyed "doing" for her, which sometimes meant "getting her deals." In one instance, after Margaret appeared on a television show called "Who Said That?" Bill talked the program's business manager into swapping the television set they owed her (for prior appearances) for a Crosley Shelvador refrigerator, double oven electric push-button range, a Crosley-built double sink and cabinets for her two past appearances and "for one or two more in the future."[178] He also built a television set from a kit which she used in her office in Suite 329 and which was widely believed to be the only one in the Senate Office Building that worked.

Domestic details of all sorts, including interior decorating, fascinated him. When Margaret built her house in Maine on Neil Hill, he wrote to his parents with enthusiasm about the texture of the carpet (a twist) and the color (light medium green). The living room was to be painted a Blue Spruce Green, and the drapes were to be a dark oyster gray. One chair and couch were to be gold, while another chair and couch would be light gray-green velour. "Margaret's bedroom will have the blue colors Mother picked," he wrote, "while the inside guest bedroom will be an antique white with maroon drapes. The guest bathroom will be a light green. The outside guest bedroom," he told them, "will be a primary maroon wall with chintz drapes that we had at the apartment."[179]

Bill's involvement with all aspects of Margaret's life was made easier by the fact that he was not especially gregarious. Unlike Clyde, who surrounded himself with people, Bill had many acquaintances—mostly other military men—but few close friends. His parents, his Air Force career, Margaret, and politics, it seemed, were his world. Lewis himself compared the Senate suite to a home. He wrote to his parents that he had installed a "radio-phonograph wire recorder so that the office is almost like an apartment. We can see the television at night and I have the soft, deep tone radio on low during the day. It gives the reception room a very quaint, and restful atmosphere. Even Margaret approves. This together with the refrigerator and my bar just about completes the home atmosphere."[180]

Politically, one of Bill's most valuable assets was his knowledge about what was going on outside the Smith camp. But his information came with a price tag. Frequently, he tipped the scales in a negative direction about people whose loyalties were mixed, but who were not really Margaret's enemies.

Theirs was a complex and an unconventional alliance of enormous depth. Although in public Bill was a dutiful and restrained Administrative Assistant and Margaret his boss, in reality from the beginning they were a unit of one. Until his death at age 69 in 1982, he handled all of Margaret's business and legal affairs. He drove her back and forth to Maine on campaign trips home, shielded her and lived in her shadow. His one interest, she was to say later was "his dedication, his devotion to my career"—a role which by 1971 would cause *Washington Post* columnist Maxine Chesire to dub him "Svengali" and others to refer to him as "a shadow senator."[181] Like Clyde, Bill was playful and even spontaneous, but he was not unfaithful. And his belief in her was "a great incentive." "He was so dedicated that perhaps that was one thing that pushed me on as it did. I didn't want to let him down."[182]

To Bill's loyalty, Margaret responded in kind. In return for his solicitousness, she kept a keen eye on the promotion lists of reserve officers and threw her support to matters such as Unification and reserve benefits that were of interest to Bill. He was her "memory" and the "brains" (though he would not let her say that), someone who would have done himself much of what she accomplished "if only he had been in the Senate." More than anything, he understood Margaret's need to play her part on a wider stage than marriage, and he helped to make that possible. Nine years before her death and four years after the death of Bill Lewis, she told a *Washington Post* reporter: "Some people wondered why Bill Lewis and I never married. Well our relationship wasn't based on that. He was 15 years younger, for one thing. Of course we had a relationship, of course we loved each other. But not like that. Looking back, I wish I would have made more time for love."[183] At the core of the enterprise was their life's work. Politics could be discussed at all hours, a plan or strategy devised, a resolution achieved, and equanimity restored. They were spiritual twins, unlost and reunited in an enterprise of importance and mutual benefit. Their ties were as deep as childhood, more constant than sexual passion, and more enduring than sexual love. Bill treasured best the sure-footed Margaret, perhaps the self Margaret liked best. In 1949 he wrote to his parents with pride: "Next Wednesday she will go to Augusta to a meeting of the State [GOP] Committee. She has that chin set and intends to let them have it full force if they try to push her around."[184] It was a reductive vision of the hero, but in a world that still relegated women to the home, for Margaret it was enough.

6. *"I Have Here in My Hand"*

FOR FOUR LONG YEARS Joe McCarthy cast a long shadow over the country, the Republican Party, and Margaret. Finally in 1954 his hand was all but played out. Some parts of that unraveling are central to Margaret's story.

On 17 July 1950, just six months after Joe's Wheeling, West Virginia speech, the Tydings Committee released a 313-page final report which excoriated McCarthy, refuted his charges, and repudiated his methods. The report revealed the origins of McCarthy's figures— 205, 57, and 81— and cleared the names of those individuals McCarthy had accused by name. Moreover, it pointed out that not a single Communist had been found in the loyalty files Truman had made available. With the Republicans crying "foul," McCarthy bellowed that the Tydings Report was "a signal to the traitors, Communists, and fellow travellers in our Government that they need have no fear of exposure from this Administration." And he vowed to get even.[185]

In those days, mail poured into McCarthy's office at the rate of 25,000 letters a day, and a spy planted in McCarthy's office by Drew Pearson early in 1951 told of contributions that sometimes reached more than $1000 a day.[186] Quite likely, much of the money he received found its way to the track, where McCarthy engaged in serious betting. But some was reserved by McCarthy and his friends for a special kind of horse-race: fielding candidates to defeat those who had become McCarthy's enemies.

The 1950 Maryland Senate race became such a contest. John Marshall Butler was a tall, graying Baltimore attorney who had never run for public office but was "eager to be a senator and was willing to engage in a strenuous campaign."[187] In early June 1950, he became McCarthy's choice to unseat Millard Tydings. After squeaking through the primary election, Butler mounted a McCarthy-like campaign in the general election and beat Tydings by a majority of 43,100 votes, an anomalous outcome in a traditionally Democratic state. Though Maryland Democrats were bitterly divided and Democratic vote totals in that state had been diminishing for some time, Millard Tydings' defeat for a fifth term was widely attributed to Joe McCarthy.[188] His support was also credited, though to a lesser extent, for Republican victories in races won by Everett

Dirksen [Ill.], Wallace Bennett [Utah], Claude Pepper [Fla.] and Frank Graham [N.C.].[189]

In January 1951, a few days after McCarthy bumped her from the Permanent Investigations sub-committee in favor of Richard Nixon, Margaret became a member of the Senate Rules Committee and was appointed to its Privileges and Elections sub-committee. At the sub-committee's first meeting, Margaret and freshman Democrat Mike Monroney [Okla.] were commissioned to investigate a complaint filed by Millard Tydings about the 1950 Maryland Senate race. Although they both protested, claiming that lawyers would be a more proper choice, their protests were ignored by the more senior members of the committee who, Margaret believed, were "attempting to dodge a most unpleasant task."[190] The key complaint from Tydings was John Butler's use of a four-page tabloid called "From the Record," 300,000 of which had been distributed across the state of Maryland. The tabloid was a collage of excerpts from editorials hostile to the Tydings Committee, photos of "State Department Pro-Communists," and assorted allegations that impugned Tydings' loyalty. One photograph especially drew attention. Tydings, a combat hero, was caught on film in rapt conversation with Earl Browder, head of the American Communist Party. In fact, it was a composite of a 1938 photo of Tydings which had been reversed and juxtaposed with a recent photo of Browder. McCarthy denied having had any hand in the photo and criticized its use, saying of the Butler-Tydings race, "I think it was one of the cleanest campaigns in the country."[191]

Ironically, because of her assignment to the Privileges and Elections sub-committee, Margaret was positioned to be far more of a nuisance to McCarthy than she had ever been before. As soon as McCarthy supporter Ken Wherry, the ranking Republican on the full Rules Committee, realized that fact, he offered to have her transferred to another sub-committee and off the Maryland investigation "since it involved Senator McCarthy and might embarrass . . . [her]."[192] Margaret responded coyly that she had not asked for the assignment but realized the chores were "a sort of freshman duty" and she would do them without shirking. On the other hand, if Senator Wherry wanted to remove her from the investigation, that, of course, was his decision to make. Shortly thereafter Robert Hendrickson, one of the original signers of the Declaration of

Conscience—who in June would commend McCarthy on his anti-Marshall speech—called Margaret to offer to swap his Pennsylvania and New York investigation assignments for her Maryland assignment, saying that he had been "selfish in taking the other states." Nothing came of Wherry's attempt to oust her. Instead, at the next Elections sub-committee meeting, Iowa Democrat and Chairman Guy Gillette announced that he was adding two more members and increasing the size of the sub-committee to four. All of the members of the Elections sub-committee were now serving on the Maryland Committee except Gillette, who had exercised his prerogative as chairman of the larger sub-committee to keep himself out of the line of fire.[193] The sub-committee began public hearings on 20 February 1951. They lasted until 11 April.

Various witnesses, including Millard Tydings and Jean Kerr (then secretary to Joe McCarthy and later his wife), testified. Despite three invitations, McCarthy himself did not appear, and the investigation closed without McCarthy's testimony. The sub-committee report was unequivocal in its condemnation of the Butler campaign. The Maryland election, declared the report, "brought into sharp focus certain campaign tactics and practices that can best be characterized as . . . destructive of fundamental American principles. The sub-committee, unreservedly denounces, condemns, and censures these tactics." Margaret believed that the investigation underscored the truth—that "the idea for the tabloid was the suggestion of McCarthy," though the sub-committee settled for calling McCarthy "a leading and potent force in the campaign against Tydings."[194] By a vote of nine to three, the report was accepted by the full Rules Committee with Smith and Hendrickson joining the Democrats, and McCarthy, Wherry and Jenner voting no.

On 6 August, William Burton Benton, a first-term Democrat from Connecticut, self-made millionaire, former Assistant Secretary of State for Public Affairs, and former vice-president of the University of Chicago under Robert Maynard Hutchins, introduced S.Res. 187 to consider expulsion of McCarthy on the basis of the Maryland Report. Margaret was unhappy with the proposal, though she was glad of the attention it directed to the Maryland campaign. Censure, rather than expulsion, was what Benton should have proposed, she thought. Censure required only a simple majority; expulsion required a two-thirds vote of the Senate.

They would never be able to get the votes they needed for expulsion.

But for the hubris of McCarthy, the Benton resolution might have been filed and forgotten. But McCarthy received the permission of the Rules Committee, of which he was still a member, to file a minority report. On 20 August, he read a two-hour reply to the Maryland Election Report on the floor of the Senate, during which time he aggressively defended all aspects of the John Butler campaign and assailed Margaret and Senator Hendrickson for failing to excuse themselves from the Monroney sub-committee. Hendrickson allowed McCarthy to put him on the defensive and suggested that his "arm had been twisted to make him sign the report."195 But Margaret answered Joe on the Senate floor. "Opposition to Communism," she began, "is surely not the exclusive possession of Senator McCarthy. Nor does differing with him on tactics automatically make one a Communist or a protector of Communism." In all, her answer to his two-hour tirade lasted two minutes, and she again placed her Declaration of Conscience in the *Congressional Record*.196 Only this time she was not alone in taking on McCarthy. President Truman soon lashed out against "scaremongers and hatemongers" in a speech to the American Legion. From the Senate, Thomas Hennings, to whom McCarthy had written suggesting that he disqualify himself from the Gillette sub-committee (which was to hear Benton's charges) assailed McCarthy's "devious means and irrelevant attacks."197 By October even Ohio Senator Robert Taft was telling reporters that McCarthy had "overstated his charges" in some cases, specifically in his speech against Marshall.198

On 24 September 1951 Margaret wrote to the chairman of the parent Rules Committee and pointed out that McCarthy had raised a point which should be settled as soon as possible. She asked for a ruling as to whether she should be disqualified or not from the Elections sub-committee when it heard Benton. When the committee met on 26 September, McCarthy requested by letter that the committee not disqualify her. She should do that herself. The committee voted 11-0 that Margaret should not be disqualified.199

On 28 September 1951 Benton testified before Gillette and his sub-committee. Four months later, on 18 January 1952, they submitted a 300-page confidential report. In the meantime, Ken Wherry died, leaving a

Republican vacancy on the Rules and Appropriations Committees and their sub-committees, and giving the Republicans a chance to dilute the Gillette sub-committee, by moving Margaret and Hendrickson to vacancies now created on other committees. The ranking Republican on Rules, Henry Cabot Lodge, appointed Idaho conservative Herman Welker and McCarthy supporter Everett Dirksen of Illinois to the Gillette sub-committee and proposed to move Margaret to the sub-committee on Rules and Hendrickson to the Library sub-committee assignment that was now open.[200]

Eventually, when McCarthy began to crow that Hendrickson "was doing the right thing by resigning," Hendrickson changed his mind, not wishing to "run out in the 'midst of a trial,' so to speak, despite Joe McCarthy's wishes to the contrary."[201] Ignoring the criticism from the press and howls from the Democrats that she should not be permitted to leave the Elections sub-committee, Margaret nonetheless moved enthusiastically to take advantage of the opportunity to win some respite from the battle she and she alone (much of the time) had been waging. She was delighted, she told the press, to be appointed to the more prestigious sub-committee on Rules.

After almost a year of investigation, the Gillette sub-committee hearings on the Benton resolution did little more than suggest, often by innuendo, the seamier side of McCarthy's activities. Right-wing newspapers discounted it, while the liberal press serialized it. Nonetheless by 1953, Herbert H. Lehman of New York, who had written one of the most glowing letters Margaret received after her Declaration of Conscience speech, had become Joe's most outspoken critic in the Senate. He warned of "creeping McCarthyism," which he described as "a subtle poison which has already eaten deep into the muscles and sinews of our body politic."[202] During the month of July alone, McCarthy was denounced by Senators J. William Fulbright [D-Ark.], Mike Monroney [D-Okla.], Arthur Eisenhower (the President's brother), and the powerful John L. McClellan [D-Ark.].

By the time McCarthy began his investigation of the Army in August 1953, even his friends had begun to doubt him. No one could take on the Army and win. By early 1954, McCarthy had finally pushed even Eisenhower too far. On 9 March, Republican Senator Ralph Flanders, a

73-year-old Vermont native, denounced McCarthy on the floor of the Senate. McCarthy belonged to a "one-man party" and "its name is 'McCarthyism,' a title which he has proudly accepted."[203] On 10 March at his press conference Eisenhower praised Flanders. By this time, writes Reeves, "Americans were realizing that Joe was not just an Irish, two-fist-ed, anti-Communist. He was a rather frightening right-wing extremist who was capable of attacking anyone who stood in his path. Journalists, clergymen, professors, engineers, librarians, senators, generals, Cabinet members, the President—no one was safe."[204]

In 1953, at the beginning of McCarthy's downward spiral, he decided to carry his "politics of revenge" to Maine.[205] The move was trumpeted in a Walter Winchell column on 25 August 1953, when Lee Mortimer, who was substituting for Winchell, announced: "Joe will fight back, tak-ing to the hustings in the states of his opponents, and especially in Maine where La Smith is up for re-election in 1954. (Remember what happened to Tydings?)"[206]

7. Shadow Boxing

JOE'S SURROGATE in Maine's 1954 primary election was to be thirty-four-year-old Robert L. Jones from Biddeford, Maine, a young man of little means and an ardent admirer of the senator from Wisconsin. In fact, there was an intensity about the young man which faintly echoed the intensity of his hero. And there were in his dark good looks a resem-blance to Joe as well. After graduating from Bates College in Lewiston, Maine, he had been a teacher in Phillips, Maine and then alumnae director at Bates, before moving to Washington, D.C. to work on the Senate staff of Owen Brewster. After Brewster's defeat in 1953, he became a research assistant to Senator Charles Potter [R-Mich.]. During the 1954 primary race, Bill Lewis characterized him in a note to the file as a shameless self-promoter who tended to misrepresent and upgrade his positions whenever possible, calling himself an administrative assistant or executive assistant, when he was no more than fourth or fifth on the staffs of these two senators.[207] Confirming Jones' tendency to exaggerate his own importance was a report in the *Bangor Daily News*. "In speech after speech, he [Jones] tells of sitting in for Potter on sessions of the

Senate commerce and rules committees and McCarthy's Senate investigations subcommittee. Occasionally he refers to himself as 'having been a member of those committees.'"[208]

In November 1953 McCarthy visited two Maine cities, ostensibly to speak to veterans groups. Although the appearances were characterized as "non-political," he happened to have in his company one Robert L. Jones, whom he introduced to the crowds and called a "fine fellow doing a fine job in Washington."[209] These speaking engagements sparked a rumor that Jones would run against Margaret. On 19 February 1954 Jones was suddenly fired from his $8500 a year job by Senator Potter because, after sitting in for Potter while McCarthy cross-examined Brig. Gen. Ralph Zwicker about the Peress case—which precipitated McCarthy's battle with the Army—Jones issued a statement in Potter's name supporting McCarthy and approving McCarthy's charge that the Army was coddling Communists.[210] Jones was also laying plans to oppose Margaret while he was still on Potter's payroll, and this said Potter, "reflected on me and my office."[211] "I have all I can do to take care of political matters in Michigan," said Potter, "without getting involved in other states."[212] Three days after he was fired, on 22 February, Jones announced his candidacy for the United States Senate, a complete reversal of the position he had steadfastly maintained as recently as 25 January, when he gave May Craig a written statement saying that he would not be a candidate for any political office in Maine.[213] He also said that he wasn't fired. He quit.[214]

In his announcement Jones referred to "the fumbling inadequacy of our senior representative," the recent loss of a destroyer contract by the Bath Iron Works and the low wholesale price of potatoes. But the issue on which he intended to make the election turn was the "bitter showdown in Maine between the forces of Americanism and international liberalism."[215]

Ordinarily, a fellow with so little experience and no elective office in his background would have drawn sniggers perhaps, but little serious news coverage in a contest with Margaret. But because of McCarthy's involvement, and the recent example of Tydings and what McCarthy had been able to do in Maryland, both the press and the Smith camp took the candidacy very seriously.

In reality, the Jones boy, as friends and foes alike called him, never was much of a threat. But that didn't become clear for a while. Most felt that he talked a lot and said nothing. He was a family man with a wife and four children to support, but there was little about him that suggested strength or stability. A story that was widely circulated during the primary was that in Phillips, where he had taught school, Jones had left a dying dog, his pet, at the town dump to die. Later someone had come to the dump, spotted the dog, taken pity on it and nursed it back to health.[216] Unfortunately for him, the persona he projected was compatible with such a tale.

Moreover, his ties with outsiders were far too strong for the tastes of the voters of Maine. "Sure he's a Biddeford boy," said a Republican lawyer from Jones' home county of York, "but he hasn't been around here much. He's been in Washington, and Biddeford is sort of a technical residence."[217] Some even noticed how he aped his hero—clearing his throat, suppressing a burp, repeating initial phrases.

Like McCarthy, Jones promised a "bare-knuckles" campaign, and he promptly attacked Margaret for being a "silent, puzzled, uninformed and weak-willed opponent of communism," and a supporter of the United Nations Educational, Social and Cultural Organization (UNESCO), "which as we know advocates a system of education demanding that our children give their first loyalty to world citizenship rather than to the United States." Subsequently, he characterized Margaret as a "do nothing, say nothing senator," who was "neglectful of the economic interests of her home state."[218] He also claimed: "We need a Senator who is young." Margaret was 56, Jones 34.[219]

Margaret responded by referring to her record—a sound strategy since Jones had none of his own to run on—and ignoring his attacks. Consistent with her strategy of previous years, she never mentioned Jones by name, and she spent most of her time in Washington, flying home to Maine only on weekends.

By February, McCarthy seemed to have figured out that he was overmatched in challenging Margaret in Maine. He loudly proclaimed that he was taking "no part in any primary campaign in Maine or anywhere else" and backed out of a Lewiston speech he had promised to give on 7 March.[220] His "Communist-hunting committee, a touch of laryngitis and traffic injury suffered by Mrs. McCarthy" were all reasons for his sudden change in plans.[221]

McCarthy's survival instincts served him well this time. Even if Margaret had been less wise and Jones less foolish, Margaret still would have won by a wide margin. The principal difference between the Maryland race and the Maine race was that unlike Tydings, Margaret was not vulnerable. Of course she had enemies, but they were far from organized. And neither Jones' callowness nor his assault on her as an internationalist liberal galvanized them into a group of formidable opponents.

In point of fact, McCarthy had selected the wrong candidate, the wrong strategy, and the wrong site for the battle. During the campaign, a story was heard about a young man, a stranger in town, who had waited at the barbershop in line for over an hour to get a haircut. The barber, who had been cutting hair for fifty years in Skowhegan, remarked to a customer that "Bob Jones has as much chance in this race as a snowball out on Maine Street today," whereupon the stranger jumped to his feet, slapped on his hat and stormed out of the shop. Some folks said that it must have been Bob Jones. Others knew that it couldn't have been Jones, because Jones hadn't so much as put his toe into Somerset County in the whole campaign. That evening the barber, who knew almost everyone in the county, told the story to every one he saw. In its way, although Jones was from Biddeford, it was a tale of native transcendence over a sinister outer world, a blend of suspicion and nostalgia. And the town devoured it.[222] They told and retold the story, lingering over it during late morning coffee, savoring the sweetness of their tribal strength and solidarity.

The same tale had been told at the beginning, during the cold, dark month of February, before the sounds of the black and yellow warbler ushered in the spring. The editor of a small newspaper in the coastal town of Rockland, offended by an "apparent flood of out-of-state political slush funds and the swift spreading of the sinister shadow of Joe McCarthy," had been moved to offer on 25 February "a prompt and vigorous declaration for Mrs. Smith, come what may." He fired the opening gun in his newspaper's pro-Smith campaign and issued what would also stand as the campaign's most enduring valedictory. "We are for Senator Smith—foot, horse, and artillery," he said, "and we are proud to align ourselves and our newspaper. Loyalty," he added, "knows no compromise. It is absolute or it is nothing."[223] Little more needed to be said.

When Maine went to polls on 22 June, McCarthy received the biggest set-back of his career. Margaret won the race by 80,000 votes with Jones carrying only 4 of 621 precincts. From the first town reporting in, tiny Brighton with a 5-0 tally, to the Maine fishing port of Rockland, which went for Margaret 1140 to 155, to Skowhegan, with a margin of 1134 to 116, to the shoe manufacturing city of Gardiner with a 1035-257 tally, rural Maine rallied to Margaret Chase Smith.[224] They were "voting against McCarthy's man." And, perhaps unconsciously, they were expressing their view of a world that valued three-piece suits and a fancy college degree far more than it valued common sense and hard work. They were for Margaret, "foot, horse, and artillery." After four lonely years of fighting McCarthy, Margaret should have been able to enjoy the sweetness of that moment.

But in that June victory was October's first chill. In his clumsy way, Jones had touched upon Margaret's true vulnerabilities—the absence of an agenda, heightening economic distress in Maine, and growing tendency to confuse criticism with enmity, lapses with defection. Referring to the latter early in the campaign, Jones had predicted "a great hidden vote—people who will vote for me, but don't come out in the open because they don't want to be on a blacklist for six years if I should lose."[225]

Lending credence to the "blacklist" reference is a 34-page memo, written in 1954 by Bill Lewis which lists by name Margaret's enemies and suspected enemies, as well as those who actually made negative comments about Margaret and those who were reported to have made them. Even ambivalent statements were taken as a sign that the maker of the remarks had "gone over to the other side." In one short paragraph, the term "rabid McCarthyites" is used three times in reference to three (out-of-state) couples. Throughout the memo, numerous references to "plotting" and conspiracy" appear.[226] New to the list of defectors, which already included Marion Martin, Selma Wagg, Owen Brewster and May Craig, was the name of Katherine Graham, publisher of the *Washington Post*, who, Margaret believed, was denying her the same amount of column space she was giving to other Senators.[227] The Smith camp feared that the BPW—the only group which would remain steadfast throughout Margaret's political career—was slipping away, some disillusioned by

Margaret's abortive non-try for the vice presidential nomination, others attracted to the Jones/McCarthy candidacy. Comments in letters from individual women in the 1954 file actually confirm some slippage among the BPW, though support from several women's groups, especially the BPW, generally remained strong. Nonetheless, Margaret and Bill could not erase from their memories a remark made by Jones on 10 April 1954. "I think the women elected Mrs. Smith in 1948. Strangely though," he continued, "more than half of the 4,000 letters I received urging me to run against her came from women. Something seems to have gone wrong with her support there."[228]

On a deeper level, despite her sweeping affirmation by the Maine electorate, Margaret was still chafing at her four-year treatment by Eisenhower and the national GOP, symptomatic of which was McCarthy's incursion into Maine. For four years the Republican Party had not merely tolerated but embraced McCarthy. And though her victory over Jones resulted in a congratulatory telegram from Eisenhower, the gesture meant much less than it would have two years earlier. By 1954, Joe's conduct during the Army-McCarthy hearings had raised such serious doubts about his effectiveness as a politician and anti-Communist crusader, and his style and tactics so appalled the American public that the Army's counsel Joseph Welch observed: "If the hearings had accomplished nothing else, the Army had been able to keep McCarthy on television long enough for the public to get a good look at him." President Eisenhower "agreed."[229] That fall McCarthy's censure was proposed, and a campaign to force a special recall election in Wisconsin ("Joe Must Go") failed by a narrow margin. Public opinion was running against him, and Joe was "becoming heartbroken and increasingly alcoholic."[230] To Margaret, Eisenhower's support only after McCarthy hit the skids was an empty and hypocritical gesture.[231] From her vantage point, the vision and courage she displayed in 1950 should have earned her the thanks of a grateful Party and a place at the table of Party leaders. Instead she had practically been shunned. In a world drawn increasingly toward relativism rather than absolutes—about which Democrat Adlai Stevenson in his unsuccessful 1952 campaign for the presidency had quipped: "some of us worship in churches, some in synagogues, some on golf courses"— few seemed sure about who was brave, what was courageous.

Today historians and television journalists assessing the fifties laud the distinguished journalist Edward R. Murrow, who devoted his entire broadcast of "See It Now" on 9 March 1953 to an attack on McCarthy. Though such courage should not be minimized, his was a far less risky gamble than the one taken by the female freshman senator from Maine three years earlier, who easily could have kept her own counsel, bided her time, and protected her store of political chips. After her speech, Bill seemed to be the only one to stand firm, and his spin that not only had she been the first to denounce McCarthy but had outmaneuvered and outwitted McCarthy at every turn became between them a bond and an article of faith, along with the corollary that she had destroyed "his paralytic power over the U.S." with her victory over Jones. But even that fiction offered little comfort. The political pragmatist in her, schooled by Clyde, knew otherwise. The seeds of McCarthy's end were in Joe McCarthy himself. She had been less an agent of his destruction, than an actor on the same stage, throwing herself into a part her restless spirit could not resist. But at least, unlike Eisenhower, she had played a part that was heroic. She had dealt with McCarthy as though he were a "lawless adult delinquent," observed Senator Charles Potter, and "slapped him down with dignity."[232] In return, Margaret might have added, she had herself been slapped down by the Party.

Her victory in Maine over Jones—which symbolized a larger victory over McCarthy and his kind of American politics—was thus not enough to still the angry voice within. McCarthy's untrammeled romp in the Senate and his incursion into her home territory stirred up feelings that went as deep as childhood: dreams denied, marginalization, betrayal. For much of her life she had been able to beat them back, first through her marriage to Clyde and later through her hard work in Congress which "guaranteed" her congressional seat. But McCarthy had managed to resurrect them. And in the primary and subsequently the general elections of 1954, those fears, fanned by Bill's insecurities and the trickle of hate mail occasioned by her Declaration of Conscience, along with her memory of how smear had been used against Clyde to deprive him of the Governor's chair, formed a siege mentality that sadly became a primary component of all future Smith campaigns. In this humor, Margaret's campaign for the general election began.

8. *Beginnings*

THE GENERAL ELECTION should have been easier for Margaret than the primary challenge. Her opponent was a friend and a Republican — or so she had thought. He had signed her nomination papers, had been her guest for lunch, and had asked her to speak to his history and government class at Colby College. She had met him through the alumnae secretary at Colby, who used to bring the Colby basketball team to breakfast at the Smith home when Clyde was in Congress. The alumnae secretary had remained friendly with Margaret after Clyde's death and his introduction of Paul Fullam had been enough to hasten the friendship. When Fullam called in April 1954 to ask her what she would think of his running against her, she replied, "I thought you were a Republican. I'm sure you are joking." Not until the next day did she read in the newspaper that he might be a candidate.[233] The campaign was off to a very bad start.

Meanwhile, a few days before Fullam announced his candidacy, a student at Colby wrote to warn her that Fullam was "the type of politician who says one thing to you and another behind your back." The young man, who knew Margaret because she had helped him when he was in the military, was to begin law school at the University of Chicago in the fall and, from Margaret's perspective, had no reason to lie. His letter was straightforward and credible, but it ended on a mysterious note, bound to stimulate the Smith camp's paranoid impulses. "I understand he called you from Princeton last week to inquire after your health. [He had.] Did you know that he has already signed your papers? He tells all these things plus a lot more that I do not wish to mention in a letter to a political discussion group that I belong to. Last week," the writer continued, "I asked him if I could quote him on his statement to the class 'that it is time we must recognize Red China and let them be admitted to the U.N.'. There is much more, plus rumors, that seem to me more like malicious slander, that I've had to listen to."[234]

In May, after Fullam had officially entered the race, he wrote to Margaret again. "Professor Fullam has discussed how he intends to conduct his campaign with our political discussion groups here at Colby," he said. "He claims Jones is wrong in assailing your voting record and thinks that the important things to bring into the public eye are *the issues* involved."[235]

The warning had a nasty sound to it, but other than Fullam's and Margaret's contrary positions on the admission of Red China to the United Nations, Margaret couldn't be sure what was meant by *the issues*. Even by June it was not clear, for one day the political novice and Harvard-educated professor was lecturing the electorate on the importance of India with its 368 million people (as compared to Indo-China), and the next day he was declaring his intention to show Maine voters the "difference between historians and politicians."[236]

By August, his focus had sharpened. Fullam left talk of India behind and turned his attention to what he claimed had prompted him to heed "the call to be a candidate for the United States Senate: the weakening of the country's defenses by the Republicans." In the parlance of Fullam's post-election spin—possibly in anticipation of a return bout in 1960—he had been prompted to run by "the fear in his little son's eyes when the five-year old heard the Boston plane go over and asked tremulously: 'Is that plane carrying the bomb?'"[237] Specifically, Fullam objected to the cuts in defense that were part of Eisenhower's defense package. "To keep government out of business is a worthy objective," he said, "but not the defense business and not at this time. We are economizing our way out of any possibility of retaliating to the Russian program of taking the world piece-meal."[238]

This line of attack was a curious one, especially in light of the position Margaret had carved out for herself. One year and five months into Eisenhower's first term, Margaret had made headlines across the country when she posed 38 questions to the Secretary of Defense, Charles E. Wilson, on the Administration's proposed budget cuts for the Air Force. Fully earning the characterization which appeared in *Collier's* that same year—"as full of sparks as a blacksmith's shop"—she had challenged him to explain how $5 billion could be pared off the Air Force budget "and still make it more powerful than it was, and who, by the way, had ordered the Air Force cut from 143 to 120 wings?"[239] When Wilson, (on leave from his presidency of the General Motors Company and a multi-millionaire) "brushed off" Senator Smith and stubbornly evaded her questions, Margaret threw down her list and acidly asked for written answers "from someone capable of supplying them."[240] The episode prompted a Herblock cartoon in the *Washington Post* and caused the editor to observe that Secretary Wilson was "learning about women from her."[241] The truth was, gender-related insights were the least of what Secretary Wilson was learning from this single-minded politician who always did her homework, never missed a vote, and expected both the military brass and cabinet members to be something other than evasive and unresponsive.

If she had a vulnerability on defense, it derived from her support (albeit tepid) of Eisenhower's so-called "new look" defense policy, a decision to pare back defense spending and increase the nation's reliance on nuclear and air power, rather than military manpower. The strategy would cut nearly 40,000 civilian employees from the Defense Department (primarily through attrition) and hold up, or cancel, most U.S. military building programs.[242] Even so, she made it clear to Maine voters that she would see to it that Maine got its fair share of dollars. In February 1954 she had demonstrated the extent to which she intended to make good on that promise when she engaged in an acrimonious debate with fellow Republican Leverett Saltonstall [Mass.] on the floor of the Senate. At issue was a $53 million contract which had gone to Fore River shipyard at Quincy, Massachusetts at a cost of $6.5 million above the bid of the Bath Iron Works. In a widely quoted statement, Margaret promised to "fight to reverse this Navy decision with every available means," and would, if necessary, "fight to amend the next Navy appropriation bill to eliminate the money."[243] Such pugnacity not only played well in Maine, but it also bolstered her long-standing record of support for defense and insulated her from blame, even in the event that Eisenhower's "new look" military policy did actually weaken the nation's defenses as Fullam, along with the national Democratic Party, were predicting.

Equally puzzling were Fullam's charges that she had failed to support federal aid to education and had "forgotten Maine." The first was an improbable line of attack on a senator who had been an early advocate of the school lunch program. The second ignored her style of treating constituent problems with the obsessiveness of a country pastor whose daily meals depended on the good will of parishioners. But in truth a vulnerability Margaret shared with all Maine Republicans was Maine's economic health. And in this sense, "forgotten Maine" was explosive.

During the Republicans' virtual lock on Maine politics since 1910, the state's economic health had steadily deteriorated, and by 1954 more than twenty-five per cent of Maine's workers depended for their livelihoods on industries which were in dramatic states of decline.[244] The key to Maine's post-war depression was the southward migration of the textile industry. But in addition, between 1940 and 1960 Maine's farm community would decline by 52 per cent, while cheap labor in the South, combined with increased competition, adverse tariff rates, and a drop in the value of lumber would reduce employment in Maine's forestry industry by 41.5 per cent.[245] Increasingly Maine's young people trying to find jobs were forced to leave the state. Many who remained lived in conditions that were "worse than the over-all urban conditions in the entire country," including the "shanty-towns of the South and the slums of the great cities." In 1955, the *Bangor Daily News* reported that 1.8 per cent of Bangor's 8,787 homes were without a toilet, "which means that within the city limits there are 158 privys or nothing but bushes. There are 246 homes with no piped running water. There are homes where the heating system is so bad that water must be kept running all the time so the rusty pipes won't freeze. The pipes in the basement are not connected to a sewer, and the water freezes on the cellar floor. The flush, kept running perpetually, overflows. The refuse collects in the hopper at first. The odor rises. Time goes on, more excrement is dumped into the hopper. It overflows on the basement floor. The wooden seat, at first merely discolored, begins to rot. . . . During the winter the slimy, filthy mess is frozen. When spring comes, it will thaw."[246]

Exploiting the festering economic situation in 1954 was a politically obscure Waterville attorney named Ed Muskie who, in his first bid for public office, would defeat Republican Governor Burton Cross and thereby usher in an era of two-party politics in Maine. In his 1954 campaign, he travelled over 20,000 miles, spent his days shaking hands and ringing doorbells, and his nights delivering speeches. He was well-schooled in the psyche of Maine, and he effectively capitalized on statewide dissatisfaction with a Republican state government that had grown increasingly remote and unresponsive to the state's economic woes. Paul Fullam, in his race against a much tougher opponent, tried to follow suit. He accused the Eisenhower Administration of soothing "us with the reassurance that we have patches of economic distress, but are actually in a period of healthy prosperity." Fullam observed acidly, "Maine just happens to be one of those patches."[247] But unlike Muskie, Fullam was not able to tie Margaret to the problems well enough to attract the number of votes he needed.

In truth, the real issue in Fullam's campaign was never publicly aired. It was Fullam's private belief that Margaret was "beyond her depth" in dealing with matters of public policy and government, an inadequacy "she managed to conceal . . . by clever wiles and dodges." As he wrote to a friend, "Operation Margaret is a favor-dispensing service which has managed to build over the years a solid corps of blind followers who identify with her personal integrity and womanly honor . . . I say this not in malice but in charity; I shall take my stand on the issues and rise or fall on that ground. Perhaps to the stock-jobbing in ships, to lobsters and potatoes, I shall be able to add consideration for the future in which our children must live."[248]

Fullam came closest to articulating his real views in a speech he delivered two weeks before the general election in Muskie's hometown of Rumford, Maine. The theme he used was: "Are you proud?" And every issue he raised was prefaced by that question to Margaret. "Are you proud of your state with its rising unemployment rate? . . . Are you proud that you voted for the cut in the school lunch program?"[249] And so on.

By this point in the campaign, Margaret's already thin patience had all but evaporated, sorely tried not only by Fullam, but by those who rushed to support him. Despite the refusal of other Democratic Senators to come into Maine and campaign against her, John F. Kennedy, the junior senator from Massachusetts—who was not campaigning for the Democratic senator in his own home state—came to Maine and told voters that not only their state but the entire New England area would be better represented by Fullam than Smith. In a Bill Lewis memo to the file on the 1954 elections, Lewis also noted that "Mrs. Roosevelt came into the State and called for the defeat of Margaret Smith."[250]

In addition, several of the people whose approval had always been important to Margaret, men like Dr. J. S. Bixler, President of Colby, now showed themselves to be people who only "represented themselves to be friends and supporters . . . [and] turned out to be the opposite." Over the

years, starting in 1943, Bixler had written to Margaret in the most solici-
tous ways, had flattered her ("We know that it will profit by your honesty
and clear-headedness") and as late as 26 February 1954 had sent her a
note to say "your friends here hope that you will not be disturbed by the
comments of your new opponent," adding, "it simply serves to make
them rally around your standard the more eagerly." Especially galling
was the fact that Bixler was the one who had urged Paul Fullam to run
for the Senate against Margaret, a role Bixler described with some pride
to Margaret's old mentor, Herbert C. Libby.[251]

The President of Bowdoin College, Kenneth Sills, similarly disappointed her. Sills had long been a leading Democrat in Maine, and
Margaret would have understood if he had come out for the entire
Democratic ticket. But Fullam seemed to receive most of Sills' attention,
with Sills even appearing on television to urge the election of Fullam
over Smith.

The dean of women at Colby, in addressing a meeting of Girls State
there a few days before the election, told them how wonderful it was that
Maine would have an opportunity to vote for "a true and sincere and
forthright person for the Senate, as contrasted with a mere politician."[252]
At this point, Margaret's well-established intelligence network dramatically worked against her, making it harder for her to remain positive in
the face of what could only be seen as betrayal.

Fullam's "Are you proud that you voted for the twenty-million-dollar
cut for TB control? . . . To recommit the Taft-Hartley Act? Proud of the
foreign aid cut? I don't think this constitutes a record of which to be
proud, but a record to hide behind generalizations" was the last straw.[253]
Not only had she voted against recommitting the Taft-Hartley Act
Amendments, and against foreign aid cuts, but she had voted for two and
a half million dollars more for TB control than the budget requested. A
$20 million cut was not even proposed.

Moreover, the tone of such questions from a former supporter was a
ploy "designed to shame [her] publicly." They "literally pointed a finger
of shame at me and made grave misrepresentations."[254] So Margaret
decided to fall back on the strategy of 1948. She would answer his charges
in the last television appearance of the campaign, on the eve of the election.

At 11:05 P.M. Margaret told voters that throughout the campaign she had refrained from attacking her opponent. "Instead," she said, "I have called him honorable, capable, and likeable—and not a man to stoop to pettiness and meanness. . . . To my surprise and disappointment, my opponent has become increasingly personal and erroneous in his attacks on me. When I said so the other day, he accused me of trying to keep my public record private and secret—and of not revealing and discussing my record with the people. At the end of this address I shall give you the biggest political surprise of this campaign—so keep tuned in."[255]

What followed was an all-points attack on Fullam which painted him as a liar and a dissembler. At the end of the speech, Margaret revealed that Fullam had signed her primary paper "representing that [he] was a Republican and that [he] was proposing [her] nomination for United States Senator and the nomination of no one else but Margaret Chase Smith." In signing Margaret's primary paper, Fullam had certainly represented himself to be a registered Republican. If he was not a registered Republican, he was ineligible to sign the paper. At the very least, such a "mistake" made him look like someone who was sailing under false colors, which was exactly the impression Margaret and Bill wanted to create. As Margaret spoke she held up the primary nomination paper to the camera so that viewers could see the notarized signature of Paul Fullam, which Bill Lewis had instructed the cameraman to zoom in on "close on the signature."[256] Margaret held the paper steady, pointed to Paul Fullam's signature and signed off.

The speech's ending was dramatic, but its most poignant moment came earlier when Margaret tried to shore up what she feared was her flagging support from Maine's educated elite. With Bixler's defection and Sills' very public support for Fullam, she worried that others might take their cue from the education establishment and wind up in Fullam's column.

"The colleges of Maine are not ashamed of me," she said, "they are proud enough that our own great Colby College gave me an honorary degree of Master of Arts . . . citing me for statesmanship and devotion to duty. Bowdoin College was proud enough of me to award an honorary degree of Doctor of Laws . . . and your telecast guest, who has often praised my record, handed that degree to me." The University of Maine, as well, "has expressed its pride in my record by awarding me an honorary Doctor of Laws."[257]

But the words had a hollow ring. Academics pay little attention to such things as honorary degrees, and to think otherwise merely perpetuated the perception that Margaret did not understand the values which prevail on college campuses.

The ploy was motivated by desperation. Or so it must have seemed. The small voice within her which she usually silenced by hard work, diligent preparation—and by never missing a roll call vote—now reminded Margaret that she didn't have the credentials of her opponent, and that she was being abandoned by the people who counted. Her carefully cultivated invincibility, her unerring capacity for handling all unpleasantness with tolerant civility had vanished. Was she really good enough? In his efforts to unseat her, Fullam had stumbled across a Margaret Chase Smith that neither he, nor anyone else, had seen before. It was a short step to the conclusion that once on the defensive, Margaret could be beaten. Perhaps not now. But eventually she could be defeated.

As her speech came in the campaign's last hour, Fullam had no time for rebuttal before voters went to the polls the next day. Although the speech created an accurate impression that Fullam's characterizations of her voting record had been largely incorrect, the tactic, as her opponents noted, bore a chilling resemblance to Joe McCarthy's—from the fact that her attacks were unanswerable (given their timing), to her use of a piece of paper bearing Fullam's signature, to her failure to warn Fullam that she would be delivering the speech. After the telecast, Fullam sent a telegram to the press. "I repeat what Mr. Welch said to Senator McCarthy, as sure there is a God in Heaven your evil will not prevail."[258] Though the campaign closed on the most bitter note of Margaret's career thus far, she defeated Paul Fullam by 40,000 votes, with a final tally of 144,530 to 102,075, 58.4 percent as compared with 71.4 percent of the vote in 1948.[259]

Five days after the election, Paul Fullam answered Margaret's election eve attack with a speech of his own over WCSH-TV. He said that he had signed Margaret's paper because he preferred her to Jones, and that he was a registered Republican only because when he came to Maine, he was told that was the only way to make his vote count. He excused her eleventh-hour attack on him but pointed out that she had allowed him no time to answer it. "Regardless of what interpretation one wants to put on the broadcast," he said, "the fact remains that [had] Senator Smith appeared on an early evening broadcast . . . she might have . . . allowed me an opportunity for an answer. That she withheld that attack until 11:05 when a glance at the radio schedule undoubtedly told her advisors that I was appearing at the same hour in Bangor . . . violates every principle of fair play in any tradition." In criticizing her voting record he had "used accurate figures compiled by the Democratic National Committee and checked in the *Congressional Record*" and she could only "have gotten the impression that he was being inaccurate from secondhand information garnered at political rallies."[260]

On balance the speech was graceful, though unyielding. In it Fullam came across as a good loser. "Senator," he said, "we pledge you our fullest confidence and support. In the exacting months and years ahead. And we shall pray for your success."[261]

In retrospect, Margaret's tactics did not appear to be warranted by the campaign of Paul Fullam, who himself had said when he was offered the nomination that he had "no illusions about the possibility of beating Senator Smith."[262] Nor was her shrillness worthy of a woman whom most of Maine felt represented the best there was in politics.

Moreover, in the passage of months following the election, one would have predicted that Margaret's world would have quickly settled back into place. Once more she was safe from attacks from the left and — after her drubbing of Jones — from the right. Yet the memory of the 1954 election would not go away. Six months after the election in response to a letter from him, Margaret wrote to Arthur M. Schlesinger, "those who now control the Democratic organization in Maine — apparently encouraged Mr. Fullam to do what he did to me. I cannot believe the rank and file of Democrats in Maine, if they knew the truth about the matter, would likewise encourage such tactics." The end of the letter stands as her final view of the matter. "I have experienced many things in politics," she said, "but none as shocking as this."[263]

What the Democrats may have learned through Paul Fullam was not to be used to advantage until 1972. Neither of Margaret's next two Democratic opponents would push very far beyond her voting record. In a postscript to the election, however, on 14 June 1955, Colby College honored Paul A. Fullam, chairman of the college's Department of History and Government, with an honorary Doctorate of Humane Letters. Within a week Fullam, who had been ill before he entered the Senate race, was dead from a heart attack at the age of 48. The Democrats now had a martyr.

9. *The Eisenhower Presidency*

MARGARET WAS NEVER TO CRACK even the outer edge of Eisenhower's inner circle, though after the 1954 primary, Eisenhower ended his long neglect and began courting her. For the moment, Margaret seemed to have the opportunity, if not to reach the inner circle of the Eisenhower White House, at least to come in out of the cold. In the spring of 1955, Margaret invited Eisenhower to come to Maine. Unlike Roosevelt and Truman, whom she had also invited, Eisenhower accepted.

Maine cooperated enthusiastically. Even the weather was glorious, with a blue sky and wispy clouds. Though it was still June, the afternoon of the 25th promised to be a scorcher. Along the way to the Skowhegan fairgrounds where the President was to speak, hundreds of white and red and yellow pennants hung across the streets, while flags flew from the roofs of homes and lined the route he would take. A large truck with a red-lettered sign, "WELCOME PRESIDENT IKE," was parked at an angle to the road. At the fairgrounds, a green and white canopy had been erected over the speaker's platform to shield the president, Governor Muskie, and Margaret, from the sun. At Margaret's home on Neil Hill, red and green chairs had been placed on the lawn and bouquets of roses arranged on the dinner tables.[264] The land jutted skyward to form a hilltop from which could be seen all of Skowhegan, and over which hawks and eagles soared, wheeling on updrafts from the river below.

During the intense 1948 senatorial campaign, thoughts of building a house on Neil Hill had been a source of escape and solace for Margaret. The land had been in the Neil family since before Margaret was born. And before that in the hands of Benjamin Moor, who had received it as a grant from the Kennebec Proprietors for his service in the Revolutionary War. At one time, John Glidden Neil was a colonel of militia and a land trader who owned most of Elm Street. But the land he chose for himself and his wife, and on which they lived virtually to the end of their long lives, was the fruit of the Revolutionary War which over time became known as Neil Hill.[265] Land there did not often change hands, and when it did, it was usually passed on to members of the family. Newcomers to Skowhegan did not live on Neil Hill, nor poor people, nor those who might want to develop it. In 1946 Roland Patten, who still worked in Margaret's office, became the buyer of record of a lot on Neil Hill. He had sold his home earlier and had no residence in Maine. He might want to return to Neil Hill, he told the owner, and she agreed to sell the land to him. On 28 August 1946 the land was transferred to Margaret.[266]

One evening as Margaret waited in Boston to catch the commuter plane to Maine, she took an envelope from the stack of mail she had brought with her from Washington and began sketching. After she had been engrossed in the sketch for some time, a voice behind her said, "Good evening, Mrs. Smith, how are you spending these three hours, drawing pictures?" She looked up to discover a man she knew from Auburn, Maine, who happened to be an architect. She told him she was trying to outline what she had in mind for her new house. "Let me take it and see what I can do with it," he offered.[267]

She wanted the house set back from the street and nestled into the hill. The side facing the street was to be traditional with small paned windows—the side facing the river, modern with a lot of glass. The house was to be planned so that "in her later years, she could have people living in the same house, but not living with her."[268] Like Margaret herself, the house was to look traditional, but would in fact be unconventional, an amalgam of old and new, an understated frame house with a spectacular view, larger in size than it looked, and with expensive touches like a stone wall and flagstone walk.

The house was not the sort of house Clyde would ever have built. Not grand enough. Nor, with its offsetting tensions of old and new, would Margaret's family have chosen it, though they were probably impressed with it. The house was totally Margaret's, the first home she had ever called her own, the first home which had felt right to her as an adult. And it had never looked better than it did on 25 June 1955 when the president of the United States was her guest. The pine, fir, spruce and hemlock she and Bill had planted two years before had grown rapidly, blending the house with the land and creating a lush, emerald green backdrop for the drama about to unfold.

Margaret invited everyone in Maine to come and see the president, and by two o'clock, traffic had begun to get heavy, as five thousand people descended on the fairgrounds. At two-thirty the Skowhegan band began to play and the dignitaries arrived. Over fifty officials took their places on the speaker's platform. At 4:30, Eisenhower gave a 20-minute speech to an enthusiastic audience.[269] This was the first time that a sitting United States president had given an address in Maine.

Supper that evening was a choice between lobster or (Eisenhower's favorite) charcoal-broiled steak with his own special sauce. Over 70 people picnicked on the lawn and west veranda at Neil Hill.[270] Newsmen hovered about and automobiles lined the narrow road which led down the hill to town. The day had about it the quality of a dream, marred only by Eisenhower's dour chief of staff, former New Hampshire Congressman, Sherman Adams, who was once described by Joseph Alsop as "a little man with a face that looked frostbitten."[271] When Adams learned that Margaret had been given a "yes" to her invitation from his boss, he had arranged an excursion for Ike to western Maine where he could fly fish, an outing which threatened to leave Eisenhower with no time for Skowhegan. Adams was "in a position to take it all away from me," Margaret noted, "but Eisenhower stayed with it and came."[272] Even so, Adam's influence with Eisenhower remained an unpleasant reminder of her own vulnerability and her lack of real clout with the president.

Three months after Eisenhower visited Skowhegan, he had a heart attack. Until then, everyone assumed he would run for a second term. For seven weeks the president was confined to the hospital, and in the months which followed, while Eisenhower worked on a limited schedule, party leaders "alternated between hope and despair as they tried to interpret conflicting reports about Eisenhower's state of mind."[273] Quickly speculation heated up about Nixon's chance of remaining on the ticket. On 29 January 1956 Margaret granted an interview to Mary Cremmen, a writer for the *Boston Sunday Globe*. With a large "IKE IN 1956" button propped on a shelf, Margaret made her pitch that "if President Eisenhower doesn't run again, the Republican Party would greatly increase its voting members by nominating a woman for Vice President on the ticket."274

Eisenhower delayed making an announcement until he was told by his physicians that he was healthy enough to "bear the physical burdens of another term." And on 29 February he announced his intention to run.275 Two weeks later, when 22,000 Republican voters wrote in Richard Nixon's name in the New Hampshire primary, the number two spot on the ticket appeared to belong to Nixon.

In late March, sensing that Nixon had the nomination wrapped up, Margaret claimed that a woman didn't have a chance of being nominated under the convention system because such nominations are the spoils of backroom deals negotiated by political bosses. The only way a woman could be nominated was through direct primary votes.276 Privately, her ambition had carried her again in the direction of the number two spot on the Republican ticket. After all, in the six years since her Declaration of Conscience, she had demonstrated an exemplary level of party regularity and consistently defended Eisenhower's "new look" in national defense and his economic policies. Lecturing in her column that "differences between Republican Members does the Party no good," she had also delivered an encomium for Bob Taft.277 Although she believed there should be greater economy and cuts in government spending, such a difference of opinion with the White House, she told readers of her column, was no excuse for Republicans "engaging in bitter attacks upon each other or in questioning the loyalty of each other."278 She had even stumped the state of Oregon for Senator Guy Gordon whose voting record, from the perspective of the *New Republic*, was "even more antiliberal" than that of Mrs. Smith's old enemy Joe McCarthy."279 She had, it seemed, fallen back on what one pundit characterized as her "residual Republican mysticism"—the belief that the Republican Party was "the nation's most efficient instrument of government" which, once the "raging frustrations of its twenty-year minority [was] ended" would "ditch McCarthyism and acquire a sobering sense of responsibility."280

In June 1956, with the Republican Convention scheduled for August, concerns about Eisenhower's health re-surfaced when he underwent an operation for ileitis (an inflammation of the small intestine). But in July, with little more than a month left before the convention, he passed the word through GOP congressional leaders that he would run again and was in "much better" health than before his surgery.[281] Eisenhower's health magnified the importance of his runningmate, and despite Eisenhower's strong endorsement of him at the end of April, rumors began to circulate once again that Nixon might be dropped from the ticket. Although Nixon had the support of most Republican leaders, political scholar George H. Mayer explains that, "he was an anathema to the Democrats, who regarded him as a 'McCarthy in a white collar.'" He frightened "away thousands of discerning, independent Democrats who were presumed to be fretting about the President's health."[282]

On 1 August, less than three weeks before the Republican Convention in San Francisco, Eisenhower held his first news conference since undergoing abdominal surgery on 9 June and declared the Republican Convention "open" to anyone who wanted to run for vice president. Despite Eisenhower's claim that the convention was "open," however, the only candidate he mentioned by name as acceptable to him was Richard M. Nixon.[283]

The day after Eisenhower's announcement, Maine newspapers began speculating about the impact of his statement on Margaret's chances for the vice presidential nomination. "Last spring [13 April 1956]. . . Maine's Republicans at their state convention passed a resolution instructing Maine's convention delegates to nominate Mrs. Smith as Maine's favorite daughter choice for Republican vice president," the *Bangor Daily News* reminded its readers. "The catch line in the resolution, so far as the senator was concerned, were the words, 'if feasible.' At the time and until Stassen's 'dump Nixon' drive started this week, Senator Smith has had little to say on the subject. Her friends have indicated that while she was tremendously pleased at the honor . . . she would not stand in the way of party unity. . . . Yesterday's press conference in Washington changed all of that."[284] The next day's edition of the *Bangor Daily News* ran an "article with the headline: "Way Seen Open to Nominate Mrs. Smith Vice President," though Margaret's refusal to speak at San Francisco during opening night oratory on 20 August suggests that she was determined to remain aloof from a contest that she could not win.

Behind the scenes, a different drama was playing out. On 1 August, the same day Eisenhower announced an "open convention," Margaret gave John H. Weston, chairman of the Maine Republican State Committee, her interpretation of the resolution passed at the Maine GOP convention. Her view, simply stated, was that their endorsement "was a binding instruction on the delegates to the national convention. The only qualification was in the words 'if feasible' and their meaning obviously referred to the situation where there would not be an open convention on the selection of the Vice Presidential nominee but rather that President Eisenhower after being nominated would declare that he wanted Nixon nominated and no other name placed in nomination." The recent statement of Eisenhower at his press conference that he would not "foreclose selection" removed the qualifying words "if feasible" and obligated the Maine delegation "to place my name in nomination for Vice President of the United States."[285]

Despite Margaret's efforts and Eisenhower's assertion that he wanted an open convention, however, Margaret had less chance in 1956 than she had had in 1952. That the Republican Party was not ready to put any woman on the ballot is likely. But, in addition, the conservatives who dominated the Party still found Margaret unacceptable. To them, her Declaration of Conscience had been the first shot in a war to which there could be no truce, even though she was arguably becoming more conservative. Not only had her diminished percentage in the 1954 Senate contest weakened her hand, but the purported dwindling support from the Maine BPW had since been confirmed. When a friend wrote to suggest to Margaret that the Maine BPW should be asked to join in the 13 April endorsement by Maine Republicans, Margaret wrote back: "You are most kind and thoughtful but I would rather that you would not request the Federation to endorse me. . . . Such a request might be embarrassing for a goodly number of members of the various county clubs since such members are actually opposed to me but would hesitate openly and publicly in saying so." An example she gave to her correspondent was the Republican Women's Club in Fred Payne's county (Lincoln County), who were "very much opposed to me. Its President is Margot Kenne Lee, who for years has waged a malicious and vicious campaign against me and who managed Jones' campaign in that area of the State."[286]

Then, there was Eisenhower himself. In a party that was deeply divided,

Eisenhower had become "the decade's pre-eminent symbol of conciliation and consolidation," chief advocate of a "great middle-of-the-road
philosophy."[287] And he was neither drawn to Margaret nor was he about
to borrow trouble by choosing a running mate who was a political moderate and who, historically, had a mind of her own. Nixon's 48 percent
support among Independents and 66 percent among Republicans
clinched the decision.

On 21 August John Weston called from California to say that things
were happening very fast. Rumors were circulating that all the vice presidential hopefuls were going to withdraw their names and Nixon would
be nominated by acclamation. Weston asked permission to withdraw her
name. Margaret countered with the argument that since she had not
entered her name, she could not be the one to withdraw it. If others started to do so, the Maine delegation should delay until there was a motion
for acclamation and then accede to it. In any case, her name should be
withdrawn only after the others had withdrawn.

She further suggested that Congressman Jonas of North Carolina
might want to second her nomination "since he wanted to do this four
years ago," or Isabella Jones, who "would also want to as she started the
movement in 1952."[288] What Weston didn't tell her, but what she learned
later, was that in the Maine delegation's first caucus, a rump group, led
by young Peter Garland of Saco, had proposed a motion to table
Margaret's nomination, presumably to enable the delegates to get aboard
the Nixon campaign as early as possible. Primarily because of the arguments made by Owen Brewster, the motion was defeated.[289]

On 22 August when Eisenhower announced in San Francisco that his
disarmament aide Harold E. Stassen had "realized that the mass of the
Republican delegates wanted Nixon, and therefore Stassen wanted to
second the vice-president's nomination," it became clear to everyone that
the "Bump Nixon" campaign had been derailed.[290] Less clear to the
Maine delegation was what they should do about it. On 22 August at
10:30 A.M. John Weston called Margaret from San Francisco and again
asked for authority to withdraw her name.

Once again Margaret would not give him the authorization he
requested, but told him that she would understand whatever he did. She
said that she was especially sensitive because of a story by May Craig

which predicted that Weston would be calling Margaret and asking for her withdrawal.[291] Later she claimed that she wanted to avoid the appearance that her withdrawal was "a put-up job." Closer to truth was an unwillingness to be detoured from her instinctual quest for achievement.

That evening the team of Eisenhower-Nixon was unanimously renominated for the 1956 political contest. After Louisiana cast all twenty of its votes for Richard Nixon, the Secretary of the Republican Convention called on Maine. Stepping to the microphone was John Weston, a Fryeburg horse and cattle dealer, who announced to the convention and the television audience, "Mr. Chairman, in April the Republican State Convention, desiring to honor its distinguished senator and one of the Nation's outstanding Republican leaders, the Honorable Margaret Chase Smith, instructed the Maine delegation to place her name in nomination at this Convention for Vice President of the United States if such action appeared feasible. . . . The Maine delegation had hoped to have this high honor and to recognize her great service to the Nation as Maine's favorite daughter. However, as circumstances have developed, . . . Maine is happy to join in supporting the renomination of our great Vice President, Richard M. Nixon. The State of Maine casts 16 ballots for Nixon."[292]

After the convention was over, Margaret wrote immediately to the Maine delegates to thank them for their support. She also thanked rump group leader Peter Garland, though her letter ended with the line: "I am particularly appreciative of your part, knowing that it was not easy for you to join in such approval of me."[293] He did not miss her meaning.[294] When she wrote to him a second time she became more explicit. "What my letter referred to was what an ardent friend of mine reported from a conversation my friend had with you prior to your leaving Maine for San Francisco. My friend reported that you had expressed your personal disapproval of me and my voting record and had expressed your opposition to placing my name in nomination for Vice President."[295] By 1956, it was clear to most that the Smith camp tolerated no divided loyalties. The politician's stock-in-trade of always leaving the door open to convert enemies to friends had vanished.

10. *Out In The Cold*

FOR THE REST OF THE DECADE and for much of her time in the Senate, Margaret remained as solitary as a Maine winter. Despite her sporadic displays of Party regularity, McCarthy's hold on the loyalty of the Party's leaders caused the atmosphere of the Senate to improve very little for Margaret, even after his fall from power. In 1954 she returned from a worldwide trip during which she had met with numerous heads of state—all covered by Edward R. Murrow and broadcast on "See It Now" on CBS—to cast a quiet vote in favor of McCarthy's censure. But, even as the votes were being cast, Republicans like Rhode Island Senator Styles Bridges and Richard Nixon were trying to save McCarthy by deleting the word "censure." The Republicans split 22-22, with the overall vote 67 to 22 for censure. The 22 who voted against censure included most of the leadership of the Republican party, among them Everett Dirkson and Barry Goldwater.

On 2 May 1957 when McCarthy died, "senators of all persuasions did their best to mourn a departed colleague." Arkansas Democrat John McClellan said, "He will be missed from the Senate and the American scene," while the Eisenhowers extended "profound sympathy" to Jean. Said Harry Truman, "Too bad. I'm very sorry to hear the news of the senator's death." Dean Acheson told reporters he had "no comment at all" and quoted a Latin phrase which he translated as: "Say nothing about the dead unless it is good."[296] Margaret sent condolences to Mrs. McCarthy and her daughter Tierney. But in June, when staff members of the Government Operations Committee, which McCarthy had once headed, drafted a resolution eulogizing McCarthy's conduct and describing him in terms that suggested he was a martyr, Margaret refused to sign. There was nothing unusual in a Senate committee's voting a motion of condolence for the family of a deceased member, but it was unusual to ask committee members to sign it. Moreover, Margaret saw no reason to praise in death a record she found odious while McCarthy was alive. Her colleagues were of a different turn of mind. The document was signed by committee chairman, John McClellan, the six other Democratic members and five of the six Republicans.[297]

In the "company town" Washington had become under Eisenhower,

Margaret found no solace, and in the style of the cabinet officers Eisenhower had brought into the Administration to "serve," she observed an arrogance that was repugnant. Like former General Motors President, now Eisenhower's Secretary of Defense, Charles E. Wilson, most of the cabinet had been drawn from the upper reaches of business and were in accord with Wilson's view that he hadn't come to Washington "to run a grocery store."[298] They were men who flourished once the war ended, who got rich selling automobiles or making airplanes or running conglomerates. They were spiritual cousins to Jay Gatsby and had made brilliant climbs from Main Street to Darien or Grosse Pointe or Shaker Heights in the course of becoming America's aristocracy, though they were aristocratic in neither taste nor temperament. They had learned to drink Scotch and play bridge. They were avid golfers and enjoyed a good cigar. They were refined, well tailored and self-righteous. In Joe Alsop's phrase, they "behaved as though they were somehow sanctified because they had sacrificed their often large business jobs to serve and live in Washington."[299] They were men exuberant about an America which had offered them so many rewards for talent and hard work, and they cherished the belief that they had "gotten there" the hard way. With them and their wives, Margaret—whose arduous climb was still very fresh and for whom public service was a genuine privilege, not a sacrifice—found little to like.

Margaret's impatience with such men was the impatience of someone who had won her place and who believed that respect was due—for the office, as well as the person. Self-respect would not allow her to ignore their arrogance, or smile at their snubs, even though her disapproval meant nothing to them. All that it meant was that Margaret was different. And to be different was not a good thing. To these men who made large donations to the Republican and Democratic National Committees and bankrolled campaigns, she was an oddity rather than a mystery. To the corporate moguls, bankers and soft drink executives—players, all, who surrounded Eisenhower—Margaret was quite simply "other." Their arrogance and contempt for details, and perhaps their contempt for women—who in their capacity as secretaries and clerks concerned themselves with matters of "little consequence"—was symbolic of the values of big business which had come to permeate the federal government. It was also symptomatic of a federal payroll that had climbed from 630,000 civilian employees under Herbert Hoover to 2,561,000 the year Eisenhower took office and a government whose budget had increased twenty-fold, from $3,863,000,000 to $85,400,000,000.[300] To men who administered budgets of this size and who were themselves 'captains of industry,' congressional prerogative meant little, especially when the term was applied to a female senator from a small rural state.

Conflict between Margaret and Secretary Wilson was a matter of "when," not "if." It began when Wilson cut five billion dollars from the defense budget, stating that he could get more defense for less money. As a member of both Armed Services and Appropriations, Margaret quickly framed 30 written questions, asking Wilson in May 1953 how two minus one equaled three. At another point she inquired who was responsible for the condition of North African air bases. After Joe McCarthy accused the Army of "coddling Communists," Margaret asked Wilson if that were so. When Wilson replied "no," Margaret asked if that was an off-the-cuff reply, or did he know. On 15 July 1954 at a Senate Armed Services hearing on Defense Department loyalty programs, Wilson volunteered that he had thought Mrs. Smith's last question "rather mean" and he had "resented" it. On second thought, however, he and his aides had concluded that it was a pretty good question, and so he had "ordered review of all past loyalty checks for all branches of the service." By doing this, he would be "in a better position to answer questions." Smiled Margaret, "Then maybe together we've made some progress."[301]

As the decade wore on, Margaret's Maine impulses and her ongoing creation of herself continued to isolate her. Having moved further and further from her Party and her president, she was also out of step with the "homogenized" America of the fifties. In a culture David Reisman described as dominated by peer group approval rather than rugged individualism—a culture in which several thousand homeowners in Levitt Town willingly abided a rule which mandated that grass be cut at least once a week and laundry washed on specific days—Margaret's solitary path, though still playing well in Maine, had diminishing appeal outside of that region. A shift in allegiance from the individualistic Protestant ethic to what William H. Whyte, Jr. in The Organization Man, called "an organization ethic" did not bode well for her. Nor was a widespread belief in "'belongingness' as the ultimate need of the individual" an ally to one whose construct of a hero had little to do with quiescence and neutrality.[302]

At the same time, for reasons not entirely unrelated to the somnolent state of the nation, Margaret embodied the dreams of a dwindling number of women across the country. In September 1956, a New Jersey attorney named Emma Dillon wrote to Margaret to express her indignation at Margaret's treatment by the GOP. Her assessment reflects the frustration of a shrinking but faithful band of women who were unswerving supporters of Margaret and who believed—with some justification—that the Party's ongoing snub was an outgrowth of gender attitudes as well as style. "Somewhere along the line there seems to be an idea that the Women's Division of our party should concern itself only with tea parties," Dillon wrote to Presidential Assistant Bernard Shanely. "Maybe so, but it is my observation that most women are not interested in this phase and a great many react unfavorably to the fact that both political parties take the attitude that women cannot comprehend, or do not want to have the same treatment that is given the men of the parties. . . . Margaret Chase Smith to a very great number of people in this country is *the* outstanding woman. She symbolizes to the young women who have ambitions and to the parents of girls who have ambitions for them, the same thing the President symbolizes to boys and their parents."[303]

Unfortunately women like Emma Dillon, who had come to political maturity in the post-suffrage era, were a vanishing breed. None of the handful of telegrams sent to Weston during the 1956 Republican Convention had urged him to hold out for Margaret. Several were sent by women, but all of them either supported Nixon, or threw support to a candidate other than Margaret.[304] The bright promise of 1948 was not to be fulfilled by the women of the Fifties.

Once World War II ended and servicemen began to return from overseas, public sentiment concerning women's place had swung back to its pre-war position. The traditional male role was accorded increased attention and prestige—as Margaret herself witnessed with the number of veterans elected to Congress in 1946 and 1948—and women were expected to return to their proper sphere.[305] At first women followed the script, voluntarily or otherwise. Between September 1945 and November 1946, one million women were laid off and another 2.25 million left work. As historian William Chafe observes, however, by 1949 a great many had found their way back into the work force. In California, for example, in 1949, "twice as many were employed as had been employed in 1940. Nationwide, the female labor force had increased without the war."[306] Even so, women's return to the labor force by the late forties and early fifties did not signal a redefinition of female role or progress in the fight for equality. The taste of freedom, increased autonomy, and the desire for a higher standard of living had brought women back.[307]

In the years following Margaret's primary victory over "the Jones boy" Americans rediscovered the frontier and called it the suburbs. They deserted cities, bought houses (financed through low-interest mortgages and assisted by veterans benefits), and commuted to work. On Saturdays, they washed their cars and mowed their lawns, and on Sundays they went to church. Over a million new homes were being built each year, all needing stoves, refrigerators, small appliances and television sets.[308] By the mid-fifties Americans were experiencing material abundance inconceivable to most of the peoples of the world and unimaginable to earlier generations of Americans. In the wake of this prosperity, older values, values in which Margaret still believed—like economy and frugality, the staples of earlier, leaner times—could not compete with the hedonism and materialism of the fifties. Luxuries which no one had in the war years were suddenly within reach for cash or credit, thus giving rise to the "second" paycheck. Wives by the millions thus went into the job market: to buy the washer-dryer, to screen in the porch, to pay for the cottage on the lake, in other words, to provide the family with some of the "extras."[309]

With these working women, Margaret had surprisingly little in common. They were chauffeuring children and balancing jobs (which quite often offered no upward mobility), while trying to "make the home an oasis of comfort and serenity for [their] harried husband[s]."[310]

Nor were they raising their daughters to re-evaluate woman's place. The results of hundreds of questionnaires distributed by *Mademoiselle* during the fifties led that magazine's editors to conclude that young women preferred to be well-rounded rather than excel, to regard family as "the ultimate measure of success," and to look forward—in the idiom of historian William Leuchtenburg—to uneventful, relaxed marriages of "thoroughly barbecued bliss."[311] The altar, as another historian put it, "remained the only acceptable destination for single girls, and those who managed to make it with prize grooms in tow became celebrities."[312] Consequently, women with whom Margaret continued to feel a bond and to whom she remained a powerful symbol were middle-class home-makers and club women, many of whom, like her, had passed through middle age by the fifties. Soon they would be classified cruelly by the youth culture that was in ascendence simply as "old."

Only in Maine, where change was less rapid, was her support secure. Social and economic changes, compounded by awareness within both parties that women voted, if at all, with their husbands, rather than as a bloc—and therefore were not "players"—were to consign Margaret to the sidelines and further erode any lingering hope that she might become a politician with national clout.

11. A *Quantum Leap* in Destructive Power

ON 1 MARCH 1954 on Bikini Atoll in the Pacific, the United States carried out its first test of a deliverable hydrogen bomb, a weapon scientists described as seven hundred times more powerful than the atomic bomb used at Hiroshima. Within hours of the explosion, "fallout" drifted over several atolls in the Marshall Island chain and almost immediately inflicted radiation sickness on more than two hundred of the islanders, who were evacuated two days later by the Navy. The twenty-three man crew of the *Fukuru Maru*, a Japanese fishing boat which was inadvertently within a hundred miles of the blast, all returned to Japan suffering from radiation sickness. As one historian characterized the panic with which the world responded, "shock, outrage, and fear spread around the world. Many imagined that the hydrogen bomb might poison the entire earth."[313]

Should such a weapon fall into the hands of the Soviet Union or Red China, one hardly wanted to imagine what might happen. On 29 March when the Administration announced that another hydrogen explosion had occurred the preceding Friday in the mid-Pacific testing area, imagination alone wasn't required. Prime Minister Churchill discussed the matter in the House of Commons, India's Prime Minister Nehru called for an end to experiments with the hydrogen bomb, and Socialists in the Japanese Diet demanded government assurances that the United States would not stockpile atomic weapons in Japan.[314] Reports came from Japan that Communist agents were trying to steal samples of the ashes "to analyze them and that U.S. secret agents were trying to fool them." And in the House of Representatives, Rep. McCormack [D-Mass.] told his colleagues that "a Communist attack against the U.S., powered by atomic weapons, would cost from 10 to 30 million casualties."[315]

In an attempt to calm public fear, Rear Admiral Lewis L. Strauss, USNR, head of the Atomic Energy Commission [AEC], read a prepared statement on 31 March in which he emphasized that although the test on 1 March "was a very large blast," nonetheless "at no time was the testing out of control."[316] By his side was President Eisenhower. When a reporter asked Strauss to describe the hydrogen bomb, he said, "Well, the nature of the H-bomb is that, in effect, it can be made as large as you wish . . . that is to say, an H-bomb can be made as—large enough to take out a city." Incredulous, the reporter asked him how big a city, to which Strauss answered, "Any city." "Any city, New York?" the reporter asked. "The metropolitan area, yes," Strauss replied. On 1 April 1954, the *New York Times* reported "H-Bomb Can Wipe Out Any City, Strauss Reports."[317] As Strauss biographer Richard Pfau described the forces thus set in motion, "Strauss realized that he had deflected public attention from the dangers of fallout by raising the specter of mass destruction."[318] To little avail, concern about mass destruction had been raised earlier by Robert Oppenheimer, Albert Einstein, and Harvard's James B. Conant. In 1949, twelve American physicists had responded to President Truman's directive to the AEC to develop the hydrogen, or "super bomb" with moral outrage. "We believe that no nation has the right to use such a bomb," they declared, "no matter how righteous its cause. The bomb is no longer a weapon of war but a means of extermination of whole populations. Its use would be a betrayal of all standards of morality and of Christian civilization itself."[319] But in June of 1950 when North Korean troops crossed the 38th Parallel to invade the South, objections to the more lethal bomb diminished. And even before the start of the Korean War, advocates of the H-bomb had an ally on the AEC—Lewis A. Strauss.[320]

On 8 April Margaret Chase Smith reacted in her column to the 1954 explosion. "What has been told the American people is very sobering. The fact that one H-bomb could wipe out and destroy New York City, the largest city in the world, has brought home to many of us the magnitude of this awesome power that could destroy the world. . . . The people are concerned," she continued. "They show it in their letters to me. . . . They want to know what defenses are being set up. They have a greater interest in and appreciation for the Civil Defense program."[321]

Twenty-nine million Americans believed that their families would not survive an atomic war on this continent, and an even greater number— 44 million—felt that where they lived would be wiped out. When people were asked on 15 June 1956 whether the H-bomb would be used against America in the event of another world war, 64 million adults believed it would.[322]

Margaret's own response was prompted by the same impulse that had propelled her to do battle with Joe McCarthy—a firmly held notion of good and evil which grew out of a belief that the universe was "under the direct and immediate supervision of God."[323] "Individually," she said after the second H-bomb test, "we are dealing with our everyday problems. . . . There's not much that any one of us can do about the hydrogen bomb." Matters requiring courage and faith are problems "that only the individual can conquer himself. For courage and faith cannot be supplied by others. Nor can it be doled out by the government. In the final analysis, all of us must turn to Almighty God and we must dedicate ourselves to Him and give our daily prayers that His will will be done in this world."[324]

Temporarily setting aside her ambivalence about Eisenhower, she observed that his "spiritual attitude" was "in the best tradition of our nation" and "may well be the fortress that ultimately repels those who have desecrated the American way of life."[325] Though she had never been an avid churchgoer, Margaret's refuge in faith contains echoes of early New England, especially in her use of Biblical quotations and her faith that Almighty God was marching with America.

Four months after the H-bomb test, Margaret was scrutinizing Communism with the same clear-eyed vision. The face of evil she had seen in war-torn Europe was evident in the growing threat of international Communism. On 11 June 1954 she warned of the Communists' attack on the Church and cautioned that people had to be on their guard against Communist attempts to make Jews, Catholics and Protestants hate each other through phony superpatriotism. "Such evil behavior," she wrote in her column "is nothing less than a sin against God and the church. It is a violation of the Golden Rule—'Do unto others as you would have them do unto you'—and a violation of the Ninth Commandment of not bearing false witness against your neighbor."[326]

Indochina now became a fixed point in the geography of her spiritual imagination. That region's struggle against Communism was a morality play in which Communism was not merely the enemy, but evil incarnate. From April on, she spoke freely and often about the "impending crisis" in Indochina, the resistance offered by French and Vietnam forces, and the danger of the Reds taking over in Southeast Asia.[327] Defeating the Communists would not be a mere victory; it would be a triumph of good over evil.

In deference to Eisenhower's non-intervention stand, when French efforts became insufficient to mount a winning defense for Indo-China, she advocated using the Nationalist China forces of Chiang Kai-shek. "Since the only really basic and legitimate issue of the people of Indo-China against France is that of the colonialism they hate," she said, "I believe that France should promise the Associated States of Laos, Cambodia and Viet Nam their full independence, and as soon as possible should give it to them."[328]

At home, she advocated outlawing the Communist Party and sponsored a bill, S-200, which would accomplish just that, though it died in committee for lack of support from the attorney general's office. In addition, she introduced a resolution calling for the boycotting of Guatemala and coffee in an attempt to stop the flow of funds into Communist hands in that country. She also supported armed shipments to Nicaragua and Honduras to aid the anti-Communist forces there.[329]

Of a piece with her anti-Communism was a growing intransigence which divided the world ever more readily into heroes and villains. Those who opposed arms shipments became to Margaret "bleeding hearts," while those who favored diplomacy in tackling the Communists were "namby-pamby."[330] Much about her state of mind can be inferred from a broadcast on 23 May 1954. "I think we should deal directly with the problems instead of beating around the bush with a lot of diplomatic talk. . . ," she said. "We might as well do away with the diplomatic niceties and face the fact that the Reds have established a beachhead [in Latin America] for subversive assault on the freedom of the Western Hemisphere."331 Increasingly Margaret's psychic and cultural terrain dominated her public utterances and signalled the full flowering of Margaret's tendency to consult her moral compass on all matters, even those devoid of moral import. The Jimmy Stewart promotion is a case in point.

Soon after Eisenhower began his second term, he forwarded to the Senate nominations for three Reserve major generals and eight brigadier generals, all of whom had been recommended for promotion by the Air Force. Margaret knew some of the men, and in several instances admired their records as regular officers. But their records as Reservists did not conform to the standards she had helped establish in numerous Reserve bills and resolutions, including the Reserve Officer Personnel Act of 1954, which required a minimum of two weeks of active duty per year. Besides, the Air Reserve Officers Association [ARA], which in 1955 has named Margaret their "Sweetheart," saw the promotions as cronyism of the worst sort. Through Bill, their protests went directly to Margaret.332 Soon Bill was examining the profile sheets of the nominees and drafting a letter for Margaret to the Secretary of the Air Force in which were described "very disturbing facts in the following individual cases."333

Of the eleven men, the most famous and the most objectionable was James Maitland Stewart, a handsome, boyish movie-star-qua-pilot who had flown more than 20 bombing missions over Germany during World War II and had become commander of a B-17 wing in the Eighth Air Force. He also played the part of Lindbergh in *Spirit of St. Louis* and starred in *Strategic Air Command*. To millions of adoring Americans, he was "Jimmie" Stewart, America's archetypal male. To the Air Force, he was their best recruiting device. To the ARA, he was someone "deficient on active duty training requirements," whose record did not qualify him to be promoted to brigadier general.334 Based on his three-year hiatus from active duty, Margaret questioned whether he was even qualified for the Ready Reserve, much less . . . the Reserve."335

Inquiry into the eleven nominations began with formal letters to the Air Force and a request from Margaret to Richard Russell, chairman of the Senate Armed Services Committee for a hearing. On 2 May 1957

Lieutenant General Emmett "Rosie" O'Donnell, Jr., deputy Chief of Staff for Personnel and former combat flier, appeared on behalf of the Air Force. His attitude was "openly derogatory" and his dismissal of Margaret as a "skirt"—an actual characterization that got back to her—could easily be inferred from his manner.[336]

Why, Margaret wanted to know, was Stewart up for promotion when 1900 other eligible colonels (a list which included Bill) had been ignored? Why "though he was not qualified to fly any Air Force plane in operation" and "in eleven years as a Reservist . . . had taken only one 15-day tour of duty, this only last year just before he was to come up for promotion" was he being advanced to a position that could place him as "deputy director of the Strategic Air Command—literally the No. 3 job in SAC importance if war comes?" Why were Brigadier General Robert L. Smith, President of Pioneer Air Lines of Dallas and a good friend of Senator Lyndon B. Johnson, "whose record isn't good enough either," and Colonel John Alison of Northrup Aircraft who "had not done a single 1-day tour of duty in nine years" and Colonel John Beverly Montgomery, who was using the Air Force Reserve to draw the maximum retirement pay of 75% of the base pay of a major general, while putting in only 15 days in 26 months, being promoted?[337] Margaret—in contrast to O'Donnell, who contradicted himself and substituted bluster for fact—had done her homework.

Assessing her performance, the *Bangor Daily News* observed that Reserve Lieutenant Colonel "Smith had the upper hand, in some respects. She had already put in 15 days of active duty as a reservist in the current fiscal year . . . and could claim more active Reserve duty than some of the nominees."[338] O'Donnell's rejoinder that, after all, "active participation" wasn't the most important factor in determining promotions contradicted his earlier testimony, that 68,000 reservists had been dropped from the rolls for not meeting this very requirement, noted the newspaper. The Maine press was willing to see Margaret's dispute with O'Donnell as a matter of principle.

Margaret's questions and O'Donnell's answers resulted in eighty-three pages of testimony which, as a courtesy, O'Donnell was allowed to edit prior to printing, so long as he stuck to grammatical corrections and expansion of testimony without changing the sense of his answers.

O'Donnell, however, changed forty-three out of forty-nine pages of his answers to Margaret, six pages in answer to Senator Stennis [D-Miss.] and three out of three in answer to Senator Barrett [R-Wyoming]. The Committee delayed action on the promotions for four months.

During those four months, the Air Force went on the offensive. Margaret's intransigence, they said, came about because Bill was not on the promotion list and because she wanted to extend her own commission in the WAFS, which was to expire automatically on 14 December when she reached the age of 60. News leaks from the Pentagon implied that "she was peeved because she was not made Commander of the WAFS in time of war."339 Officially, Margaret ignored the slurs and waited the Air Force out.340

On Thursday morning, 22 August 1957, Margaret appeared at the Senate Committee Room about five minutes before the scheduled 10:30 meeting time, with a nine-page statement in hand. The committee went into executive session, Margaret read her statement, and the Stewart nomination was rejected 13 to 0. The nomination of Colonel John Beverly Montgomery, about which she felt even more strongly than the Stewart nomination, was rejected by an 11-2 vote. The next day after the Senate had confirmed the promotions of nine of the eleven officers, Margaret placed her statement against the promotions in the *Congressional Record*. In it she accused O'Donnell of misstatements of fact, "extensive false testimony," and "wholesale rewriting of the transcript" of his testimony to the Senate Armed Services Committee.341 Noted Drew Pearson when O'Donnell's testimony came back from the Pentagon, "O'Donnell had deleted his answers. They would have made him look sick."342 Later, when Pearson dismissed the rumors that Bill was "holding up other promotions because he was not promoted himself," his final take on the whole situation was that "it doesn't pay to argue with [the] lady."343 For the time being, the bout on Stewart had gone in Margaret's favor, including her very public spat with O'Donnell.

Within two years, however, Jimmy Stewart and O'Donnell both were promoted. In 1959, O'Donnell became the top air commander in the Pacific, a job which carried with it four stars, and Jimmy Stewart became a Reserve brigadier general after putting in some flying time. Though Margaret did not support the promotion of O'Donnell because of his earlier "serious misrepresentation and untruthful statements," after obstructing the Stewart promotion for several months, she finally gave in, observing that Stewart had the "poorest and smallest" reserve training of all twenty-nine officers in the promotion list.[344] The average American might well have wondered what all of the fuss had been about.

Margaret had a point. Bigwigs with connections should not have been promoted ahead of others who were playing by the rules. On a more lofty level, an editorial in the *Lewiston Evening Journal* suggested that she had tried to "prevent the sort of situation which faced Abraham Lincoln during the Civil War when he found the Union Army loaded with officers of high rank and little experience."[345] But others might well have asked: Was it worth all of the fuss? And why pick on the likable Stewart, anyway? The answer is as complex as Margaret herself. From the fifties on, Margaret increasingly saw the world around her as a morality play. "Malenkov Is Evil; We Hate Him; But He Is Strong Man of Russia," proclaimed the headline of her 16 March 1954 "Washington and You" column.[346] This tendency to frame choices within the context of truth and falsehood, good and evil, and which intensified with age was a somewhat rigid extension of the authority of scripture. But the impulse was not limited to matters which clearly resonated as moral choices. In the Stewart matter, apart from the question of equity, most likely at stake was precisely what the Air Force claimed—that Bill, a full Reserve colonel, had not been proposed for promotion. Since 1950, as the world grew alien, the one person who represented both certainty and continuity, who was with her "foot, horse, and artillery," was Bill. Side by side the two of them had battled foes whose objectives were less worthy and whose motives were less pure. Or so they believed. But their style covered far more uncertainty than their enemies ever realized and was often a substitute for ideas. In contrast to the battle with Joe McCarthy, most of Margaret's later contests were frail, pale skirmishes of little moment. But virtually . all, like her shattering vote against confirmation of Lewis L. Strauss, were conducted on high moral ground.

On the same day in 1959 that the Armed Services Committee voted to promote O'Donnell, Margaret cast a historic vote against the confirmation of Eisenhower's controversial nominee for Secretary of Commerce, Lewis L. Strauss. Strauss had "out McCarthied McCarthy" by removing Dr. Robert Oppenheimer's security clearance and putting him on trial in 1954 while Strauss was chairman of the AEC, a tactic not likely to have won Margaret's approval.347 Moreover, questions about Strauss' integrity had again surfaced when the AEC contracted with the investor-owned Dixon Yates power company, rather than the federally financed Tennessee Valley Authority [TVA] as a power supplier for the AEC's Oak Ridge National Laboratory. Providing capitol to Dixon-Yates was First Boston Corporation, whose vice president "had acted as an unpaid consultant to the Bureau of the Budget on this contract." When this conflict of interest was discovered, Strauss denied all knowledge of the impropriety and "said he would approve the contract again if the circumstances were the same."348 Margaret, who at Eisenhower's urging, had voted for the Dixon-Yates contract and later described it as the "only vote in her entire Congressional service that she . . . would change if given another chance," had several reasons not to look favorably upon Admiral Strauss' candidacy for a cabinet post.349

Eisenhower badly wanted Strauss' nomination confirmed, and Senator Barry Goldwater of Arizona became his field general, even speaking for several hours until senators, flying back to the capitol for the vote, could arrive. Magnifying the vote's importance was the fact that Senate Majority Leader Lyndon B. Johnson had decided to make the confirmation a show of Democratic strength.

Finally the roll call began, and Strauss built up an early lead 21-12. Slowly the nays diminished his lead until it stood at 42-42. "Of the eleven Senators yet to vote," writes Strauss's biographer, "Strauss expected the support of four . . . and he believed that Margaret Chase Smith of Maine, a loyal Republican and Stuart Symington of Missouri, former Secretary of the Air Force with whom he had worked closely . . . both would vote for him, giving him confirmation by a majority of one. 'Mrs. Smith,' the clerk announced. 'Nay,' came the quiet but unmistakable response."350 When Symington voted "Nay" as well, the nomination was defeated 49 to 46. When Margaret voted, Senator Barry Goldwater, Chairman of the Republican Senatorial Campaign Committee, the group responsible for making campaign contributions to individual candidates, "banged his fist on his desk and cursed audibly. 'She won't get one cent of money from my committee for re-election,' he exclaimed."351 In his autobiography,

Waging Peace, Eisenhower called Margaret and fellow nay-sayer William Langer (N.D.), "two short-sighted Republicans who alone among the members of their party voted with the Democrats against Admiral Strauss."352 He also described "the Senate rejection of Admiral Strauss as one of the most depressing official disappointments I experienced during eight years in the White House."353 It was only the ninth time in 170 years that the Senate had failed to consent to a cabinet appointment.354

Margaret, it seemed, was to permanently occupy the fringes of the Republican Party. By the spring of 1960, Illinois Senator Everett Dirksen told Margaret that he had talked with President Eisenhower about arrangements for Republican senators to have their pictures taken with him, a rather common practice, especially around election time. "Margaret," said Dirksen, "I hate to tell you this but Ike said he would be happy to have his picture taken with every Republican senator but that Smith woman."355

One more vote like the Strauss vote, and even in Maine her independence might well have cost her more than that. As the 1960 election was heating up, Horace A. Hildreth, Margaret's old rival, announced at a dinner meeting of the UPI Broadcasters of Maine that he believed Margaret could be defeated by Second District Representative Frank Coffin, a Democrat from Lewiston. Although he later claimed to have been misunderstood, he predicted that she would be beatable "if she casts some more votes such as she cast on the confirmation of Admiral Strauss."356

12. *Passages*

BY THE SIXTIES, it was official. Margaret had slipped from what seemed a permanent position as one of America's most admired women. Perhaps it was her lack of glamour. Certainly her displacement reflects the vulnerability of most public figures to America's insatiable appetite for new faces and beauty (Eleanor Roosevelt's continuing hold notwithstanding). And the thread of confrontation which ran through accounts of her doings in Washington and the growing perception that she thought herself "bigger" than the party—a belief given credence by her continued refusal even to attend Republican National Conventions—took their toll.

In addition there was a dearth of important legislation bearing her name, the fact that she was aging, and her growing obsession with not missing a roll call vote, which caused her to put process ahead of people.

Other factors contributed as well. In April 1954 she decided to discontinue her column, "Washington and You," which had been carried in some 30 newspapers across the country for the past five years. Moreover, from 1954 on, there was about her communications a growing shrillness, even with constituents. In March 1958, a Lewiston man wrote to ask her opinion on why Maine's young people were being drawn to the Democratic, rather than the Republican, Party. Her first answer, which was polite, but not very insightful, did not satisfy him. He wrote back by return mail, pointing out that she had not really answered why "the Republican organization is losing all the new, young, intelligent voters." To his query she responded with growing impatience which culminated in the following accusation: "Your recent letter troubles me. I sense that you have not written to me in complete frankness but rather seem to want to spare me from some harsh words. . . . You know as well as anyone that the Republican Organization has always been unfriendly to me—and that I have always had to run on my own usually confronted with active behind-the-scenes opposition from . . . [them]. That is why I am puzzled that you press me so sharply to answer the question about the Republican Organization and to feel that your doing so strongly indicates that you have a feeling against me. Sincerely, Margaret Chase Smith." Such letters contributed mightily to what came to be called her "waspishness" and did much to erode her standing.[357] But there were also societal causes for her slippage.

She had brought to public office an understanding of people and process based on the values of a village, and was not prepared for the changes already underway by the end of the fifties. In 1959, Columbia University instructor Charles Van Doren shocked millions of Americans when he admitted that his television quiz role was fixed. But when Columbia tried to fire him, letters at NBC ran 5 to 1 against his firing and students rallied to protest it. When rock 'n roll stars Buddy Holly, Ritchie Valens and the Big Bopper—people Margaret had never heard of—were killed in a plane crash, they were mourned by millions. In 1960 four African-Americans asked to be served at a white lunch counter in

Greensboro, N.C., sparking sit-ins by more than 70,000 blacks and whites in more than 100 cities. Herman Kahn's *On Thermonuclear War*, published in 1960, discussed how, with careful planning, only 20 to 30 million Americans would be killed in a nuclear attack. The sexual revolution launched by Enovid 10, the first oral contraceptive (marketed at 55 cents a pill), made Margaret's moral toughness and puritanism anachronistic in a culture whose tastes ran to books like *Peyton Place* and films like "Some Like It Hot." For very few of the changes ushered in during the sixties was Margaret prepared. She was, in Marshall McLuhan's parlance, a "hot" image suddenly misplaced in a milieu which demanded a persona that was not merely "cold," but cool.

Her speech to the District of Columbia BPW in celebration of their fiftieth anniversary in 1969 suggests a public figure unwilling or unable to abandon a highly developed moral code and sense of personal responsibility, despite society's shift to the belief that "all measurements of value were relative." After congratulating the audience on their "acquisition of financial and economic security" and "their growing . . . independence from men" over the past fifty years, she turned her attention to the pill, and "the physical and biological security and freedom that the pill has so suddenly and explosively brought." Although she claimed that she did not intend "to evaluate the pill in terms of moral standards," her attitude was clear when she likened its consequences to "see through" dresses and 'micro-mini skirts.' Women are now in a new age—although I'm not so sure I would call it a Golden Age." But they are in "an age of unprecedented power in which they are more openly, more candidly, and more honestly pursuing rather than pretending to be pursued whether it be for economic security, personal achievement, or men. They are doing it with twin authoritative powers of economic security and biological security. My caution to those of my own sex is: Such power should be very carefully exercised lest it ultimately be the self-destruction of woman and her rightful and responsible place in civilization rather than 'man-kind.'"

To the mostly younger BPW audience, this must have sounded like a call to return to the pedestal, and they listened "in chilly silence, a chill that persisted throughout the reception."[358] Stunned by this rebuff from her most important source of organized support, Margaret was oblivious that she was drawing on the mores of a restrictive village culture that had all but disappeared and which women in the vanguard of the sixties had long since rejected on their way to full liberation.359

* * * * * *

In contrast to the frantic pace of social change elsewhere, in Silver Spring at the wooded, peaceful place they called Quaint Acres, Bill's and Margaret's lives were taken up with the concerns of country gentry—a wounded chipmunk, a nest of blue jays, a marauding cat. Over the years, they had established a pattern of aloofness from the cocktail party-dinner circuit that creates a semblance of camaraderie in social Washington and opted for a rhythm that was soothing and reassuring to them both. Up at six-thirty, Margaret commuted to the District, lunched at her desk, and then drove home with Bill around eight in the evening. Weekends were spent out-of-doors working in the yard, swimming in the pool, or catching up on correspondence. Holidays and adjournment meant trips to Maine, where Margaret's brother Wilbur and sister Evelyn still lived. From Neil Hill, Bill and Margaret would set off in the car without a fixed destination. Frequently they motored to Harmony, Farmington, or Kingfield—all the places in which Margaret had campaigned when she first ran for Congress, places in which she still knew people by name. Sometimes she indulged in a winter vacation as the guest of Ohio Representative Frances Bolton at her palatial Florida home in Palm Beach. She and Margaret had become friends when they both were in the House, and she would give a seconding speech for Margaret's nomination for the Presidency in 1964.

In some ways, Bill was good for Margaret. He smoothed her out, took care of her, and handled the things that would have bothered her, but for him. In both Maryland and Maine, he created homes to which he and Margaret could escape the world. One day in the fall of 1949 he had told Margaret that he was going down to the coast early the next morning, that he had a place he wanted her to see on Cundy's Harbor. They set out at dawn, picking their way toward the coast until they came to a narrow bridge which led out to one of the small, mist-enshrouded islands. Once across, they found a small store where they stopped and had a glass of milk and a doughnut for breakfast. Then they followed the road to what seemed like the end of the island and Bill stopped the car. They were both looking at the place he wanted her to have. The owner would sell one of the small houses, but he wouldn't sell the land, he said.[360] When he pointed to the land he wanted for her, Margaret laughed. She couldn't imagine it. She thought of Banker and her mother, and of how Carrie had worked for her money. The Chases and the Murrays—hard working people all. But not people who owned places on the coast.

Bill bought the house, and eventually the rest of the point—all six acres of it. Nine years later Margaret built her own house, the one they called "the white house." In the meantime, she stayed at Bill's, a small brown house—a cabin, really—with Margaret's room a small cozy space that delighted her. Cundy's was the Maine of tourists: a picturesque harbor with working lobster boats, set against a backdrop of fir trees and hemlocks. Away from the village, the hard-surfaced road turns to dirt, and a peninsula, jutting into the Atlantic, offers at every turn a glimpse of deep water, islands and inlets, a myriad of vistas. While Bill's father was alive, he and his dad would go to the point and cut trees and work the dogs and talk to the lobstermen as they motored into the harbor. Later, after his father died, Bill and Margaret would go there alone—Margaret to catch up on correspondence and Bill to work on the land—and both to drink in the clear sharp beauty of Maine. Neil Hill, Cundy's, and Quaint Acres, all refuges from a public life that with each year sapped more of their energies.

Of the two of them, Bill was "the reader," and through him came much of the information Margaret needed. He would skim books and summarize them, an arrangement which seemed efficient and logical, but which kept her from seeing and fully understanding the profound changes that were taking place. Moreover, in their years together they had come to resemble one another in the way that long-married couples often do. Hence, some of Margaret's least attractive impulses—her suspiciousness of strangers, her tendency to be judgmental, her relentless drive, and her Yankee frugality—were mirrored in Bill. And she had no way and no reason to reassess these habits. Had Bill been her husband, his negative influence would have been limited to non-working hours. But he was with her constantly on Capitol Hill and in Silver Spring, and thus neither in her private nor her professional life was there room for fresh ideas or other, younger people, especially males. Her office consisted of female secretaries who, except for Blanche Bernier Hudon (now Margaret's private secretary on a $7,099 salary) typed and handled the mail. They knew very little about the inner workings of the office. In addition, Margaret had hired Joseph "Spike" Bernier, Blanche's brother and her sister Laura's husband, who was paid a $15,731 salary to be a Jack-of-all-trades, a combination of chauffeur, handyman, confidante, and messenger. Finally, there was Bill, who earned $16,300 and was the team's quarterback.[361] At no time were there interns, snappy young lawyers fresh out of the Ivy Leagues—the sort recruited by John Kennedy and other young congressmen—staffers full of energy, arrogance and ideas that could keep her connected.

Despite her growing isolation, Margaret easily won a third term to the Senate in 1960. The Republicans ran no one against her in the primary, and in the general election, in the face of a well-muscled Maine Democratic Party, the faithful turned out and gave her a 96,000 vote majority over Lucia Cormier, a Muskie protégé. Despite the novelty of two women squaring off over a Senate seat—a situation which earned them a spot on the cover of *Time* magazine—the race was never close. Cormier's remote personality made Margaret seem warm by comparison, and her liberal platform seemed little different from Margaret's moderate-to-liberal record. Maine saw no reason *not* to vote for Margaret.

13. Camelot and Beyond

THE THREE YEARS of John Kennedy's presidency, which would be remembered by some as Camelot, were, ironically, years which provided glimpses of a younger Margaret—the same young woman who had voted against her party and for Lend-Lease, the same freshman senator who had quietly but firmly stood up to McCarthy. On 30 March 1961 when she learned that the Snark missile base in Presque Isle, Maine, was to be closed, she spoke briefly on the floor of the Senate. Although her speech was less memorable than her Declaration of Conscience, it resonated with the something like the same political courage.

> Mr. President, this morning at 9 o'clock I received from the Department of the Air Force notification that it had been decided to close the Snark missile base at Presque Isle.

I regret that in the rapidly changing character of the security and defense of our country—and specifically in the development of the missile program—the long anticipated inactivation and termination of the now outmoded Snark program and the resulting scheduled closing of the Presque Isle Air Force Base have now become realities, as a result of the decision by President Kennedy.

The far easier course for me to pursue politically would be to vigorously protest this action and, as a Republican senator, to point out that the decision was made by a Democratic president, and to make a political attack on the decision of President Kennedy.

The far safer course for me to pursue politically would be to demand that the now outmoded Snark program be continued, so that the Presque Isle Air Force Base be kept operating, to aid the economy of the area and to avoid the impact and dislocation that its closing is bound to have on the economy of the area.

But in all good conscience I cannot do this, for this would simply be playing politics with our national security, our national defense and our taxpayers' dollar. It would be submitting to the economic philosophy that our national defense establishment and our national security program must be operated primarily for the local economy.

I shall do what I can to help the Presque Isle area absorb the economic impact of this unpleasant decision made by President Kennedy; and while I can understand and appreciate the concern of the area, I am confident that the great majority of the people of the area are not only fair-minded about this long anticipated development but are also of such admirable self-reliance that they will meet the impact well and successfully.

By her third term, Margaret was the third-highest ranking GOP member on the Senate Armed Services Committee and the fifth-ranking Republican on Appropriations. She also held membership on the Space Committee, for which she had given up her place on Government Operations, a slot taken by the junior Senator from Maine, Democrat Edmund S. Muskie (who after two terms as governor had been elected to the Senate in September 1958). When Kennedy came to office on 20 January 1961 as a minority president who had made foreign policy a centerpiece of his campaign, Margaret was well positioned to exert pressure on him. The principal battles she would fight were the Cuban missile crisis and the Nuclear Test Ban Treaty. Of the two, the first contained more substance. The second launched her bid for the presidency in 1964.

To say that Margaret was *not* dazzled by the Kennedy charm is an understatement. She had worked with him on the New England Senatorial Conference and served with him in the House in 1947 and 1948. In the Senate, they had both been members of the Reorganization sub-committee of Government Operations. None of these contacts with him had been positive for her. His breezy style annoyed her, his indifference to the legislative process insulted her, his brother Bobby's connection with Joe McCarthy made her wary, and his incursion into Maine in the 1954 race on behalf of her opponent infuriated her. Even so, his "Let us never negotiate out of fear. But let us never fear to negotiate" impressed her. The posture was eminently reasonable but with a fine, tough edge. And he further disarmed her on 23 March 1961, when in a televised press conference he pointed to a map, "eloquently explained why we had to stand firm on Laos—and . . . issued an ultimatum to Khrushchev to get Communist forces out of Laos." But when Khrushchev called Kennedy's bluff and defied the ultimatum, "and Communist aggression increased in Laos," Margaret "was disillusioned. Kennedy had failed to back up his strong words."[362]

On 21 September 1961, in what was described as "one of her rare speeches from the Senate floor," she "took the Kennedy Administration to task for what she interpreted as its apparent failure of nerve and lack of will with respect to nuclear weapons."[363] Specifically, she was alarmed at the new stress placed by the Kennedy Administration on the use of conventional weapons in the ongoing struggle with the Soviets over Berlin. "If today, and in the days immediately ahead, we fail to meet the Soviets at the ultimate levels of will and purpose," she said, "the danger will be greatly widened that we will have no choice later on but to meet them at the ultimate levels of force and violence; either that or submit to their will. How much farther do you think Khrushchev would go if he was confident the over-all military advantage was on his side?"[364]

Margaret chided the administration for "turning to emphasis on conventional weapons" when the U.S. needed to increase its nuclear superiority over Russia, and urged the president to be a risk-taker and to draw the line. We have played into the hands of Nikita Khruschev "for the kind of warfare in which he knows he can beat us," she said. By depending on conventional warfare, we appear to be admitting that "we do not have the will to use that one power with which we can stop him. In short, we have the nuclear capability, but not the nuclear credibility."[365] Margaret's position that the United States should not limit itself to conventional weapons but should use nuclear tactical weapons wherever and whenever appropriate was on the record.

White House reaction was swift. Defense Secretary Robert McNamara claimed that the U.S. *would* use atomic weapons if necessary, and Attorney General Robert Kennedy also made it clear that in the event of war, atomic weapons *would* be used. Moscow reaction was less swift, but more heated. Nikita Khrushchev's reply was sent to Britain's former Defense Secretary Emanuel Shinwell, who, with 58 other M.P.'s, had urged Russia to cease nuclear testing. "Who can remain calm and indifferent to such provocative statements made . . . by this woman, blinded by savage hatred toward the community of socialist countries?" he asked. "It is hard to believe how this woman, if she is not the devil in disguise, can make such a malicious, man-hating call. She should understand that in the fire of nuclear war, millions of people would perish, including her own children, if she has any. Even the wildest of animals, a tigress even, worries about her cubs, licks and pities them." Observed Margaret, who *Time* noted was "a childless widow," "Mr. Khruschev is angry because American officials have grown more firm since my speech."[366]

Thirteen months later, when the Cuban missile crisis occurred on 22 October 1962, however, Margaret felt vindicated. Kennedy's response sounded as though it had been drafted by Margaret herself. "Let no one doubt that this is a difficult and dangerous course on which we have set out," he said. "No one can perceive precisely what course it will take or what costs or casualties will be incurred. But the greatest danger of all would be to do nothing."[367] He also announced that he was establishing a blockade and warned that he had "directed the armed forces to prepare for any eventualities." Any missile launched from Cuba against any nation in the Western Hemisphere would be regarded "as an attack by the Soviet Union on the United States, requiring a full retaliatory response upon the Soviet Union."[368] Missiles already in Cuba had to be removed. Within seven days, Khrushchev agreed to remove the missiles.

Margaret's second bout with Kennedy occurred on 24 September 1963, when Margaret cast "a very troubled vote" against the Nuclear Test Ban Treaty between the United States and Russia. Though she knew that most of her constituency favored the test ban and that her vote would be used against her in the 1966 race, she became one of 19 senators to vote against it. The treaty was ratified 80 to 19.[369] Said Margaret: "I have tried very hard to find a basis for which I could conscientiously vote for ratification of the treaty. I regret to say that the issues have not supplied such a basis. On the other hand it has been argued with sincerity . . . that one could not conscientiously vote against the treaty because such a vote would be a vote against peace. . . . I cannot challenge that argument. . . . But in equal degree, I cannot challenge with complete certainty the argument made that the treaty may be a first step toward the undermining of our national security."[370] Shortly after the vote occurred, President Kennedy was handed a note by his secretary while meeting with the German ambassador. He had instructed his staff to advise him the minute the vote was taken—and, apparently, whether he had been successful with Margaret. The note read: "Test-ban vote 80-19. Mrs. Smith went wrong."[371] Ted Sorenson, Kennedy's alter-ego, was later to describe Margaret as one of two enemies that Senator Kennedy had in the Senate."[372]

One of the other 18 Senators to vote against the treaty was Barry Goldwater, an arch-conservative from Arizona who was already a front-runner for the Republican nomination for President in 1964. Their agreement on foreign policy matters provided an opportunity for Bill to plant the improbable idea that Goldwater and Smith would be excellent running mates. The day after the vote and several weeks after Margaret gave the first of several speeches against the treaty, the *Lewiston Evening Journal* aired a story quoting Margaret to say that she was "startled by the mail she has received urging her to run on the GOP ticket next year." Despite her assurance that she was "realistic enough to know that she [didn't] have a chance," the first of several trial balloons had been launched.[373]

In November, Margaret promised to announce her intentions regarding the presidential race on December 5 in a speech at the Women's

National Press Club. Her self-described position was "less liberal than that of Nelson Rockefeller and less conservative than that of Barry Goldwater," though as one editor who could usually be counted on to support Margaret observed, this was a "statement which could apply to other 'dark horse' leaders within the GOP. . . . Rockefeller and Goldwater between them represent the 'extremes' of Republican philosophy." He also warned that "there is much reason to doubt a majority of the voting public is prepared to place a member of the female sex in the White House." Though Rockefeller was hurt by his divorce and remarriage, and "the New York Governor would lose many women's votes because of this, Mrs. Smith would, if named the GOP's Presidential candidate, lose the vote of many men."[374] Margaret's beginning could not be described as auspicious.

Suddenly, on 21 November 1963, America went into mourning. On a campaign swing through Dallas, John F. Kennedy had been assassinated. He was the first president to die in office since Franklin Delano Roosevelt died of cerebral hemorrhage in April 1945, and he was the first to be assassinated since William G. McKinley was shot in 1901. The day after the assassination, amidst the speeches and ceremony and collective public grief, Margaret very quietly honored his memory in the Senate chamber by plucking a red rose from her lapel and placing it on the desk he had once occupied. The idea had originated with Mike Mansfield, though Margaret "was deeply pleased to do it."[375] According to the *Lewiston Evening Journal*, "she moved so quickly that most observers missed the incident. The rose lay untouched through the brief official session of the Senate. As the day ended it was still there in the fading light of the darkening chamber."[376] Meanwhile, on a plane from Dallas, the new president, Lyndon Baines Johnson, was being sworn in by Federal Judge Sarah T. Hughes, former president of the BPW and Democratic nominee for vice president in 1952.

In deference to Kennedy's death, Margaret decided to delay the announcement of her candidacy until 27 January, the date for which the Women's National Press Club Meeting had been re-scheduled. As the luncheon date approached, speculation in the press increased, and both Margaret and Bill were plagued with questions of whether she would run.

When Bill distributed copies of her speech to the press that morning before the luncheon, recipients discovered that the conclusion with

Margaret's final decision was omitted. She had written two endings, and she had kept them to herself. She claimed that not even Bill knew which one she would use. After keeping the audience in suspense right up to the end, Margaret concluded: "And so, because of the many reasons compelling me not to run, I have decided that I shall enter the New Hampshire Presidential preferential primary and the Illinois primary."

The announcement was the high point of Margaret's presidential campaign. It suggested that she was not out of touch, for it contained echoes of some of the most noble themes of the sixties and clearly aligned her cause with the cause of civility and tolerance and commitment to social justice. "In my opinion, any hatred or bigotry—even the slightest hatred or bigotry—is too much for our nation and to be deplored. But I cannot agree with those who contend that now there is greater hatred and bigotry than ever existed before in our country. Instead I believe that our country is far freer of bigotry and hatred than it was ten years ago. . . . Who can deny that the rights of negroes are greater in 1964 than they were in 1954? Who can deny that there has been progress on civil rights in the past decade? Perhaps not as much as there should have been. But who can . . . say that we have . . . become more bigoted in 1964 on civil rights than we were in 1954?"[377] The words did not have the luster nor the grace of a Kennedy phrase, but they were clearly in the tradition of what Kennedy had called "the common enemies of man: Tyranny, poverty, disease and war itself." And they were spoken with some moral authority, as she had supported Truman's efforts to end racial discrimination, supported Eisenhower's decision to send troops to Central High School in Little Rock, Arkansas and voted for the 1957 civil rights bill, which set up a Commission on Civil Rights and authorized federal suits in support of African-Americans denied the right to vote. She also became a co-sponsor of a second Civil Rights Act introduced in 1959, which was passed in spite of a southern filibuster of 125 consecutive hours and which ultimately increased federal authority over suffrage

With others of her age, she privately held to a form of garden variety racism which included the use of terms like "half-breed," to refer to the offspring of racially-mixed unions. But her commitment to the national interest and to the principle of equity pulled more strongly on her than racial prejudice, and so she voted for the Civil Rights Act of 1964 and the

Voting Rights Act of 1965. After five years of civil disorder: the burning of Watts, Detroit, Dayton, Ohio and Cambridge, Maryland, the arrests of over 70,000 people, and open revolt on college campuses, however, she voted against court-ordered busing, funding for the integration of metropolitan schools, and the withholding of federal aid for refusing to bus. Civil order was and would remain far more important to her than broadened civil rights.[378]

Her announcement to the Women's National Press Club also made it clear that her candidacy was symbolic. Through her "for the first time women of the United States had an opportunity to break the barrier against women being seriously considered for the Presidency of the United States." She was, she said, "pioneering the way for a woman in the future . . . to make the way easier for her to be elected President."[379]

Margaret entered the first-in-the-nation preferential presidential primary in New Hampshire behind Goldwater and Rockefeller, who had announced their presidential candidacies much earlier. Her Maine supporters predicted that Margaret's chances in a three-way race would be "'pretty good' because her candidacy would be a 'way out' for many not desiring to vote for either Goldwater or Rockefeller." Others in the Maine GOP, while pulling for Margaret and commending her courage, said "they had to take a realistic view in predicting she will be battling against great odds."[380] The number of entrants in the New Hampshire primary later expanded to include former Minnesota Governor Harold Stassen and two write-in candidates: 1960 presidential nominee Richard Nixon and ambassador to Saigon, Henry Cabot Lodge.

On Monday morning, 10 February after a twelve-hour drive from Washington that got Bill and Margaret to Colebrook, New Hampshire at 4 A.M. Sunday morning, Margaret hit the campaign trail in Pittsburg, New Hampshire, near the Canadian border at 6:30 A.M. The first voters she approached "were two startled loggers loading pulpwood on a truck at the roadside." The temperature hovered at thirty degrees below zero.[381]

There were no organized receptions and no coached crowds, just Margaret and the folks from New Hampshire. "The people have a chance to see and talk with me and then ask questions," she told reporters, "making it possible for them to make up their minds about me."382 The campaign was populist in impulse and low-key. Margaret wore no hat or any kind of head covering. She dressed in a short beaver jacket with light ankle boots. During the day she sipped coffee, not only in restaurants but perched on stools in diners. From bobbin mills to country stores, she never asked for peoples' votes, just reminded them of her twenty-three years in the House and Senate and her unbroken record on more than 1,600 roll call votes. "I never walk out on a vote or dodge an issue," she said. "I am always willing to stand up and be counted no matter how controversial the issue."383

After a week in New Hampshire following Margaret's campaign, Lorin Arnold, the *Bangor Daily News*' political columnist, announced to his readers that he was "persuaded she cannot win." On the nearly 1,000 miles he spent covering her campaign, he had talked with the "many varied Republicans from all walks of life that she had met" and came away with the impression that they would not vote for her. "Practically all of those folk, meeting the senator for the first time," he wrote, "immediately became exceedingly fond of her and were noticeably impressed by her charm, graciousness and ability as a senator. They admired her courage in taking this big step but took the stand that the presidency was no place for Senator Smith or any other woman—not yet, at least."384 The warm receptions from "nice people" would not convert into votes.

Arnold's predictive powers proved impressive. On 10 March Henry Cabot Lodge flattened all other contenders in the New Hampshire primary with an unanticipated write-in victory. Unofficial returns two days later put Lodge at 33,521 (35.4%), Barry Goldwater 21,775 (23%); Nelson Rockefeller 19,496 (20.6%); Richard Nixon 15,752 (16.6%); Margaret Chase Smith received 2,812 votes and Harold Stassen 1,285 votes.385

The next primary was in Illinois in April, a race she had successfully entered by the skin of her teeth only twenty minutes before the deadline.386 In Illinois there was potential for Margaret to make a worse showing than she had in New Hampshire.

The Illinois Young Republicans who had obtained enough signatures for Margaret's name to appear on the ballot had reason to fear repercussions from the Goldwater people "who dominated the Republican Illinois organization." But they told the press that they were "really pushing Margaret for Vice President."387 Everett Dirksen, state Republican leader and former McCarthy supporter, was "openly unhappy about Margaret's candidacy in his own state of Illinois." And Charles Percy, the handsome, successful Republican candidate for governor of Illinois in 1964 and board chairman of Bell and Howell, like the other leading Republicans of the state, gave Margaret a wide berth. But in Illinois, unlike New Hampshire, Margaret had one big advantage. The women were organized and supportive.

To the surprise of experts, who had predicted that she would get less than 10% of the vote, and thanks to the work to Mrs. Murray "Vi" Dawson and her group of women, Margaret got a quarter of a million—or 30% of the vote. Goldwater won in Illinois, but by a much smaller margin than had been predicted. Though Margaret publicly gave credit to a "small band of brilliant young men [referring to the Young Republicans] and dedicated women" who had helped her to achieve her vote in Illinois, privately she credited the women with making it happen.[388] In New Hampshire she spent $250 and finished almost last. Then she went to Illinois, spent only $85 and made a showing. "For $335, I didn't do badly," she said.[389] Illinois, however, was to provide her last good news.

In Oregon, where she did not campaign owing to travel costs and distance, she came in a disappointing fifth, as she had in New Hampshire. In the Massachusetts primary, which was held on 28 April, Lodge once again swept to victory while Margaret finished fifth.

The last test before the convention came on 2 June in the California primary, a contest which Margaret had not chosen to enter. When the electors narrowly chose a slate of 86 Goldwater delegates, it became clear that none of the dark horses would be able to take the nomination away from the Arizona senator, despite some last minute maneuvering by Governor William Scranton of Pennsylvania. California had put Goldwater "within reach of the 665 delegates needed for the nomination."[390] On the eve of the convention on 12 July with the Republican Party poised to turn away from the moderate majority that had dominated it for forty years, Margaret arrived in San Francisco with only 16 votes in hand—all 14 votes of the Maine delegation, plus the votes of North Dakota's John Rouzie and Vermont's George Aiken.[391] Aiken, now 75 and a twenty-five year veteran of the Senate, was to nominate her.[392]

Though by now Margaret was a contender for the nomination in spirit only, she was greeted at the airport by "Vi" Dawson and "her girls" as though a conquering hero. They cheered and applauded and waved "Smith-for-President" signs, while a brass band played "Hello Maggie." They had set up headquarters on Market Street under the direction of Marion Otsea, chairman of the Smith California committee, and had already prepared for a floor demonstration following Senator Aiken's nominating speech. As Margaret said later, "I never had any intention of giving up until the final vote was cast." Neither did "the girls."393

On Monday, 13 July a bitter fight broke out in the platform committee between liberals, who "believed they were making a desperate effort to rescue the party from oblivion," and Goldwaterites "who regarded the wrangle over the platform as a final effort to discredit their standard-bearer before a national television audience."394 The upshot was a memorable display of bad manners by Goldwater supporters in the galleries on Tuesday night, 14 July when Nelson Rockefeller stepped to the rostrum at 8:45 to begin the platform fight.395 It was, in the view of a fellow observer and Republican, "not only the dramatic high point of the convention, but the truest distillation of this convention's spirit: tough, intransigent, abrasive. Rockefeller had barely started denouncing the John Birch Society in his speech calling for adoption of the antiextremist plank, when the booing began. Rockefeller could scarcely complete a sentence without being interrupted by a volley of boos." Only a small fraction of the boos, he recalled, were coming from the delegates on the floor; most were coming from the galleries, where "the rank and file of the Goldwater Movement" was sitting. "This was their day, and they weren't going to let Nelson Rockefeller spoil it for them." But that sentiment wasn't confined to the galleries. On the floor, "one alternate delegate from Louisiana nudged his neighbor, pointed to the spectators booing Nelson Rockefeller, and said approvingly, 'Look at that; it's America up there.'"396

On Wednesday, 15 July the convention neared its climax. For seven long hours, eight names were placed before the convention in endless nominating and seconding speeches, despite an outcome which was obvious to everyone. In a box above the convention floor, in defiance of the tradition which called for candidates to be absent during their nominating speech, Margaret watched as Senator Aiken finally strode to the microphone to place her name in nomination.

"I intend to nominate for President one of the most capable persons I have ever known and one with whom I have been associated in public service for twenty-four years," echoed the unmistakable cadence and crispness of George Aiken's voice over the public address system of the Cow Palace. "My candidate wants the nomination solely on her record and qualifications for the job. As a result our transportation fund is busted. Our entertainment fund is shattered. Our demonstration wallet collapsed. Our conscience is intact." After reminding the audience that Margaret had "not neglected her work in the Senate to chase down delegates to this Convention," and that she had spent no money for advertising, had hired no paid workers, made no promises, and "will have nothing to do with the wheeling and dealing," he paused, then quickly concluded. "I am proud," he said, "to nominate that candidate—the Senior Senator from the Great Republican State of Maine—Senator Margaret Chase Smith."[397] Her nomination was far more improbable than Willkie's had been twenty-four years earlier.

Miraculously—because at first they had not been able to gain entrance to the floor of the arena—Smith demonstrators and cheerleaders burst onto the convention floor. The band was playing "Drink a toast to dear old Maine," cards were being held in the gallery, and "everyone was cheering and singing and the delegates were carrying Smith signs and the whole huge hall was having a good time," remembered Donna Wright of San Francisco, the organizer and director of the floor demonstration. Then, she said,

> an element we hadn't even considered came into play . . . sentiment, and respect and good wishes for a gallant lady.
>
> We had captured the audience in a genuine, spontaneous show of affection, sensed, just as much, from all reports, by individuals watching TV in their living rooms far from the electricity of the actual scene. Perhaps everyone was tired of the tension and strife of a bitter contest, perhaps they suddenly realized what Senator Smith had been trying to say was *for* something instead of *against*. . . . The Cow Palace was singing 'Boola, Boola,' Senator Smith was beaming from her box, Marion [Ostea] was waving a rose around her head, my husband [in the gallery] finally got 'Hello Maggie' [in individual large single letter signs] almost perfect and people smiled through their tears.[398]

After the floor demonstration and the seconding speeches, Goldwater was asked by a group Bill Lewis cryptically described as "Air Force-minded visitors at the convention" to allow each of the delegates pledged to him to "cast one vote for Margaret Chase Smith in honor of women nationally." The gesture would cost him very few out of the large number of delegates pledged to him, they argued, and it would potentially "gain the votes of millions of American women and at a very little cost." According to Lewis, "they were curtly rebuffed."[399]

Margaret was too liberal for Goldwater. Her historic support for the minimum wage law, social security and federal aid to schools, coupled with her recent support of the Economic Opportunity Act of 1964 ran counter to almost all of Goldwater's political impulses. Besides, Margaret's patrician manner and bearing smacked of the Eastern Establishment, spiritual home to the Rockefellers, Lodges, and Scrantons, the internationalist liberals who had long discounted Goldwater and recently vilified him. By the convention's end, Goldwater was in no mood to deal with the Eastern elite or "lukewarm Republicans." He chose as his running mate Congressman William E. Miller, "a staunchly conservative, largely unknown native of upstate New York."[400]

When the final roll call began, Margaret left the Cow Palace and missed seeing Goldwater roll up his 883 votes. She was not there to hear the vote cast for her by Joe Martin of Massachusetts, or the two votes cast for her from Alaska, or the three from North Dakota, one each from Ohio and Washington, the five from Vermont or the fourteen from Maine. She did not know that despite Lodge's superior showing in the primaries, on a technicality she had come in second, as the delegates for the other candidates allowed their votes to be shifted to Goldwater, while Margaret's 27 votes stood fast.[401]

What she did know was the same thing one of her supporters had known when a Goldwater person sneered at her and said, "You're wasting your time!" Unflustered and unflappable, the Smith supporter retorted, "You're only running—I'm making history."[402]

In the final analysis, Margaret's decision to run, as well as her decision to go to San Francisco and see the campaign through to its finish was a personal, rather than a political decision, a conclusion invited by the Smith camp's exaggerations regarding "a steady flow of mail from all fifty states urging [her] to run and to give the Republican voters a third choice between Conservative Goldwater and Liberal Rockefeller."[403] No correspondence of that magnitude is extant, although several hundred people did mail in contributions after her 27 January announcement. Nor was broad support suggested by the number of Smith organizations formed during the primaries. Even in Illinois, home to Margaret's largest core of organizers, the Vi Dawson group numbered no more than twelve.[404] The popular primary vote itself further confounds any claims to a groundswell of support.

Margaret and Bill may have been swayed by public opinion polls which showed that Goldwater's support among Republicans at no time reached 30%, not even on the eve of the convention. In fact, in April and May when most delegates were being elected, Goldwater support from Republicans stood at just 14%.[405] They certainly sensed that Goldwater conservatism was not what the rank-and-file wanted. Yet, savvy Republican that Margaret was, she must have seen the Goldwater people gaining control of the Party machinery long before the delegates were chosen. In nearby Waterville, Cyril Joly, Jr., for example, who was Goldwater's campaign chief in Maine, had begun over a year before the primaries to line up support for Goldwater. That Margaret perceived Goldwater's vice-like grip on the nomination—but too late—was suggested in 1965 at a luncheon in her honor. "If I were to run again," she said at that time, "I would organize every state and go for the delegates at least *two years in advance.*"[406]

The decision to run was a return to her quest plot. She had been born more than twenty years before the young president who had just been assassinated, more than eleven years before the vice president who succeeded him. Nineteen hundred sixty-four was the last conceivable presidential election in which Margaret might be a candidate. By the next one, she would be seventy. When she was asked by a reporter in January why she had decided to run, her response was: "There was nowhere to go but the presidency."[407] Among Republican candidates, she had more congressional experience than all of them put together. Not one had faced the odds or surmounted the obstacles she had. Her 1964 run for the Presidency was a memorial to all that she had been, and to what might have been. But it was her last hurrah.

The impact of the outcome of the race, more than the campaign itself, struck parts of America with peculiar force. In the New Bern, *North Carolina Mirror*, the editor wrote: "Harking back to the Republican National Convention in San Francisco, we hope it will be our good fortune to remember longest Senator Margaret Chase Smith. Some of the other folks there we won't mind forgetting, if such a thing is possible. This distinguished woman never really had a chance to be her party's standard bearer," the editor observed," but the *Mirror* is glad she campaigned for the nation's highest office. It gave millions of Americans a televised glimpse of one of this country's great public servants. At a gathering where true dignity was an oddity, just as it will be rather inconspicuous when the Democrats meet in Atlantic City, she managed to retain the graciousness and charm that has characterized not only her personal life but her career in Congress."[408]

There is deeply embedded in this description an unmistakable tone of nostalgia. There is, too, a longing and an embrace of earlier, more genteel times. Nowhere did the writer understand Margaret to be a *political* alternative to Goldwater, an ideological counterpoint to Goldwater conservatism or Rockefeller liberalism. Much as if she were an elder statesman on the eve of departure from office, what was nostalgically remembered was the way she conducted herself, the personage she had become. For many of her most ardent supporters, Margaret was the epitome of the gracious lady. Their highest praise cast her not as a policymaker or leader but as the gracious Grand Duchess—of the blood royal, but not in line of succession. She was, in her sixties and in the sixties, vested with power by some because she projected the manners and morals of an earlier age. This was, however, the power of an icon or a monument, not the sort prized by the likes of Lyndon Johnson or Richard Nixon. By 1964, Margaret had become America's fonder past.

14. The "Now Generation"

BY THE TIME LYNDON JOHNSON was sworn in for his first full term in 1965, the idealism of the early Civil Rights Movement had given way to nationwide race riots, sparked by conditions Malcolm X characterized not as an American dream, but an "American nightmare. . . . Three hundred and ten years we worked in this country without a dime in return." At the same time, President Kennedy's 1962 instruction to U.S. troops in Vietnam to protect themselves if fired upon but to understand that they were "not combat troops in the generally understood sense of the word" had evolved by 1965 into Lyndon Johnson's order to send the first ground troops to Orange Beach, three miles south of Danang. From the air base there, a continuous bombing campaign against North Vietnam was to be launched. Its name: Operation Rolling Thunder. As a protest of the country's involvement in southeast Asia, the first teach-in was held at the University of Michigan on 2 March 1965, while the largest took place at Berkeley, where 12,000 heard Dr. Benjamin Spock, Norman Mailer, I.F. Stone, and Senator Ernest Grueing, among others. "Flower Power" was coined by Allen Ginsberg at a Berkeley antiwar rally. Before the year was out, a group planning to destroy the Washington Monument, Statue of Liberty, and Liberty Bell was arrested, and Quaker Norman Morrison had immolated himself on the steps of the Pentagon. As the press familiarized the country with major U.S. installations like Cam Rahn Bay and Bien Hoa, as well as combat zones like the Mekong Delta, and as "body counts" continued to escalate, students across the country began to carry Viet Cong and North Vietnam flags and demonstrate. Their chant: "Hey, hey, LBJ, how many kids did you kill today?" was to drive Johnson from the White House. Against this backdrop of disorder, Margaret continued to function as the symbol of Maine's present-past, though the nastiness of the political climate took a toll on her as well. In 1965 she wrote to J. Edgar Hoover to request an investigation of her staff, including Bill. Before she ran for office the next year, she wanted to be sure that she would be spared "even the slightest and most remote possibility of . . . embarrassment."[409]

In Maine, as in Washington, there were signs of unease. On Tuesday, 25 May 1965, the now-minority Republicans in the Maine House walked out in a body as the House passed an order that one of them called "a complete insult" to U.S. Senator Margaret Chase Smith. The walkout, of about ten minutes duration, occurred when the clerk read aloud a Senate-amended order revising a House tribute to Margaret which had been presented by a Republican leader to commemorate the recent (May 19) announcement of her candidacy for re-election and congratulate "the

67 year-old senator on a 25-year congressional career in which 'she had worked tirelessly for her fellow citizens . . . fearlessly for good government, a strong national defense and legislation to improve the American way of life.'" That resolution had been amended on the motion of Democratic state senator Mary Chisholm of Cape Elizabeth to focus on Margaret's roll call record and her age. As reported in the *Bangor Daily News*, Chisholm's version congratulated the "grand old lady" for her "unparalleled record of not having missed roll call votes. . . ." It omitted much of the language of the original resolution but said she had become known for "wearing a fresh rosebud every day" and "ordering the Senate secretary to send her one." The protested version was later rescinded and the original resolution tabled until Wednesday.[410]

On Thursday, 28 May the Maine House voted to kill the original resolution which had congratulated Margaret on her twenty-five years and her fine record in Congress. The Democrats' position was expressed in caucus by Speaker Dana W. Childs of Portland, who reminded fellow Democrats of Paul Fullam's 1954 campaign, when "Senator Smith appeared on television and displayed one of her nomination petitions . . . showing Fullam as a signer and thus, Margaret claimed, backing her candidacy. If we're endorsing what her position is," Childs said, "we'll have to answer for it in the next election." Observed another, there will be "program after program on television showing this order if it should be passed. She is a crafty little lady. She's a crafty politician. She'll use it— the resolution order—to bury us just as she buried Paul Fullam." The original resolution was defeated on a 73-66 party line vote.[411]

Meanwhile on 1 June Margaret, who took no public position on the maneuverings in Maine, celebrated the anniversary of her Declaration of Conscience speech and the tenth straight year in which she had been recorded on every roll-call, a total (after two votes on 2 June) of 1,978 without a miss. The following week, when she cast her 2000th Senate vote—a vote on an amendment to the foreign aid authorization bill which failed, 80 to 2—the Senate, led by Everett Dirkson [R-Ill], passed a resolution honoring her. In seven speeches she heard the accolades she had longed to hear for fifteen years and the applause, too, as she was given three standing ovations by fellow senators. Uncharacteristically, Margaret broke down and sobbed as she responded with thanks. Her iconographic function as the Senate's "grand old lady" was complete. She had been canonized and enshrined in a resolution, though neither she nor Bill understood it quite that way.

Had Washington been less hospitable to Margaret she might have decided to call it quits after the fourth term she would win in 1966. But at last she was having fun. And besides, what else was she to do, she would have responded, had she been asked.

For the first time since she sat in the Senate, she had a friend in the White House. Margaret had known Lyndon Johnson ever since 1945, when they both served on the House Naval Affairs Committee. His ascent to the Senate had occurred in 1948, the same year as her own, and the two had been casual friends for many years. Unlike his predecessor, whose urbanity and intellectualism made her uneasy and defensive, Lyndon Johnson's Texas hill country pragmatism was enough like Margaret's own to draw her to him. And unlike an increasing number of Americans who saw him through the prism of Vietnam and heard his words with what Richard Rovere in the *New Yorker* described as "distrust and disbelief," Margaret both believed in what he said and respected what he stood for.[412]

Along with most of her colleagues in the Eighty-Ninth Congress, she supported Johnson's domestic program, even though she was displeased with Johnson's failure to reverse a decision made during the Kennedy years to close the Kittery-Portsmouth shipyard as of 1974. The matter remained unresolved until 1971 when President Nixon finally rescinded the closure order. She voted for Johnson's final Medicare-Social Security bill, which included a Medicare program for the elderly and increased Social Security benefits, a $6.5 billion package.[413] She was especially enthusiastic about Johnson's $4.5 billion public works Big Rivers and Harbors bill, which included $227 million for the Dickey-Lincoln School Hydro-electric project along Maine's St. John River, a project which was never completed, however.[414] She supported his Elementary and Secondary Education Act, which provided more than a billion dollars in grants for indigent pupils, and the Higher Education Act which assisted college students. On Vietnam, too, she and the President were in accord. On 3 December 1965 when Margaret spoke at Bangor High School and made her final statement for the year regarding the conduct of the war in Southeast Asia, she said simply, "I support President Johnson's policy in Viet Nam and will continue to do so."[415]

Ties between Margaret and President Johnson were further strengthened by Johnson's long-standing interest in Bill Lewis. Johnson had first noticed Bill in 1945 when Johnson was assigned by his mentor, Speaker Sam Rayburn, to the House Naval Affairs Committee. Bill impressed the Texan, and he offered Bill a chance to become "an LBJ boy," which Bill declined.[416] Later after he won a seat in the United States Senate and was presumably preparing for his leap to the White House, he offered Bill a job in the Justice Department. After Bill again turned him down, Johnson remained what Bill later described as "deeply irritated," but by the time Johnson became president, he was treating Bill as an intimate. During the last six months of the Johnson presidency, Bill was a White House guest five times, including a luncheon alone with the President. Johnson once asked Bill to the White House to discuss with him "a special confidential mission." The day Bill was promoted to major general (Ret), 10 February 1966, Lyndon B. Johnson tendered his congratulations by telegram.[417]

The biggest event of Margaret's political calendar in 1966 was her upcoming re-election, though as the editor of the *Lewiston Evening Journal* wrote a week before the date of that event: "From the time U.S. Senator Margaret Chase Smith announced her decision to seek re-election, it was a foregone conclusion that she would be returned to office. Senator Smith has the enviable record over the years of being the top votegetter in . . . Maine. The mere fact that she is heading the Republican ticket this year," the editor cooed, "is certain to reflect itself favorably in the vote totals garnered by other GOP candidates. Our lady senator is just this popular."[418] Margaret's opponent, Democrat Elmer H. Violette, a state legislator and lawyer from Van Buren, carried on what the newspaper called a "dignified and thought-provoking campaign," but Margaret's victory was never in any doubt.

On 8 November she defeated Violette 188,291 to 131,136. The pundits had been correct, though at least one noted that her margin of victory was less than in previous years. And beneath the expansiveness of the *Lewiston Evening Journal* editorial, was a cautionary note. "We . . . doubt whether the Democrats can hope to defeat her regardless of the candidate they may choose," the editor wrote. Thus, "we would think the soundest Democratic strategy would be to run a respectable but sacrificial nominee, and look ahead to 1972."[419] The advice proved prophetic.

With the retirement of Leverett Saltonstall, who had first been sworn in with her, Margaret began her fourth term as the ranking Republican on the Senate Armed Services Committee, in line for the chairmanship in the event of reversal in party power. She also became the third-ranking Republican on the powerful Appropriations Committee, while retaining her top party position on the Aeronautics and Space Sciences Committee.[420] On 11 January 1967 she was chosen by her 35 male colleagues to preside over the Senate Republican Conference. The election put her at the forefront of the minority Republican Party and meant that she would attend bipartisan sessions at the White House. In each of these positions, Vietnam and questions regarding the efficacy of U.S. policy daily confronted her. For the first few months of 1967, the Republicans and Margaret were silent on Vietnam, primarily because the party was "massively in support of a determined line in Vietnam."[421] When Margaret did speak out, in late January, although she indicted the administration for "seriously faulty judgement: resulting in shortages of both bombs and pilots . . . and a deterioration of combat readiness in many military units," she defended Johnson's "firmness" and said she would "continue to support him against his critics, most notably from within his own political party, who urge a pull-out and literally a surrender in Vietnam."[422] Her stance put her squarely at odds with students and faculty across the country who were demonstrating in massive numbers against a war in which draft calls had reached 50,000 per month and deferments had been abolished.

After twelve months that saw a president announce that he would not seek and would not accept another term and during which time troop levels rose to over one-half million, Margaret told the Republican National Committee on 9 September 1967 that what the Republicans needed was a peace candidate for the 1968 presidential race. Though in the past she had consistently supported the campaign to expand the bombings of vital military targets in North Vietnam, she told the Republican National Committee: "We have had a Democratic administration for nearly seven years now and it is bogged down in an increasingly unpopular war and apparently incapable of either winning that war or bringing the fighting to an honorable conclusion." She said that voters wanted a president like Eisenhower, who could bring peace, "give us physical security at home instead of wrath, crime on the streets, massive defiance of law and order, and tolerance of traitors, and give us tax cuts instead of tax raises."[423] Her recommendation did not mean, however, that she was joining the doves and the protesters. Her attention had simply shifted from one evil—the Communist take-over of South Vietnam—to a still greater evil: civil disorder at home.

On 20 January 1969, with a promise to unite the country and a mandate to get the country out of Vietnam, Richard M. Nixon became the thirty-seventh president of the United States by the narrowest margin since 1912. "The greatest honor history can bestow is the title of peacemaker," he said. "This honor now beckons America—the chance to help lead the world at last out of the valley of turmoil and onto that high ground of peace that men have dreamed of since the dawn of civilization." Then he turned his attention to the deep divisions of the country. "The simple things are the things most needed today if we are to surmount what divides us, and cement what unites us. To lower our voices would be a simple thing. In these difficult years, America has suffered from a fever of words: from inflated rhetoric that promises more than it can deliver; from angry rhetoric that fans discontents into hatreds; from bombastic rhetoric that postures instead of persuading. We cannot learn from one another until we stop shouting at one another."[424] Nixon's sentiments seemed to Margaret to be just what the country needed.

Despite Nixon's promise to expedite withdrawal from Vietnam, talks dragged on with no sign of progress. In February what one writer called "a midwinter contagion" of student protest broke out across several of the nation's campuses. At the University of Chicago, students seized the administration building and occupied it for two weeks to protest the dismissal of an instructor. At the University of California campus at Berkeley, police arrested 22 students, as protesters trashed the cafeteria and the library. In Madison, 10,000 marchers, chanting freedom songs and singing "America" walked from the campus to the state capitol.[425]

Little, it seemed, had changed in the month which had elapsed since the cold, gray, windy day of Nixon's inauguration when hundreds of young anti-war protesters had lined the route, while on Pennsylvania Avenue demonstrators burned small American flags the Boy Scouts had distributed and "a barrage of sticks, stones, beer cans, bottles and obscenities hit the vehicle" in which Nixon was riding. It was, writes Nixon biographer Stephen Ambrose, "the first disruption of an inaugural parade or ceremony in the 180 years of the American Presidency. Not even in 1861 had anything like this occurred."[426]

In June 1969, six months after he took the oath of office, President Nixon turned to a strategy called "Vietnamization." "Nixon hated doing it," wrote Ambrose, "but the American political system imposed it on the President. He could not escalate on the ground; stalemate was unacceptable; withdrawal was the only choice." Nixon's decision to begin a "phased, slow motion retreat," however, has been called "the worst mistake of his Presidency." Wrote his biographer, "because the war went on, tension and division filled the land, and the Nixon haters went into a frenzy," even though he set a goal that America would be out of Vietnam by the end of 1970.[427]

After a temporary lull, anti-war activities reignited in October, with a "moratorium" attracting as many as a million participants from New York City to San Francisco. On 15 October hundreds of people descended on Washington, D.C. for a single mass rally. In Maine about 150 of Bowdoin College's 900 students attended a protest meeting in the college chapel. Senator Muskie returned to his alma mater, Bates College, to make a major address, in which he supported student protests, and Democratic Senator George McGovern of South Dakota, who took a similar tack, addressed a University of Maine gathering. The commander of Maine's Veterans of Foreign Wars called the moratorium "shameful" and asked for a display of American flags to counteract it. In Waterville, Cy Joly urged all motorists to drive with their lights on to show support for the president's policies. And in Skowhegan, William G. Lessard said "these demonstrators will seek to undermine the bargaining position of the President in the Paris talks and thus will further endanger the lives of our fighting men in Vietnam."[428] Maine, like much of the rest of the nation was divided.

Margaret, who never liked the "old" Nixon, nonetheless leaped to defend him from his critics. She was appalled that Nixon was being excoriated for not pulling troops out of Vietnam quickly enough and shocked at what she saw as the hypocrisy of the protesters. Nixon was actually the first President to reverse the flow of troops and begin withdrawal of forces. In her view, the liberals' fault-finding with Nixon exceeded all bounds of reasonableness.

On 15 December 1969, Nixon announced a further reduction of fifty thousand troops in Vietnam, bringing the total to 115,500 since taking office. This pace, however, was not fast enough for the "doves"—the "extremists," as Margaret called them, nor "for the crassly pragmatic politicians, who had supported Presidents Kennedy and Johnson on getting us combat-involved and escalated and who suddenly attacked President Nixon for failing to get us out completely."429

On 29 April 1970, in an address from the Oval Office, Nixon announced that the United States was going to "clean out" major North Vietnamese and Vietcong occupied territories in Cambodia. "This is not an invasion of Cambodia. Once the enemy is driven out, the United States will not occupy the area." In fact, he promised, "we will withdraw."430 Read the *New York Times* headline: "PRESIDENT'S GAMBLE: WIDEN WAR TO END IT MORE QUICKLY." As part of the attack, and without Secretary of Defense Melvin Laird's knowledge, Nixon ordered air attacks by more than a hundred fighter-bombers on anti-aircraft sites and logistical support facilities in North Vietnam. Nixon tried to keep the missions secret, but on 2 May the story broke. The "doves" were furious, and even Nixon's supporters were caught off guard. The air attack on North Vietnam and the assault on North Vietnamese sanctuaries in supposedly neutral Cambodia heightened the already deep divisions within the United States.

On 4 May thirty-seven college presidents sent Nixon a letter urging him to "demonstrate unequivocally his determination to end the war promptly." The Cambodian invasion and the renewed bombing of North Vietnam, they wrote, had generated "severe and widespread apprehensions on our campuses." The letter's signatories included the presidents of Johns Hopkins, the University of Pennsylvania, Princeton, Columbia and Notre Dame.431 That afternoon, on the campus of Kent State University, four students, two of them young women, were shot and killed in a volley of gunfire from the Ohio National Guard who had been called out earlier by the governor in response to the burning of the ROTC building on campus. Almost instantaneously across the country, hundreds of thousands boycotted classes and demonstrated. On some campuses, notably Notre Dame, Tulane, Rutgers, the University of Miami, and Boston University, fires and fire bombings were reported.[432]

In Maine, a group of striking students from virtually all of Maine's colleges released a telegram that they were sending to Maine's senior senator. "Return home," it said, "and address yourself to the people whom you represent."[433] The telegram never arrived. Margaret read about it in the newspaper and responded, though she was put off from the start by its tone.

15. Colby College and the 1972 Senate Election

MAY NINTH dawned bright and brisk and there was the promise of high blue in the sky and an abundance of sun. A jewel of a day for Maine in early May. It was a Saturday, and there were no classes being held on the 500-acre Colby campus located just outside Waterville on Mayflower Hill. Margaret stood on the steps of the library, its modified Georgian Colonial design a monument to tradition and order. She gazed at the faces of the 2000 students who had come to Colby from colleges all across Maine to protest Nixon's Cambodian policy. The girls had long, straight hair, often parted in the middle, which they wore loose, shoulder-length or longer. Many of the boys had long hair, too, and beards. Most were in shirt sleeve and wore sun glasses. Quite a few looked like children of Maine—well groomed, neatly dressed, respectful. For that she was grateful.

Her right hip, which was to be operated on within three months, was hurting her and she couldn't seem to shake the memory of the 1954 race.[434] Colby was where Paul Fullam had taught. She had been given her first honorary degree by Colby and Colby was the sort of school she as a young girl would have given anything to attend. Did these students not appreciate how fortunate they were?

Earlier that day President Nixon had tried to communicate with student protesters in Washington at the Lincoln Memorial, but after asking students from California who "had come three thousand miles to show their concern about the war . . . how they liked surfing," he had done more talking than listening.435 In contrast, Margaret had come to Colby to listen and answer questions.436

Tall, congenial Ed Muskie had come to score points against the Nixon administration. Not only had he run on the Democratic ticket with Hubert Humphrey in the 1968 presidential race, but his name was often mentioned as a presidential candidate for 1972. Since 1967 he had been holding hearings all over the country on both the environment and the war in Vietnam, establishing nationwide his solidly liberal credentials.

Muskie and Margaret were not friends, and the contrast between the two senators was bound to work against Margaret. At 6'2" Muskie towered a foot over Margaret. At 55, his lanky frame and long, narrow face invited comparison with Lincoln, and his vigor made him seem younger than his 55 years. In contrast, Margaret was having difficulty standing because of the pain in her hip. Robbed of her usual level of high energy, she seemed frail and older than her 72 years. And from the beginning, because her pro-administration views were known well in advance of the meeting, she was on the defensive.

Muskie offered the students a plan, an "immediate, standstill cease-fire throughout Indochina," with troops to be withdrawn over an 18-month period. Margaret told the students that she had come to listen and try to answer their questions, not to make a speech or lecture. But she refused to duck the issue at hand, or turn on a president with whom she fundamentally agreed. What the president had done in Cambodia, she said, was a sensible military move. And he should be "given the time and opportunity to meet his commitments."437

Had the day ended there, Margaret might have been able to declare victory and go home, her brave and plucky defense of Nixon's policy winning grudging respect. But it did not end there. When one student asked her how her mail had been running on Cambodia, she "turned to aide William Lewis and asked audibly: 'Bill, how has the mail been running on Cambodia?' He answered: '6 to 1 against the invasion.'" The students gasped. As the *New York Times* opined, "for those who had been told to write to their congresswoman rather than demonstrate, her response was hardly encouraging."438

Another student asked "how he could trust a President who lied to the American people about the presence of U.S. troops in Laos?" Margaret responded that there were no troops in Laos. Immediately, a Bowdoin student and former army lieutenant named "Brownie" Carson who had been wounded in Laos was produced, a move Margaret believed was designed to embarrass her. "'Brownie' got up and told how he had been wounded and half of his platoon wiped out in Laos the year before."[439]

For Margaret, the confrontation at Colby was "perhaps the most unpleasant experience of [her] entire public service career."[440] Three times during the grueling ninety minutes it was suggested to Bill that the "questioning be terminated—first by the President of Colby, second by their public relations officer, and finally by the Colby student president presiding." But Margaret would not let them run her off. She and Bill waved off their offers. She was there for the duration.[441] She would stay until they had no more questions.

The editor of the *Lewiston Evening Journal* gave Margaret high marks for the day. She went to Colby College "and refused to engage in the political game. Had she done so she might have been tempted to tell the students she disagreed with Nixon's Cambodian troop decision. Instead, she told the truth." Muskie's call for an "immediate standstill cease fire throughout Indochina," on the other hand, "would be wonderful if the enemy would stop firing," the editor observed.[442]

Margaret's detractors said her valor that day was eclipsed by evidence which argued that she was out of touch. As *Maine Times* editor John Cole, who was there, put it, "There she was, the highest ranking Republican on the Armed Service Committee, and she seemed to have almost no idea what was happening in the war, and no idea how the students felt about it. It was just a sad performance by an old lady out of touch with reality."[443] The article, which did not appear until 1972, just ten days prior to the primary election in which Margaret was facing a tough, rich young challenger for her seat, provided a compelling reason to the large percentage of voters who were undecided not to vote for Margaret. The image of an old woman sadly out of touch with reality was a theme taken up by both of her opponents in 1972. On other issues—even the war—Margaret could bounce back between 1970 and 1972, but on the subject of age, she could do nothing. Colby gave the age issue validity.

Her way of coping with what she had seen at Colby was to make a second Declaration of Conscience speech. This time she would address the anarchism of the Left. As she had done in 1950 when she consulted Walter Lippmann about her first Declaration of Conscience speech, in 1970 she talked with Howard K. Smith, a T.V. commentator whose views were compatible with hers, about her second. He agreed with her slant, applauded her timing and pointed her to a recent editorial in the *Wall Street Journal*, which Margaret found not only helpful but "discreet and wise." While the editorial provided the "flavor," Bill and Margaret were the sole authors.[444]

On 1 June 1970, Margaret made her second Declaration of Conscience speech, twenty years to the day after her first. In outline, it followed the first, contrasting the errors of the Left with what she had seen in 1950 as the errors of the Right, and calling for a return to the basic principles of Americanism: "the right to criticize; the right to hold unpopular beliefs; the right to protest; the right to independent thought . . . and the right to dissent against dissenters." Her most memorable words came at the end. "Extremism bent upon polarization of our people . . . [is] increasingly forcing upon the American people the narrow choice between anarchy and repression. And make no mistake about it, if that narrow choice has to be made, the American people, even if with reluctance and misgiving, will choose repression. For an overwhelming majority of Americans believe that: Trespass is trespass—whether on campus or off. Violence is violence—whether on the campus or off. Arson is arson—whether on the campus or off. Killing is killing— whether on the campus or off. The campus cannot degenerate," she said, "into a privileged sanctuary for obscenity, trespass, violence, arson, and killing with special immunity for participants in such acts. Ironically, the excesses of dissent on the extreme left can result in repression of dissent. For repression is preferable to anarchy and nihilism to most Americans."[445]

The speech was meant to be a model of restraint and good sense. And it reflected the views of many who longed for order amidst competing forces of social change. But it did not receive the acclaim of her earlier Declaration, even in Maine. While public reaction was characterized in her political biography as "overwhelmingly favorable," and mail "heavier and more favorable that it had been on the first Declaration," and though she received praise from public figures ranging from Walter

Lippmann and Ted Kennedy to conservative Senator John Williams [R-Del.] and Richard Nixon, the public paid little attention to it.[446]

One reason was that instead of alleviating fears, she gave listeners a high-minded scolding. And a scolding is not what the protesters, or anyone else, wanted to hear. Not quite hidden beneath her words—and common to those with similiar evaluative frameworks—was a frustration with the times that resulted in a contraction of empathy and a surfeit of suspicion. Her 1968 reply to an anguished letter from a Brooks, Maine woman whose duaghter's fiancé had been killed in Vietnam, and who blamed Margaret for not helping him get a humanitarian transfer after the death of his brother, is illustrative. Margaret wrote: "it is a rather disheartening and disillusioning experience for me to be held accountable by your minister for sending him [the fiancé] back and by your daughter for his death when the decision . . . was strictly the power of the Marine Corps and not mine. I wonder if you, your daughter, and your minister hold Senator Muskie and Representative Kyros accountable and to blame as you do me—and if you have not, why you have singled me out for exclusive blame. Sincerely, Margaret Chase Smith."

On a par with the sub-text of her speeches and letters—especially among protesters—was awareness of her continuing alliance with a White House involved in a declared war with students. Just before Kent State and after the announcement that the U.S. was invading Cambodia, Nixon had referred to the privileged protesting kids as "bums." "You see these bums, you know, blowing up the campuses," he had said. "Listen, the boys that are on the college campuses today are the luckiest people in the world . . . and here they are burning up the books, I mean storming around this issue." As historian Stephen Ambrose observed, his words hurt. No more dramatic proofs exists than the response of the father of Allison Krause, one of the victims of Kent State, who told a reporter after the tragedy, "My child was not a bum."[447]

Yet here was Margaret, defending a man who had lied both about Laos and Cambodia, and whose feelings about students—and by inference about the act of protest itself—was reflected in Nixon's epithet. Perhaps to both of them, kids were just "bums."

In 1972 Margaret almost didn't run. For the first time in her life, she thought about walking away from politics. Both her primary opponent, Robert Monks, a 39-year-old industrialist, and her opponent in the general election, Democratic Representative William Hathaway, announced their candidacies before she did. Uncharacteristically, Margaret wavered. Nineteen months after the Colby affair, on 9 December 1971, Bill Lewis had been stricken with a severe heart attack. Margaret was with him when it happened. He had taken her for a routine medical checkup during a lull in the Senate. Neither of them was to return to the capitol that day. Margaret moved into the VIP suite at Walter Reed and stayed by Bill's side for almost two weeks, until he was out of danger.

Almost immediately, news of the heart attack fueled rumors that Margaret would not run again. Though Margaret had taken out nomination papers for the June primary on 3 December, she had not yet announced whether she intended to seek another term when a story appeared, speculating that Bill's condition might cause her not to run.[448]

Along with her age, her dependence on Bill would become an issue in the campaign, with opponents claiming that she depended too heavily on Bill for advice and that he operated as a de facto senator. Though the charge would prove unsettling to Margaret, a more immediate concern was her health. In 1968, she had undergone hip surgery on her congenitally dislocated left hip. A hip replacement on her right hip had been performed on 8 July 1970, with surgery to replace her left hip occurring on 25 August 1971. She also suffered from age related macular degeneration, which greatly interfered with her sight. For some time, her secretary had been preparing her notes on 8 x 9 sheets in large black hand lettering.[449] These impairments were related to the more damaging issue of her age. Raised by her opponent at the very outset of the campaign, his use of her age helped to make up her mind that she *should* run for a fifth term.

Robert Augustus Gardner Monks was tall (6'6"), ruggedly handsome, young and rich, a Kennedyesque figure, who was a political amateur. Monks had a Phi Beta Kappa key and a law degree from Harvard Law School, and he represented the part of the world that had most often discounted George Chase's daughter. After seven years with a Boston law firm, he had bought out his wife's coal and oil business and expanded it into a multimillion-dollar enterprise. In 1970, he sold his interest in the company and moved to his wife's family's estate on Cape Elizabeth. For most of his life he had lived in Boston and spent weekends and summer vacations in Maine. Monks had lived in Maine only one year before declaring his candidacy. In that time, he had visited every town and community and set up a computerized list of Republicans. His full-time staff of 25-30 were working out of two offices in Portland and several field offices in Bangor and Augusta. With the help of part-time and volunteer staff, every registered Republican in the state was being canvassed and new ones registered by the thousands. The cost of his campaign was estimated at a minimum of $250,000.[450] When Monks began his campaign, he said that if Margaret were re-elected she would be 81 when her term expired. That turned into a statement that she was 81, and she would be 87 when her term expired.[451] Margaret announced on 7 February 1972 that she would seek a fifth term.

The contest with Monks inspired low flying on both sides. Though Margaret seldom referred to Monks by name, she tried to exploit Monks' Massachusetts roots. "It's much easier to sit on the sidelines or come in from another state and tell what's wrong," she said, "than it is to be here and carry through and do things that build the party."[452] Her campaign workers were more direct. As the *Brunswick Times Record* reported: "Nearly every Smith organizer will tell a reporter Monks is listed in the Boston Social Register with a Cambridge, Massachusetts address and that he was the largest contributor ($2,500) to Congressman William D. Hathaway's re-election campaign in 1969."[453]

In speaking with women's groups, she generously drew from the threadbare speech she had delivered as early as the Forties and as recently as the 1964 presidential campaign—"The Challenge to Women." The theme was 'woman's place is everywhere.' But the quotations in the newspaper made Margaret sound as though she had grown more conservative about woman's place. "The greatest contribution a woman can make is in her home and in improving her community," she said. "Basically the home is the number one place for a woman."[454] As reported by the *Aroostook Republican News*, the sentiment was a retreat from Margaret's usual stance.

Monks, on the other hand, spoke in towns across the state, waging a person-to-person campaign. He tied his rhetoric to key issues like the aged, the environment, the economy, and fisheries, and he made a concerted effort to attract young, uncommitted voters. He criticized Margaret for not maintaining an office in Maine and concentrating most of her energies on military affairs. As a result, he said, the problems of Maine such as job development and environmental protection had assumed "a lesser priority." He therefore proposed to open a system of local offices throughout the state, staffed by people "expert in governmental approaches to our state's more pressing problem areas." Help would thus be available for Maine's senior citizens and for matters which ranged from economic development to environmental protection and enhancement.[455]

Margaret's answer to Monks' charge, which echoed Jones' earlier claim that Margaret had forgotten Maine, was simple and predictable. She was elected to represent the people of Maine in Washington, so she stayed there and did her job. Besides, until she underwent hip surgery, she had come to Maine once a month. After her surgery, she had been there once every six weeks, a good record by Senate standards.

On Monks' plan for area offices, she withheld comment. She preferred the old-style politics she had learned at Clyde's elbow. Absent regional surrogates, Margaret and Bill were points of first and last appeal. They personally accumulated a great many IOUs. In this way they could reward the faithful and punish the wayward. It was local politics at the national level, national clout with local control. And for Margaret it had worked for thirty years.

When Monks became more aggressive in late spring and focused on issues of Maine's economy: "One of every three families in Maine . . . has cash income of less than $5000; Maine has the lowest per capita income figure in New England . . . $741 less than the New England average; in the 1960s, Maine had an outward migration of over 50,000 people . . . most of these people were young . . . ; since 1968, Maine has lost 9,000 jobs in its six basic industries . . . employment in these industries has increased nationally," Margaret most often chose simply to ignore his charges.[456]

When she did respond, as in an interview on the *CBS Evening News* with Walter Cronkite on 15 June 1972, Margaret said, "Well, I've been inquiring around about the high unemployment and the figures show that there is unemployment, but that people who want to work can find work." There was not much else she could have said that would have been as damaging to her credibility with Maine's working poor.

Responded Monks: "That's grotesque—I mean it's really grotesque. You've just got to travel this state and see some people to—that's just grotesque. There are places where there are good men and good women who want to work and there's no jobs. Somerset County, where the senator comes from, has got 15 percent unemployment. Old Town has got one person in five out of work. There are good people out of work in Maine communities who cannot get jobs, believe me."457 The *Somerset Reporter*, Margaret's hometown newspaper, agreed with Monks.458

Even before the CBS interview, the *Somerset Reporter* had taken an unusual position on its hometown senator. In January, the editor proclaimed that he had had enough of Margaret Chase Smith, and he subjected her qualifications to withering satire. "Both Robert A.G. Monks . . . and Representative William Hathaway, who has the Democratic nod in his pocket, hold degrees from Harvard and Harvard Law. Senator Smith tops that educational nonsense by holding some 60 honorary degrees, give or take a few. Both Monks and Hathaway are successful lawyers and/or businessmen. But the Senator can easily negate those qualifications by pointing to her background with the *Somerset Reporter*, one of the County's leading organs of public opinion, and as girls' basketball coach at Skowhegan High. Where Senator Smith is known throughout the world, Monks and Hathaway are known in some parts of Maine." Calling Margaret a "one-woman show," the editor called Monks and Hathaway "the first serious breath of fresh air that Maine voters can breathe come voting time."459

Nonetheles, in June, despite the falling away of some of Margaret's customary support and Bob Monks' outspending Margaret by 45 to 1, when the voters went to the polls, enough of the faithful showed up to give Margaret a two-to-one victory: 76,964 to 38,345. With Margaret spending just a penny a vote and Monks spending $10 a vote for every vote he received, pundits were confirmed in speculations made before election day that Monks' chief drawback was "his ostentatious show of money—large campaign staff, expensive media effort." The decision by Monks "only served to highlight the traditional frugality of Mrs. Smith's campaigns."460

For all of his education and success—at least as the world understood success—Bobby Monks could not a shed a public style that was "formal, polite, responsive and energetic," but something apart from the man inside. Monks had "small threads of disquiet here and there making it impossible for the man to completely relax, and thus make it possible for his audience to relax with him." Robert Monks was never able to meet the public without this "inner tension."[461] In contrast, in spite of numerous signs that Margaret's powers were declining, she was in her element. Campaigning was what she knew how to do best. It energized her. It made her feel young and loved and appreciated. People stood in line for 45 minutes just to shake her hand. Tears welled up as someone recounted the story of the son Margaret helped locate overseas. Bouquets of roses, her trademark, almost always appeared and were presented, and Margaret took peoples' hands and looked them in the eye. "This is a wonderful, wonderful meeting," she would tell them, "and I hope you'll get on the phone to your friends and tell them what a delightful time we've had together."[462] And they did.

Even so, the primary campaign exacted a high price. Republicans— particularly in towns like Bath and Brunswick where economies were severely depressed—would not turn out for Margaret in the general election in November. One such Republican, who had even signed Margaret's nomination petition, said he was "tired of a candidate who doesn't work for the party and support local candidates. She forgets who got her in Washington, and she's never around like Muskie and Kyros to help local people. If she is knocked off," he continued, "the politicians will get the idea that they can't lose touch with the grass roots."[463] Other Republicans, like Dr. Fred Whittaker, president of the Bangor Theological Seminary, were at odds with Margaret over her support of the war in Vietnam, an issue which did not become important in the primary race because Monks, like Margaret, supported Richard Nixon. Substantial numbers of these voters would cast their ballots for Hathaway.

For many, the age issue and a related concern that she was out of touch remained nettlesome. Despite the fact that Margaret had been quite sprightly during the primary campaign, the voters had seen her only on weekends and rarely had a chance to judge her acumen or sharpness on the issues. The primary election brought into focus the age and acuity issue, and it continued to hang in the air like late afternoon fog.

Nor did Hathaway want to see the fog dispelled. His polls showed that age was a great chink in Margaret's armor, but his instincts told him to tread softly. The solution was Senator Ed Muskie, who was not up for re-election and thus could shoulder risks that Hathaway needed to avoid. On 19 October, in answer to the question of whether age should be a factor in the race between Smith and Hathaway, Muskie responded that "the Senate ought to have the benefit of relative youth." Then he added: "I hope that I have the good sense not to seek to stay in the Senate past the age of 70."[464]

Hathaway in the meantime continued the campaign style he had adopted during his own primary race. The newspapers characterized it as "old-fashioned politics." Rather than seek out the largest possible crowds, he maintained a flexible itinerary which allowed him to converse a half an hour with a country store owner or a housewife, making up the time at other stops along the way.[465] It was an echo of Margaret's earlier campaigns. Like Margaret, he had been sent to Congress by the Second District, the largest east of the Mississippi, and he walked in Margaret Chase Smith's shadow through the small mill towns, the picturesque fishing villages and the crumbling, once-proud cities. In fact, reported the *Wall Street Journal*, he was "doing his best to repeat Senator Smith's original campaign success. He visited each of Maine's 495 cities and towns during the first half of this year, and by November 7 he plans to have revisited half of them."[466]

Polls commissioned by the Republican Party showed Hathaway trailing by better than 45% to 55% in his own district, though Hathaway claimed that his own polls showed the race to be much closer—perhaps just three or four points.[467]

When asked whether she had identified any problems in running against Rep. Hathaway, Margaret answered truthfully, "I don't think I have any particular weak spots." So confident is she, reported the *Wall Street Journal*, "that she says nothing in her speeches about her accomplishments for Maine. Instead, she mostly encourages support of local Republicans and extols President Nixon's record. When asked by a reporter to spell out what she has done for Maine, she declines, saying,

'I don't think I have to go around and say what I've done for Maine. My record speaks for itself.'"[468]

While Hathaway was hewing to the formula that had first elected Margaret to the Senate—leaving his Portland hotel at 5:15 A.M. "to drive 80 miles north to Waterville so he could stand in the early-morning cold and greet workers at a Scott Paper Co. plant" and hustling through the day "from factory to shopping center to railroad yard to shake as many hands as possible"—Margaret was waging a low profile campaign. She favored gatherings set up so that she could see a large of numbers of voters—all of whom had turned out to see her. "On a recent weekend," reported the *Journal*, "she flew into Portland on a late Friday afternoon and spoke briefly at a bean supper. Saturday she arrived at her home in Skowhegan and that night she spoke to a Portland group of party faithful. Afterwards, people lined up to greet her, addressing her as 'Mahgret.' She greeted many by their first names, recalling past meetings and giving regards for friends and relatives."[469] But she didn't travel down too many dirt roads to lonely farmhouses in the summer and fall of 1972. Nor did she meet with fishermen before dawn as she had when she was younger. Her rural power base would just have to hold together on its own.

Although Margaret appeared to be campaigning less for the general election than she had for the primary, Hathaway would prove to be a much tougher opponent than the "carpetbagger" Monks. He was forty-eight, and a decorated World War II veteran. He was pleasant and soft-spoken and projected an image much like the younger Margaret. He sought people out, listened carefully to them as they talked, and seemed genuinely eager to help them. His first big boost came from the normally neutral Maine Teacher's Association, which gave him their endorsement.[470] On the other hand, Margaret received unusually enthusiastic support from the Nixon Administration, including a place on the program of the Republican National Convention to second the nomination of Spiro T. Agnew for vice president, and an attempted campaign appearance by Julie Nixon, whose plane could not land because of the weather.

Hathaway's most important break came in September, less than two months before the election. Ralph Nader's "Citizens Look at Congress" published a lengthy profile of Margaret. It was not merely unflattering, it was a hatchet job, far worse because of its vaunted non-partisanship than the *New York Times* article written by Cambridge-based freelance writer, Berkeley Rice, which had appeared just before the primary election bearing the title "Is the Great Lady from Maine Out of Touch?"[471]

The Nader Report began with an 'inside look' at the relationship between Margaret and Bill. The last sentence on the first page read, "William Lewis, Jr. is as close to being a surrogate Senator as one can be." This point of view was developed more fully on the next page.[472]

After sketching her biography, the report observed, "The Margaret Chase Smith success story is reminiscent of a Horatio Alger story. But unlike Alger's heroes, Smith's power rests more in her title than with what she does with it; in her style more than her actions. And her actions bear inferences of a courtly, majestic grande dame. A reporter who has observed her for four years noted that her demand for privacy is so encompassing that she sweeps through her business with a kind of majestic isolation."

Referring to her Declaration of Conscience as "what Capitol Hill observers call 'a finest hour,' critics," they said, "wonder if a member of congress should not have more than one 'finest hour' in 32 years."[473]

The report's most damaging section was its analysis of Margaret's voting pattern from 1966 to 1972. According to the report, she voted for Vietnam war funds and against foreign aid. She also opposed cuts in defense spending, voting against the anti-ballistic-missile system desired by the military brass in 1969, only because she believed that better technology would soon be available with less danger of nuclear fall-out. This part of the analysis was fairly accurate, though she supported foreign aid more frequently than the Nader report suggests. Public Works and space also got more of her votes than are revealed in the Nader Report. But it was in the area of domestic spending that the Nader report was most misleading. Although her vote against a poverty program cut in vocational training in 1963 and her vote for hospital care benefits for the elderly for 1964 were both accurately included in the Nader catalogue of votes, the majority of votes listed—seven out of nine on measures such as child care, Project Headstart, and manpower training increases—were inaccurately reported.

When Lyndon Johnson was in the White House, Margaret's voting pattern on domestic matters was generally liberal. As a matter of fact, most of the time she and Senator Muskie voted the same way. On 12

December 1967, they both voted for a $14.2 billion three-year extension of the Elementary and Secondary Education Act, and a $2.73 billion foreign aid appropriation for the current fiscal year.[474] They both voted for final passage of amendments to the Social Security program, providing for increased benefits of $7.2 billion through 1969, a boost of 15%. They both voted in favor of a bill authorizing $4.65 billion over two years for the War on Poverty and against an amendment to eliminate the $2.8. billion emergency job program for the cities. Even with Nixon in the White House—other than her votes on military spending—Margaret's record was that of a moderate. In 1972 she and Muskie both voted to override President Nixon's veto of the 1972 Water Pollution bill and for the establishment of the Consumer Protection Agency. On 13 September 1972 she and Muskie both voted for the $33.6 billion federal revenue sharing bill. Though the two senators certainly had their differences, on many non-defense issues they voted the same way, contrary to what the Nader Report implies. Even a cursory review of one year of Margaret's votes reveals that the Nader Report ignored other votes that were consistently "liberal." Had they been considered, the conclusion that the "Senator is more conservative than moderate" could not have been so glibly made.

On the Dickey-Lincoln School Hydroelectric Project, an issue for which Margaret, Muskie and Hathaway had fought very hard, and for which they all wanted to claim credit, the report's deficiencies are particularly clear. After merely noting Margaret's support for the hydroelectric project, "along with all members of the Maine congressional delegation," the report alleged that the differences in Hathaway and Smith's support was in what it called "their styles." Hathaway "fills the *Congressional Record* and newsletters with his support of the project and his concern about a lack of electric power and its high cost to New England. Smith," it continued, "who produces no newsletter for back home readers, seldom indicates interest in the *Congressional Record*." Beyond the naiveté of this observation, with its implication that material placed in the *Congressional Record* affected voting or measured effectiveness, the reduction of Hathaway and Smith's hard work to a matter of style was a disservice to both candidates, but especially to Margaret.

Margaret had used all of her considerable senatorial pull with her colleagues who passed the bill, and with Lyndon Johnson who continued to support it, despite its rejection by the House. Most likely Margaret's support for the bill convinced Richard Nixon to continue to include the item in his budget, even though the House persisted in rejecting it. Hathaway, for his part, also worked very hard, but against greater odds in the lower House and with less success than Margaret. On this score, the perspective of a disinterested contemporary is revealing. Said Senator Spessard Holland, a Florida Democrat, "If anyone ever fought for a project in which she was interested, she did." He remembered the conference committee sessions when Dickey-Lincoln School funds were compromised at $875,000 after the House had rejected out-of-hand the budget request of $1.6 billion. "The scrap put up by the distinguished Senior Senator from Maine," Holland said, "is something I shall long remember."[475]

To some, Ralph Nader had become, by 1972, a cult figure. He had been the first to successfully tackle General Motors and show that they were putting profit ahead of safety and good design. He was a Harvard Law graduate, a consumer advocate and a "giant killer." He was welcome on virtually every college campus in America. His group's profile on Margaret, no matter how flawed, was bound to affect the decisions of younger voters.

Also likely to affect young voters was an assault launched by the feminist National Organization of Women (NOW), an organization which Margaret had refused to join when it was founded in 1966.[476] Despite Margaret's advocacy of the Equal Rights Amendment, the co-founder of Maine's chapter of NOW announced in 1972 that she was committed to "nagging and bugging" Margaret until she recognized "the fundamental issues of women's liberation." She also called Margaret "an elitist" who represented "everything women in the liberation movement want to eliminate."[477] Two months before the Maine chapter's denunciation of Margaret, a feminist newsletter, "The Woman Activist," analyzed senators' voting records on issues of importance to women. Not only did Democrats score much better than Republicans, but Margaret scored only 25% "because of one absence and two antifeminist votes." The survey covered four votes.[478]

In August the personal narrative of five women who had travelled from Portland, Maine, to Washington, D.C. to protest the war in Vietnam gained some notoriety when it appeared in a publication called *North Country*. These five women, carrying two babies, visited the office of

Margaret Chase Smith. "We did our duty," wrote its author, Barbara Woodbury "and visited Senator Smith, wistfully hoping that being a woman, she would share our concerns for human life. That turned out not to be the case, however. . . . On the long ride home through endless detours of a flood-ravaged countryside we came to two conclusions," said Woodbury, "people in Washington need to cultivate the old-fashioned traits of honor and compassion; and Maine voters who believe in the value of life will not find Margaret Chase Smith worthy of their vote."[479]

The Democrats were organized as they had never been before. And they were hitting Margaret with everything they could find. But the unexpected source of unwitting assistance was Margaret herself.

From the end of the primary until October, Margaret seemed unwilling to answer the question posed by both newspapers and the Democratic candidate: What have you done for Maine? Margaret was of two minds on the matter. First of all, she felt that she had answered it—countless times since the primary. And secondly, she didn't feel that after thirty-two years she needed to recite her accomplishments. She didn't need "to go out and say what I've done because the people of Maine know what I've done." It was what one commentator referred to as her Popeye-like "I yam what I yam" approach.[480]

Finally, after she became convinced of the necessity to appear more responsive, she gave her answer to the *Maine Sunday Telegram* in October. She listed the Dickey-Lincoln School power project, her success in keeping the Kittery-Portsmouth Naval Shipyard open, her role in gaining a $3 million survey of the Passamaquoddy Tidal Power Project, her success with the Rivers and Harbors projects throughout Maine, and her efforts on behalf of the Bath Iron Works. Numerous "small projects," like getting the Coast Guard to keep the Kennebec River open during the winter, handling hardship discharges, providing assistance for passports, pensions and social security payments ended the list.

The list was respectable. It represented steady effort and attention to detail. But it did not reflect sponsorship of any major legislation or important bills. That was not what she did best. Nor with a steady flow of Democrats in and out of the White House and a Democratic-dominated Congress was that a reasonable expectation.

And the list came too late. Wrote the editor of the *Portsmouth Herald*

(N.H.) on 13 October, "Perhaps 'people know' her record, but perhaps a lot of younger voters in Maine don't remember, because it has been so long since Sen. Smith has really done one heck of a lot. . . . Let us hope the voters of Maine remember her with honor, but forget her in the polling booths this November. It is time for a change."[481]

A worse blow came three weeks later when the *Somerset Reporter*, her hometown paper which had been bought in recent years by the *Bangor Daily News*, announced its support for Hathaway. The date was 2 November, five days before the general election. After the editor alluded to the Nader Report and cited polls which showed that the gap between Margaret and Hathaway was much closer than previously expected, only .6 of a percentage point according to the *Bangor Daily News* poll, he concluded, "At 74, Mrs. Smith can no longer possibly have the stamina necessary to keep pace with the gruelling daily schedule demanded of an effective U.S. Senator. If elected, she will be 80 by the time her term of office is complete. . . . We feel compelled to strongly urge you to vote for William D. Hathaway for U.S. Senator on November 7."[482]

*　*　*　*　*　*

On earlier election days, Margaret followed Clyde's custom of going to the Municipal Building where the voting booths were set up and talking and shaking hands with people all day, at times looking over the outside check lists. The last few years, she had been detained in Washington and had not made an appearance. On 7 November 1972, even though she was in Skowhegan, she decided against going to the polls. She would vote by absentee ballot.

Before 7:00 in the morning, she and Bill got in the car and pulled out of Skowhegan, heading for Portland where she was to have lunch with her attorney Mert Henry at the Cumberland Club. This time the ride, which often soothed her, did not give her the feeling of escape that it usually provided. She felt uneasy.

On the return trip from Portland, they stopped by Bill's place at Cundy's Harbor to pick up a television set so they could watch the evening's returns. After a few hours, they left for Skowhegan. Both of them felt unsettled after the fast pace of the final weeks.

Margaret prepared some dinner and around nine-thirty people started dropping in. Red roses arrived. Then more old friends, supporters,
and family. They munched on sandwiches and cookies, drank coffee and
talked. There was about the group the quiet ease of people who had
known each other for a very long time. Outwardly Margaret seemed like
herself, but she didn't have the same enthusiasm as in other years.
Perhaps she was just tired, she thought.

Then the returns started coming in. Radios and television sets were
turned up. Margaret was on the phone. The early returns didn't sound
right.[483] As soon as she heard the returns from Auburn, she knew something was very wrong.

Auburn was on the Republican side of the river. Lewiston, on the
other side of the Androscoggin, was Democratic. She had worked the
fringes of Lewiston, the small villages on the edge, but never the town
itself, a big textile area and solidly Democratic, home to Bates College.
It couldn't be budged. But Auburn—Auburn was conservative
Republican. It was where Wallace White had been born and raised, the
center of the Maine shoe industry. What had happened to all of her support there? How had Auburn slipped away? And when?

They were questions she would ask herself again and again as the
returns came in. The low hum of conversation stopped as the crowd realized what was happening. Franklin County, that most rural of counties
held, but not by many votes. Next came Oxford County—except for
Rumford (Muskie's hometown)—Margaret Chase Smith country for
sure. All those little towns—Norway and Waterford, Peru and Sweden,
Byron and Gilead. She had visited them all, and could see them as clearly as if she had been there yesterday. Then the announcer said, reporting
from Oxford County, Hathaway: 9,533; Smith: 8,382. When she heard
these totals, she knew what had happened. Her supporters hadn't turned
out. They "worked their fingers off in the primaries, sat on their hands
and said I was going to win [the general election] anyway."[484] But she was
only partly correct. In Auburn, in heavily Democratic Androscoggin
County, 72.3 percent of the total registered voters turned out for
Tuesday's general election, just 885 ballots short of the 1960 record when
John F. Kennedy won the presidency over Richard Nixon.[485] Moreover,
though Androscoggin County boosted Hathaway's lead by nearly 13,000

votes—25,832 to 13,369—it neatly divided its vote between President
Nixon and Democratic nominee George McGovern 19,566 to 19,386, in
contrast to the sharp imbalance of the Senate vote, an outcome which
suggests strong anti-Smith sentiment.[486] She had been overconfident,
Margaret later admitted. While Hathaway effectively used television ads,
she "didn't buy any television time, or radio time or any newspapers
ads"—at least none to amount to anything.[487] Anywhere she went, she
said, she made news. Why buy time? Besides, "If I had changed in 1972
[and used television] people would have said: 'Well, she's getting pan-
icky. 'So we talked it over, and I said no, I'm not going to do it."[488] Of
Oxford County's 28,813 registered voters, only 18,000 voted in the general election. She was almost 4,000 votes shy of her 1960 tally in Oxford,
and she and Hathaway together drew 2500 fewer votes than she and
Cormier had received in 1960. Hathaway's 1000 vote increase would not
have mattered had the Smith faithful turned out. In the end, one-third of
Maine's 615,546 registered voters failed to vote. The final tally was Smith:
197,040; Hathaway 224,270. Even in Skowhegan they had not voted for
her. Much of Maine appears to have taken the advice of the *Portsmouth
Herald* editor. They had "remembered with honor" but forgotten her in
the polling booths in November. The time had come for a change.

The friends who had come to celebrate didn't know whether to stay
or leave. They had never seen Margaret lose an election. Before long
most had left the warmth of her home for the raw November night. She
watched as cars pulled away, headed back down the hill to town. A single row of automobile headlights blazing like a funeral procession in the
late night. As they disappeared, stillness returned to Neil Hill. The lights
of the town flickered off one by one. Skowhegan retired for the night.

EPILOGUE

THE FIRST THREE MONTHS were the worst. Newsmen dogging her path, hoping for stories on how distraught she was. The phone ringing constantly. Speculation on her loss continuing as the AP named the upset Maine's top news story of 1972. Her stoney silence fueling rumors that she had gone into hiding.

After a while, Margaret stopped blaming herself and realized that age had beaten her as much as anything else, though overconfidence had played a part as well. In January when she would have begun her fifth term, thirteen new Senators were sworn in. On average, they were 22 years younger than those they replaced. Of her old friends, only George Aiken still going strong at 80, remained. Even Bill Hathaway, reportedly "delighted but shocked" at his success, when asked to single out the biggest reason for his victory answered: "Age." Margaret was 75, Hathaway 48.[489]

In February she gave her first interview since the election. After clearing up the impression that she was a "hermit, hiding in a hovel, licking my wounds," she told a *Maine Sunday Telegram* reporter simply: "They wanted someone younger."[490] Soon the tragedy of Watergate would remind her that there was much she would not miss about Washington. Calling it the "bitter fruits of crass pragmatism," Watergate was for too many not a reprehensible act, but "getting caught in the act."[491] At least she would not have to defend the indefensible acts of a Republican president.

Perhaps that was when the healing began.

Or perhaps it was during the three years she travelled to the West and the South as a visiting professor in the Woodrow Wilson Fellowship Program. Using Silver Spring as a base, she and Bill travelled to eight colleges a year between 1973 and 1976, with stays that ranged from a few days to several weeks at each institution. Her honorarium (Bill was unpaid) was $1500 per week.[492] The role was one she relished. Students were respectful, faculty interested, and administrators eager to lavish attention on her. Her discussions of honesty in government, which were presented against the backdrop of Watergate, were sharply relevant, and thus to her audiences Margaret frequently seemed less like a little old lady who was out of touch than a visionary whose time had come. Or at least that was Margaret's perception of their reactions. But even these infusions of hero worship did not quiet her restless spirit. And travel itself began to take its toll. Washington from the air still projected a timeless serenity, for only the grandeur of its public buildings was evident. But on take-off, the spaghetti roads and acres of automobiles—increasing each year—even the litter alongside the highway—formed an alien reality which grew increasingly difficult to ignore.

During this time, Bill had entered into discussions with Northwood Institute, a business college originating in Midland, Michigan, which was interested in sponsoring a Margaret Chase Smith Library in Skowhegan, in exchange for her properties and the use of her name for fundraising purposes. Bill saw Northwood as a way to protect Margaret's assets from taxes.[493] More than that, it was a reason to go home.

But a bizarre incident in 1974 almost eliminated that option. Still smarting from Skowhegan's rejection of her in 1972, Margaret was ill-prepared to receive a notice from the Skowhegan Board of Voters Registration informing her that her name had been removed from the voting lists because she was a nonresident. Though the choice had been made locally, it was the result of a Maine Secretary of State's directive to local boards to purge from their voter lists anyone ineligible because they lived elsewhere. In a state with a sizable summer population, the policy amounted to house cleaning. But the chair of the Skowhegan Board took the policy literally and wrote to Margaret to tell her that her name was being removed. Margaret was incensed.[494] Promptly she appealed the decision of the Board, only to lose the appeal and witness the initiation of an inquiry into her taxes.[495] She now knew there was more going on than someone's overzealous enthusiasm for following the policy of the secretary of state.[496] At this point, she asked her Maine attorney, Merton Henry, a former campaign aide and source of advice, to look into the matter. He wrote to Bill that "residence is a matter of intention" and at least a sixty days notice had to be given to remove someone's name from the voting list.[497] The selectmen, unwilling to support the board in what seemed a lapse in judgement and was clearly a public relations nightmare, overturned the decision and restored Margaret's right to vote. As late as 1977, Margaret alluded in a letter to the fact that she and the Northwood Library Board "wonder[ed] about keeping the library in Skowhegan in such a . . . hostile environment."[498] The issue receded when the library was given tax-exempt status and the charge of $1,611 in unpaid taxes was dropped. Margaret had once again risen to battle and won. In the process, her pre-eminence had been at least partly re-established, and the belief that she still had more friends than enemies in Skowhegan began to take hold, banishing many of the doubts that had arisen even before 1972. With the library under construction, Bill and Margaret spent more time in Skowhegan than they had in recent years. Maine was where the healing would be completed. Then with the library almost finished, on 26 May 1982 Bill died at Cundy's Harbor. He had been laying carpet inside his small brown house, and his heart had simply stopped. Almost forty years from the time they met, her best friend was gone. And for the first time in as many years, Margaret was alone.

At first she felt lost without Bill to protect her. But then she discovered that she didn't really need protection. Even without her generous Senate pension which in 1988 exceeded $88,000, she was, thanks to her own frugality and the inheritance Bill had left her, well-fixed. In addition, other than failing eyesight, she was in good health, and spry, and there was much left to do. The library was completed by August 1982 and was ready for visitors. Politicians from Maine and reporters from Washington still called her, and from 14 December through Christmas the house was filled with roses sent by admirers from all over the country. They never forgot her.

Increasingly, as the Women's Movement looked for heroes, some claimed Margaret, citing her as a great inspiration. When she heard this, she smiled to herself, remembering the gathering in Houston of all the "important women" to which she had not been invited, and the snubs from Bella Abzug and NOW. If she had helped them, that was fine, she would say, "But I'm no feminist." Herbert Libby would have been proud. On the Monday before the Houston conference opened, Margaret Chase Smith received a telegram from Bella Abzug which said: "If we don't hear from you in response to our invitation for you to attend our conference, the invitation is withdrawn," Margaret never received an invitation, but according to her, "NOW had given it to the press that they had invited me and I had turned it down."[499]

With the passage of time, Margaret and Skowhegan forgave each other, and Skowhegan once again began to boast of their most famous citizen. The governor established a Margaret Chase Smith Day, while Skowhegan named its two bridges and an elementary school after her. After all, it was said, she had been the only one down there in Washington willing to take on Joe McCarthy. And she had looked out for national defense even as she let the bureaucrats know that the people were in charge. Not the generals, not the admirals, not the president himself, but the people. The Murrays and Chases and Emerys and Smiths. The people on small farms and those on shift work at the glove factory. The ones who fought for the country and most often didn't come home. The people who raised their families and paid the politicians' salaries. And she was heard to say that she didn't regret a day of it. No sir. She said she wouldn't have had it any other way.

On her 90th birthday in December 1987, she was honored in Augusta, the same city Clyde had entered a young man and left a seasoned politician. What would he have said about her? That she had fought well, and for the right things? That she had mastered all the things he had taught her, and then some? He, more than most, would have enjoyed the irony in Senator Muskie's remark that Muskie and the Democrats both recognized her power, "which was considerable." And he would have smiled at the tribute of Congresswoman (later Senator) Olympia Snowe, who called Margaret a "trailblazer for women, whether she chooses to claim that or not." But it was Senator Mitchell's comments which would have pleased him most. For George Mitchell, who had worked his way through Bowdoin as a janitor, came the closest to understanding the source of her power. "Margaret Chase Smith embodies our best conception of ourselves," he said. "She puts before us a vision of what we all aspire to but seldom achieve." Mitchell had got it right. It was her raw instinct for most often doing the right thing and doing it well that Clyde had first noticed.

But Margaret's own words captured her spirit best. After all the speeches had been given, all the celebratory words used up, Margaret rose to thank the three hundred for coming. She steadied herself at the podium behind a large bouquet of red roses sent by President Reagan and his wife Nancy, while the audience stood, warmly applauding her. Finally she raised her hands, and the room grew quiet. For a moment, she was younger and straighter and full of pepper, tart-tongued, and the ageless, flat Yankee twang which sounded patrician came over the microphone. The woman who was a Maine legend and who had just listened to an evening of eulogies was not about to yield to the sentimentality of the moment. With perfect timing, emphasizing the irony of her remark, she quipped: "I'm wonderful. I know it. . . . It's been a little hard to take and still keep my feet on the ground." And then she broke into a broad smile as the audience, again on its feet, alternatively laughed and applauded.

To see her in such a setting was to witness something mystical. People could not get enough of her. That quality punctuated the newspaper articles which compared her to royalty, the television and radio interviews which always ended up talking about the legend that was Margaret Chase Smith.

In December 1993, an article appeared in the newspaper about Margaret Chase Smith's 96th birthday. Dozens of friends and admirers had honored her at the Governor's Mansion in Augusta. Once again, as if twenty years had not elapsed since she was last in the spotlight, when someone asked her why she wasn't running for governor, she turned and with no flicker of a smile told him: "That wouldn't be a bad idea just to get people to vote." And then, as though the thought had just occurred to her, she asked, "Is it too late?"

On 29 May 1995, the succession of strategies which had propelled a restless spirit toward excellence for most of her 97 years were no longer needed. At 4:40 P.M. she died in her bedroom at Neil Hill after eight days in a coma from a massive stroke. All of Maine was invited to the memorial service which was held on 16 June.

At 1 P.M. when the parade of buses hired for the occasion to transport people from the fairgrounds to the ceremony began to deposit their passengers at the foot of Neil Hill, squiggly lines of heat were drifting across the blacktop road, and soon only the rose and blue spikes of the lupine along the road seemed starched and fresh. As the faithful straggled past the large white frame, black-shuttered Coburn house at the foot of the hill, they talked in low voices about how early they had left home that morning, about the robust green of the young summer day, and widely agreed that Margaret herself would have approved of the bright sun and cloudless sky.

"I've never seen the grounds look lovelier," exclaimed one middle-aged woman, who, with an elderly woman, had just finished the climb to the summit. And indeed, the showy rhododendron of deep pink and white were in full bloom, as were the red geraniums which lined the flag-stone walks. Slowly, the two women began to drift toward the large, white tent which had been erected for the service. By 2 P.M. several hundred filled the tent and to the chords of "Joyful, Joyful, We Adore Thee" the crowd rose and sang its heart out. Everyone who was anyone in Maine politics was there, including former Senator Edmund Muskie, former Governors John Reed, Kenneth Curtis, and John McKernan, and Senator Olympia Snowe. Senator William Cohen, who like Margaret had represented the Second Congressional District in the House before being elected to the Senate, tried to put into words what Margaret had meant to him and to Maine. "She dug the well for me and many of the elected officials who are here to commemorate and celebrate her life," he said.[500]

Governor Angus King captured a formidable Margaret that many in attendance had seen at one time or another. He talked about his anxiety in telling her that he had worked on Bill Hathaway's 1972 campaign. Finally, he decided to write her a letter to which she replied, "Dear Angus King: It is perfectly all right with me that you once worked for Bill Hathaway. Sincerely, Margaret Chase Smith."[501] The youthful King elicited a chuckle from the extended Smith family which filled the tent.

Then, as one, on that nearly-still June afternoon, the voices rose and swelled in the final hymn: "Mine eyes have seen the glory of the coming of the Lord; He is trampling out the vintage where the grapes of wrath are stored; He hath loosed the fateful lightening of His terrible swift sword; His truth is marching on." The woman who always seemed to know who she was and where she had come from was home to stay. Maine individualism and ties to the past tugged at old and young alike. But each had as well a unique memory of Margaret, visions of which could be glimpsed like bright ribbons, fluttering on the softest of breezes.

ENDNOTES

ABBREVIATIONS USED IN ENDNOTES

ARN Aroostook Republican News
BDN Bangor Daily News
BG Boston Globe
BPW National Federation of Business and Professional Women
BSG Boston Sunday Globe
BTR Brunswick Times-Record
DKJ Daily Kennebec Journal
DOC Declaration of Conscience
ES Evening Sentinel
IR Independent Reporter
LDS Lewiston Daily Sun
LEJ Lewiston Evening Journal
LS Lewiston Sun
MCS Margaret Chase Smith
MCSA Margaret Chase Smith Archives
MH Miami Herald
MST Maine Sunday Telegram
MT Maine Times
NC North Country
NYT New York Times
PA Pittsfield Advertiser
PEE Portland Evening Express
PH Portsmouth Herald
PI Post-Intelligencer
PPH Portland Press Herald
PST Portland Sunday Telegraph
RCG Rockland Courier Gazette
SR Somerset Reporter
WDN Washington Daily News
WES Washington Evening Star
WMS Waterville Morning Sentinel
WPM Washington Post Magazine
WPTH Washington Post Times Herald
WS Waterville Sentinel
WSJ Wall Street Journal
WT Washington Times
W&Y "Washington and You"

INTRODUCTION

1 Louise Coburn Collection, Miller Library, Colby College Archives; Marilyn Mavrinac, "Genteel Conflict: The Early Years of Coeducation at Colby College," The Colby Alumnus, Dec. 1986, 12-17.

2 Mavrinac, 13-14; for parallel strategies in the suffragist movement see Eleanor Flexner, *Century of Struggle* (Cambridge, Mass: Harvard University Press, 1959), 151-3, 216, 110-13; William L. O'Neill, *Everyone Was Brave* (Chicago: Chicago University Press, 1969), 18-24, 33-38; William Chafe, *The American Woman* (Oxford: Oxford University Press, 1975), 11-14; Barbara Welter, "The Cult of True Womanhood: 1820-1860," *American Quarterly*, XVIII (Summer 1966), 162.

3 O'Neil, *Everyone*, 4-5.

4 Nancy F. Cott, *The Bonds of Womanhood*, (New Haven: Yale University Press, 1977), 125; also see Carl Degler, *At Odds: Women and the Family in America from the Revolution to the Present*, (New York: Oxford University Press, 1981), 343.

5 Taylor, *Liberty Men and Great Proprietors: The Revolutionary Settlement on the Maine Frontier, 1760-1820* (Chapel Hill: University of North Carolina Press, 1993), 63.

6 Ibid., 8.

7 U.S. Department of Commerce, Bureau of the Census, data compiled from 1900, 1910 and 1940 census returns.

8 Maine Development Commission, *Facts about Maine: The Offer of the Pine Tree State*, 1946, 14.

9 Perry Miller and Thomas H. Johnson, *The Puritans* (New York: American Book Company, 1938), 284. Quotations from Perry Miller and Thomas Johnson's work are henceforth cited using the following abbreviation: TP

10 John Winthrop, "A Modell of Christian Charity," quoted in *The Puritans*, 199.

11 Carolyn G. Heilbrun, *Writing a Woman's Life*, (Ballantine Books: New York, 1988), 49.

PART ONE

1 For a discussion of the major proprietary claims to the District of Maine and their impact on the agrarian dream, see Taylor, *Liberty Men and Great Proprietors*, 12; Abnakis were called Tarrateens by the Puritans.

2 Father Sebastian Rasles, Missionary of the Society of Jesus in New France to Monsieur his Brother, "The Jesuit Relations and Allied Documents: Travels and Explorations of the Jesuit Missionaries in New France, 1610-1791,"

ed. Reuben Gold Thwaites in *The Indians of North America*, ed. Edna Kenton, vol. 2 (New York: Harcourt, Brace and Co., 1927), 365-6. Quotations from Edna Kenton's work are henceforth cited using the following abbreviation: INA.

3 INA, 368.

4 Ibid.

5 Ibid.

6 Ibid.

7 The manuscript dictionary eventually came into the possession of Harvard University, in whose library it is preserved. The box in which Father Rasles kept his manuscript is the property of the Maine historical society. The document was published in 1853 by John Pickering in *American Academy of Arts and Sciences Memoirs*, new series, Vol. 1, 375-574.

8 For a full account see James P. Baxter's *New France in New England*, William Allen, *The History of Norridgewock* (Norridgewock: 1849); William D. Williamson, *The History of the State of Maine* (Hallowell: 1832).

9 INA, 499.

10 Henry David Thoreau, *The Maine Woods* (New York: Harper and Row, 1987), xxxix, xli, xlii.

11 Frederick Webb Hodge, ed., *Handbook of American Indians*, Smithsonian Bureau of American Ethnology Bulletin No. 30 (Washington, D.C., 1911) 2-4; Thoreau, *The Maine Woods*, xxxix.

12 Thoreau, *The Maine Woods*, xliv.

13 Kenneth A. Lockridge, *A New England Town: The First Hundred Years* (New York: W.W. Norton, 1985), 4.

14 TP, 46.

15 Ibid, 59-60.

16 Ibid, 61.

17 Lockridge, *A New England Town*, 4-8.

18 Charles E. Clark, *The Eastern Frontier: The Settlement of Northern New England 1610-1763* (New York: Knopf, 1970), 82.

19 For genealogical information I am indebted to the following sources which will be used for the remainder of this chapter without attribution: Joshua Coffin, *History of Newbury, Newburyport and West Newbury from 1635-1843* (Boston: 1845 Chase and Chamberlin); *Descendants of Aquila and Thomas Chase* (Derry, NH: 1928); *Revolutionary War Pension File #S-36964*, National Archives, Washington, D.C.; MCSA.

20 Lockridge, *A New England Town*, 40. During this period, Newbury remained a Puritan stronghold which produced three prominent Puritan clergymen:

John Clark of Exeter, Samuel Emery of Wells, and Samuel Moody of York. Clark, *Eastern Frontier*, 82.

21 Taylor, *Liberty Men*, 63.

22 Thoreau, *The Maine Woods*, 20.

23 INA, 386-7.

24 David C. Smith, "Maine's Changing Landscape to 1820," in Charles Clark, James Leamon, and Karen Bowden, eds., *Maine in the Early Republic*, published for the Maine Historical Society (Hanover, NH: University Press of New England, 1988), 15.

25 Ibid.

26 Robert Frost, "The Road Not Taken," 1916.

27 Alan S. Taylor, "Nathan Barlow's Journey: Mysticism and Popular Protest on the Northeastern Frontier," Charles Clark et al, eds., *Maine in the Early Republic*, 100-115.

28 Edward Augustus Kendall, *Travels Through the Northern Parts of the United States in the Years 1807 and 1808*, vol. 3 (New York: I. Riley, 1809), 89.

29 Taylor, *Liberty Men and Great Proprietors*, 173-4.

30 Louise Coburn, *Skowhegan on the Kennebec*, vol. 2 (Skowhegan, Maine: Independent Reporter Press), 603.

31 Ibid., 606-610.

32 *Maine: A Guide 'Down East,'* The American Guide Series, Federal Writers' Project of the Works Progress Administration for the State of Maine (Boston: 1937), 45.

33 TP, 37.

34 Anecdote file, Margaret Chase Smith Archives (hereafter cited as AF).

35 AF.

36 Ibid.

37 Ibid.

38 Ibid.

39 Ibid.

40 Quoted by A. Poulin, Jr., "Poetry and the Landscape of Epiphany: On Translating the Poetry of Anne Herbert," in Anne Hebert: *Selected Poems*, trans. A. Poulin, Jr. (Brockport, NY: B.O.A. Editions, Ltd., 1987), 150.

41 AF.

42 Ibid.

43 Ibid.

44 Ibid.

45 Patricia Wallace, *Politics of Conscience* (Westport, CT: Praeger, 1995), 6, notes that Margaret's baptized name was recorded at the church of Notre

Dame de Lourdes in Skowhegan as Margueritte Mandeline Chase. Smith's sensitivity about the French version of her name is discussed in footnote ten, 203-4. "When Margaret Chase Smith learned that I had received the baptismal certificate [from the Church of Notre Dame de Lourdes in Skowhegan], she wrote to say that she was sending a copy of her birth certificate giving 'the correct names of myself and my mother and father.'" The significance of the datum is not explained by Wallace, and the reader is led to infer that some kind of cover-up was going on by Smith. Just as likely, however, is the possibility that several clerical errors were made in the Notre Dame de Lourdes document. Surely that must be the explanation for the substitution of the exotic and improbable "Mandeline" for the French "Madeline." Lending credence to this explanation is a note in the Birth Records file of the Margaret Chase Smith Archives from Francis E. Croteau to Margaret Chase Smith, February 1952: "It was well your mother came in. As she probably wrote you, it was necessary to execute depositions correcting all her children's records. Someone had written your first name in the record in pencil without authority. The record at Augusta [Maine] was, therefore, not corrected. I have reported to the Division of Vital Statistics so that your record is complete there and at this office. Should it be destroyed by fire at one place it will be available at the other," (a reference to the Skowhegan fire which destroyed all of Margaret's birth records except those in the Church of Notre Dame de Lourdes). I have already noted in this work that Lambert Morin changed his name to the anglicized John Murray, suggesting an unease with the role of the ethnic, and I have argued that his legacy to Margaret was a dual insecurity in position and a hunger to secure position. But I do not believe that the baptismal certificate itself advances this discussion.

46 AF.
47 MCS, interview with author, 23 July 1983.
48 Wallace, *Conscience*, 6.
49 AF.
50 Ibid.
51 Ibid.
52 Ibid.
53 MCS, interview with author, 6 August 1983.
54 AF.
55 Ibid.
56 E.A. Robinson, "Bewick Finzer," 1916.
57 Beverly Smith, "The Senator from the Five-and-Ten," *The Saturday Evening Post*, 11 September 1948, 146.

58 AF.

59 Ibid.

60 Second and Final Account, Estate of Clyde Smith, Clyde Smith File, MCSA.

61 IR, 6 March 1913, 1.

62 Richard Hofstadter, *The Age of Reform* (New York: Vintage Books, 1955), 64.

63 AF.

64 Hofstadter, *The Age of Reform*, 5.

65 AF.

66 Ibid.

67 MCS, interview with author, 13 August 1983; also see Frank Graham, Jr., *Margaret Chase Smith: Woman of Courage* (New York: John Day Co., 1964), 19-20.

68 MCS, interview with author, 13 August 1983.

69 AF.

70 A small notice appeared in *The Independent Reporter*, 11 November 1915, 5: "Mrs. Frances Kelly arrived Tuesday evening from a visit in Newport, Plymouth, and Pittsfield. During her absence, Miss Margaret Chase substituted as night operator in the New England Telephone Office."

71 MCS, interview with author, 6 August 1983.

72 Ibid.

73 LEJ, 20 May 1961, Magazine section, 10A.

74 *The Lever*, published by Skowhegan High School, March 1916, 6, Lever folder, MCSA.

75 MCS, interview with author, 31 July 1983.

76 IR, 2 March 1916, 1.

77 MST, 18 July 1976, 12A.

78 Helen Vandercook, *The Campfire Girls at Sunrise Hill* (Philadelphia: John C. Winston Co., 1913), 7, 9, 72-73, italics mine.

79 MST, 18 July 1976, 12A.

80 AF.

81 By 1922, women in positions as stenographers, etc. were making as much as $26 per week or slightly more than $1000 per year nationally. However, salaries in Skowhegan lagged behind these national data by at least half, so a good wage for Margaret after some years of experience was $18-$28, the salary she received between 1919 and 1927.

82 Scrapbook, Vol. 6, 120, MCSA.

83 Undated, Eldina Pratt to Clyde Smith, Clyde Smith file, MCSA.

84 Ibid.

85 IR, n.d., Scrapbook, Vol. 6, 109, MCSA.

86 Ibid.

87 Undated notes, Clyde Smith, Clyde Smith file, MCSA.

88 IR, n.d., Scrapbook, Vol. 6, 109, MCSA.

89 Ibid.

90 "Clyde Harold Smith Legislator," Scrapbook, Vol. 5, 99, MCSA.

91 William Allen White, *Autobiography* (New York: Macmillan Company, 1946), 350.

92 Ibid., 337.

93 William A. Robinson, *Thomas Reed, Parliametarian* (New York: Dodd, Mead, 1930), 333.

94 White, *Autobiography*, 336.

95 Robinson, *Thomas Reed, Parliamentarian*, 380.

96 Ibid., 379.

97 Samuel Leland Powers, *Portraits of Half a Century* (Boston: Little, Brown & Co, 1925), 264.

98 Orlando O. Stealey, *Twenty Years in the Press Gallery* (New York: author, 1906), 412-13, quoted in Barbara W. Tuchman, *Proud Tower* (New York: The Macmillan Co., 1966), 141-2.

99 Robinson, *Thomas Reed, Parliamentarian*, 374.

100 24 April 1940, *Congressional Record*, 76th Cong., 1st sess., Appendix, 2557-2558, reprinted from 1903 speech.

101 Ibid.

102 Tuchman, *Proud Tower*, 167.

103 Undated IR, Scrapbook, Vol. 6, 120, MCSA.

104 IR, 1940, Scrapbook, Vol. 6, 104, MCSA.

105 SR, 23 April 1908, 1.

106 Coburn, *Skowhegan on the Kennebec*, Vol. 2, 882.

107 Ibid, 921-2.

108 Mrs. Elizabeth Sealy, interview with author, 29 April 1992.

109 Coburn, *Skowhegan on the Kennebec*, Vol. 2, 507.

110 Ibid., 498.

111 Ernest L. Butler, Butler and Butler, Attorneys-at-law, to Margaret Chase Smith, 11 February 1948, Clyde Smith file, MCSA.

112 Graham, *Margaret Chase Smith*, 21.

113 AF.

114 Clyde Smith file, MCSA; for reference to Clyde's election see IR, 11 November 1915, 5.

115 MCS, interview with author, 6 August 1983.

116 AF.

117 Ibid.

118 MCS, interview with author, 13 August 1983.

119 AF.

120 IR, 13 April 1916, 1.

121 AF.

122 MCSA, Class of 1916 folder.

123 AF.

124 MCS, interview with author, 31 July 1983.

125 AF.

126 Ibid.

127 MCS, interview with author, 6 August 1983.

128 AF.

129 MCS, interview with author, 6 August 1983.

130 Ibid.

131 Ibid.

132 Graham, *Margaret Chase Smith*, 21.

133 AF.

134 IR, 8 November 1917, 6.

135 IR, 6 December 1917, 1.

136 Roland Patten to Clyde Smith, 1930, Clyde Smith file, MCSA.

137 AF.

138 IR, 25 April 1918, 8; IR, 24 April 1919, 2.

139 See Robert H. Wiebe, *The Search for Order* (New York: Hill and Wang, 1967) 1-83.

140 IR, 6 December 1917, 1, italics mine.

141 Coburn, *Skowhegan*, vol. 1, 290.

142 Ibid., 287.

143 IR, 18 April 1918, 1.

144 Ibid.

145 IR, 17 May 1934, 5A.

146 IR, 6 September 1917, 1, Supplement.

147 IR, 12 September 1918, 1.

148 IR, 2 January 1919, 1.

149 IR, 27 March 1919, 1.

150 IR, 13 December 1917, 1.

151 IR, 6 June 1918, 1.

152 *Maine Guide*, 47.

153 IR, 29 May 1919, 11.

154 IR, 5 June, 1919, 1, 2.

155 AF.

156 IR, 23 October 1919, 6.

157 Maine Telephone & Telegraph Company to Margaret Chase Smith, 6 January 1920, MCSA.

158 IR, 23 October 1919, 6; 9 October 1919, 1; 8 April 1920, 1.

159 Coburn, *Skowhegan*, vol. 2, 510.

160 MCS Speech 1938, Earliest Speeches, 19, MCSA.

161 Ibid.

162 AF.

163 MCS Speech, Earliest Speeches, 19, MCSA.

164 AF.

165 Ibid.

166 Scrapbook, Vol. 9, 5, MCSA.

167 Roland T. Patten to Clyde H. Smith, 21 March 1930, MCSA.

168 AF.

169 Coburn, *Skowhegan*, vol. 2, 882.

170 AF. See Anne Firor Scott, *Natural Allies: Women's Associations in American History* (Urbana: University of Illinois Press, 1992).

171 Scrapbook, Vol. 9, MCSA.

172 AF.

173 The 21 December Dyer letter is not extant. Clyde H. Smith to Lena M. Dyer, 23 December 1920, (no signature, on letterhead: Office of Selectmen, Assessors and Overseers of Poor, Town of Skowhegan. Initials CHS/HPB) Clyde Smith file, MCSA.

174 IR, 6 October 1921, 3.

175 Scrapbook, Vol. 1, 16 MCS Archives, DKJ, 7 May 1923, 2; DKJ, 24 May 1923, 2.

176 Coburn, *Skowhegan*, vol. 2, 885.

177 *A History of the National Federation of Business and Professional Women's Clubs, Inc. 1914-1944* (New York: National Federation of Business and Professional Women, 1944), 12. Quotations from *A History* are henceforth cited using the following abbreviation: HBPW.

178 HBPW, 13-14.

179 Ibid., 20.

180 Ibid., 17-20.

181 Ibid., 21-22.

182 Ibid., 115.

183 AF.

184 Scrapbook, Vol. 9, 8, MCSA.

185 Ibid.

186 Ibid.

187 Ibid., 7.

188 AF.

189 Ibid.

190 Ibid.

191 Scrapbook, Vol. 9, 8, MCSA.

192 DKJ, 14 June 1923, 5; IR, 19 August 1920, 1; 2 September 1920, 1,4.

193 AF.

194 Scrapbook, Vol. 9, 24, MCSA.

195 Margaret Chase Smith, Speeches, Vol. 1925, 13, MCSA.

196 Ibid.

197 Scrapbook, Vol. 9, 18, MCSA.

198 AF.

199 Business and Professional Women's Club File, Maine Convention folder, 1927 booklet, MCSA.

200 Scrapbook, Vol. 9, 20, MCSA.

201 Ibid., 17, MCSA.

202 *Maine Guide*, 65, 245; IR, 23 August 1928, 3B.

203 IR, 7 June 1928, 1; 18 October 1928, 6A.

204 IR, 19 October 1928, 6A; 12 January 1928, 3B.

205 Mary R. Melendy, *The Perfect Woman A Complete Medical Guide for Women*, (K.T. Bolond, 1901), 47.

206 Wallace, *Conscience*, 31, suggests that in 1929 speculation began that Clyde was the father of an illegitimate child who grew up in Skowhegan and was "never denied as being Clyde's daughter." The rumor has not been confirmed.

207 DKJ, 15 May 1930,2.

208 Ibid.

PART TWO

1 Beryl Markham, *West with the Night* (San Francisco: North Point Press, 1983), 131.

2 AF.

3 Campaign Diary, MCSA.

4 BDN, 8 April 1940, 1; DKJ, 8 April 1940, 1.

5 Clyde Smith to his constituents, 7 April 1940, Clyde Smith file, MCSA; Scrapbook, Vol. 6, 115, MCSA.

6 IR, 31 December 1936, 1A; 28 January 1937, 1, 4A. See Margaret Chase Smith,

Declaration of Conscience (New York: Doubleday & Co., 1972), 65 (hereafter cited as DOC) for a discussion of pressures on Clyde from constituents to appoint Margaret as his secretary. Though it is further claimed by Margaret that she became Clyde's "top staff member," the preponderance of the evidence suggests otherwise.

7 WES, 8 April 1940, 1.

8 LEJ, 8 April 1940, 1; Scrapbook, Vol. 6, 113, MCSA.

9 Scrapbook, Vol. 6, 110, MCSA.

10 LEJ, 8 April 1940, 1.

11 Scrapbook, Vol. 6, 115; Clyde Smith to his constituents, 7 April 1940, Clyde Smith file, MCSA.

12 AF.

13 IR, 18 May 1939, 4A.

14 WMS, 12 April 1940, 1; Scrapbook, Vol. 6, 117, MCSA.

15 Kathryn Byrne, "The Fatal Day Never Came," unpublished, 13 June 1947, 4, Clyde Smith file, MCSA.

16 WS, 9 April 1940, 1.

17 BDN, 14 May 1940, 1.

18 BDN, 16 May 1940, 1.

19 Campaign Diary, MCSA.

20 May Craig, "Inside in Washington," PPH, 12 April 1940, 4.

21 John A. Kolmer, M.D., Director Research Institute of Cutaneous Medicine, to Benjamin B. Foster, M.D., 21 December 1938; Clyde Smith to Dr. Benjamin B. Foster, 17 January, 1939: Clyde Smith to Dr. John A. Kolmer, 17 January 1939, Clyde Smith file, MCSA. As defined by *Dorland's Illustrated Medical Dictionary*, 28th ed., s.v. "tabes dorsalis" is "parenchymatous neurosyphilis in which there is slowly progressive degeneration of the posterior columns and posterior roots and ganglia of the spinal cord, occurring 15 to 20 years after the initial infection of syphilis, characterized by lancinating lightning pains, urinary incontinence, ataxia, impaired position and vibratory sense, optic atrophy, hypotonia, hyperreflexia, and trophic joint degeneration."

22 IR, 27-30 March 1930, 1.

23 LEJ, 7 March 1935, 9.

24 IR, 25 May 1916, 3.

25 MCS, interview with author 23 July 1983.

26 In March 1931 Clyde fended off charges that his connections with the New England Culvert Co. had resulted in that company's receiving the majority of state contracts for steel culverts, presumably because of Clyde's position as a highway commissioner. See LEJ, 18 March 1931, 1, 3.

27 Claire Callahan, "A Woman with Two Jobs," *Ladies Home Journal*, October 1930, 114, quoted in Chafe, *American Woman*, 106.

28 MCS, interview with author, 11 August 1983.

29 Ibid.

30 McCall's, October 1928, 2, Otis Lee Wiese, editorial; Elizabeth Cook, "The Kitchen Sink Complex," *Ladies Home Journal*, September 1931, 12.

31 MCS, interview with author, 11 August 1983.

32 Ibid.

33 AF.

34 AF.

35 See Chafe, *American Woman*, 199-225 for complete discussion of the cross-currents of the post-war period.

36 Margaret Davidson, "Kitchen for a Lady Senator," *Ladies Home Journal*, November 1956, 204-6.

37 Margaret Chase Smith, "No Place for a Woman?" *Ladies Home Journal*, February 1952, 50,83.

38 MCS, interview with author, 11 August 1983.

39 MCS, interview with author, 31 July 1983.

40 Undated correspondence, Clyde Smith to MCS, (circa 1932), Springfield, Mass., Clyde Smith file, MCSA.

41 LEJ, 1 January 1932, 7.

42 PEN, 13 January 1932, 26.

43 In 1929 the Rowen and Moore Shoe Co. announced an indefinite shut-down of the plant due to "a widespread depression in the shoe business..., a condition which Rowen and Moore, Inc., has not alone suffered from" IR, 24 January 1929, 1, 4. At the same time it was reported that Clyde himself "seriously considered placing additional funds in the business, taking over the directing reins of the plant with the hopes of building up the business to such an extent that it will yield returns to the many local investors." In 1930, when three truckloads of shoes were stolen from Rowen and Moore's successor, the Northeastern Shoe Co., Clyde became the company's assignee in the recovery of the stolen merchandise. Although Northeastern's ledger shows that he received $626.10 for "salary and expenses" from January 1930 to April 1932, he spent $1000 during that same time for travel, phone calls, postage, etc. as Northeastern's assignee, a net loss of approximately $350, Clyde Smith file, Ledger, Northeastern Shoe Co., Personal Expenses as Assignee, 26 January 1930 to 28 March 1932, 31-5, MCSA. His primary source of revenue — rental property income — yielded approximately $2,455.75 annually. After mortgage payments, repairs, upkeep, taxes, and periods of vacancy, rentals would have

been enough to add a margin of comfort to a solid financial base, but they were hardly sufficient to support the style of living enjoyed on Fairview Avenue, Clyde Smith file, estate Clyde Smith Folder, MCSA. Further evidence of the Smith's precarious financial status in these years is provided by Margaret's decision to take in tourists, a fairly common practice and one followed by the Myron Smiths, though not one of which Clyde approved. After six weeks, at Clyde's urging, Margaret abandoned the tourist home business, AF.

44 Clyde Smith to MCS, 7 December 1932, Middletown, Ohio; Undated letter Clyde Smith to MCS, Middletown, Ohio; Undated letter Clyde Smith to MCS, Springfield, Mass.; Undated letter Clyde Smith to MCS, Geneva, New York; Clyde Smith to MCS, 4 December 1932, Clyde Smith file, MCSA.

45 IR, 14 December 1933, 1B.

46 IR, 2 June 1933, 3A.

47 IR, 13 July 1933, 1, 4A.

48 IR, 5 April 1934, 1B.

49 IR, 3 May 1934, 1B.

50 LEJ, 12 September 1934, 1. In Maine, the Governor is nominated by direct primary and serves a two-year term. Maine's constitution grants wide powers to the legislature and curtails those of the Governor by creation of a seven-member Council which must approve nearly all executive actions. Until recently state elections were held biennially on the second Monday in September of even-numbered years.

51 IR, 13 September 1934, 1A.

52 Papers, Vol. 1, 1906-1937, 60, MCSA.

53 LEJ, 7 March 1935, 9.

54 Ibid.

55 Papers, Vol. 1, 1906-1937, 159, MCSA.

56 Ibid., 155.

57 LEJ, 26 November 1935, 1, 2.

58 Papers, Vol. 1, 1906-1937, 159, MCSA.

59 Ibid.

60 ES, 27 November 1935, 1. None of these letters and telegrams are extant.

61 LEJ, 31 December 1935, 1.

62 IR, 2 April 1936, 3A; 11 June 1936, 7A.

63 IR, 2 April 1936, 3A..

64 IR, 18 June 1936, 1A.

65 Ibid.

66 Papers, Vol 1, 39. Date of above not known but appears to have been clipped

from a newspaper and pasted in a scrapbook just above an entry dated May 15, 1937, MCSA.

67 AF.

68 Campaign Diary, MCSA.

69 IR, 4 June 1936, 2A.

70 IR, 16 June 1936, 1, 5A.

71 Ibid.

72 IR, 17 September 1936, 1A.

73 IR, 1 October 1936, 3A.

74 IR, 31 December 1936, 1A.

75 AF.

76 Scrapbook, Vol. 10,8, MCSA.

77 AF.

78 Ibid.

79 Ibid.

80 Ibid.

81 *Washington Times*, 27 December 1938; Scrapbook, Vol. 9, 53, MCSA, italics mine.

82 AF.

83 Abigail Q. McCarthy, "Eleanor Roosevelt as First Lady," in *Without Precedent*, ed Joan Hoff-Wilson and Marjorie Lightman (Bloomington: Indiana University Press, 1984), 218.

84 Scrapbook, Vol. 9, 49 MCSA.

85 Wiebe, *The Search for Order*, 12.

86 IR, 29 February 1940, 4A.

87 Ibid.

88 For his many insights into the hold of pastoralism on the American and European imagination, I am indebted to Leo Marx, *The Machine and the Garden*, (New York: Oxford University Press, 1964), 118-44.

89 TP, 152.

90 See Marx, *The Machine and The Garden*, 176.

91 Her victory in the 13 May primary was tantamount to election as she faced no Democratic opposition in the special election on 3 June. When that general election was held, she received a surprising 440 votes from her home county of Somerset, a sizable vote considering the election was only a formality. Other areas, like Lewiston, which cast only 196 votes, had a much smaller voter turn-out. IR, 6 June 1940, 1.

92 IR, 16 May 1940, 7A.

93 NYT, 16 May 1940, 1.

94 See MCS Papers, Miscellaneous Papers 1925-1945 for excerpts of the speech. The speech itself, delivered 27 October 1938, is not extant. See also DOC, 65-67.

95 BDN, 17 May 1940, 4.

96 See Alfred Thayer Mahon, *The Influence of Sea Power on History* (New York: Sagamore Press, 1957); *The Interest of America in Sea Power* (Boston: Little Brown, 1897).

97 IR, 6 June 1940, 3A, 29 May 1940, 1.

98 Manchester, *The Glory and the Dream*, 228. In Maine support for the armed services was more pronounced than in the country as a whole. As of 15 January 1940, Maine "was the only state above its quota in the army's nation-wide recruiting drive." According to first corps area chief of staff Col. Charles B. Meyer, the state had produced 400 new soldiers, 100 more than its quota. BDN, 16 January 1940, 3A.

99 Brann lost the Senatorial race in the general election held on 9 September, 1940 to Ralph Owen Brewster by a margin of 50,000 votes. Commented the BDN, "Bran [sic] never more than a lukewarm supporter of the New Deal until this year, warmly endorsed Roosevelt's third term candidacy and was soundly whipped." BDN, 10 September 1940, 1.

100 DOC, 67.

101 Address, Herbert C. Libby, 11 June 1940, 2, MCSA, italics mine.

102 Scrapbook, Vol. 10, 27 MCSA.

103 IR, 13 June 1940, 6A.

104 WS, 11 June 1940, Scrapbook, Vol. 10, 8, MCSA.

105 Address, Herbert C. Libby, 11 June 1940, 2, MCSA.

106 Letter Mary Low Carver to Louise Coburn, August 15, 1890, Louise Coburn Collection, Colby Archives. "I argue it [coeducation] on the ground of the home-life and for married women because he does. If I can show him that coeducation in the present course of study result in greater benefits to the home-life, I answer his argument more effectively. I say afterwards that there is no need of arguing for the benefits to society as everybody knows that an educated woman's sphere is necessarily wider than the home." Also see Ilene Kraditor's excellent discussion, *The Ideas of the Woman's Suffrage Movement, 1890-1920* (New York: Columbia University Press, 1965), 115-116; O'Neill, *Everyone*, 50-51.

107 Chafe, *American Woman*, 13; *Congressional Record*, 89th Congress, 1st Session, 4 March 1965, 4158.

108 "Conservatism in Maine," July 1940, 74, Papers, 1925-1945, MCSA.

109 Nancy Woloch, *Women and the American Experience* (New York: Alfred A.

Knopf, 1984), 455. Woloch points out that even the New Deal women, including Eleanor Roosevelt herself, avoided the label "feminist."

110 IR, 16 May 1940, 7A.

111 BDN, 14 May 1940, 4.

112 Eleanor Flexner, *Century of Struggle: The Woman's Rights Movement in the United States* (New York: Atheneum, 1974), 173.

113 DKJ, 6 January 1923, 2.

114 IR, 14 November 1940, 5A.

115 IR, 18 July 1940, 1.

116 Campaign Diary, MCSA; IR, 20 June 1940, 1A, 6A.

117 Campaign Dairy, MCSA.

118 IR, 22 August 1940, 1, 5A.

119 IR, 5 September 1940, 1.

120 Campaign Diary, MCSA.

121 IR, 12 September 1940, 3A.

122 Wallace, *Conscience*, 53.

123 See Miscellaneous Speeches 1925-1945, October 5, 1940, 187; Scrapbook, Vol 13, 76, MCSA.

124 IR, 19 September 1940, 1. Three other congresswomen were in attendance — all more senior than Margaret. Frances Bolton of Ohio; Edith Nourse Rogers of Massachusetts and Jessie Sumner of Illinois. Margaret travelled with Judge Sumner to the meeting. IR, 3 October 1940, 5A.

125 Scrapbook, Vol. 13, 60, MCSA.

126 Miscellaneous Speeches, 1925-1945, 111; Speech, 18 October 1940, Scrapbook, Vol. 13, 76, MCSA.

127 Speech, 18 October 1940, Scrapbook, Vol. 13, 76, MCSA.

128 Stephen Shadegg, *Clare Boothe Luce: A Biography* (New York: Simon and Schuster, 1970), 120.

129 William E. Leuchtenburg, *In the Shadow of FDR* (Ithaca: Cornell University Press, 1985), 163.

130 Barbara Miller Solomon, *In The Company of Educated Women: A History of Women and Higher Education in America* (New Haven: Yale University Press, 1985), 48.

131 Chafe, *American Woman*, 93.

132 LEJ, 27 January 1931, 9.

133 BDN, 12 February 1940, 6; 7 October 1940, 8.

134 A survey released in October 1940 by the National Federation of Business and Professional Women named Maine as having the largest number of women "functioning in town and city offices" in the country, with women

occupying 2,407 town and city offices, a figure which suggests the inclusion of Party workers as well as members of county and town committees in the survey. In January 1941, results of a second survey were released. Again Maine finished well in front with 473, the highest number of women in city and town offices of any state in the union. That such a dramatic disparity exists between 1940 and 1941 suggests that the criteria for inclusion changed. In the 1941 study, South Dakota reported the largest number of women in county offices (as contrasted with county and town offices) with 119, and Ohio reported the second highest with 35. Connecticut reported the largest number of women legislators, with 25. BDN, 7 October 1940, p. 8; 23 January 1941, 7. The original surveys conducted by the BPW are not extant.

135 Martin's support for women, though perhaps feminist at the core, did not translate into strident feminism. A month after the election, she warned the Bangor, Maine GOP women against placing "too much importance on the women's viewpoint" and urged them "to look at questions from the angle of the citizen, rather than that of a woman. If we do that," she said, "we will go a long way in politics." BDN, 11 December 1940, 11.

136 The only female in the Senate was Hattie Caraway of Arkansas, who had succeeded her husband in 1931. In the House, Democrat Mary Norton of New Jersey, first elected in 1925, was the most senior, followed by Representative Edith Nourse Rogers of Massachusetts, Democrat Caroline Goodwin O'Day of New York; Representative Jessie Sumner of Illinois, Representative Frances Bolton of Ohio, and Representative Jeannette Rankin of Montana.

137 Amy Vanderbilt, *Complete Book of Etiquette* (New York: Doubleday and Co., 1952), 564-565.

138 AF.

139 See Debra Walker King, "'Callin' Her Out In Name': Interpretive Strategies and Naming in African American Literature" (unpublished PhD diss., Emory University) 1994.

140 In a revision of this story, Margaret speculated that the story, to which she paid no attention, had been started in Lewiston, Maine, by "over-eager supporters trying to appeal to the French vote," AF.

141 Franklin Delano Roosevelt, "The Arsenal of Democracy," Radio Address, Washington, D.C. December 29, 1940. See NYT, 30 December 1940, 6.

142 William Manchester, *The Glory and the Dream* (New York: Bantam Books, 1980), 230.

143 MCS, "W&Y," IR, 2 January 1941, 4A. Margaret's column echoes President Roosevelt's assurance that "there is no demand for sending an American expeditionary force outside our own borders. There is no intention...to send

such a force. You can therefore, nail, nail any talk about sending armies to Europe as deliberate untruth." See NYT, 30 December 1940, 6.

144 BDN, 10 February 1941, 2.

145 MCS, "W&Y," IR, 10 February 1941, 2.

146 AF.

147 MCS, "W&Y," IR, 16 January 1941, 4A.

148 Manchester, *The Glory and The Dream*, 235. Two weeks later, another destroyer, the "Reuben James," was attacked by a U-boat in Icelandic waters. This time the ship sank, taking over one hundred hands with her. The story was widely covered by the press.

149 MCS, "W&Y," IR, 16 October 1941, 4A.

150 BDN, 14 November 1941, 1, 2.

151 Oscar Shepard, "Maine Young Republicans Oppose Policy of Isolation," BDN, 17 November 1941, 1.

152 Ibid.

153 BDN, 16 Jan 1940, 3.

154 Harry Thurston Peck, *Twenty Years of the Republic* (New York: Dodd Mead, 1906), 276. Maine's most famous mavericks include House Speaker Thomas Reed, and twentieth century Governor James Longley. A more contemporary figure, Independent candidate Ross Perot, won nearly one-third of Maine's votes in the 1992 presidential election. Nation-wide, only 55 percent of registered voters turned out, but in Maine 72 percent went to the polls, the highest voter turnout in the nation. Perot won three counties outright, including Somerset County, while Clinton took the remaining thirteen. George Bush, who made Kennebunkport a second home, took none of Maine's counties in 1992.

155 BDN, 20 December 1940, 1, 4.

156 MCS, "W&Y," IR, 9 January 1941, 4A.

157 BDN, 21 March 1941, 1, 2; BDN, 4 March 1941; BDN, 5 April 1941, 1.

158 See Manchester, *The Glory and the Dream*, 256-60.

159 MCS, interview with author, 26 July 1972.

160 Ibid.

161 Imogene Bohrer Clarke, "A Little Bird Told Me," IR, 18 December 1941, 4A.

162 Ibid.

163 Ibid.

164 *Joint Committee for Arrangements for the Commemoration of the Bicentennial*, 94th Cong., 2d sess., 1976, H. Report 94-1732, 67.

165 IR, 11 December 1941, 1.

166 Clarke, "A Little Bird Told Me," 4A.

167 Statements and Speeches, 77th Congress, 1941-1942, Vol. 1, 446, MCSA.

168 In 1940, Maine led all of the other New England states "in the production of apples, hay, oats, barley, sweet corn, wheat, eggs, butter, buckwheat, plums, dried fruit and vinegar. With one exception in each case, Maine produced more hay, milk, chickens and more acres of green peas than any other of the New England states." *Facts About Maine, The Offer of The Pine Tree State*, Maine Development Commission, 1946, 16.

169 MCS, "W&Y," IR, 16 July 1942, 4A.

170 *Congressional Record*, 77th Cong., 1st sess., 9 December 1941, 9561.

171 Scrapbook, Vol. 19, 59, MCSA.

172 Rep. Frank C. Osmers [R-N.J.] volunteered at the same time as Vreeland for the Army, though he entered as an enlisted man, while a third Representative, Lyndon B. Johnson [D-Tex] became the first member of Congress to be called up since the war with Japan began. On 11 December he was ordered to active duty as a lieutenant commander in the Naval Reserve, Robert Caro, *The Path to Power* (New York: Alfred A. Knopf, 1982), 757-8. In his column of 23 April Drew Pearson reported those on active duty: Senator Henry Cabot Lodge [Mass], Captain U.S. Army; Rep. Warren Magnuson [Wash], Lt. Commander, U.S. Navy; Rep. Frank Osmers, Corporal, U.S. Army; Rep. Eugene Worley [Texas], Lt Commander, U.S. Navy. See Drew Pearson and Robert Allen, "Washington Daily Merry-Go-Round," BDN, 23 April 1942, 6.

173 MCS, "W&Y," IR, 2 April 1942, 4A.

174 Scrapbook, Vol. 21, p. 190; Vol. 20, 101; Vol. 19, 59, MCSA; *Congressional Record*, 77th Cong., 2d sess., 1942, 9445-9446.

175 IR, 27 August 1942, 1A, 4A.

176 MCS, "W&Y," IR, 9 July 1942, 4A.

177 Donald R. Mathews, *U.S. Senators and Their World* (Chapel Hill: University of North Carolina Press, 1960), 95, 146-175.

178 MCS, "W&Y," IR, 23 January 1941, 4A.

179 MCS, "W&Y," IR, 30 October, 1941, 4A.

180 See U.S. House of Representatives, 77th Congress, 2nd Session, Committee on Military Affairs, *Hearings on H.R. 6293 to Create the Woman's Auxiliary Army Corps*, 20-21 January 1942, 51.

181 MCS, "W&Y," IR, 2 April 1942, 4A.

182 IR, 11 June 1942, 8A; Statements and Speeches, 77th Congress, 1941-1942, Vol. 1, 7 June 1942, 448, MCSA.

183 Paul Hendrickson, "Margaret Chase Smith's Gutsy Legacy," *Washington Post*, 4 August 1986, B2.

184 Scrapbook, Vol. 21, 10, MCSA.

185 For an excellent review of the history of the ERA, see Chafe, *American Woman*, 112-132.

186 MCS, "W&Y," IR, 18 February 1943, 4A; "I do not know that the measure which will come to the House floor will be in the exact wording of the Amendment framed and presented from the National Women's Party, but this organization has worded their proposal after long and careful consideration and the best legal advice, and it seems to me to be suitable language." Margaret's kind words for Alice Paul's militantly feminist NWP is out of character but probably reflects her bid for continuing BPW support. No alliance with the NWP ever materialized.

187 See "President Laughlin's Trip East," *Independent Woman*, I (Feb., 1920), 12.

188 NYT, 18 December 1942, 6.

189 Manchester, *The Glory and the Dream*, 269.

190 MCS, "W&Y," IR, 24 September 1942, 4A.

191 MCS, "W&Y, IR, 10 February 1944, 4A.

192 IR, 21 January 1943, 1, 3A.

193 See Mathews, *U.S. Senators and Their World*.

194 IR, 29 January 1943, 1, 4A.

195 Ibid.

196 Ibid.

197 IR, 18 March 1943, 4A; PI, Seattle, Washington, 22 October 1943, n.p., Congested Areas file, MCSA.

198 AF.

199 Melvin J. Maas to Admiral F. J. Horne, 21 March 1946, Bill Lewis file, MCSA.

200 AF.

201 Bill Lewis file, MCSA.

202 Although he retired from the U.S. Air Force a colonel, in February 1948 William C. Lewis, Sr. was promoted to brigadier general on the first Air Force Reserve list selected after World War II. See William C. Lewis, Jr. to Clarence E. Page, 27 April 1976, Bill Lewis file, MCS Archives; also see Headquarters Fourth Air Force of the Commanding General to Col. William C. Lewis notifying him of promotion, 4 September 1947, Bill Lewis file, MCSA.

203 Edgar B. Naught to Commandant, 12th Naval District, 20 January 1942, Bill Lewis file, MCSA.

204 Chester T. Lane, general counsel to Commandant, 12th Naval District, 20 January 1942. Bill Lewis file, MCSA.

205 Ibid.

206 MCS, "W&Y," IR, 6 May 1943, 4A; 14 October 1943, 4A.

207 WAVES (Women Accepted for Volunteer Emergency Service). In July 1942 the Naval Reserve Act was amended to provide for a women's reserve. It was not intended that women would become integral to the service but would be used in a "limited way" to release officers and enlisted men for sea duty. The amendment was proposed by Melvin Maas on 2 July 1942.. In November 1942 the U.S. Coast Guard SPAR (for Sempre Paratus, the Coast Guard's motto) was created. In February 1943, the Marines established a service for women but did not give it a name. One year after Rogers proposed it, on 15 May 1942, the Women's Auxiliary Army Corp [WAAC] had been established, though without military status. In 1943 Rogers proposed legislation which would replace the WAAC with the Women's Army Corps [WAC]. Though their role was still auxilliary, WAC would release men for combat duty and be eligible for all benefits except for dependents benefits. See Janann Sherman, "Margaret Chase Smith and Women in the Military," *The Journal of Military History* 54 (January 1990): 56-57; also see D'Ann Campbell, Women at War with America: Private Lives in a Patriotic Era (Cambridge: Harvard University Press, 1984), 70. The fact that Margaret was more than half-way through her second full term before she sponsored legislation was not unusual. In an analysis by Rochelle Jones and Peter Woll, The Private World of Congress, (New York: The Free Press, 1979), 32, the authors observe that "it is only after Members of Congress begin to feel secure and settle into their Capitol Hill careers that they begin to pursue seriously legislative activity in order to make their mark and demonstrate their power within that body. Most Members of Congress will readily admit, at least to themselves, that their constituencies interfere with Capitol Hill careers." One example, though drawn from the Senate is particularly informative. "As Nunn [Senator Sam Nunn, D-Ga.] began to build his Capitol Hill career and reputation through his sub-committee he did not sponsor any important legislation. . . Nunn was admired and respected because of his diligence and intelligence, not because of legislation which bore his name," 114.

208 Ann Cottrell, "Story of WAACS' Immorality is Laid to Nazis," WP, 4 June 1943, 11.

209 NYT, 4 June 1943, 9.

210 MCS, "W&Y," IR, 5 October 1944, 4A.

211 Ibid.

212 IR, 16 December 1943, 3A.

213 DOC, 85.

214 MCS, "W&Y," IR, 29 April 1943, 4A.

215 MCS, "W&Y," IR, 23 March 1944, 4A.

216 *Congressional Record*, 78th Cong, 2nd sess., 9 February 1944, 2454; *Congressional Record*, 78th Cong, 2nd sess., 21 March 1944, 2455.

217 Robyn Muncy, *Creating a Female Dominion in American Reform, 1890-1935* (New York: Oxford University Press, 1991), 38, 150-151.

218 IR, 20 April 1944, 1. Another explanation for Secretary Perkins' interest in Margaret can be found in the MCSA, AF. When Margaret was on her way home from the Republican state convention in the spring of 1944 she was stopped by the highway police saying they had been looking for her because of an urgent call that she was to return. She stopped in Pittsfield and found that Secretary of Labor Perkins had been trying to find her for several days. The secretary explained that the International Labor Conference (ILO) was scheduled to meet in Philadelphia. She was anxious to name Margaret as a delegate to represent the House of Representatives at those meetings. She needed an answer so that she could make a recommendation to President Roosevelt who would make the appointment. She told Margaret that it was something that Margaret could help in, that there was a need for someone with Margaret's record, her philosophy and who was a woman. After lengthy conversation, Margaret "finally said yes" and went on her way to Skowhegan, "somewhat puzzled that the effort was made to find me and wondered what was back of it." Then she remembered that Clyde had been one of five members of the House Labor Committee to write the Wage and Hour Law, "that Mary Norton . . . the Chairman of the Labor Committee was a close friend of Secretary Perkins and both of them were sincere in seeing more women in government." Margaret went to Philadelphia for the sessions as she had promised the secretary she would do.

219 MCS, "W&Y," IR, 14 December 1944, 10.

220 Scrapbook, Vol. 28, 155.

221 AF.

222 Scrapbook, Vol. 28, 155, MCSA; also see IR, 28 December 1944, 1, 4; IR, 4 January 1945, 1 3.

223 MCS, "W&Y," IR, 18 January 1945, 4.

224 MCS, "W&Y," IR, 18 January 1945, 4A.

225 IR, 19 April 1945, 1, 5.

226 DOC, 203.

227 IR, 10 May, 1945, 3. By this time, Margaret had been reappointed to the Naval Affairs Committee and appointed to five subcommittees: Discipline and Health, Naval Academy, Ordinance, Private Bills, and Submarines.

228 IR, 14 June 1945, 1.

229 IR, 15 November 1945, 1.

230 IR, 18 October 1945, 1.

231 See Sherman's insightful discussion, "Margaret Chase Smith and Women in the Military," 59.

232 MCS, "W&Y," IR, 15 November, 1945, 4A. In "Washington and You," 2 March 1944, 4A, she called attention to another difficulty encountered by women in the service: limitations on rank. She devoted the entire column to the subject of nurses, both Army and Navy. She explained that in both the Army and Navy, the nurse corps were independent of the WAC or WAVES, that while Navy nurses could hold an officer's rank, female officers in the Army held only "relative rank." That is, they were treated as officers but were actually not. "Measures," she said, "are almost complete to give them rank, however."

233 LEJ, 9 April 1946, 1.

234 LEJ, 10 September 1946, 1.

235 Edward D. Talberth, "Maine Republicans: Who Will Seek What Office Appears Uncertain Just Now," PST, 1944, Scrapbook, Vol. 23, 169, MCSA.

236 LEJ, 28 September 1946, 1.

237 IR, 27 August 1942, 4A.

238 Ibid., 1A, 4A.

PART THREE

1 See Robert H. Ferrell, "The Price of Isolation," in the *Unfinished Century*, ed. William E. Leuchtenberg (Boston: Little, Brown and Company, 1973) 465-571.

2 Dorothy Thompson, "The Lesson of Dachau," *Ladies Home Journal*, September, 1945, 6.

3 IR, 28 June 1945, 1, 3.

4 MCS, interview with author 28 December 1982.

5 MCS, interview with author 26 July 1982; DOC, 73.

6 MCS, interview with author 28 December 1982.

7 MCS, interview with author 31 July 1983.

8 Richard Bolling, *House Out of Order* (New York: E. P. Dutton, 1965), 87.

9 Ibid.

10 William C. Lewis to Carl Vinson, 28 December 1946, Bill Lewis file, MSCA.

11 William C. Lewis to Carl Vinson, 29 December 1946, Bill Lewis file, MCSA.

12 Ibid., italics mine.

13 Congested Areas subcommittee members to Honorable Frank Knox, secretary of the Navy, 15 April 1944, Bill Lewis file, MCSA.

14 Carl Vinson to Chief of Naval Personnel, 25 September 1945, Bill Lewis file, MCSA. On 28 September 1945, Bill Lewis was promoted to Lieutenant Commander.

15 Carl Vinson to Artemus Gates, 28 November 1945, Bill Lewis File, MCSA.

16 Bureau of Naval Personnel to the Honorable Carl Vinson, chairman Naval Affairs Committee, 29 May 1946, Bill Lewis file, MCSA.

17 Bureau of Naval Personnel to Carl Vinson, 29 May 1946, W. E. Lewis file, MCSA.

18 Statements and Speeches, Press release, vol. III, 1946, 571.

19 Paul Hendrickson, "The Luce Mystique," WP, 9 April 1982, D1-D2.

20 Joseph C. Goulden, *The Best Years: 1945-1950* (New York: Atheneum,1976), 133.

21 Manchester, *The Glory and the Dream*, 446.

22 LEJ, 6 November 1946, 1.

23 Marion Martin to MCS, 10 October 1946, Marion Martin file, MCSA.

24 MCS to Marion Martin, 12 September 1946, Marion Martin file, MCSA.

25 Ibid.

26 See Susan Ware, *Beyond Suffrage: Women in the New Deal* (Cambridge: Harvard University Press, 1981), 21.

27 *Time*, 8 October 1934, 59.

28 Ibid.

29 Ibid., 60.

30 Rochelle Chadakoff, ed., *Eleanor Roosevelt's My Day* (New York: Pharos Books, 1989), 63.

31 Nancy Wolock, *Women and the American Experience* (New York: Alfred A. Knopf, 1984), 452.

32 Susan Ware, *Beyond Suffrage*, 132-133. Historian Susan Ware notes that Howorth's assessment may have been exaggerated. In addition to Ware's important study, several historians have added greatly to our understanding of the networks which flourished in the pre and post suffrage period. Examples include Blanche Weisen Cook, *Eleanor Roosevelt*, vol 1 (New York: Viking, 1992); Blanche Weisen Cook, "Female Support Networks and Political Activism: Lillian Wald, Crystal Eastman and Emma Goldman," *Chrysalis*, 3 (Autumn 1977): 43-61; Carroll Smith-Rosenberg, "The Female World of Love and Ritual: Relations between Women in Nineteenth-Century America," *Signs:* Journal of Women in Culture and Society, 1 (Autumn 1975): 1-29; Elizabeth Isreals Perry, "Training for Public Life, ER and Women's Political

Networks in the 1920's," 35, and Susan Ware, "ER and Democratic Politics: Women in the Postsuffrage Era," 53-9, in *Without Precedent.*

33 Susan Ware, *Beyond Suffrage*, 133-4.

34 Frances Perkins, secretary of labor to MCS, Member of Congress, 26 June 1945, Scrapbook, Vol. 32, 121, MCSA. Perkins biographer George Martin notes that both of Perkins' parents were from Maine and that she strongly identified with the state. Since colonial times the Perkins family had farmed a holding at Newcastle, a village about sixty miles east of Portland on the Damariscotta River. Though Frances and her siblings grew up in Worcester, Massachusetts where Frances' father had found work after 1865, every summer the children were sent "home" to Newcastle to "the Brick House" in which their grandmother and uncle still lived. As Perkins' biographer notes, despite his success in Worcester, Fred Perkins "nurtured the family ties with Maine" through his "constant talk of the Natives of Maine Association, of which he was a leader. . . ." Even at age 65, Perkins still retained one-half ownership of "the Brick House" with her sister and it was to Newcastle, Maine that she travelled after leaving office in 1945. George Martin, *Madam Secretary* (Boston: Houghton Mifflin Co., 1976), 41-5, 469). Correspondence in the MCSA suggests that the two women kept in touch for many years after Frances Perkins left the cabinet.

35 They also shared the view—along with the BPW—that women should play a key role at the peace table after World War II. In fact, at the behest of Secretary Perkins, Margaret had been invited to a White House Conference in June 1944 on "How Women May Share in Post-War Policy Making." Secretary Perkins and Margaret appeared during the morning session and spoke for ten minutes each, with Margaret insisting that "women should be at these conferences from a standpoint of practical necessity rather than the insistence of a fair share of influence." In other words, women's potential for contributing stemmed from their acumen, not their gender.

36 MCS to the Honorable Carroll Reece, chairman Republican National Committee, 16 December 1946, Marion Martin file, MCSA.

37 Carroll Reece, chairman Republican National Committee to MCS, 4 January 1947, Marion Martin file, MCSA.

38 Herbert C. Libby to MCS, 18 December 1946, Marion Martin file, MCSA.

39 MCS to Herbert C. Libby, 21 December 1946, Marion Martin file, MCSA.

40 Brewster was one of seven members on Truman's Senate Special Committee to Investigate the National Defense Program, which, quite early on, became known simply as the Truman Committee. See David McCullough, *Truman*, New York: Simon & Schuster, 1992, 266-288.

41 Until this time, Margaret had not thought of Martin as a "Hildreth" person, nor were there any public signs of an alliance between them prior to Martin's appointment.

42 BDN, 2 April 1947, 1, 4.

43 Herbert C. Libby to MCS, 18 December 1946, Marion Martin file, MCSA.

44 BDN, 7 February 1947, 10.

45 BDN, 24 April, 1947, 1,2.

46 S. 1641 was a combination of S. 1527 and S. 1103, the first of which covered the WAC, the second the women in the Naval Services. Women in the Air Force were covered by amendment on 23 March 1948.

47 See D'Ann Campbell, *Women at War* 19-61.

48 Virginia Crocheron Gildersleeve, *Many a Good Crusade: Memoirs* (New York: Macmillian, 1954), 267.

49 House Hearings on H.R. 5915, 9 May 1946, 3328.

50 Senate Hearings on S. 1641, 9, 15 July 1947, 10, 43.

51 MCS, W&Y, PA, 6 February 1947.

52 DOC, 86-8.

53 Ibid., 87, 48.

54 House Hearings on S. 1641, 23 March 1948, 5833.

55 See *Congressional Record*, 80th Congress 2d sess., 6 April 1948, 4233-4; A2241-2. DOC, 91-2.

56 May Craig, "Mrs. Smith Loses House Fight; Looks to Senate," DKJ, 22 April 1948, 7.

57 *Congressional Record*, 80th Congress, 2nd sess., 21 April 1948, 4717-18.

58 DOC, 94.

59 Letter MCS to James Forrestal, 22 April 1948, Armed Services Committee File, MCSA. In 1943, James Forrestal's wife undertook a brief speaking tour in Maine, presumably with Margaret's help. As an unpaid consultant to the Navy, Mrs. Forrestal had earlier engaged the dress designer Mainbocher to design the WAVES uniform. See Townsend Hoopes and Douglas Brinkley, *Driven Patriot: The Life and Times of James Forrestal* (New York: Alfred A. Knopf, 1992), 133.

60 James V. Forrestal to Senator Chan Gurney and Congressman Paul W. Shafer, 30 April 1948, Armed Services Committee File, MCSA.

61 *Congressional Record*, 80th Congress, 2d sess., 2 June 1948 7052-57. When the House accepted the conference report integrating women into the regular armed services, Rep. George Estes of Massachusetts, who had supported Margaret's efforts in the original losing battle in the House said: "The action of the House today is tribute to the unceasing work of Margaret Smith for

recognition of the outstanding work women did during the war." Rep. Frances Bolton sent her the following telegram minutes after the roll call: "Pleased and proud vindication of your fight for women in regular status in armed services by the House today." The most prophetic statement of the day was made by Rep. Gordon Canfield of New Jersey: "The women of the armed services will never forget that it was Margaret Smith who never gave up the fight to give them regular status. The action in the House today is a victory for Margaret Smith." DKJ, 3 June 1948, 1.

62 See Sherman, "Margaret Chase Smith and the Fight For Regular Status for Women in the Military," 47-78.

63 Bar Association, *Statements and Speeches*, Vol. 5, n.p., MCSA.

64 Senate Hearings on S. 1641, 2 July 1947, 16-18.

65 Hoopes and Brinkley, *Driven Patriot*, 319.

66 Ibid., 341. Also see U.S. Congress, House of Representatives, *Select Committee on Post-War Military Policy, 78th Congress, 2nd session, 26 April 1944*, 48-68; Demetrios Caraley, *The Politics of Military Unification* (New York: Columbia University Press, 1966), 27-30.

67 Doubtless Vinson's numerous interventions to gain Bill rapid promotion fueled resentment, as personnel decisions even by sub-cabinet officers were reversed in order to further Bill's career. At the start of the January 1947 session, the depth of the Navy's resentment became clear when the now-deposed Vinson attempted to place Bill with the newly-formed Armed Services Committee. Blocking the appointment were Republicans and Navy loyalists W. Sterling Cole and George Bates, who claimed that they were doing so at the behest of the Navy legislative counsel and judge advocate general on the grounds that Bill's father was a colonel in the Army Air Corps Reserves. Vinson, it was reported later by Bill Lewis, "was shocked at their opposition and even more at the basis of their opposition. He asked "Why they had not raised the question about Lewis during the time that he had served as General Counsel of the House Naval Affairs Committee." Two months later, in early March, Vinson revealed the conversation to Bill. Aware that his future in the Navy was clouded, Bill subsequently resigned as a commander in the Naval Reserve on 28 April 1947 after he was offered a commission as a lieutenant colonel in the Army Air Corps Reserve. In his acceptance letter to the Army Air Forces, Bill explained that "his sense of loyalty (to the Navy) seemed to have been misplaced," DOC, 74, footnote.

68 Bill claimed that he "was not an employee of ARA" and that he did not receive a cent for . . . work on unification but in fact sustained substantial personal expenses for which I have not been reimbursed a cent . . . [and] . .

sustained a considerable personal loss in devoting my time to ARA. Telegram William C. Lewis, Jr. to Al Near, 18 August 1947, Bill Lewis file, MCSA.

69 "How the A.R.A. 'Delivered the Goods,'" undated memo, Bill Lewis file, MCSA.

70 Hoopes and Brinkley, *Driven Patriot*, 377.

71 DOC, 73.

72 Hoopes and Brinkley, *Driven Patriot*, 346.

73 DOC, 73-74.

74 Ibid.

75 See MCS, W&Y, 6 February, 1947; 20 February, 1947; 20 August, 1947; 28 August, 1947.

76 Ibid., 75-6.

77 DOC, 78.

78 Hoopes and Brinkley, *Driven Patriot*, 368.

79 DOC, 79-80.

80 William C. Lewis, Sr. to the Honorable Luther L. Hill, 26 July 1947, Bill Lewis file, MCSA.

81 MCS to John R. Steelman, 25 August 1947; David Niles, 30 July 1947; Harry S. Truman, 30, 1947, Papers of Harry S. Truman, Official file, Harry S. Truman Library. Bill Lewis was sponsored for the position of Assistant Secretary of the Air Force by others which included Carl Vinson, Lister Hill, the leader for unification in the Senate, Elmer Thomas, the ranking minority member of the Appropriations Subcommittee on Military Affairs in the Senate, and many members of the Armed Services and Appropriations and other congressional committees.

82 DOC, 233, footnote.

83 BDN, 2 June 1947, 6B.

84 For a contrary view see Gregory Gallant, "Margaret Chase Smith: McCarthyism and the Drive for Political Purification," (Ph.D. diss., University of Maine, 1992), 2-3.

85 MCS to Miss Alice Fraser, 19 November 1946, Bill Lewis file, Statements and Speeches, 818-820, MCSA.

86 The trip had first been proposed in the summer of 1945. BDN, 10 July 1947, 13.

87 Drew Pearson. "Merry-Go-Round," BDN, 26-27 July 1947, 10.

88 BDN, 15 August 1947, 1, city ed.

89 BDN, 1 August 1947, 12, city ed.; 28 August 1947, 7, city ed.

90 *U.S. News & World Report*, 24 September 1948, 15.

91 BDN, 22 October 1947, 1, 9, city ed.

92 Ibid., 9.

93 Ibid.

94 Ibid.

95 BDN, 3 November 1947, 1, 2, city ed.; "Sumner Sewall: A Brief Personal History," 1948 Campaign file, MCSA.

96 Edward D. Talberth, "Maine Politics," PPH, 27 Jun 1948,1.

97 DOC, 105.

98 Cotton Mather, *Magnalia Christi Americana* (Hartford, 1855), I:128-9.

99 Lorin Arnold, "Women's Vote Wooed in U. S. Senate Race," BDN, 6-7 December 1947, 1, city ed.

100 Edward D. Talberth, "Women Steal the Show," PPH, 7 March 1948, p. 5-6.

101 Arnold, "Women's Vote," 1.

102 Mildred Childs to MCS, 11 November 1947, 1948 Campaign—Correspondence file, MCSA.

103 Alonzo J. Harriman to MCS, 16 February 1948, 1948 Campaign—Correspondence file, MCSA.

104 Lydia (Mrs. Claude) Gillette to MCS, undated correspondence, 1948 Campaign—Correspondence file, MCSA.

105 Ibid.

106 Ibid.

107 Peter Mills to MCS, 19 May 1948, 1948 Campaign—Correspondence file, MCSA.

108 Lydia (Mrs. Claude) Gillette to MCS, undated correspondence, 1948 Campaign—Correspondence file, MCSA, italics mine.

109 MCS to Lydia (Mrs. Claude) Gillette, 17 December 1947, 1948 Campaign—Correspondence file, MCSA; Celia (Mrs. Fred D.) Miller to MCS, 2 March 1948, 1948 Campaign—Correspondence file, MCSA.

110 The main points of the Taft-Hartley Act were as follows. It forbade a closed shop; required a majority vote by secret ballot to ratify union shop agreements; prohibited jurisdictional strikes and secondary boycotts; allowed labor unions to sue for breach of contract; defined unfair labor practices for unions as well as employers; provided a sixty-day moratorium in any industry in interstate commerce before they could strike; required unions to make their financial affairs public; and provided an eighty-day injunction in national health-and-safety strikes. Solicitousness toward labor can be seen in MCS's correspondence with Richard W. Gustin, Sec., Maine Federation of Labor. Margaret wrote him on 30 December 1943 as follows: "No, I am sincere in wanting to see and talk with you. I don't know what you mean by my usual line of flattery. My only regret is that I don't have time to see you and other friends more often. I have it in mind and sometimes hesitate to mention it in

letters as it sounds, as you have taken it, like a usual expression. I shall be in Augusta January 20 and in Waterville February 21 as now planned. . . . If I don't see you during these visits, it may be we can arrange a special appointment later in the spring." MCS to Richard W. Gustin, 30 December 1945, General Correspondence File, MCSA.

111 William S. White, *The Taft Story* (New York: Harper and Brothers, 1954), 81.

112 Ingrid Scobie, *Center Stage* (New York: Oxford University Press, 1992),265; 262-81.

113 DOC appendix, 451.

114 MCS, interview with author, 28 December 1982.

115 Anne Dudley to MCS, 28 April 1948, 1948 Campaign—Correspondence file, MCSA.

116 MCS to Ted M. Levine, 1 September 1980, General Correspondence file, MCSA. In response to Levine's query: "Aside from your immediate family, who is one person who has played a major role in influencing your career and life?," Margaret answered: "The person is William C. Lewis, Jr. . . . He managed all my Senate campaigns and was the largest money contributor to my first campaign;" DOC, 106.

117 Undated memorandum by Lena Batchelder Haskell to MCS, reporting phone calls from Mildred Childs, 1948 Campaign—Correspondence file, MCSA; see also Mildred Childs to MCS, 13 November 1947, 1948 Campaign—Correspondence file, MCSA.

118 AF.

119 Lena Batchelder Haskell to MCS, 13 November 1947, 1948 Campaign—Correspondence file, MCSA; Celia (Mrs. Fred D.) Miller to MCS, 2 March 1948, 1948 Campaign—Correspondence file, MCSA.

120 MCS to Celia (Mrs. Fred D.) Miller, 9 March 1948, 1948 Campaign—Correspondence file, MCSA.

121 Anne Dudley to MCS, 28 April 1949, 1948 Campaign—Correspondence file, MCSA.

122 Celia (Mrs. Fred D.) Miller to MCS, March 9, 1948, 1948 Campaign—Correspondence file, MCSA.

123 DOC, 108.

124 Ibid., 108-109.

125 Ibid., 110.

126 PPH, 22 May 1948, 1; DKJ, 22 May 1948, 13.

127 Ibid.

128 Undated correspondence between Doris Ricker Marston and the Editor, PPH, 1948 Campaign—Correspondence file, MCSA.

129 Unsigned memorandum, May 1948, Campaign 1948, 1948 Campaign—Correspondence file, MCSA.

130 Ibid.; MCS to Ted M. Levine, 1 September 1980, General Correspondence File, MCSA.

131 DOC, 112.

132 PPH, 31 May 1948, Campaign 1948, Press file.

133 Undated correspondence between Doris Ricker Marston and MCS, 1948 Campaign—Correspondence file, MCSA. Also see Mrs. Robert J. Smith to MCS, 22 May 1948, 1948 Campaign—Correspondence file, MCSA.

134 DOC, 113-117.

135 *Facts About Maine*, 10, 18.

136 Walt Whitman, *Leaves of Grass*, 1892.

137 DOC, 113-117.

138 MCS, Scrapbook, Vol. 59, 258.

139 NYT, 23 June 1948, 4.

140 BDN, 24 June 1948, 1, 4.

141 "My Lost Youth," in *The Complete Works of Henry Wadsworth Longfellow*, ed. by Horace E. Scudder (Boston: Houghton Mifflin, 1893).

142 SEP, 11 September 1948, 146.

PART FOUR

1 David McCullough, *Truman* (New York: Simon and Schuster, 1992), 711, 658, 661.

2 *1948 Election Report*, 17 December 1948, prepared by George H. E. Smith, Sec. and Staff Director of the Republican Policy Committee.

3 Her predecessors were Mrs. Rebecca Felton of Georgia (1922), Mrs. Rose Long of Louisiana (1936-7), Mrs. Dixie Graves of Alabama (1937-8), Mrs. Rose Bushfield of South Dakota (1948), all filling unexpired terms; Mrs. Gladys Pile of South Dakota was elected for a two-month unexpired term in 1938; and Mrs. Hattie Caraway of Arkansas was appointed to fill the unexpired term of her husband and subsequently elected to two full terms herself (1931-1945).

4 David Emblidge, ed., *Eleanor Roosevelt, My Day*, vol. II (New York: Pharos Books, 1990), 141.

5 Elizabeth Curtice, "Our BPW in the Senate," *Independent Woman*, October 1948, 307.

6 *Newsweek*, 12 September 1949, 61, *Time*, 5 July 1948, 21, *Newsweek*, 5 July 1948, 26, *Newsweek*, 27 September 1948, 19-20, *New Republic*, 5 July 1948, 21.

7 *Time*, 5 July 1948, 21.

8 DKJ, 24 June 1948, 8.

9 BDN, 24 June 1948, 4.

10 Ibid.

11 Ibid.

12 MCS, interview with author, 26 July 1982.

13 Ibid.

14 Clare Boothe Luce speech to the Republican National Convention, 21 June 1948, *Official Report of the Proceedings of the 24th Republican National Convention*, (1948), 53-61.

15 MCS, interview with author, 26 July 1982.

16 See John W. Bricker speech nominating Sen. Robert A. Taft, 23 June 1948, *Official Report of the Proceedings of the 24th Republican National Convention*, 212-17.

17 DKJ, 26 June 1948, 1.

18 BDN, 15 September 1948, 1, city edition.

19 The 1946 elections drew 183 World War II veterans as congressional candidates. With the victories of 69, one in seven members of the 80th Congress was a veteran of the recent war. Goulden, *The Best Years*, 229.

20 Goulden, *The Best Years*, 229.

21 Bess Furman, "Senator Margaret Smith Appeals to Queen Juliana to Halt Fighting," NYT, 4 January 1949, 1,8.

22 BDN, 4 January 1949, 1, 2.

23 "Gentlewoman from Maine," *Ladies Home Journal*, January 1961, 111.

24 Lilian Rixey, "Mrs. Smith Really Goes to Town," *Collier's*, 29 July 1950, 44.

25 BDN, 3 January 1949, 18.

26 Furman, "Senator Appeals," 1, 8.

27 "Her Nomination a Victory for Us All," *Independent Woman*, August 1948, 225. Also see in *Independent Woman*: Clara Belle Thompson and Margaret Lukes Wise, "Can You Take Responsibility?," February 1943, 44-58; Violet Moss, "New Women in a New World," October 1943, 293-314; Martha Strayer, "Washington—as the New Congress Convenes," January 1945, 2-20; Dorothy D. Crook, "Representing American Women," February 1946, 37-59; Sara Sparks, "How to Run for Public Office," April 1947, 101; Geneva F. McQuatters, "The 80th Congress Gets Underway," March 1947, 81-2; Emma Carr Bivine, "And Then There Were Seven," January 1947, 25; Alice Fraser, "Two New but not Too New," January 1947, 2-27.

28 LEJ, 3 January 1949, 10.

29 Ann Fields, "Will Margaret Chase Smith Ever Be President?" *Coronet*, November 1951, 100.

30 Susan H. Hartmann, "Prescriptions for Penelope: Literature on Women's Obligations to Returning World War II Veterans," *Women's Studies*, 5 (1978): 223.

31 Alma Lutz papers, quoted in the "Case for the Equal Rights Amendment," Woman's Party pamphlet, nd, Box 2, Schlesinger Library.

32 B. Smith, "Senator from the Five and Ten," SEP, 11 September 1948, 36-7.

33 BDN, 4 January 1949, 2.

34 William Lewis, undated memorandum to file, Marion Martin file, MCSA.

35 Ibid.

36 MCS, interview with author, 28 December 1982.

37 AF, BDN, 30 December 1948, 8; Rixey, "Mrs. Smith Really Goes," 44.

38 MCS, Interview with author, 23 July 1983.

39 Mathews, *U.S. Senators and their World*, 92.

40 Graham, *Margaret Chase Smith*, 65.

41 BDN, 15 July 1949, 6.

42 BDN, 8 September 1949, 1.

43 LEJ, 19 September 1949, 5.

44 See *Time*, 3 October 1949, 10.

45 LEJ, 8 October 1949, 1.

46 BDN, 19-20 February 1949, 2, Aroostook ed; 31 Jan. 1949, 6.

47 BDN, 21 February 1949, 14.

48 Thomas C. Reeves, *The Life and Times of Joe McCarthy* (New York: Stein and Day, 1982), 110, hereafter cited as LT.

49 See David Caute, *The Great Fear: The Anti-Communist Purge Under Truman and Eisenhower* (New York: Simon and Schuster, 1978) 70-81, quoted in LT, 209.

50 Mayer, *Party*, 478.

51 LT, 222-3.

52 The unmentioned source of the figure 205 (according to Reeves) was a letter written on 26 July 1946, by then-Secretary of State James F. Byrnes to Democratic Congressman Adolph Sabath of Illinois and subsequently inserted in the Congressional Record. The letter "was a reply to an inquiry about the screening of approximately 4,000 federal employees who were transferred to the State Department from wartime agencies. Some 3,000 case histories had been examined, Byrnes stated, resulting in a recommendation against permanent employment in 285 cases." Reeves notes, "to date, 79 had been 'separated from service,' 26 because they were aliens and therefore ineligible for peacetime government employment. Seventy-nine subtracted from 285 is 206; a slip in arithmetic made it 205," LT,224. Also see Richard H. Rovere, *Senator Joe McCarthy* (New York: Harcourt Brace, 1959).

53 LT, 224.

54 NYT, 14 February 1950, 1.

55 Speeches and Statements, 15 November 1948, American Woman's Association; Senator-elect MCS at the 40th Anniversary of Grocery Manufacturers of America, 16 November 1948, Waldorf-Astoria, New York.

56 LT, 242-3.

57 See David McCullough, *Truman*, 766.

58 DOC, 6-7.

59 Ibid. In the fifties, 63% of the Democrats and 45% of the Republicans serving in the Senate were lawyers; 17% of the Democrats and 40% of the Republicans were businessmen, 7% of the Democrats and 8% of the Republicans were farmers, 7% of the Democrats and 1% of the Republicans were professionals. The remaining 10% was equally divided among other professions, 5% Democrat, 5% Republican. [Mathews, *U S. Senators and their World*, 36]

60 DOC, 7.

61 MCS, interview with author, 26 July 1982.

62 LT, 13.

63 MCS, interview with author, 28 December 1982; LT, 79.

64 LEJ, 11 February 11, 1950, 1.

65 LT, 245-7.

66 *Congressional Record*, 80th Cong., 2nd sess., 21 February 1950, 2062-2068; *Congressional Record*, 80th Cong., 2nd sess., 22 February 1950, 2129-2150.

67 LT, 250.

68 LT, 251-260.

69 WP, 15 March 1950, 1, 2.

70 LEJ, 21 March 1950, 1.

71 LT, 283.

72 LEJ, 1 May 1950, 1.

73 Ibid., 12.

74 MCS, "W&Y," LS, 1 March 1950, University of Maine, Folger Library Microfilm Collection.

75 Ibid.

76 MCS, interview with author, 23 July 1983.

77 Ibid.

78 This version differs from Lewis' claim that Margaret was reluctant to take on McCarthy (see DOC, 9). It also differs in detail from Lewis' version which suggests that the speech was drafted before he and Margaret left for Maine. His version casts Margaret as a virtually unwilling hero whose spirit of cooperation caused her to invite others to join the crusade. Wallace, *Conscience*,

relies on the Lewis' version in her work. But his view is consistent neither with the account this interviewer received from Margaret Chase Smith nor with her character as this author has come to understand it.

79 William James, "The Moral Equivalent of War," *Atlantic Readings No. 10* (Boston: Atlantic Monthly Press, 1910), 1-16.

80 See Rovere, *Senator Joe*; Michael Paul Rogin, *The Intellectuals and McCarthy: The Radical Specter* (Cambridge, Mass: The MIT Press, 1967).

81 MCS, "W&Y," LS, 16 February 1950, University of Maine, Folger Library, Microfilm Collection.

82 DOC, 10.

83 MCS, interview with author, 23 July 1983; Unless otherwise stated, the sequence of events surrounding Smith's Declaration of Conscience is drawn from the 23 July interview and will be cited in the text as I, 7-23.

84 I, 7-23.

85 DOC, 17.

86 I, 7-23.

87 Ibid.

88 Ibid.

89 DOC, 11-12.

90 I, 7-23.

91 In the Bill Lewis' note in DOC, 11-13, it is suggested that "this was literally the moment of truth between May and Margaret...because the incident removed any possible impression or idea that May was MCS's mentor."

92 DOC, 12-13.

93 Ibid., 14.

94 Ibid., 15-17.

95 NYT, 2 June 1950, 11.

96 DOC, 15.

97 NYT, 2 June 1950, 11; WP, 12 June 1950, 1.

98 DOC, 15.

99 Bill Lewis to Leo Cherne, 20 Feb 1977, McCarthy: Tail Gunner Joe, Correspondence file, MCSA. Bill relates an incident which occurred one year after Margaret delivered her DOC. In 1951 for two hours and forty-five minutes on the floor of the Senate, McCarthy assailed General George C. Marshall, Truman's Secretary of Defense, as a "mysterious, powerful" figure who, along with Dean Acheson, was involved in "a conspiracy on a scale so immense as to dwarf any previous such venture in the history of man. A conspiracy of infamy so black that, when it is finally exposed, its principal shall

be forever deserving of the maledictions of all honest men." When McCarthy finished no one came to Marshall's defense, though Margaret registered her disapproval by reaffirming her Declaration of Conscience. Later that week, when Margaret and Bill were having dinner in the Senate dining room, Hubert Humphrey stopped by their table. "Margaret, you're doing a whale of a job. Keep it up." Turning toward him, Margaret said, 'Hubert, if you think I'm doing such a good job, why don't you join me?' He threw up his hands and said, 'Oh my God, that would be political suicide.'" See also *Congressional Record*, 82nd Congress, 1st sess., 14 June 1951, 6556-6603.

100 DOC, 18.

101 DOC file, MCSA.

102 *Chicago Tribune*, 10 June 1950, 7-10H; also see DOC file, MCSA.

103 DOC, 21.

104 Harold L. Ickes, "And A Woman Shall Lead Them," *New Republic*, 19 June, 1950, 10.

105 *Newsweek*, 12 June 1950, 25.

106 Ibid.

107 Gallant, "Margaret Chase Smith, McCarthyism and the Drive for Political Purification," 32.

108 LEJ, 3 June 1950, 4.

109 David M. Oshinsky, *A Conspiracy So Immense* (New York: the Free Press, 1983), 165.

110 Rovere, *Senator Joe*, 5-6.

111 Rixey, "Mrs. Smith Really Goes to Town," 20.

112 Ibid., 44.

113 LEJ, 5 August 1950, 1, 9.

114 LEJ, 27 January 1951, 4.

115 DOC, 23.

116 Ibid., 24.

117 Scrapbook, Vol. 95, 103, MCSA.

118 LEJ, 26 November 1951, 1, 10.

119 MCS to Owen Brewster, 5 December 1949, Brewster file, MCSA. "As to your generous remarks about my being on the national ticket, I am most appreciative. . . . However, I am just as realistically aware as you are that I don't have any chance of being placed on the ticket."

120 Jonathan Edwards, *Seventy Resolutions*, Resolution #7; ___ to MCS, n.d., DOC Correspondence file, Anti-Smith folder, MCSA; ___ to MCS, n.d., DOC Correspondence file, Anti-Smith folder, MCSA.

121 LEJ, 1 July 1952, 2.

122 LT, 423. The quotation is in error. Although Sen. H. Alexander Smith [R-N.J.] was considered by Margaret and Bill Lewis, they finally chose Sen. Robert Hendrickson [R-N.J.] to sign the Declaration of Conscience.

123 Graham, *Margaret Chase Smith*, 91. In a letter dated 6 August 1952 to Mrs. Mabel Tracey from MCS, Margaret specifically denies the story that [her] speaking time was cut from 15 minutes to three minutes, but by that date she was also looking ahead and trying not to court further disapproval from the Republican Party.

124 MCS to Guy Gabrielson, 20 June 1952, 1952 Vice Presidential file, MCSA; LEJ, 9 July 1952, 4.

125 Mayer, *Party*, 487-491.

126 Ibid., 486, 491.

127 MCS to Priscilla Owens, 4 March 1952, 1952 Vice Presidential file, MCSA.

128 Dorothy Titchener to MCS, 12 May 1952, 1952 Vice Presidential file, MCSA.

129 Undated note to file, 1952 Vice Presidential file, MCSA.

130 *History of the BPW*, 87-88.

131 Fanny Hurst, "Women . . . Sleeping Beauty of Politics," *Independent Woman*, July 1945, 194.

132 Bertha Adkins, telephone conversation with Bill Lewis, 28 July 1952, transcript, 1952 Republican National Convention file, MCSA.

133 Ibid.

134 Undated memorandum by Bill Lewis to file, part I, 1952 General Relations file, MCSA.

135 James Blenn Perkins to MCS, 15 July 1952, 1952 Vice Presidential file, MCSA.

136 LEJ, 8 July 1952, 6.

137 Undated memorandum, part II, p. 1, William C. Lewis to file, re phone conversation with Bertha Adkins, Republican National Committee, 28 July 1952, MCSA. "People called me from the Convention and said Senator Smith had picked up 31 votes and had some 200 votes definitely pledged to her and that if they could get Alabama to stand aside with the person they intended to nominate, they might nominate Senator Smith." Bertha Adkins: "I had heard only around 100. I had certainly hoped her name would be put in nomination." Also see Bertha Adkins, telephone conversation with Bill Lewis, 28 July 1952, transcript, Republican National Convention file, MCSA.

138 LT, 427.

139 LT, 422.

140 Ibid.

141 Mayer, *Party*, 491.

142 Ibid.

143 *Independent Woman*, August 1951, 226.

144 James Blenn Perkins to MCS, 15 July 1952, 1952 Vice Presidential file, MCSA.

145 See BPW Report on Progress, 14 July 1952, BPW Archives, Washington, D.C.

146 Undated memorandum, Bill Lewis to file, 1952 Vice Presidential file, MCSA.

147 Clare Boothe Luce to MCS, 13 August 1952; MCS to Clare Boothe Luce, 15 August 1952, 1952 Vice Presidential file, MCSA.

148 Undated memorandum, Bill Lewis to file, 1952 Vice Presidential file, MCSA.

149 James Blenn Perkins to MCS, 15 July 1952, 1952 Vice Presidential file, MCSA.

150 *Official Report of the Proceedings of the 25th Republican Convention* (1952) Republican National Committee, see especially 169-177.

151 Edmund Fuller, "The Career Woman Who Lectured the Pope," *Wall Street Journal*, 15 March 1982, n.p., BPW Archives.

152 MCS, interview with author, 27 December 1982.

153 See letter Mrs. Paul (Dorothy) Titchener, 9 February 1970, 1952 Vice Presidential file, MCSA.

154 MCS, interview with author, 27 December 1982.

155 Isabella J. Jones to MCS, 17 July 1952, 1952 Vice Presidential file, MCSA.

156 Two telegrams, MCS to Bertha Adkins, 27 dated July 1952, 1952 Vice Presidential file, MCSA.

157 MCS to Clare Boothe Luce, 15 August 1952, 1952 Vice Presidential file, MCSA.

158 MCS to Clare Boothe Luce, 29 July 1952, 1952 Vice Presidential file, MCSA.

159 Clare Boothe Luce to MCS, 13 August 1952, 1952 Vice Presidential file, MCSA.

160 MCS to Clare Boothe Luce, 15 August 1952, 1952 Vice Presidential file, MCSA.

161 MCS to the Honorable Richard Nixon, 25 July 25, 1952 Republican Campaign file, MCSA.

162 DOC, 125.

163 Ibid., 134.

164 Ibid., 135-6.

165 MCS, interview with author, 28 December 1982.

166 MCS, interview with author, 6 August 1983.

167 James Blenn Perkins to MCS, 15 July 1952, 1952 Vice Presidential file, MCSA.

168 MCS to Clare Boothe Luce, 15 August 1952, 1952 Vice Presidential file, MCSA.

169 Isabella Jones file, BPW Archives; Women's Division, Republican National Committee, 1959, BPW Archives.

170 Undated letter, Dorothy Titchener to MCS, 1952 Vice Presidential file, MCSA.

171 Undated memorandum, Bill Lewis to file, Marion Martin file, MCSA. In Wallace, *Conscience* 58, the author repeats the rumor and provides hearsay linking May Craig and Smith. No proof is provided. In the course of my research, no evidence was uncovered linking Craig and Smith. My characterization of this rumor as smear and lie does not represent a moral judgment by the author. There is simply no evidence that her sexual preference was for women.

172 DOC, 138-9.

173 MCS, "W&Y," LS, 29 June 1950, Microfilm Collection, Folger Library, University of Maine.

174 MCS, interview with author, 28 December 1982.

175 MCS, interview with author, 31 July 1983.

176 Ibid. No public hint of impropriety in the Smith-Lewis living arrangements can be found; instead, critics like Don Larrabee, PPH and Maxine Cheshire, MH, WP columnist, concentrated on Bill's influence over Margaret. Wrote Larrabee in December 1971: "He [Lewis] is treated with all the courtesy, honor and respect accorded the Senator herself. He is universally recognized as her alter ego without whom no major decision has been made for almost a quarter of a century." Quoted by Maxine Chesire, "Ailing Aide Keeps Senator from Seat," MH, 1 January 1972, 4-c.

177 MCS, interview with author, 28 December 1982.

178 Undated letter, Bill Lewis to General and Mrs. William C. Lewis, Bill Lewis file, MCSA.

179 Ibid.; during the time Bill Lewis, Sr. headed the ARA, the Lewises kept an apartment in Washington, DOC.

180 Ibid.

181 MCS, interview with author, 28 December 1982; MCS to Ted Levine, 1 September 1980, General Correspondence file, MCSA; BDN; 31 October 1972, editorial, n.p., Election file, MCSA.

182 MCS, interview with author, 28 December 1982, MCSA.

183 Ibid.; Hendrickson, "Gutsy Legacy," B2.

184 Bill Lewis to General and Mrs. William C. Lewis, 1 December 1949, Bill Lewis file, MCSA.

185 LT, 318. Also see Mayer, *Party*, 479.

186 LT, 318.

187 LT, 336.

188 Mayer, *Party*, 479.

189 Richard Fried, *Men Against McCarthy* (New York: Columbia University Press, 1976) 95-121; NYT, 7 July 1951, p. 1; Julian Pleasants and Augustus Burns, Frank *Porter Graham and the 1950 Senate Race in North Carolina* (Chapel Hill: University of North Carolina, 1990), 98.

190 DOC, 24.

191 LT, 339-40. Also see *U.S. News and World Report*, September 1951, 31.

192 DOC, 25.

193 Ibid., 24-26.

194 LT, 364.

195 DOC, 29.

196 Ibid. 30; *Congressional Record*, 82nd Cong., 1st sess., 20 August 1951, 11584.

197 *Congressional Record*, 82nd Congress, 1st sess., 21 September 1951, 11857-58.

198 WDN, 23 October 1951, 1.

199 DOC, 31.

200 LT, 395-6. Also see DOC, 32-3.

201 LT, 396.

202 NYT, 30 April 1953, 1.

203 *Congressional Record*, 83rd Cong., 2nd sess., 9 March 1954, 2886.

204 LT, 563.

205 The term is not uncommon but has been used most recently in Pleasants and Burns, *Frank Porter Graham and the 1950 Senatorial Race in North Carolina*.

206 DOC, 51.

207 Undated memorandum, Bill Lewis to file, 1954 Election file, MCSA.

208 Douglas B. Cornell, "AP Writer Sees 'Young Jones' Running Hard But Uphill Battle With Senator Smith For Primary Win." BDN, 8 June 1954, 3 city ed.

209 James D. Ewing, "Maine Sniffs McCarthy Behind Jones Candidacy," WPTH, 28 March 1954, 1954 Election file, MCSA.

210 *Newsweek*, 28 June 1954, 23.

211 Ibid.

212 BDN, 23 February 1954, 1.

213 May Craig, "Inside Washington," PPH, n.p., 1954 Election file, MCSA.

214 Ibid.

215 May Craig, "Inside Washington," PPH, 3 March 1954, n.p., 1954 Election file, MCSA; NYT, 23 February 1954.
216 Undated memorandum, Bill Lewis to file, 1954 Election file, MCSA.
217 Douglas P. Cornell, "AP Writer Sees 'Young Jones' Running Hard But Uphill with Senator Smith for Primary Win," BDN, 8 June 1954, 3 city ed.
218 PEE, 24 February 1954, n.p., 1954 Election file, MCSA.
219 Ibid.
220 BDN, 22 February 1954, n.p., 1954 Election file, MCSA.
221 PEE, 24 February 1954, n.p., 1954 Election file, MCSA.
222 Ibid.
223 RCG, 9 March 1954, n.p., editor quotes from his earlier editorial in the RCG which appeared on February 25, 1954 and is not extant, 1954 Election file, MCSA.
224 D. Cornell, "Swamps GOP Rival by 5-1 Margin at State Primary Polls, BDN, 2 June 1954, 1.
225 Douglas B. Cornell, "AP Writer Sees," 3 city edition.
226 Undated memorandum, Bill Lewis to file, 1954 Election file, MCSA.
227 MCS, interview with author, 28 December 1982.
228 Paul Craigue, "Counts 50,000 Votes as His . . .," BG, 11 April 1954, n.p., 1954 Election file, MCSA; BDN, 6 April 1954, 14, city edition. The Bangor BPW endorsed Margaret's nomination and reelection in 1954, pointing to "her distinguished service to the State of Maine and to the U.S." during her eight years service in the House and six years in the United States Senate. The Maine Division of the American Association of University Women followed suit and on 17 May 1954 endorsed Margaret as the most qualified candidate for the U.S. Senate." BDN, 17 May 1954, 7, City edition. On 7 June 1954, "the Maine Federation of Business and Professional Women's Clubs at its concluding sessions at the Bangor House Sunday adopted a resolution endorsing the candidacy of Senator Margaret Chase Smith for renomination and election. The two-day convention was attended by more than 200 business and professional women from Fort Kent to Kittery." BDN, 7 June 1954, 1, City edition.
229 LT, 636.
230 LT, 637.
231 Threads of anti-Eisenhower ran through conversations with MCS and appeared to subtly shade many of her decisions, such as her refusal to help Elizabeth Arden, the cosmetics mogul who had a home in the Belgrade Lakes area, to organize the women of Maine for Eisenhower. MCS interview with author, 23 July 1983.

232 Scrapbook, Vol. 310, 7, MCSA.

233 MCS to Jack Alex, 19 April 1954, 1954 Correspondence/Campaign file, MCSA; BDN, 17-18 April 1954, 1, city ed.

234 Jack Alex to MCS, 15 April 1954, 1954 Correspondence/Campaign file, MCSA.

235 Jack Alex to MCS, 25 May 1954, 1954 Correspondence/Campaign file, MCSA. italics mine.

236 BDN, 14 June 1954, 17, City edition.

237 PPH, 18 September 1954, n.p.

238 LDS, 13 September 1954, n.p., 1954 Election file, MCSA.

239 "A Mighty Smith is She," Collier's, 7 August 1953, 51; Statements and Speeches, Vol. 10, 163, MCSA.

240 LEJ, 22 May 1953, 4; Time, 1 June 1953, 16; LEJ, 27 May 1953, 1; Statements and Speeches, Vol. 10, 163, MCSA.

241 BDN, 19 June 1953, 4.

242 Time, 1 June 1953, 16. Eisenhower's more cautious approach to military spending grew out of his assessment of the effect of high budget deficits on the economy. He believed that such deficits posed a greater threat to the country than could any immediate military threat from the Soviet Union.

243 BDN, 15 February 1954, 4; BDN, 16 February 1954, 18; BDN, 19 February 1954, 1.

244 In 1910, the Democrats won their first victory in Maine in 32 years. Another victory came in 1914 when the Republican Party was divided by a split between Regulars and Progressives, a anomaly that occurred again in 1932. Thus declines in Maine's economic health could fairly be said to have happened during the Republicans' watch.

245 Census Bureau, 21-93.

246 BDN, 10 March 1955, 1.

247 PPH, 3 September 1954, A. P. 1954 Election file, MCSA.

248 Peggy Lamson, Few Are Chosen, (Boston: Houghton Mifflin Co., 1968), 19.

249 DOC, 151.

250 Undated memorandum, Bill Lewis to file, 1954 Election file, MCSA. This may have influenced Margaret's willingness to debate Eleanor Roosevelt on "Face the Nation," 4 November 1956. The "debate" was set up by the National Committees of the two parties and the two women were assigned to defend their party's nominee for the Presidency—Dwight Eisenhower and Adlai Stevenson. In style, Margaret's presentation seemed scripted, while Mrs. Roosevelt's was more extemporaneous; on the issues, the debate was a draw. Margaret believed, however, that her attention to costume made a big

difference in viewer approval. She chose a simple black dress with a single strand of pearls to contrast with Mrs. Roosevelt's beige shantung suit and hat. Her avowed pleasure in "outmaneuvering" Mrs. Roosevelt in this way strikes a petty note which is in sharp contrast to the deference Margaret displayed toward Mrs. Roosevelt prior to 1954. See DOC, 203-11.

251 Undated memorandum, Bill Lewis to file, Paul Fullam file, 1954 Election file, MCSA.

252 Ibid.

253 DOC, 151. Quotations from Margaret Chase Smith's 12 September 1954 speech are taken from DOC, 151-63.

254 Ibid., 154.

255 Ibid., 153.

256 Ibid., 162.

257 Ibid., 160.

258 Ibid., 163.

259 BDN, 15 September 1954, 1.

260 PPH, 18 September 1954, 1954, n.p., Election file, MCSA.

261 Ibid.

262 MCS to Arthur M. Schlesinger, Jr., 4 February 1955, 1954 Correspondence/Campaign file, MCSA.

263 Ibid.

264 LEJ, 27 June 1955, 1, 7.

265 Coburn, *Skowhegan*, Vol. II, 696.

266 AF.

267 Ibid.

268 Ibid.

269 BDN, 25 June 1955, 1, 7.

270 MCS, interview with author, 26 July 1982.

271 Joseph W. Alsop, "Witness to the Persecution," WPM, 2 February 1992, 32.

272 MCS, interview with author, 26 July 1982.

273 Mayer, *Party*, 501.

274 BSG, 29 January 1956, n.p., 1956 Vice Presidential file, MCSA.

275 Mayer, *Party*, 501.

276 LEJ, 23 March 1956, 4.

277 MCS, "W&Y," BDN, 18 March 1954, 22; MCS, "W&Y," BDN, 14 April 1954, 14; MCS, "W&Y," BDN, 14 May 1954, 14.

278 MCS, "W&Y," BDN, 15 April 1954, 24.

279 *New Republic*, 16 August 1964, 5.

280 Duncan Aikman, "Maverick from Maine," *Nation*, 15 September 1951, 204.

281 BDN, 11 July 1956, 1.

282 Mayer, *Party*, 502.

283 BDN, 3 August 1956, 1.

284 BDN, 2 August 1956, 2.

285 MCS to the Honorable John F. Weston, 1 August 1956, 1956 Vice Presidential file, MCSA.

286 MCS to Melva Day, 17 May 1956, 1956 Vice Presidential file, MCSA.

287 Arthur M. Schlesinger, Jr., ed., *History of U. S. Political Parties (1945-1972)*, vol. IV (New York: Chelsea House Publications, 1973), 2991.

288 MCS, memorandum to file, 21 August 1956, 1956 Vice Presidential file, MCSA.

289 Drew Pearson, "Describes Close Door Argument By Maine GOP . . . On Nominating . . . Smith," BDN, 24 August 1956, 8; MCS to Peter Garland, 24 August 1956, 12 September 1956,; Peter Garland to MCS, 5 September 1956, 1956 Vice Presidential file, MCSA.

290 BDN, 23 August 1956, 1.

291 MCS, Memorandum to file, 22 August 1956, 1956 Vice Presidential file, MCSA.

292 *Official Proceedings of the Twenty-sixth Republican National Convention*, 20-23 August 1956, Republican National Committee, 314.

293 MCS to Peter Garland, 24 August 1956, 1956 Vice Presidential file, MCSA.

294 Peter Garland to MCS, 5 September 1956, 1956 Vice Presidential file, MCSA.

295 MCS to Peter Garland, 12 September 1956, 1956 Vice Presidential file, MCSA.

296 LT, 672-3.

297 McCarthy file, Death folder, MCSA.

298 Quoted in Manchester, *Glory and the Dream*, 648.

299 Alsop, "Witness to the Persecution," 28.

300 Manchester, *Glory and the Dream*, 649.

301 BDN, 16 July 1954, 4.

302 See William H. Whyte, *The Organization Man* (New York: Simon and Schuster, 1956); David Riesman, *The Lonely Crowd: A Study of the Changing American Character* (New Haven: Yale University Press, 1950). Also see Leuchtenburg, "Consumer Culture and the Cold War," in *The Unfinished Century*, 743-57.

303 Emma E. Dillon to MCS, 29 September 1956, 1956 Vice Presidential file, MCSA, italics mine.

304 See Telegram folder, 1956 Vice Presidential file, MCSA.

305 See Eleanor Straub, "Government Policy Toward Civilian Women During World War II," (PhD. dissertation, Emory University, 1973), 162, 358; Leila Rupp, *Mobilizing Women for War: Germany and American Propaganda, 1939-1945*, (Princeton: Princeton University Press, 1978); Richard Polenberg, *War and Society: The U.S. 1941-1945*, (Philadelphia: Lippincott, 1972).

306 Chafe, *American Woman*, 181-182.

307 Woloch, *Women and the American Experience*, 469.

308 By 1953 two-thirds of American families had television sets. By 1957 Americans owned 47 million sets. By the mid-sixties 94 percent of American households owned at least one set. See Leuchtenburg, "Consumer Culture," 739-40.

309 In 1948 only one in four homemakers with children had jobs, but by 1960, two out of five of such women were at work. Between 1940 and 1960, the proportion of working wives doubled, and after 1949, three-fifths of those who entered the labor market were married women. See Chafe, *American Woman*, 181-194.

310 Chafe, *American Woman*, 217.

311 Leuchtenburg, "Consumer Culture," 748.

312 Manchester, *The Glory and the Dream*, 761.

313 Richard Pfau, *No Sacrifice Too Great*, (Charlottesville: University of Virginia Press, 1984), 164.

314 BDN, 30 March 1954, 1, 2.

315 Ibid., 1.

316 Pfau, *No Sacrifice*, 165.

317 NYT, 1 April 1954, 1.

318 Pfau, *No Sacrifice*, 166.

319 Manchester, *The Glory and the Dream*, 572.

320 Ibid.

321 MCS, "W&Y," BDN, 8 April 1954, 26.

322 Gallup Poll, BDN, 16 July 1956, 1.

323 TP, 8.

324 MCS, "W&Y," BDN, 31 March 1954, 16; also see MCS, "W&Y," BDN, 8 April 1954, 26.

325 BDN, 11 March 1954, 18.

326 MCS, "W&Y," BDN, 7 June 1954, 14.

327 MCS, "W&Y," BDN, 27 April 1954, 10.

328 Ibid.

329 MCS, "W&Y," BDN, 19 May 1954, 10; MCS, "W&Y," BDN, 25 May 1954, 10.

330 MCS, "W&Y," 3 June 1954, 24.

331 Statements, Speeches, Vol. II, Broadcast for May Craig, 23 May 1954, MCSA.

332 BDN, 25 June 1955, 12.

333 DOC, 216-18.

334 Ibid., 221.

335 DOC, 222.

336 Ibid, 226.

337 Drew Pearson, "Senator Smith Wins Battle with Air Force," BDN, 29 August 1957, 24; Graham, *Margaret Chase Smith*, 122; BDN, 27 August 1957, 6, City edition; Drew Pearson, "'Rosie' O'Donnell, Senator Smith For Our Promotions," BDN, 28 May 1959, 20.

338 BDN, 3 May 1957, 14.

339 Pearson, "'Rosie' O'Donnell, Senator Smith For Our Promotions," 20.

340 Pearson, "Senator Smith Wins Battle," 24.

341 See *Congressional Record*, 84th Cong., 2nd sess., 1957, 16708-16719.

342 Pearson, "'Rosie' O'Donnell, Senator Smith For Our Promotions," 20.

343 Pearson, "Senator Smith Wins Battle," 24.

344 Armed Services Committee, Air Force Personnel File, Emmett O'Donnell Folder; James M. Stewart File, Ruth H. Morrison Folder, MCSA.

345 Editorial, LEJ, 21 August 1961, 4.

346 BDN, 16 March 1954, 10.

347 James Reston, "Dr. Oppenheimer Suspended by A.E.C. in Security Review; Scientist Defends Record," NYT, 13 April 1954, 1, 15.

348 Lamson, *Few Are Chosen*, 26.

349 DOC, 139.

350 Pfau, *No Sacrifice*, 239.

351 Drew Pearson, "Says Senator Smith in Vote on Strauss Risked GOP Support for Reelection," BDN, 24 June 1959, 14.

352 Dwight D. Eisenhower, *Waging Peace*, (New York: Doubleday and Co., 1965), 396. William Langer [R-N.D.] had been one of two Republicans to vote contrary to the wishes of Eisenhower in the Dixon-Yates contract in 1954. The other Republican was Senator John Sherman Cooper of Kentucky.

353 Eisenhower, *Waging Peace*, 396.

354 Pfau, *No Sacrifice*, 228.

355 DOC, 289.

356 PST, 27 September 1959; 4 October 1959, 16B.

357 LEJ, 27 April 1962, 4; MCS to Benjamin L. Berman, 28 March 1958, Correspondence file, Anti-Smith folder, MCSA.

358 See Paul Johnson, *Modern Times: The World from the Twenties to the Eighties* (New York: Harper and Row, 1983), 11; DOC, 98-101.

359 See Wiebe, *The Search for Order*, 12.

360 AF.

361 BDN, 7 July 1959, 6, city ed.

362 DOC, 260.

363 *Nation*, 7 October 1961, 7.

364 *Time*, 29 September 1961, 16.

365 Ibid.

366 Ibid.

367 LEJ, 23 October 1962, 1, 2.

368 Ibid, 2.

369 DOC, 326.

370 Ibid.

371 BDN, 27 August 1964, 4, city ed.

372 JFK Library Oral History Project, John H. Kelso interview, 23.

373 BDN, 27 August 1964, City Edition, 10; LEJ, 7 November 1963, 1; 18 November 1963, 4; 8 November 1963, 4.

374 Ibid.

375 DOC, 310.

376 LEJ, 26 November 1963, 2.

377 DOC, 363-372.

378. Civil Rights file, Segregation Folder, MCSA; MCS, interview with author, 23 July 1983; Hugh Davis Graham and Ted Robert Gurr, *Violence in America: Historical and Comparative Perspectives, a report submitted to the National Commission on the Causes and Prevention of Violence* (New York: Bantam Books, 1969), 576.

379 DOC, 369.

380 Lorin Arnold, "Can She Win in N.H.?," BDN, 28 Jan 1964, 1.

381 DOC, 375.

382 Lorin Arnold, "Low-Key Campaign," BDN, 11 Feb 1964, 1.

383 BDN, 12 February 1964, 1.

384 Lorin Arnold, "Can She Win?" BDN, 15-16 Feb 1964, 1.

385 BDN, 12 March 1964, 1.

386 BDN, 28 January 1964, 4.

387 DOC, 376-378; BDN, 18 April 1964, 5.

388 Ibid.

389 AF.

390 See George H. Mayer's chapter "The Amateur Hour and After," in *The Republican Party*, 528-558.

391 DOC, 380.

392 Stephen Hess and David S. Broder, *The Republican Establishment: The Present and Future of the G.O.P.* (New York: Harper and Row, 1967), 296.

393 AF.

394 Mayer, *Party*, 545.

395 Robert D. Novak, *The Agony of the G.O.P. 1964*, (New York: Macmillan Co., 1965), 452-453.

396 Ibid., 453.

397 DOC, 383-387.

398 Ibid., 388.

399 Ibid.

400 Mayer, *Party*, 546.

401 Joe Martin's vote was lost when his alternate voted for Goldwater after Martin had retired for the evening. DOC, 389.

402 AF.

403 DOC, 358.

404 AF.

405 Mayer, *Party*, 535.

406 BDN, 16 July 1965, 2, italics mine.

407 BDN, 29 January 1964, 1, city ed.

408 DOC, 390.

409 MCS to J. Edgar Hoover, 2 March 1965, U.S. Dept. of Justice, FBI file.

410 BDN, 26 May 1965, 1,2.

411 BDN, 28 May 1965, 1,2.

412 Richard Rovere, "Letter from Washington," the *New Yorker*, 23 Sept 1967, 157-168.

413 BDN, 29 July 1965, 1, 2.

414 BDN, 21 October 1965, 1, 4. The benefits of the bill to Maine were reduced power costs, heightened economic activity, and preservation of the Allagash wilderness area. When the St. Johns' section of the bill was first derailed by the House, it was Johnson's intervention (at Margaret's request) that restored it. Subsequent derailments delayed appropriations.

415 BDN, 3 December 1965, 1, 2.

416 Bill Lewis to Carl Vinson, 19 November 1973, Bill Lewis file, MCSA.

417 DKJ, n.d., Bill Lewis file, MCSA.

418 LEJ, 4 November 1966, 4.

419 LEJ, 3 January 1966, 4.

420 LEJ, 16 Nov 1966, 25.

421 BDN, 16 January 1967, 6.

422 BDN, 24 January 1967, 1; 21 March 1967, 1.

423 BDN, 9 September 1967, 1.

424 NYT, 21 January 1969, 1.

425 BDN, 14 February 1969, 1, 10.

426 Stephen E. Ambrose, *Nixon: The Triumph of a Politician 1962-1972*, vol II (New York: Simon and Schuster, 1989), 245.

427 Ibid., 278.

428 LEJ, 15 October 1969, 1.

429 DOC, 426

430 Ambrose, *Nixon*, 345-50.

431 NYT, 5 May 1970, 1.

432 Ibid.

433 DOC, 428.

434 The pivotal role the 1954 race played in the 1970 debacle at Colby is an inferential leap based on consistent threads, but not fully-formed opinions expressed by conversation by MCS over an extended period.

435 Ambrose, *Nixon*, 357.

436 DOC, 429.

437 Berkeley Rice, "Is the Great Lady from Maine Out of Touch?," NYT Magazine Section, 11 June 1972, 50.

438 Ibid.

439 Ibid.

440 DOC, 429.

441 Ibid.

442 LEJ, 12 May 1970, 4.

443 Rice, "Great Lady," 50.

444 DOC, 430.

445 Ibid., 431-435.

446 Ibid., 436.

447 MCS to Mrs. Harriet Lanphier, 28 June 1968, Correspondence file, Anti-Smith folder, MCSA; Ambrose, *Nixon*, 351.

448 LEJ, 3 December 1971, 7; Cheshire, "Ailing Aide Keeps Senator," 4-c; Maxinee Cheshire, "Veteran aide's illness may revise plans of Maine Sen. Smith,: BSG, 9 January 1972, A-10.

449 Editorial, BDN, 31 October 1972, n.p., General Election file, 1972; AF.

450 Rice, "Great Lady," 50. Margaret later estimated it at $2 million.

451 MCS, interview with author, 23 July 1983.

452 PPH, 7 June 1972, 11; Scrapbook, 1972, 11, MCSA.

453 Ernie Stalworth, "Smith Backers Predict Victory," BTR, 7 June 1972, 1.

454 ARN, 10 May 1972, 8A.

455 Statement by Bob Monks, 17 February 1972, 1972 Election file, MCSA.

456 "A Time to Look at the Facts," Monks for U.S. Senate Committee, 19 June 1972, 1972 Election file, MCSA.

457 Transcript, "CBS Evening News," 15 June 1972, 1972 Election file, MCSA.

458 Editorial, SR, 2 November 1972, 4A.

459 Editorial, SR, 27 January 1972, 4A.

460 Jim Brunelle, "Grueling Schedule Pays for Monks," MT, 2 April 1972, 4JW; Dave Swearingen, "Senator Margaret Chase Smith Again Proves a Winner," LEJ, 20 June 1972, 1.

461 John Cole, "Bob Monks Makes a Run for the Roses," MT, May 1972, 2.

462 Ibid., 4.

463 BTR, 7 June 1972, 10.

464 LEJ, 19 October 1972, 36.

465 LEJ, 9 June 1972, 1.

466 David Gumpert, "Senator Smith of Maine is a Little Old Lady, But Can You Say That?," WSJ, 9 October 1972, 1.

467 Ibid, 23.

468 Ibid.

469 Ibid, 1, 23.

470 LEJ, 11 September 1972, 4, 10.

471 Rice, "great Lady," 1, 50.

472 Gay Cook and Dale Pullen, *Margaret Chase Smith, Republican Senator from Maine*, Ralph Nadar Congressional Project, "Citizens Look at Congress," (New York: Grossman Publishers, 1972) 2.

473 Ibid.

474 BDN, 12 December 1967, 1C.

475 BDN, 18 November 1967, 24.

476 Scrapbook, Vol. 387, 175, MCSA.

477 PPH, 28 June 1972, 1.

478 NYT, 23 April 1972, 53.

479 NC, 6 July 1972, 5, 1972 Election file, MCSA.

480 Donald C. Hansen, "Sen. Smith and the Popeye Factor," PPH, 19 October 1972, 14.

481 PH (N.H.), 13 October 1972, 4.

482 Editorial, SR, 2 November 1972, 4A.

483 AF.

484 MCS, interview with author, 23 July 1983.

485 LEJ, 8 November 1972, 9.

486 Ibid.

487 MCS, interview with author, 23 July, 1983.

488 Ibid.

489 LEJ, 8 February 1973, 13; 1 February 1973, 23.

490 LEJ, 5 February 1973, 8.

491 LEJ, 1 June 1973, 11.

492 Woodrow Wilson Fellowship Foundation file, MCSA; Don Larrabee, "Former Senator Smith to Follow Once Again Career of Teaching," PPH, 26 July 1973, 1,7.

493 MCS, interview with author, 26 July 1983.

494 Scrapbook, Vol. 368, p. 70, MCSA.

495 Board of Voters Registration File, Correspondence folder, MCSA.

496 MCS, interview with author, 26 July 1983; 28 December 1982.

497 Merton Henry to Bill Lewis, 17 May 1974, Board of Voters Registration File, Correspondence folder, MCSA.

498 NYT, 13 June 1974, 7; MCS to Donald Atkinson, 29 June 1977, Board of Voters Registration, Correspondence folder, MCSA.

499 MCS, interview with author, 26 July 1982.

500 BDN, 17-18 June 1995, A-2.

501 Ibid.

SELECTED WORKS CONSULTED

PRINCIPAL MANUSCRIPT COLLECTIONS CONSULTED

Most of the primary source materials for this book are in the Margaret Chase Smith Library [MCSL] in Skowhegan, Maine. They comprise more than 300,000 files and 100 volumes of scrapbooks, in addition to films and video recordings. Included in the holdings are the Clyde Smith Papers and the William C. Lewis, Jr., Papers, as well as manuscripts and personal correspondence of persons too numerous to list here. A complete catalogue is available from MCSL.

Another collection consulated was the Frances Perkins Papers at Columbia University, New York City, which was useful in confirming the friendship that existed between Margaret Chase Smith and Frances Perkins. At the Schlesinger Library, Radcliffe College, I benefited from the Peggy Lamson interviews of Frances Bolton and her son, Oliver Bolton, 25, 26 April 1967, and from her interview of Smith, 22 May 1967, which mirrored several of my own sessions with Smith. The Clare Boothe Luce Papers at the Library of Congress were instructive, though they did not yield any new information about Luce's and Smith's 1952 conflict resulting from Smith's failed vice presidential bid. I have also benefited from correspondence in the Harry S. Truman Library in Independence, Missouri, which documents Smith's steady attention to constituent concerns between 1945-1953, and to materials in the John F. Kennedy Library which document the strained relations between Smith and the Kennedy Staff. The Louise Coburn Papers at Colby College, Waterville, Maine, were useful in Skowhegan social history.

The Papers of Pluma Batten, Martha May Eliot, Francis J. Flaff, Florence L. C. Kitchelt, Emma Guffey Miller, Pauline Newman, Adelaide Fish Hawley Cumming at the Schlesinger Library, Radcliffe College, contain Smith correspondence.

Other collections containing correspondence are the Blair Moody Papers and the Stella Osborn Papers, Bentley Historical Library, University of Michigan, Ann Arbor, Michigan; the Papers of Bernard Baruch, Alice Hager, James Pike, and Dorothy Thompson at the George Arents Research Library, Syracuse University, Syracuse, New York; the Millicent Todd Bingham Papers and the Walter Lippman Papers at the Sterling Memorial Library, Yale University, New Haven, Connecticut; the Curtis P. Nettles Papers, Cornell University Library, Ithica, New York; the George D. Aiken Papers, University of Vermont, Burlington, Vermont; Stanley R. Tupper Papers, Fogler Library, University of Maine, Orono, Maine; the Edmund S. Muskie Papers, Bates College Library, Lewiston, Maine; the Dwight D. Eisenhower Library, Abilene, Kansas.

In addition to the collection of the National Federation of Business and Professional Women's Clubs, Washington, D.C., other library and archival sources were: Maine Historical Society, Portland Maine; Maine State Library, Augusta, Maine; Portland Public Library, Portland, Maine; Skowhegan Public Library, Skowhegan, Maine. The following oral history projects were also consulted: Maurine Neuberger, 1970, Roswell Gilpatric, 1970, and John H. Kelso, 1970, John F. Kennedy Library Oral History Interview, Boston, Mass., all typescripts; Margaret Chase Smith and William C. Lewis, Jr., 20 August 1975, Lyndon Baines Johnson Library, Austin, Texas, typescript.

DOCUMENTS

U.S. Congress. House. Committee on Naval Affairs. "Report Covering Various
Assignments Pertaining to Women in the Naval Services." *Naval Affairs Committee
Hearings and Reports, 1943-1946.*
    U.S. Congress. House. *Congressional Record.* 1937-1948.
    U.S. Congress. Senate. *Congressional Record.* 1949-1972.
    Guide to Research Collections of Former United States Senators 1789-1982.
Washington, D.C.: Historical Office, United States Senate, 1983.
    Sicherman, Barbara, et al., eds. *Notable American Women: The Modern Period.*
Cambridge, Mass.: Harvard University Press, 1980.
    Official Report of the *Proceedings of the Republican National Convention*, 1920-48.
    Women in the Public Service. Washington, D.C.: Women's Division, Republican
National Committee, 1956-60.

NEWSPAPERS AND MAGAZINES

The Skowhegan Independent Reporter, 1915-72, complete run.
Lewiston Evening Journal, 1960-72, complete run.
Bangor Daily News, 1951-60, complete run; 1964-72, complete run.
Independent Woman, Jan. 1943-Aug. 1948, complete run.
Kennebec Journal, selected issues; *Portland Press Herald,* selected issues; *Maine
Sunday Telegram,* selected issues; *New York Times,* selected issues; *Washington Post,*
selected issues; *Washington Star,* selected issues; *Waterville Sentinel,* selected issues; *Wall
Street Journal,* selected issues.
    Also consulted were selected issues of *Time, Newsweek, Colliers, Life, Ladies Home
Journal, Cornet, Good Housekeeping, Fortune, Harper's, Look, McCall's, New York Times
Magazine, Parade, Reader's Digest, Saturday Evening Post.*

SMITH'S WRITINGS

Statements and Speeches (45 vols).
"Washington and You," 1951-57, complete run.
Smith, Margaret Chase. *Declaration of Conscience.* Garden City, N.Y.: Doubleday, 1972.

INTERVIEWS

Crane, Henrietta. Interview with author. 29 April 1992, Skowhegan, Maine. Notes.
    Hall, Hoyt. Interview with author. 7 August 1982, 28 April 1992, 29 April 1992,
Athens, Maine. Notes.
    Hall, Marion. Interview with author, 29 April 1992, Athens, Maine. Notes.
    MacCampbell, James. Interview with author. 28 December 1982, 29 December
1982, Skowhegan, Maine. Notes.
    Potter, Jackie. Interview (telephone) with author. 5 June 1995. Notes.
    Smith, Margaret Chase. Interviews with author. 28 December 1982, 29 December
1982, Skowhegan, Maine. Tape recording.

_____. Interview with author. 4 July 1983, Lakewood, Maine. Notes.

———· Interview with author. 23 July 1983, Norridgewock, Farmington Falls, Belgrade, Winthrop, Lisbon Falls, Topsham, Cundy's Harbor, Maine. Tape recording.

———· Interview with author. 26 July 1983, Skowhegan, Maine. Tape recording.

———· Interview with author. 31 July 1983, Solon, Athens, Harmony, Hartland, Farming-ton, Maine. Tape recording.

———· Interview with author. 6 August 1983, Kingfield, Maine. Tape recording.

———· Interview with author. 7 August 1983. Athens, Maine. Notes.

———· Interview with author. 11 August 1983, Rumford, Naples, Rangeley, Maine. Tape recording.

———· Interview with author. 13 August 1983, Augusta, Brunswick, Lewiston, Auburn, Cundy's Harbor, Maine. Tape recording.

———· Interview (telephone) with author. 22 October 1984. Notes.

———· Interview with author. 12 August 1990. Skowhegan, Maine. Notes.

———· Interview with author. 28 April 1992. Skowhegan, Maine. Notes.

Shaw, Ruth. Interview with author. 28 April 1992, Skowhegan, Maine. Notes.

Stockwell, Angela. Interview with author. 3, 22, 30 July 1982; 7 August 1982; 28 April 1992; 21 October 1992. Athens, Maine. Notes.

BOOKS ON MARGARET CHASE SMITH

Agger, Lee. *Women of Maine*. Portland, Maine: Guy Gannett, 1982.

Fleming, Alice. *The Senator from Maine, Margaret Chase Smith*. New York: Thomas Crowell, 1969.

Gallant, Gregory P. *Margaret Chase Smith: McCarthyism and the Drive for Political Purification*. Ph.D. dissertation, University of Maine, 1992.

Graham, Frank. *Margaret Chase Smith: Women of Courage*. New York: John Day Company, 1954.

Lamson, Peggy. *Few Are Chosen: American Women in Political Life Today*. Boston: Houghton Mifflin, 1968.

Wallace, Patricia. *Politics of Conscience*. Westport, Conn.: Praeger, 1995.

SELECTED SOURCES NOT PREVIOUSLY CITED IN TEXTUAL NOTES

A. HISTORICAL BACKGROUND: MAINE

Chase, Mary Ellen. *A Goodly Heritage*. New York: Henry Holt, 1992.

Coffin, Robert P.Tristram. Works (an indispensable source of information about Maine people and the Maine landscape, and Smith's favorite author).

Dwight, Timothy. *Travels in New England and New York, 1821-22*. New Haven: Timothy Dwight, 1821.

Williamson, William D. *The History of the State of Maine*. Hallowell, Me: Glazier, Masters, 1832.

B. POLITICS

Ambrose, Stephen. *Eisenhower: Soldier and President.* New York: Simon and Schuster, 1990.

Degler, Carl. *At Odds.* New York: Oxford University Press, 1980.

Donovan, Robert J. *Tumultuous Years: The Presidency of Harry S. Truman, 1949-1953.* New York: Norton, 1982.

Forrestal, James. *The Forrestal Diaries.* Edited by Walter Millis. New York: Viking, 1951.

Gallup, George. *The Gallup Polls: Public Opinion, 1935-1971.* New York: Random House, 1972.

Goodwin, Doris Kearns. *No Ordinary Time.* New York: Simon and Schuster, 1994.

Hartmann, Susan M. *Truman and the 80th Congress.* Columbia, Missouri: University of Missouri Press, 1971.

Lash, Joseph P. *Eleanor and Franklin.* New York: Norton, 1971.

Nixon, Richard. *In the Arena: A Memoir of Victory, Defeat and Renewal.* New York: Simon and Schuster, 1990.

Pearson, Drew. *Drew Pearson Diaries 1949-1959.* Edited by Tyler Abell. New York: Holt, Rinehart and Winston, 1974.

Schlesinger, Arthur M., Jr. *The Imperial Presidency.* Boston: Houghton Mifflin, 1973.
——— *Robert Kennedy and His Times.* Boston: Houghton Mifflin, 1978

Turner, Kathleen. *Lyndon Johnson's Dual War: Vietnam and the Press.* Chicago: University of Chicago Press, 1985.

C. WOMEN

Berry, Mary Frances.*Why ERA Failed.* Bloomington, Ind.:Indiana University Press, 1986.

Chafe, William H. *Women and Equality: Changing Patterns in American Culture.* New York: Oxford University Press, 1979.

Davis, Allen. *American Heroine: The Life and Legend of Jane Addams.* New York: Oxford University Press, 1973 (MCS: *Beyond Convention* has benefited from the rich body of narratives, documents, biographies and memoirs by feminists, reformers and politicians too numerous to list here).

Elshtain, Jean Bethke. *Public Man, Private Woman.* Princeton: Princeton University Press, 1981.

Gelb, Joyce, and Marian Paley. *Women and Public Policy.* Princeton: Princeton University Press, 1982.

Kelley, Florence. *The Autobiography of Florence Kelley.* Edited by Kathryn K. Sklar. Chicago: University of Chicago Press, 1986

Klein, Ethel. *Gender Politics.* Cambridge, Mass.: Harvard University Press, 1984.

Rosenberg, Marie B., and Len V. Bergstrom, eds. *Women and Society: A Critical Review of the Literature with a Selected Annotated Bibliography.* London: Sage, 1975.

Scott, Anne F. *Making the Invisible Woman Visible.* Urbana: Univ. of Illinois Press, 1984.

Smith-Rosenberg, Carroll. *Disorderly Conduct: Visions of Gender in Victorian America.* New York: Alfred A. Knopf, 1985.

Ware, Susan. *Partner and I: Molly Dewson, Feminism, and New Deal Politics.* New Haven, Conn.: Yale University Press, 1987.

INDEX

R

Rankin, Jeannette, 127
Rasles, Father Sebastian, 1–2, 6
Reece, Carroll, 155, 159, 184, 197
Reed, John, 334
Reed, Thomas Brackett, 35–36, 54
Reid, Helen Rogers, 156
Reid conference, 157
Republican National Committee,
    158–160, 184, 219
Republican National Convention
    1940, 113, 116
    1948, 196–198, 200
    1952, 222–228
    1956, 264
    1964, 297–299
    1972, 321
Republicans, regaining control in 1946,
    154
Rice, Berkeley, 322
Ripley, Wallace, 189
Robinson, George, 172
Rockefeller, Nelson, 292, 294, 297
Rogers, Edith Nourse, 130, 132, 148,
    174
roll call votes, 113, 258, 303
Roosevelt, Eleanor, 105, 142, 156-7, 195
Roosevelt, Franklin D., 94, 142
    National defense speech, 107
    third term election, 118
    Lend-lease "chat," 121
Rouzie, John, 296

S

Saltonstall, Leverett, 253
Scolten, Adrian, 199
Scranton, William, 296
Scribner, Charles, 97–98
"*See* It Now" broadcast, 268
Senate Armed Services Committee,

288, 306
Senate Republican Conference, 306
Senate Rules Committee, 240
Sewall, Sumner, 113, 145, 177
the Shawmut years, 16–19
Sheppard, Harry, 170
Shinwell, Emanuel, 290
shipbuilding industry, 124–125. *See also*
    Bath Iron Works and Kittery-
    Portsmouth shipyard
Short, Dewey, 165–166
Sills, Kenneth, 256
the Sixties, 283–309
    cultural milieu, 283–284, 301–302
Skowhegan
    MCS childhood years in, 16–25
    MCS adolescent years in, 26–48
    WWI parade, 55–57
Skowhegan Republican Committee, 69
smear sheets, 184, 187
Smith, Albra, 32, 89–90
Smith, Angie Bartlett(mother), 32
Smith, Clyde
    childhood, 31–33
    Hartland years, 33–39
    early political career, 34–28, 52–54
    mentors, 34–37
    marriage to Edna Page, 39–41
    newspaper, 40–41
    attraction between MCS, 42–43, 50
    age difference with MCS, 42, 88
    rumors, 51, 61, 80, 185–186
    career in Maine legislature, 55, 69
    World War I parade, 56–57
    prenuptial party, 67
    mentor to MCS, 75, 86, 92
    highway commission, 74–75
    marriage to MCS, 76, 88–93, 101–102
    jobs held, 87
    gubernatorial campaign, 95–96, 98–99
    tractor scandal, 97–98
    U.S. House of Representatives, 100-102

BAKER & TAYLOR